Point of Sale

Point of Sale

· ·

Analyzing Media Retail

EDITED BY DANIEL HERBERT AND DEREK JOHNSON

Rutgers University Press

New Brunswick, Camden, and Newark, New Jersey, and London

Library of Congress Cataloging-in-Publication Data

Names: Herbert, Daniel, 1974– editor. | Johnson, Derek, 1979– editor.
Title: Point of sale : analyzing media retail / edited by Daniel Herbert and Derek Johnson.
Description: New Brunswick, New Jersey : Rutgers University Press, [2019] | Includes biblio-
graphical references and index.
Identifiers: LCCN 2019012235 | ISBN 9780813595528 (pbk.) | ISBN 9780813595535 (cloth)
Subjects: LCSH: Selling—Mass media. | Mass media—Economic aspects. | Retail trade. |
Electronic commerce.
Classification: LCC HF5439.M267 P65 2019 | DDC 658.8/7—dc23
LC record available at https://lccn.loc.gov/2019012235

A British Cataloging-in-Publication record for this book is available from the British Library.

∞ The paper used in this publication meets the requirements of the American National
Standard for Information Sciences—Permanence of Paper for Printed Library Materials,
ANSI Z39.48-1992.

www.rutgersuniversitypress.org

Manufactured in the United States of America

DH—for Clara and Fiona
DJ—for Dahlia and Annika

Contents

Part III: Practices and Participation in Media Retail Communities

Point of Sale

Introduction

• •

Media Studies in the
Retail Apocalypse

DEREK JOHNSON AND
DANIEL HERBERT

Ironically, as twenty-first-century retail industries face impending doom, their relevance to the critical understanding of media products, entertainment experiences, and the popular culture of buying and selling media might be even more keenly felt. In the United States, retail economies had by 2017 entered a state of crisis literally described in apocalyptic terms.[1] Reflecting on the growth of online shopping, abandoned suburban shopping malls, and shifts in consumer spending, the *Atlantic* described closures for JCPenney, RadioShack, Macy's, and Sears—once foundations of the retail sector—as a "meltdown" and "extinction-level event."[2] So prevalent was this doomsday cult that "retail apocalypse" had its own Wikipedia page.[3] Following a record-breaking loss of 105 million square feet of retail space in 2017, CNBC reported that another 90 million had evaporated by April 2018, with more still to disappear as Toys "R" Us claimed bankruptcy.[4] These visions of shopping Armageddon extended beyond the United States as well. BBC News pondered the impact of the retail apocalypse in Canada,[5] while the *Financial Times* noted in 2017 the global scope of distressed retail assets, as French mall operator Unibail-Rodamco purchased London and New York shopping centers and the British operator Hammerson similarly sought to buy competitor Intu.[6] A world of retail shopping appeared to teeter on the brink.

This discourse of industrial collapse explicitly highlighted media, entertainment, and popular culture as failing retail products. Retailers such as Walmart and Amazon make considerable revenue by selling media of all types and play crucial roles in the circulation and delivery of countless media commodities through their brick-and-mortar locations and online portals. Yet *Business Insider* identified media such as books, games, and music—as well as consumer products like toys, which are highly dependent on shared branding with media blockbusters—as retail sectors likely to be "hit the most" by this apocalyptic downturn.[7] The *Atlantic* even invoked distressed media industries to explain the destruction facing retail, framing the apocalypse as a problem of "bundles." Just as smaller cable channels would not generate enough demand to survive on their own if not bundled with anchors like ESPN, shopping malls and big-box developments depended on anchor stores to support and build visibility for smaller retail endeavors. Thus the story of the retail apocalypse was like a rerun of the disruptions already faced by media industries like television, where networks and channels faced threats from new, nonlinear, disaggregated streaming portals that allowed their users to construct their own online television experiences.[8] Amazon, Netflix, Apple, and Google might be considered the four horsemen of this shared apocalypse, having equally disrupted brick-and-mortar retail and the dominant pathways in which media products circulated.

Yet the relationship between retailing and media extended beyond perceptions of parallel industries in decline. As much as media goods represented significant retail economies under threat, some analysts eyed new media technologies as the means of developing the retail forms and practices of the future. Nikki Baird, vice president of innovation at retail enterprise solution provider Aptos, tied the failure of retail businesses to its reluctant embrace of a process of digital transformation in which consumers migrated across multiple social media channels.[9] In her view, the retail meltdown came from the misrecognition of the power of media in the world of shopping, against which she proposed greater integration between retail and digital media platforms. Similarly, *Forbes* contributor Steven Barnes stared down the apocalypse with his vision of a "new dawn" or "evolution" in which retailers would increasingly rely on new media technologies, using data to build stronger customer profiles, deploying mobile apps to replace the check-out process, and building experiential stores that support loyalty, affinity, and community.[10] Beyond blind faith in digital platforms, this vision for new retail stores looked to the realm of meaning, identity, and narrative pleasure in which media entertainment content has long traded. In this imagined future, the store could sell "a lifestyle on top of products,"[11] cultivating consumer subjectivities and identities that have long been the province of branded media culture.[12] Whether adopting the power of media to generate "willed affinities"[13] or its capacity to build an "intensity" of interest,[14] the retail store of the future was increasingly imagined as one that might learn from media industries to build more meaningful relationships with consumers. As such, retail industry cheerleaders figured retail and media entertainment in partnership. Shopping center developer Stephen Congel recommended that forward-looking retailers consider "mixed-use development" strategies that look across industry lines to sectors like entertainment.[15] Although analysts located the future of retail in other arenas too—the *Atlantic* saw promise in the self-driving car[16]—the "digitally transformed retail"[17] envisioned by Baird and others depended significantly on media as a platform for that evolution. In this sense, media products may have been implicated in the retail apocalypse, but the power of media technologies and branding also pointed to potential retail regenesis.

Whether in this present crisis or historically, the worlds of media and retail cannot be separated, and *Point of Sale: Analyzing Media Retail* represents the first significant attempt to center media retail in the study of popular media culture. Bringing together fifteen essays by media scholars attuned to both contemporary changes and the history of retail as a fundamental yet underexplored part of the culture industries, this book calls our attention to retail as a crucial aspect of media culture. Instead of the old adage "distribution, distribution, distribution!" that informs a political economy of media that is focused on players such as Disney, Warner Bros., NBC, and Sony, this collection asks how companies like Amazon, Walmart, and Target play just as powerful of roles in the business and everyday experiences of popular culture by acting as the last-mile interface between distributors' products and consumers. Indeed, those retailers may sometimes be *more* powerful, not only shaping consumer access to media products but also flexing their muscles to influence the practices of distributors and producers. Further, the recent attention to "production, production, production!" prompted by "production studies,"[18] has revealed how the media industries are composed of communities whose values and practices shape media content. Yet this focus on production also overlooks how media culture is similarly informed by the beliefs, norms, and practices of retail professionals and countless media shoppers.

By investigating media retail, this book specifically examines those companies, storefronts, and consumer experiences surrounding the sale of books, movies, television, music, comic books, video games, and other forms of popular culture and entertainment. We argue that the retailing of media matters in part because of the centrality of cultural texts like movies, games, books, and songs to the formation of individual and communal identities. Indeed, media remains a unique and significant commodity because of the narratives, meanings, and identities that they carry, and to some extent, media products may demand special attention separate from soaps, groceries, and other consumable goods also purchased at retail. However, given the mediatization of culture more generally,[19] it is also undeniable that when branded, soaps and groceries often operate through similar logics and experiences of narrative, meaning, and identity. It is therefore doubly important to give specific consideration to film, television, games, and other media product in retail space, as these commodities can inform how retail sells a wider range of products as entertainment. A focus on media retail asks us to identify what makes media products unique to the retail industry and in retail space while simultaneously investigating the relationships between media forms and other consumer products sharing that space.

Media retail transactions appear to be occurring everywhere, from gas stations and grocery stores to television sets, computers, and phones. Indeed, this book's investment in retail is motivated by the rapid changes happening in the circulation and consumption of media due to the advent of digital technologies and online platforms. The growth of e-tailers like Amazon and iTunes and their disruption of traditional retail dynamics have gone hand-in-hand with a proliferation in the very ways in which media are sold, such as with electronic sell-through (EST), transactional video on demand (TVOD), and subscription video on demand (SVOD), options that now exist alongside the pay-per-view (PPV) services offered by cable companies, rental kiosks like Redbox, and the physical media continuing to be sold at big-box stores like Target, Best Buy, and Costco. Further, many media retailers offer multiple forms of access, such as with Walmart's Vudu digital platform, which has both "rental" and "sell-through" options, or Amazon, which sells tangible and digital media products in a wide variety of ways. It seems as if there is some retailer—and some method for engaging in media transactions—to match every desire and sensibility.

Yet media retail must equally be considered from a historical view trained on legacy institutions that may not be as outwardly exciting in the digital era but whose power in relation to media retail remains underexplored. Walmart is significant not just because of its development of new digital storefronts but also for being the site at which media has been bought and sold for decades— where books, compact discs, and VHS cassettes could be acquired, to say nothing of the hardware of media platforms themselves. It is also at retail that consumers have long purchased media technology: radio sets, televisions, stereo receivers, recording and production equipment, video game consoles, personal computers, and much more. Indeed, the rise of platform studies[20] creates productive opportunities for examining retail as the site at which media machines are first desired, made meaningful, and experienced by their users, thanks to the salesmanship and presentation of retail forces courting consumer transactions. As we pay attention to media platforms alongside content, retail provides a salient site of analysis. Retail is the site of the experience of buying media things, whether that be excited families buying a new, big-ticket luxury entertainment item or audio-visual entertainment purchased in the course of mundane, everyday occurrences.

While retail constitutes this important element of media industry and culture, few media scholars have examined this vital area of research. In 2014, Joseph Turow noted this lack of media studies scholarship on retail, calling on media scholars to engage more concertedly with the topic.[21] Elsewhere, Turow examines retail marketing, and although he does not focus on the retailing of media, his work highlights the ways in which digital, interactive retailing provides companies with abundant information about consumers' choices, tastes, and habits.[22] One of the few others to have directly engaged the topic of *media retailing* is Avi Santo, whose work appears in this volume.[23] In their attention to specific media forms, other scholars have provided illuminating analyses of the retailing of movies and home video,[24] books,[25] comic books,[26] music,[27] and video games.[28] This scholarship is notable for examining how retailers and retail environments have shaped the circulation, meaning, and significance of those media commodities, and in that respect, this collection builds upon a remarkable foundation. However, in this focus on individual media and types of products or commodities, there remains an opportunity to build a stronger framework for addressing media retail more broadly and systematically.

A number of media and cultural studies scholars have also examined retail in relation to broader topics. Excellent work on children's media culture by Ellen Seiter, for instance, examines the role of retailers and retailing.[29] Other scholars, including Anne Friedberg and Margaret Morse, have investigated retailing and shopping to examine historical changes in visual and cultural conventions.[30] Some work examines how American cinema has promoted consumerism,[31] while other scholarship explores how citizens interact with media texts, stars, brands, and commodities in politically resistant ways.[32] Additionally, many media scholars have tackled subjects we might consider retail-adjacent. Derek Johnson's work on media franchising, for example, looks at licensing arrangements that support the marketing of toys and media-branded goods, while Jonathan Gray's analysis of media paratexts includes promotional materials and media merchandise.[33] Further, there is now considerable scholarship on distribution—and digital distribution in particular—a process intimately connected to retail.[34] Although all these studies provide rich insights into related topics and demonstrate the contextual insights that media studies can offer, the study of retail has remained on the periphery of other concerns.

If film, media, and cultural studies have largely overlooked retail, then one can more readily find scholarly debates centered on retail and shopping within history and sociology where considerations of media are less a priority.[35] The essays in *The Shopping Experience* reveal retail and shopping as crucial aspects of contemporary society, yet none of these essays examine media.[36] Although books like *Shopping: Social and Cultural Perspectives*, *Shop 'til You Drop*, and

The Politics of Shopping offer cultural and sociological examinations of how shoppers engage with retail spaces, they similarly neglect to discuss media and retailers selling media.[37] Further, these works consistently highlight the importance of social identity within considerations of retail and shopping. Scholars have, for instance, examined the crucial roles that retailers and retailing played in establishing national cultures and identities[38] while intersecting with racial and ethnic politics.[39] Notably, a number of scholars provide historical accounts of retailing and specific types of retailing establishments, such as department stores and grocery stores, in relation to gender identity and women's social identities in particular.[40] Nevertheless, this work also largely sets media retailing to the side. In this book's effort to give media greater consideration, its essays build a dialogue with the important insights of this previous scholarship, examining how media retail relates to the politics of identity, from gender to sexuality to nation.

A rich literature about consumer culture, broadly conceived, also bears heavily upon our ideas regarding the importance of media retailing. Celia Lury, for instance, provides a theoretically informed overview of "consumer culture," including issues of commodity exchange and shopping.[41] Yet because this work does not discuss retail in detail, it opens the door for more relational studies of media, retail, and consumerism. Similarly, books like *The Consumer Society*[42] and *Consumer Society in American History*[43] provide theoretical, historical, sociological, and economic approaches to understanding consumer culture yet only briefly discuss film, television, radio, and other media. By looking specifically at media retail, we can fill a notable lacuna in the literature about shopping and consumerism.

Finally, the study of media retail can build upon abundant literature about retail from scholars working in economics, business, and similar areas like advertising.[44] Publications such as the *Journal of Retailing* and *Journal of Retailing and Consumer Services* analyze important retail industry phenomena, including consumer behavior and identities, digitalization and e-commerce, and occasionally even the retailing of media and similar topics, such as marketing, advertising, branding, and celebrity endorsements. This work investigates topics including logistics, in-store shelving strategies and practices, and retailer brand identities, among others. Although much of this scholarship is more practice- or strategy-oriented, it nevertheless provides consistent analysis of market dynamics and industrial practices useful to media studies. Indeed, scholars such as Avi Santo, Emily West, Marc Steinberg, and Ethan Tussey and Meredith Bak make critical, interdisciplinary use of such scholarship in their contributions in this collection, modeling the larger ambitions of this book. On the one hand, *Point of Sale* aims to center retail within media studies and, further, to demonstrate the utility of analyzing media retail as an important and complex cultural sector, not just one peripherally addressed in the course of investigating a single media form or commodity. On the other hand, by examining retail from a media studies perspective, this collection aims to impact the larger discourse about the roles of shopping and consumerism in contemporary society across a variety of fields within the humanities, social sciences, and business.

The approach of "critical media industry studies" proves particularly well suited to engage with the retailing of media.[45] The research and analytical methods characterizing critical media industry scholarship lend themselves to understanding the multiplicity of objects, processes, practices, themes, and problems that fall under the umbrella of "retail." As informed by critical political economy, media industry studies prepares us to examine the structure of the retail business, the role that media plays within that business, the agency of media retailers, and retailing companies within the larger media industry. Further, this approach enables historical analyses regarding the changing role of retailing within the media at various moments. Indeed, we need to better understand how retailing shaped the media industry long before Amazon or Apple appeared on the scene, making industrial histories especially valuable to those who wish to better understand our current moment.

Yet our interest in critical media industry studies does not represent an eagerness to identify a distinct subfield disengaged from the larger project of media studies equally and integrally concerned with cultural forms, social contexts, and audiences.[46] As Timothy Havens, Amanda Lotz, and Serra Tinic have asserted, critical media industry studies "accounts for the complex inter-actions among *cultural* and economic forces" (emphasis added).[47] We embrace critical media industry studies as a way of linking concerns for the political economy of media retail to the everyday experiences of those who participate in the media cultures constituted by retail contexts. Although "retail" does not appear on the "circuit of culture,"[48] this cultural studies tradition directs our attention to the ways in which retailers and shoppers engage in meaning-making activities. Through their designs, in-store advertisements, commodity arrangements, consumer relations activities, promotions, and so on, retailers organize a paratextual world that shapes how media are understood by con-sumers and audiences.[49] Retail workers—from corporate executives to branch managers to checkout clerks—constitute an important industrial community; industry research informed by cultural studies can guide scholars as we seek to understand how media retail organizes itself, makes cultural meanings out of daily work activities, and ultimately shapes media's place within culture. Finally, we need to better understand how media shoppers make sense of retail experiences from a critical perspective that contrasts with the administrative and commercially oriented knowledge of customers sought and manufactured by retailers themselves. Indeed, media industry studies equips us to examine how "shoppers" and "customers" are imagined, produced, represented, and commercialized by the retail industry.[50] In fact, we should see not only media industry studies as suitable for studying media retail but more so retail as an especially productive site for expanding and refining the media and cultural studies endeavor—particularly insofar as such research examines middle grounds and meeting places between industry and everyday cultural practices.

Media Retail as Transactional and Interactional

As the first volley in a deeper study of media retail, this book makes a case for retail as a distinct realm of media industry and culture, theorizing retail from a media studies perspective informed by the intersections of *transactional* industry market structures and *interactional* experience of them as everyday culture. By transactional, we mean to draw attention to retail as a significant locus of economic exchange in the media industries: the literal, concrete space of the market. To think of it in a conventional Marxist way, we could say that although "production" is where value is generated, it is in retail, in the market, where value is realized.[51] The complex political economy of media retail demands greater attention so that we might better understand the transactions it entails. It may sound simplistic to say that retail sectors enable media to be bought and sold, but consider in that light Hollywood's long-standing reliance on and preference for licensing libraries of intellectual properties over selling them away in more permanent ways. Strictly speaking, studio films and television programs were not often bought and sold but borrowed and returned. While licensing certainly involves financial transactions, too, the existence of media retail sectors requires us to develop specific models for making sense of these unique types of transactions. Instead of looking to film and television industries to start making sense of these transactions, we might instead look to distributional models based in "publishing" that have a longer history of supporting direct sales transactions in books, music, comics, and more. In this vein, scholars such as Derek Kompare have offered new understandings of screen media as potential objects of retail exchange, when the publishing model of the emerging market for DVDs at the turn of the twenty-first century enabled television to be truly bought, sold, and owned.[52] In comic book studies, Matthew Pustz, Benjamin Woo, and others have similarly recognized how transitions from drug store sales to specialty retailing altered the transactions involving the medium, encouraging collecting, speculating, reselling, and habitual purchase (while also creating new social dynamics that limited participation in such transactions).[53]

A political economy of media retail affords a deeper understanding of companies that have not yet been adequately integrated into our critical mappings of the culture industries. Retailing has long been crucial to the media industries, whether we think of the sale of recorded music, tickets at a movie theater, or especially the movies and television programs that became discrete consumer products on home video. For the most part, the companies that have sold these goods and services have been separate from the companies that produce and distribute these media, yet such retailers still play a powerful role in the media industries at large. Amazon.com sold more than $10 billion of media commodities in the first half of 2015 alone.[54] That same year, the more traditional brick-and-mortar retailer Walmart remained "the studios' largest customer" and "the number one retailer of packaged media"—even with DVD sales having peaked more than a decade earlier.[55] However, companies like Amazon, Netflix, Apple, Google, and others appear so disruptive and threatening to conventional, legacy media retail businesses precisely because they have converged the industrial functions of media distribution, retailing, and exhibition. Not only do these companies deliver digital media streams; they also control digital platforms that serve as virtual storefronts that shoppers use to weigh their entertainment options. Furthermore, these companies offer the interfaces through which people view media. If the classic Hollywood studios held power because they controlled production, distribution, and exhibition, while contemporary media conglomerates benefit from being both vertically and horizontally integrated, then we should also recognize the power that some retailers have over the media commodity chain. By conjoining media distribution and exhibition with retail, these companies create new industrial alignments while allowing consumers to shop for, purchase, and consume media as part of a single experience. Further, digital media service providers like Netflix and Amazon wield an unusual amount of power because of the massive amounts of data they can collect about consumers' retail behaviors and choices.

While the point of sale is the time and space of the transaction, a transactional approach to media retail also considers all the practices and labor roles that enable those transactions. If we start where the work of the media distributor usually ends, we can follow the last mile of media's journey to the consumer through a number of important processes including the work of retail buyers who gauge the potential for consumer transactions and order enough stock to meet that demand; the design work of organizing retail space and integrating media into storefronts (both brick-and-mortar and digital); the labor of salespeople whose knowledge, cultural capital, and expertise in relation to media might contribute to potential sales; and of course the decision-making that goes into pricing media, putting it on sale as a loss leader or on clearance to make way for something more valuable. All this labor we might better understand—if only as a starting point—by considering its political-economic role in supporting media retail transactions.

By calling attention to labor, we can also emphasize the role that people play in the retailing of media. Indeed, in analyzing media retail, we must remember how all sorts of people—citizens, shoppers, consumers, employees, and store managers—engage with retail spaces and the media commodities found there. Thus in addition to being transactional, retail is *interactional*.[56] Any analysis of the selling of media goods necessarily involves examining consumers or, more accurately, potential consumers. Retail is the arena where media commodities find (or fail to find) audiences, making it a particularly pressured space for both media industries and publics who desire entertainment. Retail involves both salesmanship and shopping. Studying media retail therefore means studying the *interaction* of businesses, retail spaces, and shoppers navigating these spaces. In media retail, the practices and strategies that shape the commodification of culture intersect with audiences and their meaningful practices of consumption in everyday life.

Media retail is thus an economic, social, and cultural phenomenon. It is the arena in which the values of media are declared, debated, and accepted or rejected. In shaping their storefronts, their aisles and shelves, their interior displays, and their checkout areas, retailers hold powerful sway over a vast amount of the media space encountered in public life. Retailers decide what media to order; how to stock, face, and make it available to customers; when to encourage consumption through sales and other promotions; and where to place media products in meaningful relation to one another. Simultaneously, shoppers move through these spaces, guided by their desires and assessing the value of the various commodities they encounter. These interactions are value-making activities and consequently prove crucial to understanding the value media hold in culture.

As a category that defines people in relation to retail businesses, spaces, and material goods, the "shopper" is an abstracted figure. Yet just as scholarship on media reception has shown how cultural backgrounds and identities inform media consumption, so too are social identities articulated in relation to media retailers, spaces, commodities, and shopping experiences. Retailing orbits all manner of conventionally defined social categories, including gender, sexuality, class, race, ethnicity, and generation, among others. Such categories are not inherent but rather are perpetually constructed, negotiated, and reconstructed, with media retail providing a space for these processes of identity construction. Because these social categories are value-laden, they matter to the media retailers who seek to garner consumer dollars, and they should matter, in a different way, to scholars who wish to understand how commerce and culture intersect.

We know that retailers target different social groups by design, whether through advertising, in-store displays and shelf positioning, product offerings, and even store location within urban, suburban, or rural geography. For instance, Target indicates that its average "guest" is around forty years old and has an annual household income of approximately $64,000; further, the company believes that half their customers have college degrees and that 43 percent have children living at home.[57] This information represents an endeavor to imagine a clientele into being and entice customers into one of the company's 1,800 locations. Similarly, Ellen Seiter details how toy stores organize their wares according to divisions of age and gender and also how these stores more indirectly address people of different races, incomes, and educational levels.[58] Identity is central to retail and so should be central to the study of media retail too. Nevertheless, we should always remember the constructedness and complexity of social identities as lived experiences, even when media retailers treat them as a fixed means of assessing potential sources of revenue. That is to say, we should be attentive to the ways in which social and cultural identities are actively produced, realized, and expressed through media retail encounters. Shoppers engage in performative acts of *taste*, which, following Bourdieu, follow social status, aspiration, and modulation.[59] As an interactional space, retail lends itself particularly well to thinking about "social fields" in which various social actors come together, interact, and affirm or adjust their unequal positions and identities within the larger culture.

The study of retail should contend with the fleeting, embodied, speculative, and deeply subjective ways in which shopping identities are formulated; this too is interactional. As Pasi Falk and Colin Campbell write, "The 'interaction' with material goods [in retail spaces] ranges from a variety of sensory experiences to acts of imagination in which the self is mirrored in the potential object of acquisition with questions which are rarely formulated and hardly ever articulated: *'is that for me?'; 'Am I like that?'; 'Could that be (part of) me?'; 'Could I be like that?'; 'Would I like to be like that?'*, and so on."[60] Questions like these occur as a matter of course in shopping experiences and are integral to the retailing of media goods and services. However difficult to study, we should keep these questions and experiences in mind as we study media retail because, no doubt, retailers themselves account for interactional processes.

A Media Studies Shopping List

Due to the multidimensional nature of media retail, this collection is necessarily interdisciplinary in scope and offers analyses from a diverse range of research methods, including political economy, cultural studies, feminist and queer studies, and cultural geography, among others. Despite these different approaches, these essays are all animated by an understanding of media retail as transactional in its production of markets while simultaneously interactional in orienting media consumption around the axes of meaning, identity, and community. To keep the transactional and the interactional in tension, the following chapters address three core questions. First, they explore how and why digital media technologies have changed the business of retailing entertainment culture while transforming the scope of retail more broadly. Second, they investigate the status of media brands as commodities in retail space, revealing how media goods are positioned and how that positioning implicates media and consumers in the politics of meaning and identity. Third, they consider how transactions and interactions in these narrative spaces support everyday forms of community, practice, and participation for retailers and shoppers alike.

Our first set of essays focuses on the shifting relationships between retail and new media technologies. To theorize the interrelationships between media and retail industries, Daniel Herbert explores the emergence of "multifunctional" business models wherein these industries converge. His chapter focuses on the ways in which corporations bend conventional categorical distinctions and invest in media technology to position themselves across the boundaries of different hardware and software commodities. Thus Circuit City and its investment in the DIVX media format represent both an early failure of this multifunctional logic and an important precedent for understanding tech companies like Apple and Amazon that integrate media production, distribution, and retail. Examining Amazon as a multifunctional media retailer, Emily West investigates its long-standing interest in bookselling to argue that the company has transformed not just the venues for book transactions but also the publishing models in which content is created. For West, Amazon is, as a book retailer, emblematic of digital capitalism's ability to continually commodify traditional media products while developing platforms that transform retail from a public, shared experience into a personalized, differentiated one. Together, these first two chapters reveal the significance of media within the digital retail economy, both as a product and as a platform for its continuing evolution.

To provide context for this digital retail economy, Gregory Steirer problematizes the everyday experiences of media retail by unearthing the legal foundations that structure them in the United States. By refusing copyright holders control over what purchasers do with a copy of an intellectual good (beyond the prohibition of reproduction and public exhibition), the "first sale doctrine" imagines media retail into being, establishing the right not just for consumers to resell but also for industries to set up trade in media commodities. As Steirer argues, media retail would have developed very differently without this protection—and his discussion of the efforts that media industries have made to circumvent the first sale doctrine reveals media retail as a cultural formation continually under legal and technological reconstruction. In light of these shifts, Heikki Tyni and Olli Sotamaa examine crowdfunding in digital video game development to uncover new relationships in the buying and selling of media goods. While participants in crowdfunding campaigns typically imagine themselves as helping produce a game, the authors instead recognize that commitment of funds as a form of preordering. This "retailization" of development, they argue, furthermore turns the production of games into a spectacle where consumers act as sales agents to attract larger communities of financial support. Elizabeth Affuso also reveals the new possibilities that digital economies hold for media retail, considering the celebrity apps that curate shopping experiences for their users. As she argues, celebrities have been pushed into digital retailing by an alliance between entrepreneurialism and branding, where the celebrity image on the app platform functions as both a media commodity to be sold and the storefront itself. What emerges is a new retail model based in subscription, where celebrity apps provide a portal to digital mediated shopping experiences (some material, some virtual) tied to microtransactions and clublike feelings of belonging. Through this identification with spectacle and celebrity, shopping becomes media entertainment, suggesting new possibilities for pleasure and looking in digital retail economies.

The second group of essays looks beyond technologies and platforms that enable the transactions and interactions of media retail to consider the role of branded media products in the consumer-facing storefront—and, of course, the politics and power dynamics behind the construction of those retail products and spaces. For the first three of these essays, in fact, franchised comic book brands like *Wonder Woman* become a significant site of interest, revealing both the importance of media brands to retail and the multifaceted ways in which they are deployed as merchandise. Although media scholars have long embraced the concept of "flow" to describe the experiences constructed for consumers by television programmers and other industry gatekeepers, Avi Santo adapts that model to retail space. Examining the practices of shelf slotting and merchandise facing, he enables us to think about contemporary retail as a mediated space that generates continuities and discontinuities between different products. In his attention to how media brands like *Wonder Woman* circulate in these retail flows, his chapter also shows how the environment in which media are sold supports—or potentially disrupts—products' potential participation in hegemonic constructions of gender, age, and other meaningful ideological formations. Ethan Tussey and Meredith Bak take a complementary approach by investigating the display of media-branded toys lines in retail environments, yet they combine this spatial approach with a concern for retailer brands that interoperate with the media brand. Examining the case of DC Super Hero Girls—a toy brand spun-off from the DC Comics superhero media franchise—the authors show how efforts to build greater appeal to younger female consumers with a message of feminist empowerment depended significantly on a limited-term exclusive arrangement with Target, a U.S. retailer that embraced identification with progressive politics to appeal to a middle-class clientele. In the space of Target—and its specific branding and shelving practices—gendered play practices validated a shared feminist brand identity. For Santo, *Wonder Woman* is a brand whose ideological valences depend on its retail positioning, whereas for Tussey and Bak, it represents the potential for toys to sit at the center of media constellations branded at retail.

Yet Courtney Brannon Donoghue sees that same franchise as only a starting point for considering wider relationships between female-driven films and retail marketing campaigns as media merchandising strategies move beyond blockbuster comic book fare to offer adult shoppers a means of consumer participation in the ambivalent politics of feminist empowerment. Moving discussion beyond the girl power presented in toy retail, Brannon Donoghue figures prayer beads, sex toys, and other licensed merchandise targeted to women (as well as the retail spaces in which they are sold) in relation to a marketplace feminism than aligns media fandom with shopping. Her chapter thus encourages studies of media retail to consider how retail strategies figure in the production of new media markets and consumer identities. In response, Tim J. Anderson explores efforts the recording industry made in the 1990s to introduce music commodities into retail sites that hoped to cultivate different clienteles than the record shops that fostered toxic forms of masculine consumption. Middle-class lifestyle branding and digital music sales both "streamlined" the record-buying process for women previously excluded by the specialty record ship. Anderson demonstrates how different retail models support distinct social contexts in which media products and consumer cultures can be constructed. Equally concerned with the reconstruction of retail environments that are hostile to women but refocusing these issues through the lens of sexuality and race, Lynn Comella's chapter examines how sex-positive feminists reclaimed and remade the retail norms of the sex shop to challenge the hegemony of white male heterosexual pleasure and carve out a space for queer women and women of color in this media marketplace. While this involved new ways of presenting and shelving sex-positive products—as Santo, Tussey, and Bak might emphasize—the entrepreneurs behind these efforts also participated in new media production endeavors to create the magazine and video products this new retail environment demanded. In her emphasis on these entrepreneurs' efforts to create a space for inclusivity and community in these retail locales, Comella highlights how the interactions of media retail bear upon multiple forms of identity and identification.

The final five chapters embrace this turn toward community to consider the practices and forms of participation that emerge from and around media in retail contexts, ranging from the experiences of those who work in the store to those who shop in it. These begin with two essays focused on comic book retailing. Benjamin Woo and Nasreen Rajani reflect on the persistence of the comic book shop within comic-reading communities, highlighting their significance as the primary site of struggle over diversity within that fan culture.

Although the authors recognize the white, masculinist, heterosexual norms in these shopping spaces, they also reveal the ways in which retailers and their employees negotiate and navigate these tensions in the attempt to build a sense of community in their stores. By focusing on a project of "retail reform," the chapter reveals media retail as a site of political action. Against the primacy of the comic book shop, however, Erin Hanna posits events like San Diego Comic-Con (SDCC) as equally significant sites of media transaction producing comics fandom. Tracing the organization of SDCC from its emergence in the 1970s until today, she figures the event as a vital site of interaction between retailers and comic fans—one reshaped over time as SDCC adapted to new retail models and cultivated a cultural economy oriented toward exclusive convention collectibles. With many fans now attending to purchase items that they will resell after the event, Hanna productively blurs the boundaries between the industrial practices of retail and the consumer activities of fandom.

The last three essays examine everyday engagement within specific sites of media retail. Examining the impact of video-on-demand services on diasporic video stores throughout the United States, Evan Elkins reveals that underneath anxieties about perceived obsolescence amid changing media technologies, geographies, and audiences, these retail outlets continue to operate "translocally," serving as important hubs in the global flow of people and media commodities. Through his interactions with store operators, Elkins reveals retail environments as crucial sites of tension between local communities and transnational identities within global media culture. Similarly concerned with the role of media retailers in everyday localities, Marc Steinberg explains how the convenience store serves as a hub for the production and consumption of the anime "media mix" in Japan. He demonstrates both the logistical power of the convenience store in the delivery and supply of branded products and also its mediating power as a site of promotion, consumption, and narrative imagination. Through daily encounters, the convenience store shapes the geographies and temporalities of the media mix experience—encouraging further study of media retail as a site of everyday participation. Derek Johnson explores those possibilities by considering market experiences in retail environments as an integral, participatory component of media pleasure and narrative fantasy rather than merely the perfunctory acquisition of media commodities. Identifying theme parks as only one such type of retail fantasy, his chapter explains how the Wizarding World of Harry Potter offers visitors a form of transactional participation in the franchise story world—ultimately revealing the retail point of sale as the point of entry into the meanings and ideologies of media culture, where shopping proves to be as significant and mediated as the media commodity itself.

Retail is crucial to the consumer culture in which we live and a force that challenges critical media studies to develop stronger understandings of that culture. Ultimately, by considering the transactional and interactional dimensions of media retail, these chapters lay the groundwork for a new and vital area of inquiry in media and cultural studies that not only generates better schema for understanding the operations of industry but also puts industry studies in greater dialogue with the study of media and consumer culture. Retail is a routine aspect of our media-driven social lives, and this very routineness has kept it from our scrutiny. This book seeks to change that routine, setting an agenda that makes retail and retail shopping experiences into distinct foci for media analysis. And even if those routines are changing—subject even to the industrial apocalypses imagined in retail reporting—we might better understand those shifts in media culture by thinking about the transactions and interactions in which we are engaged.

Notes

1 Matt Townsend, Jenny Surane, Emma Orr, and Christopher Cannon, "America's 'Retail Apocalypse' Is Really Just Beginning," *Bloomberg*, 8 Nov. 2017, https://www.bloomberg.com/graphics/2017-retail-debt/.

2 Derek Thompson, "What in the World Is Causing the Retail Meltdown of 2017?," *Atlantic*, 10 Apr. 2017, https://www.theatlantic.com/business/archive/2017/04/retail-meltdown-of-2017/522384/. Although the term does not appear in the text of the article, the title of the web version heralds "The Great Retail Apocalypse of 2017."

3 "Retail Apocalypse," *Wikipedia*, accessed 18 May 2019, https://en.wikipedia.org/wiki/Retail_apocalypse.

4 Lauren Thomas, "The Amount of Retail Space Closing in 2018 Is on Pace to Break a Record," *CNBC*, 18 Apr. 2018, https://www.cnbc.com/2018/04/18/the-amount-of-retail-space-closing-in-2018-is-on-pace-to-break-record.html.

5 Robin Levinson-King, "Who Will the 'Retail Apocalypse' Claim in 2018?," *BBC News*, 3 Jan. 2018, http://www.bbc.com/news/world-us-canada-42418902.

6 Miles Johnson, "'Retail Apocalypse' Trade Prompts Contrarian Bets," *Financial Times*, 18 Dec. 2017.

7 Wolf Richter, "Here Are the Type of Stores Getting Hit Hardest by the Retail Apocalypse," *Business Insider*, 26 Feb. 2018, http://www.businessinsider.com/here-are-the-types-of-stores-getting-hit-the-hardest-by-the-retail-apocalypse-2018-2.

8 Amanda Lotz, *Portals: A Treatise on Internet-Delivered Television* (Ann Arbor: University of Michigan Press, 2017); Amanda Lotz, *We Now Disrupt This Broadcast* (Cambridge: MIT Press, 2018); Amanda Lotz, *The Television Will Be Revolutionized* (New York: New York University Press, 2014); Derek Johnson, ed., *From Networks to Netflix: A Guide to Changing Channels* (New York: Routledge, 2018).

9 Nikki Baird, "Retail Apocalypse Explained: Retailers Have Not Actually Embraced Digital Transformation," *Forbes*, 12 Mar. 2018, https://www.forbes.com/sites/nikkibaird/2018/03/12/retail-apocalypse-explained-retailers-have-not-actually-embraced-digital-transformation/#5337c0b22806.

10 Steven Barnes, "Retail's New Dawn: The End of the So-Called Retail Apocalypse," *Forbes*, 26 Feb. 2018, https://www.forbes.com/sites/stevenbarr/2018/02/26/retails-new-dawn-the-end-of-the-so-called-retail-apocalypse/#48b703a45170.

11 Marc Bain, "Footlocker CEO Says 'Retail Apocalypse' Headlines Are Missing the Point," *Quartz*, 4 May 2018, https://qz.com/1270413/foot-lockers-ceo-says-retail -apocalypse-headlines-miss-the-point/.

12 Laurie Ouellette, *Lifestyle TV* (New York: Routledge, 2018); and Laurie Ouellette and James Hay, *Better Living through Reality TV: Television and Post-Welfare Citizenship* (Malden, Mass.: Wiley-Blackwell, 2008).

13 John Caldwell, "Cultures of Production: Studying Industry's Deep Texts, Reflexive Rituals, and Managed Self-Disclosures," in *Media Industries: History, Theory, and Method*, eds. Jennifer Holt and Alisa Perren (Malden, Mass.: Wiley-Blackwell, 2009), 200.

14 Michael Curtin, "On Edge: Culture Industries in the Neo-Network Era," in *Making and Selling Culture*, ed. Richard Ohmann (Hanover, Pa.: Wesleyan University Press, 1996), 197.

15 Stephen Congel, "Five Steps to Surviving the Retail Apocalypse," *Forbes*, 4 Apr. 2018, https://www.forbes.com/sites/forbesrealestatecouncil/2018/04/04/five-steps-to -surviving-the-so-called-retail-apocalypse/#71eb80d49975.

16 Thompson, "What in the World."

17 Baird, "Retail Apocalypse."

18 John Caldwell, *Production Culture: Industrial Reflexivity and Critical Practice in Film and Television* (Durham, N.C.: Duke University Press, 2008); Vicki Mayer, Miranda Banks, and John Caldwell, eds., *Production Studies: Cultural Studies of Media Industries* (New York: Routledge, 2009); Vicki Mayer, *Below the Line: Production and Production Studies in the New Television Economy* (Durham, N.C.: Duke University Press, 2011).

19 Stig Hjarvard, *The Mediatization of Culture and Society* (London: Routledge, 2013).

20 See Tarleton Gillespie, "The Politics of 'Platforms,'" *New Media and Society* 12, no. 3 (2010): 347–364; and Nick Montfort and Ian Bogost, *Racing the Beam* (Cambridge: MIT Press, 2009).

21 Joseph Turow, "The Case for Studying In-Store Media," *Media Industries Journal* 1, no. 1 (2014): 62–68, https://quod.lib.umich.edu/m/mij/15031809.0001.112/-case -for-studying-in-store-media?rgn=main;view=fulltext.

22 Joseph Turow, *The Aisles Have Eyes: How Retailers Track Your Shopping, Strip Your Privacy, and Define Your Power* (New Haven, Conn.: Yale University Press, 2017).

23 Avi Santo, "Retail Tales and Tribulations: Transmedia Brands, Consumer Products, and the Significance of Shop Talk," *Cinema Journal* 58, no. 2 (Spring 2019): 115–141; Avi Santo, "Fans and Merchandise," in *The Routledge Companion to Media Fandom*, eds. Suzanne Scott and Melissa Click (New York: Routledge, 2017): 329–336.

24 Joshua Greenberg, *From Betamax to Blockbuster: Video Stores and the Invention of Movies on Video* (Cambridge: MIT Press, 2008); Daniel Herbert, *Videoland: Movie Culture at the American Video Store* (Berkeley: University of California Press, 2014).

25 Laura J. Miller, *Reluctant Capitalists: Bookselling and the Culture of Consumption* (Chicago: University of Chicago Press, 2006); Janice A. Radway, *A Feeling for Books: The Book-of-the-Month Club, Literary Taste, and Middle-Class Desire* (Chapel Hill: University of North Carolina Press, 1997); Ted Striphas, *The Late Age of Print: Everyday Book Culture, From Consumerism to Control* (New York: Columbia University Press, 2009); John Thompson, *Merchants of Culture: The Publishing Business in the Twenty-First Century* (New York: Plume, 2010).

26 Randy Duncan and Matthew J. Smith, *The Power of Comics: History, Form and Culture* (New York: Continuum 2009); Matthew Pustz, *Comic Book Culture: Fanboys*

and True Believers (Jackson: University Press of Mississippi, 1999); Benjamin Woo, *Getting a Life: The Social Worlds of Geek Culture* (Montreal: McGill-Queen's University Press, 2018).

27 Tim J. Anderson, *Popular Music in a Digital Music Economy: Problems and Practices for an Emerging Service Industry* (New York: Routledge, 2014); Jeremy Wade Morris, *Selling Digital Music, Formatting Culture* (Berkeley: University of California Press, 2015).

28 Carly A. Kocurek, *Coin-Operated Americans: Rebooting Boyhood at the Video Game Arcade* (Minneapolis: University of Minnesota Press, 2015).

29 Ellen Seiter, *Sold Separately: Children and Parents in Consumer Culture* (New Brunswick, N.J.: Rutgers University Press, 1993).

30 Anne Friedberg, *Window Shopping: Cinema and the Postmodern* (Berkeley: University of California Press, 1994); Margaret Morse, "An Ontology of Everyday Distraction: The Freeway, The Mall, and Television," in *Logics of Television: Essays in Cultural Criticism*, ed. Patricia Mellencamp (Bloomington: Indiana University Press, 1990).

31 David Desser and Garth S. Jowett, eds., *Hollywood Goes Shopping* (Minneapolis: University of Minnesota Press, 2000).

32 Roopali Mukherjee and Sarah Banet-Weiser, eds., *Commodity Activism* (New York: New York University Press, 2012).

33 Derek Johnson, *Media Franchising: Creative License and Collaboration in the Culture Industries* (New York: New York University Press, 2013); Jonathan Gray, *Show Sold Separately: Promos, Spoilers, and Other Media Paratexts* (New York: New York University Press, 2010).

34 Dina Iordanova and Stuart Cunningham, eds., *Digital Disruption: Cinema Moves On-line* (St. Andrews, Scotland: St. Andrews Film Studies, 2012); Chuck Tryon, *On-Demand Culture: Digital Delivery and the Future of Movies* (New Brunswick, N.J.: Rutgers University Press, 2013); Michael Curtin, Jennifer Holt, and Kevin Sanson, eds., *Distribution Revolution: Conversations about the Digital Future of Film and Television* (Berkeley: University of California Press, 2014); Wheeler Winston Dixon, *Streaming: Movies, Media, and Instant Access* (Lexington: University of Kentucky Press, 2013).

35 Lizbeth Cohen, *A Consumers' Republic: The Politics of Mass Consumption in Postwar America* (New York: Vintage, 2003); Daniel Thomas Cook, *The Commodification of Childhood: The Children's Clothing Industry and the Rise of the Child Consumer* (Durham, N.C.: Duke University Press, 2004); Vicki Howard, *From Main Street to Mall: The Rise and Fall of the American Department Store* (Philadelphia: University of Pennsylvania Press, 2015); Peter Ikeler, *Hard Sell: Work and Resistance in Retail Chains* (Ithaca, N.Y.: Cornell University Press, 2016); Richard Longstreth, *The American Department Store Transformed, 1920–1960* (New Haven, Conn.: Yale University Press, 2010); Ann Satterthwaite, *Going Shopping: Consumer Choices and Community Consequences* (New Haven, Conn.: Yale University Press, 2001); Lisa Scharoun, *America at the Mall: The Cultural Role of a Retail Utopia* (Jefferson, N.C.: McFarland, 2012).

36 Pasi Falk and Colin Campbell, eds., *The Shopping Experience* (London: Sage, 1997).

37 Jenny Shaw, *Shopping: Social and Cultural Perspectives* (New York: Polity Press, 2010); Arthur Asa Berger, *Shop 'til You Drop* (New York: Rowman and Littlefield, 2005); Kaela Jubas, *The Politics of Shopping* (Walnut Creek, Calif.: Left Coast Press, 2010).

38 Donica Belisle, *Retail Nation: Department Stores and the Making of Modern Canada* (Vancouver: University of British Columbia Press, 2011); Marjorie L. Hilton, *Selling*

to the Masses: Retailing in Russia, 1880–1930 (Pittsburgh: University of Pittsburgh Press, 2012).

39 Mia Bay and Ann Fabian, eds., *Race and Retail: Consumption across the Color Line* (New Brunswick, N.J.: Rutgers University Press, 2015); Elizabeth Chin, *Purchasing Power: Black Kids and American Consumer Culture* (Minneapolis: University of Minnesota Press, 2001); Alison Isenberg, *Downtown America: A History of the Place and the People Who Made It* (Chicago: University of Chicago Press, 2004); Christine Williams, *Inside Toyland: Working, Shopping, and Social Inequality* (Berkeley: University of California Press, 2006).

40 Tracey Deutsch, *Building a Housewife's Paradise: Gender, Politics, and American Grocery Stores in the Twentieth Century* (Chapel Hill: University of North Carolina Press, 2010); Erika Diane Rappaport, *Shopping for Pleasure: Women in the Making of London's West End* (Princeton, N.J.: Princeton University Press, 2000).

41 Celia Lury, *Consumer Culture* (New Brunswick, N.J.: Rutgers University Press, 2011).

42 Neva Goodwin, Frank Ackermand, and David Kiron, eds., *The Consumer Society* (Washington, DC: Island Press, 1995).

43 Lawrence Glickman, ed., *Consumer Society in American History* (Ithaca, N.Y.: Cornell University Press, 1999).

44 For example, Rick DeHerder and Dick Blatt, *Shopper Intimacy: A Practical Guide to Leveraging Marketing Intelligence to Drive Retail Success* (Upper Saddle River, N.J.: FT Press, 2011); Robin Lewis and Michael Dart, *The New Rules of Retail: Competing in the World's Toughest Marketplace* (New York: St. Martin's Press, 2014); Jim Pooler, *Why We Shop: Emotional Rewards and Retail Strategies* (Westport, Conn.: Prager, 2003).

45 Timothy Havens, Amanda Lotz, and Serra Tinic, "Critical Media Industry Studies: A Research Approach," *Communication, Culture and Critique* 2 (2009): 234–253.

46 Julie D'Acci, "Cultural Studies, Television Studies, and the Crisis in the Humanities," in *Television after TV: Essays on a Medium in Transition*, eds. Lynn Spigel and Jan Olsson (Durham, N.C.: Duke University Press, 2004), 418–445.

47 Havens, Lotz, and Tinic, "Critical Media," 237.

48 Paul du Gay, et al., *Doing Cultural Studies: The Story of the Sony Walkman* (London: Open University, 1997), 3.

49 Gray, *Show Sold Separately*.

50 Along these lines, see Derek Johnson on production studies taking an "audience turn" in "After the Industry: Can Production Studies Make an Audience Turn?," *Creative Industries Journal* 7, no. 4 (2014): 50–53.

51 Marx differentiates among distribution, *exchange*, and consumption in *Grundrisse* (London: Penguin Classics, 1973), 88–89. Admittedly, "exchange" and "retail" are not exactly synonymous, but it is nevertheless important to note that we can distinguish "retail" or sale from the process of distribution and from consumption and, further, that it is in the market where "use values" are transformed into "exchange values."

52 Derek Kompare, *Rerun Nation: How Repeats Invented American Television* (New York: Routledge, 2005).

53 Pustz, *Comic Book Culture*; Benjamin Woo, "The Android's Dungeon: Comic-Bookstores, Cultural Spaces, and the Social Practices of Audiences," *Journal of Graphic Novels and Comics* 2, no. 2 (2011): 125–136.

54 Erik Gruenwendel, "Amazon at 20," *Home Media Magazine*, Oct. 2015.

55 "Home Entertainment Visionaries," *Home Media Magazine*, 23 Feb. 2015.

56 Herbert, *Videoland*, 50.

57 "Corporate Fact Sheet," *A Bullseye View: Behind the Scenes at Target*, accessed 5 May 2018, https://corporate.target.com/press/corporate.

58 Seiter, *Sold Separately*, 208–211.

59 Pierre Bourdieu, *Distinction: A Social Critique of the Judgment of Taste*, trans. Richard Nice (Cambridge, Mass.: Harvard University Press, 1984).

60 Pasi Falk and Colin Campbell, introduction to *The Shopping Experience*, eds. Pasi Falk and Colin Campbell (London: Sage, 1997), 4.

Part I

**Retail and New Media
Technologies**

● ●

1

Industrial Crossroads or Cross Purposes?

●●●●●●●●●●●●●●●●●●●●●

Circuit City, DIVX, and the
History of Multifunctional
Media Retailers

DANIEL HERBERT

In January 2017, the *Wall Street Journal* reported that Apple Inc. planned to begin procuring original media content for a new subscription service.[1] This article noted that Apple's endeavor "could . . . mark a significant turn in strategy for Apple as it starts to become more of a media company, rather than just a distributor of other companies' media."[2] A later story on this topic placed Apple within "a crowded market, where both new and traditional media players are vying for original shows."[3] Considered together, these accounts suggest a potential shift in Apple's ontology from a "tech" company into a "media" company and, further, indicate that Apple was (merely) the latest company to expand into media.[4]

Apple's expansion followed, first, the company's previous diversification into retailing and, second, the entry of several major retailers into the media business. The first Apple Store opened in 2001, and by 2015, there were more than 450 Apple Store locations. Apple opened the iTunes Store in October 2003 as a digital platform to sell music and began selling movies and television programs through the iTunes Store in 2005 and 2006, respectively. And while Apple moved into the retail sector, retailers moved into the media business. After years of selling books, music recordings, and physical video commodities, Amazon.com Inc. began selling television programs and feature films via digital download in 2006, and in 2011, the company offered a video streaming service to members of the Amazon Prime program. Analogously, Walmart purchased Vudu Inc. in 2010, and the company continues to offer movies and television programs through the Vudu app on various smart devices.

All this points toward a new industrial alignment of the retail and media industries. Indeed, many of the most important "media" companies today are vitally, if not centrally, involved in retail. It is crucial that we interrogate this historical and industrial conjuncture because, at the minimum, it represents a rather novel innovation of vertical integration within the media industries. The current combination of media and retailing activities among multiple major corporations represents a significant consolidation of power within media culture that could significantly impact the kinds of media that get made, how media circulates, and how audiences will access and make meanings related to these media. And yet, as the stories about Apple's entry into the media business suggest, this new industrial landscape appears as a fait accompli.

This essay seeks to denaturalize the current alignment between the retail and media industries by looking at a similar but failed attempt to align the retail, tech, and media industries in a previous historical moment. Specifically, this essay examines the big-box electronics store Circuit City and the company's unsuccessful endeavor to launch the DIVX (Digital Video Express) media format during the 1990s. DIVX was a movie-on-disc platform that largely resembled the DVD (digital versatile disc). Unlike DVDs, however, DIVX discs were designed to only play within a short period of time after purchase; following this window, consumers had to pay an additional fee to continue watching. In this way, DIVX was both a video format and a business model. And whereas DVDs "became the fastest-selling item in the history of the US consumer electronics market,"[5] DIVX failed to attract consumers and was discontinued in 1999. Paul McDonald has previously detailed the rise and fall of DIVX.[6] Yet McDonald focuses more on the format than the retailer and does not address the way in which DIVX represented an attempt at an industrial convergence among the retail, media, and technology industries. Indeed, my focus is as much on Circuit City as it is on DIVX and questioning how Circuit City's foray into media technology development foreshadowed the present moment of multifunctional retailers.

In using the word *multifunctional*, I hope to specify the ways in which some retailers, including Circuit City, have diversified in ways that bend conventional industrial categories. Of course, many conglomerates have been composed of different divisions that are involved in different business sectors. One might think of Paramount Pictures, which was a division of Gulf and Western from 1966 to 1989; during this period, Gulf and Western was also involved in manufacturing and agriculture, among other industries. Similarly, the Sony Corporation bought Columbia Pictures in 1989 after years of primarily being involved in electronics manufacturing. What I am trying to distinguish, specifically, is that business endeavor that diversifies a company in a new, potentially definitional way, such as when Amazon moved from merely retailing movies to distributing movies of its own. At this point, in fact, many retailers are best thought of as multifunctional to the extent that they also operate as technology firms, media distributors, and media exhibitors, among other identities. For its part, Circuit City was involved in consumer electronics retailing, media retailing, used car sales, banking, and, with DIVX, technology development—a technology that it would sell as well.

As the Sony/Columbia example prompts us to consider, companies often engage in multifunctionality in the pursuit of "synergy." As Jennifer Holt has indicated, this buzzword has had multiple definitions, including "the commercial possibilities of mutually locking commercial ventures"[7] and "tight diversification."[8] Thus on the one hand, the idea of multifunctionality accounts for the divergent business activities, divisions, and sectors that a company might be involved with. On the other hand, history shows that various media companies created new divisions or enveloped other companies with the idea that these different units might coordinate and generate new value. This might occur, as Derek Johnson discusses, as the reexploitation of a single intellectual property across different media platforms.[9] Or, as in the case of Sony and Columbia, synergy might appear as a marriage of hardware and software.

However, as Johnson also details, synergy is an "ideal" that "often proves impractical."[10] Similarly, multifunctionality can sometimes put a company's divisions at cross-purposes. Such was the case with Circuit City's participation in the development and retailing of DIVX, as the platform created tensions within Circuit City and across the retail sector. As a *retailer*, Circuit City aimed to make money from any home video technology; thus the company sold the hardware and software for both DIVX and the competing DVD format. As a *technology firm*, Circuit City needed as many retailers as possible to carry DIVX, and yet other retailers resisted DIVX precisely because of Circuit City's "primary" function as a retailer. Thus while synergy and multifunctionality are not quite the same, this case shows how multifunctionality can fail due to, in part, a failed attempt at synergy.

Out of Control: Home Video Retailing before DIVX

In order to understand Circuit City's involvement with DIVX, one must first look to the historical development of home video in the United States.

Although it garnered vast revenues for hardware manufacturers, movie studios, and retailers, home video raised a number of problems for the movie industry. First, it entailed a brief but impactful format war between rival VCR (videocassette recorder) technologies. Second, it threatened the studios' control over video commodities and the IP (intellectual property) embedded on them. Third, it allowed for the emergence of a new sector to the business, retailing rather than theatrical exhibition, now largely defined by a rental business model and controlled by new industrial players.

Although video was used in television production in the United States during the 1950s and 1960s,[11] it wasn't until the 1970s that video technologies were used more widely. Sony released the Betamax videocassette recorder in Japan in 1975 and then in the United States in 1976.[12] JVC unveiled the competing VHS (Video Home System) format that same year, and in 1977, electronics manufacturer Matsushita asserted that it would support VHS, pitting different technology companies against one another in a format war.[13] Department stores and consumer electronics stores retailed VCR hardware.[14] These retailers positioned the VCR as an appliance that extended from television, and they treated videotapes as appendages of this appliance.[15] The promotional discourse initially situated VCRs as tools to be used for "time shifting" television programming—that is, as devices that allowed one to record and watch television shows at a time of the viewer's choosing.[16] This time-shifting ability also allowed viewers to skip over commercials, the economic bedrock of the American television industry, and several studios joined forces to sue Sony for "contributory infringement" of their intellectual property by endowing consumers with the ability to duplicate, manipulate, and potentially redistribute these works.[17]

Although this lawsuit, known as *Sony v. Universal*, found in 1984 that Sony was not responsible for consumers' uses of VCR technology, it signals the Hollywood studios' concern that home video represented a loss of control over their intellectual properties. This issue grew more pronounced as conceptions and uses of home video changed through the early 1980s and as the retailing of home video shifted toward video specialty stores, which used a rental business model. Specifically, the VCR was repositioned from being a time-shifting device for television programming (although people could still use it in this way) toward being a movie delivery vehicle.[18] And although some early video distributors tried to impose nonrental clauses in their contracts with retailers, this effort was unsuccessful due to the way in which the "first sale doctrine" was applied to videos.[19]

The first rental stores opened immediately following the release of feature films on video, and the rental industry expanded rapidly in the coming years; by 1985, more than 21,000 retailers specialized in video rental.[20] Crucially, this first wave of video retailers was composed of independently owned "mom and

pop" stores whose owners often "had no formal background in film whatso-
ever."[21] Thus the rapid expansion of the home video industry wrested control
over movies away from the Hollywood studios in two ways. First, home video
was characterized by a huge number of independent firms that did not have
established relationships with the studios. Second, the rental business model
meant that the Hollywood studios were cut out from a huge amount of home
video revenues; once a distributor sold a tape to a retailer, that retailer made all
further revenues from the rental of that tape. The selling of VCRs, meanwhile,
remained the province of consumer electronics stores.

The video rental industry consolidated through the second half of the
1980s, and by the early 1990s, a handful of chains dominated the industry,
with Blockbuster Video standing as the most prominent example. Through
this period, Hollywood made efforts to better integrate home video within the
overall operation of the industry. In 1994, the television syndication company
Viacom bought a majority stake in both Blockbuster Video and Paramount
Communications.[22] Here, a single conglomerate sought to connect media
production with distribution *and retailing*, signaling the importance of video
rental to the movie business. Prior to this, in the mid-1980s, the Hollywood
studios instituted a "two-tier" pricing system for video releases to better control the rental market.[23] Whereas the studios priced many tapes between $60
and $100, intended for video rental stores, they began pricing select movie
titles between $20 and $40 to generate a direct-to-consumer, "sell-through"
market that curtailed video rental stores' revenue base. Alternatively, some
home video distributors established leasing plans with the Hollywood studios
during the 1980s and 1990s, allowing the studios to earn a portion of the revenues earned on each rental transaction.[24] In terms of better controlling IP, the
studios worked with hardware manufacturers to install copy protection technology on VCRs and tapes from the mid-1980s onward.

DVD: Another Spin on Home Video

Nevertheless, Hollywood continued to search for solutions to the problems
posed by home video, particularly through the development of digital technologies. As a heavily encrypted, disc-based home video format, DIVX (Digital
Video Express) was designed to address a number of these issues. Yet DIVX
competed with the DVD (digital versatile disc), a technology that also represents an effort to transform both home video technology and retailing. A
number of different electronics companies sought to develop a new digital disc
format for movies, similar to music CDs; importantly, these discs were designed
as playback devices that would not *record* video signals. Yet it was specifically a
collaboration between Toshiba and Time Warner that led to the development
of the DVD in the 1990s. As Paul McDonald notes, this partnership "brought

together two of the major names in media hardware and software,"[25] and the DVD also accrued alliances among other electronics firms, including Matsushita and Pioneer, and information technology companies, such as Apple and IBM.[26] Although not all the Hollywood studios sided with the DVD Consortium immediately,[27] the invention of the DVD format nevertheless speaks to a historically specific alignment among key players in the electronics, IT, and media industries—but notably not yet retail—in a shared effort to reshape media consumption while avoiding another format war.

Promotional discourses marketed DVDs based on the discs' high video and audio quality and "bonus features."[28] Aside from behind-the-scenes documentaries and interviews, though, the DVD had other features that helped it reshape the retailing of home video. DVDs were significantly cheaper to produce than VHS tapes, allowing studios to price them between twenty and thirty dollars as sell-through commodities.[29] The DVD thus aimed to replace the VHS and the rental business model built around it. Further, an agreement was established among all the different players that ensured that DVDs would be encrypted. DVDs were put into the consumer market in North America in March of 1997.[30] Americans adopted this technology quickly, and the sell-through model came to dominate video retailing as the amount of revenue garnered by direct sales overtook that of rental over the course of 1996–2001.[31]

This shift in the business model for video retailing also entailed a change in the location where these items were sold. As video rental declined and sell-through increased in market share, the retailing of DVDs largely shifted to big-box discount chains, such as K-Mart, Target, and Walmart, as well as to big-box electronics stores like Best Buy and Circuit City. In 1999 and 2000, Best Buy sold more DVDs than any other retailer; then in 2001, Walmart overtook Best Buy as the biggest DVD retailer and earned more than $3 billion in video sales.[32] These retailers sold DVD players as well, reestablishing a link between the retailing of video hardware and software.

Enter Circuit City

From an industrial perspective, it might make sense that a company like Circuit City would want to take part in the development of a home video platform. Yet it would have been difficult to predict this endeavor based on this company's history. Circuit City was founded in 1949 as the Wards Company, based in Richmond, Virginia.[33] Originally, the company sold car tires but expanded into selling televisions and other home electronics during the 1950s.[34] It opened additional stores in the 1950s, all of which sold appliances, televisions, and other home electronics.[35] The Wards Company continued to expand in a rather haphazard manner during the 1960s and 1970s. In some cases, the company licensed space in other retail stores, while in others it acquired small chains of hardware and electronics stores.[36] What resulted was a highly fragmented set of operations, with a number of stores that had different names, business models, and even merchandise.[37] As one article put it, "There were warehouse-showrooms that sold everything from television sets to major appliances, small stores that carried just electronics items, or leased spaced inside discount department stores."[38]

In 1977, the company acquired two discount chains in the Washington, DC, area and renamed all the stores "Circuit City."[39] These locations were six to seven thousand square feet in size and specialized in audio and video equipment.[40] The company promoted these stores with significant newspaper advertising, helping create "Circuit City" as a recognizable brand. After this point, the company began specializing in the superstore retailing model. The company had opened a store in 1974 called the "Wards Loading Dock," which was a "40,000-square-foot retail warehouse showroom displaying a vast selection of audio, video and major appliance products";[41] one account states that the store offered around two thousand different products.[42] This store was successful and served as the basis for the company's subsequent "superstores." It opened a second Wards Loading Dock in Richmond in 1979 and in 1981 began opening superstores in other areas with the name "Circuit City Superstores."[43]

The Wards Company changed its name to Circuit City when it went public on the New York Stock Exchange in 1984.[44] It replaced all the former "small" Circuit City stores with superstores in 1984 and closed all non–Circuit City stores in 1986.[45] These superstores sold a wide range of appliances and consumer electronics including stoves, microwaves, washing machines, answering machines, stereo equipment, speakers, and of course, televisions and VCRs.[46] As retail spaces, these immense stores aimed to "create the illusion of both warehouse pricing and customer service."[47] Propelled by the success of this model, Circuit City continued to expand through the 1980s into the 1990s. Whereas the company had 73 stores in 1986,[48] it had 133 stores in 1989[49] and 356 stores in 1995.[50] The company had $1 billion in sales in 1987, $2 billion in 1989, and $3 billion in 1992.[51]

In the mid-1990s, Circuit City expanded beyond operating strictly as a hardware retailer to being a *media* retailer as well when it followed competitor Best Buy and began selling recorded music.[52] The 1990s were marked by a shift in music retailing, with the rapid growth of music superstores like Virgin Megastores and the entry of new competitors into the CD market, including bookstore chains as well as electronics retailers like Best Buy.[53] As of 1995, Circuit City had dedicated music-retailing areas in 220 (out of 365) of its stores.[54] Notably, Best Buy's and Circuit City's entries into music retailing were positioned within public discourse as a threat to established record stores.[55] Circuit City priced CDs as low as $11,[56] at a time when music specialty stores charged list prices, which typically ranged from $16 to $18.[57] Circuit City thus used CDs as "loss leaders," luring shoppers into the store with cheap CDs, where they might buy more profitable items. The company sold an estimated $250 million in recorded music in 1995.[58]

Circuit City entered into some unconventional business ventures during this period. The company opened its own bank in 1990.[59] Perhaps more surprising, Circuit City expanded into the used car market in 1993,[60] when it opened its first CarMax location.[61] Circuit City had no experience in selling used cars, and there were doubts among industry experts that CarMax would succeed.[62] Although CarMax split from Circuit City in 2002,[63] the endeavor demonstrates an effort to broaden the company's business.

Circles and Squares: Circuit City and DIVX

Circuit City's participation in the creation of DIVX represents another example of the company's interest in broadening its business activities. Further, DIVX constitutes a category-altering expansion for the company. As noted, DIVX was a disc-based video format that aimed to displace the VHS and, just as importantly, to compete with the DVD. Development for DIVX began in 1994.[64] The system was originally called "Zoom TV."[65] Zoom TV was a division of Ziffren, Brittenham, Branca & Fischer, a major entertainment law firm based in Los Angeles. The firm represented such clients as Woody Harrelson, Harrison Ford, and Eddie Murphy.[66] Further, this law firm helped coordinate major merger and acquisition deals in the media business, including Ted Turner's purchase of the MGM library in 1986 and Disney's purchase of Miramax in 1993.[67] In fact, Ziffren, Brittenham, Branca & Fischer aimed to be central to the consolidation of the media industries during this period, particularly with the pairing of technology and media companies. A story from 1995 in *Forbes* put it this way: "As telecommunications, electronics and computers converge, these businesses increasingly are turning to Hollywood for content to run over their wires and to put on their screens and machines. ZBB&F is right there to help."[68] More than helping, this law firm held a privileged position in the technological and structural transformation of the movie business. Thus the *Forbes* article also discussed the law firm's foray with Zoom TV, which it characterized as a "move on from being a go-between to becoming an owner."[69] The patent for Zoom TV was filed in November 1995 by a lawyer from Ziffren, Brittenham, Branca & Fischer as well as a technological consultant.[70] This was more than just a law firm but also a tech company of sorts.

Circuit City got involved early in DIVX's development. Initially, Circuit City invested $30 million to support the technological development of the format.[71] Then during the spring of 1997, Circuit City invested an additional $100 million into the platform, which was now renamed DIVX.[72] The additional $100 million endowed Circuit City with a two-thirds majority stake in the platform.[73] Some members of the DIVX group had experience in media and electronics, such as Executive Vice President Richard Sowa,[74] who had worked as the president of distribution for Playboy, which included home video and cable activities.[75] The head of DIVX was Richard Sharp, then the chairman and chief executive of Circuit City.[76] Sharp continued to be based in Circuit City's headquarters in Richmond, while DIVX headquarters were in nearby Herndon, Virginia.[77]

It is at this moment that Circuit City properly became a multifunctional retail company, no longer simply involved in the selling of appliances, consumer electronics, and recorded music but now a developer of home video technologies. To be clear, Circuit City did not produce either DIVX players or media content to be played on those devices. Yet by developing the technology and licensing it to electronics manufacturers, the company took a step toward vertical integration at the same time that it entered an entirely new business sector. DIVX therefore entailed a major branching out of Circuit City's operations in an attempt at synergy, which simultaneously created a new multifunctional identity for the company. As companies like Apple, Amazon, Walmart, and others have more recently combined media and retailing business activities, Circuit City and DIVX force us to consider the historical and industrial significance of the pairing of retail and media more generally.

Despite its control over DIVX, Circuit City depended on other companies in other business sectors for the format to succeed. Circuit City strove to secure agreements with, first, electronics manufacturers to build DIVX machines and, second, Hollywood studios to release content on the platform. Doing so was a complicated process. The mid-1990s was a moment in which the alliances around the DVD were still being forged and issues of encryption and copy protection were still being sorted out.[78] It remained unclear which movie studios would support DVD or any disc-based video format. This was, in other words, a moment in which the ultimate fate of digital videodiscs was still undecided. As of mid-1995, DIVX (as Zoom TV) was still in the process of securing deals with hardware manufacturers.[79] By the time that Circuit City publicly announced DIVX in September 1997, Disney, Universal Studios, Paramount Pictures, and DreamWorks had all agreed to release films on the format.[80] Similarly, Zenith, Panasonic, and RCA all agreed to manufacture DIVX devices.[81]

Warner Bros and Sony had already backed the DVD at this point. Earlier that year, Zoom TV / DIVX had been publicized at the Video Software Dealers Association convention, which prompted much discussion about its differences from DVD as well as the potential for a war between the two formats.[82] As noted, DVDs were released in March of 1997, while DIVX was not scheduled to arrive on the market until the following spring—and actually would not appear in stores until June 1998.[83] Thus much of the public discourse in the fall of 1997 positioned DIVX as a threat to the DVD, not just because it was a direct competitor but also because it had the potential to create confusion among consumers and retailers. One analyst stated outright, "I really hope this isn't a replay of Beta versus VHS."[84] And indeed, the DIVX/DVD rivalry is part of a longer history of competition among formats in the home video business, as it both echoes the Beta/VHS war and presages the competition between the HD DVD and Blu-Ray high-definition disc formats that occurred in the mid-2000s. This history of format wars makes DIVX all the more noteworthy, however, as the potential schism it threatened, between formats and media companies, was literally and figuratively engineered by a retailer.

The rivalry between DVD and DIVX relied substantially on the particular qualities of the DIVX format. Paul McDonald has referred to DIVX as "not really a format but an encryption system linked to a retail scheme";[85] I would emphasize the latter part of this statement, asserting that DIVX entailed a competing business model that aimed to fundamentally impact video retailing. DIVX worked like this: consumers would buy a DIVX player, which resembled a DVD player and could play other DVD discs but cost roughly $100 more.[86] Consumers could then "purchase" a DIVX disc for around $5, a fee that was in line with video rental prices at the time and was substantially lower than the $20–30 typical price for DVDs.[87] However, DIVX discs could only be played for a two-day period, after which point they would be "locked."[88] In this manner, DIVX resembled video rental, as there was a limited time for viewing, and yet the discs did not need to be returned to a retail location. If consumers wanted to watch the disc again, they could use a modem on the device, run through a phone line, to unlock the disc for another two-day period for around $3; if consumers wanted unlimited viewings, they could unlock the discs permanently for less than $20.[89] Some in the press referred to DIVX as "a DVD player for the rental market that will play encrypted discs on a pay-per-view basis,"[90] while others properly assessed that the format was "a rental/sales hybrid."[91] Thus DIVX's combination of technical functionality and price aimed to create a middle road between the traditional video rental and direct sell-through commercial models, where costumers did not need to return a video but also did not have complete ownership and control over the commodity.

To the studios that supported the format, DIVX appeared to solve a number of issues that had defined the home video market previously. For one, DIVX promised a high level of encryption, thus preventing the copying of discs. As one article put it, DIVX "solves the problem of piracy feared by Hollywood studios."[92] Second, DIVX retailing entailed revenue sharing, where the studios would get a portion of each retail transaction. This contrasted with the way in which video rental stores earned revenues on every

VHS rental transaction, cutting studios out of a continuing revenue stream. Third and finally, DIVX offered the studios an innovative means of circumventing the first sale doctrine. Although one could purchase a DIVX disc and ostensibly do with it whatever one wished, the technical system forced viewers to link a particular disc to a specific DIVX player in order for it to function. So if a customer loaned, traded, or sold that disc, the new user would have to pay to have that disc unlocked on a new device. As one critic snarkily wrote, "Perhaps the coolest feature of Divx is that you can take a disc over to a friend's house, pop it into his Divx player, and he gets billed. Excellent!"[93]

As Paul McDonald indicated, "If distributors simply wanted to withdraw a title . . . then it could be quite easily taken out of circulation at the point of supply"[94] because of the way that DIVX machines provided "permission" to view content via an online connection. This remote access feature seems especially prescient, given the way in which the contemporary electronic sell-through (EST) and rental markets work, where the purchasers of digital movie files are, in fact, licensees. DIVX was, to a great extent, a forerunner of contemporary digital rights management (DRM) systems for online media, which provide access to media content at the same time that they inhibit the duplication and unwarranted recirculation of that content.

More than just a war among video formats, DIVX created competition among different retail models for video and, crucially, among different retailers. The initial plan was for DIVX discs to be sold at conventional video rental stores.[95] Yet Blockbuster Video held off from carrying DIVX.[96] There was also resistance to the format by the Video Software Dealers of America (VSDA), the trade association that represented video stores. VSDA president Jeffrey Eves stated that because one didn't need to return DIVX discs to a store, "it would seem on its face to be designed to eliminate the need for 30,000 specialty stores throughout the country."[97] In 1999, rumors arose again that Blockbuster might begin selling DIVX, but those plans fell through.[98]

DIVX also had to compete with the sell-through market simultaneously being established for DVDs and, consequently, placed Circuit City in competition with big-box discount chains, such as Walmart, which began to dominate the DVD market. Circuit City also competed with such stores because they all carried DVD players. On the one hand, Circuit City hedged its bets by carrying both DVDs and DIVX discs. On the other hand, Circuit City was poised to compete with the discount chains precisely *through* its retailing of the software and hardware for an alternative format. In this contest, Circuit City struggled. One article cited analyst Tom Wolzien as noting that although "Circuit City commands a dominant 15% of the consumer electronics market, its video sales are dwarfed by giant retailers such as Walmart. It is at those stores where the mass market potential for any technology must ultimately be proven."[99] Best Buy refused to carry DIVX because of the format's connection to Circuit City.[100] Even Circuit City itself struggled with the format war that it had initiated by selling DVD players while it was launching DIVX. When the plans for the rollout of DIVX were being made, Circuit City chairman Richard Sharp stated it was a "'delicate issue' because Circuit City doesn't want to endanger sales of existing DVD player inventory."[101] It appears that Circuit City's multifunctional identity put it in competition with itself.

However innovative Circuit City may have been in its endeavor to develop a video technology, the company ultimately found it impossible to transform home video retailing. Following a limited release of DIVX in the summer of 1998, there was a "national roll-out" of the format in seven hundred retail locations the following October.[102] But less than a year later, in June of 1999, Circuit City discontinued DIVX.[103] The company offered a one-hundred-dollar rebate to consumers who had bought a DIVX player before its discontinuation was announced, and the company maintained the online "DIVX Central" system for two more years, allowing customers to continue "unlocking" their DIVX discs through 2001.[104] Otherwise, these DIVX players were still capable of playing DVD discs, which by that point had become the standard home video format.

Paul McDonald has detailed many of the factors that contributed to DIVX's failure:[105] DIVX players were too expensive. DIVX arrived on the market too late after the DVD. Not enough movie titles appeared on DIVX. DIVX was a "closed" system, while the DVD was "open." DIVX movies were pan and scan, while DVDs often featured widescreen films. DIVX offered none of the "bonus features" found on many DVDs. Many of these issues relate to market forces and technological differences. McDonald's account also suggests, however, that DIVX was a failure in retailing. DIVX required partnerships with not only electronics manufacturers and Hollywood studios but other consumer electronics and home video retailers as well. That is, Circuit City could not operate alone, even (or perhaps especially) as a multifunctional retailer. In order for DIVX to work, it first had to be sold to consumers, and thus it depended on partnerships or at least cooperation with other retailers. Without such external "buy in" regarding DIVX, Circuit City's multifunctional identity was merely an anomaly within the media and retailing industries, which had not proven especially open to combining these functions.

Almost all other retailers simply refused to support DIVX. One analyst asked, "Why didn't more retailers carry it, especially Best Buy? . . . The answer is: Would you put profits in the pockets of your arch competitor?"[106] This statement presents a picture that is as much about rivalries in the retail sector as it is about a war between video formats. And further, new retailing competition arose at this same time, as Blockbuster Video began renting DVDs in 1998 and Netflix began their DVD rent-by-mail service in that same year. Here we see that, in addition to sell-through giants like Walmart, companies like

Blockbuster and Netflix posed new competition to DIVX and Circuit City alike. After all, as the manifestation of a multifunctional retailer, DIVX and Circuit City were one and the same.

Conclusion: The Continued Relevance of DIVX

Circuit City went bankrupt in 2008 and stopped all operations in 2009 after a decadelong battle to rebrand itself in the face of the exploding cellular phone industry and the competition posed by online retailers (figure 1.1). Jeffrey Sconce wrote at that time about the desolation one could find inside a Circuit City store during a liquidation sale, which appears all the more relevant today, given the way in which online retailing has swept over so many brick-and-mortar retailers.[107] Sconce focuses on the way in which media commodities appear particularly devalued in this context, as old CDs and random DVDs litter the aisles like garbage in the making. Sconce provides a visceral sense of Circuit City's function as a retailer of tangible media and the frailty of this business. With this in mind, we might see the failure of the DIVX platform as foreshadowing the decline in physical media commodities and the retailers that sold them.

As an effort to conjoin the retailing, technology, and media businesses, DIVX remains relevant in a variety of ways. After Circuit City abandoned the format, former DIVX workers formed a new company called Cinea, Inc. Clearly building upon the ideas behind DIVX, Cinea worked to create media

FIG. 1.1 An abandoned Circuit City in Rockford, Illinois, its space now "for lease" (photo by Carol Johnson)

content protection technologies for use in a wide variety of platforms and venues, including "digital cinema, in-flight entertainment, high-definition DVD, and video on demand."[108] Cinea, in other words, was strictly a technology company. Circuit City, meanwhile, still held the patents for DIVX. In 2011, these patents were auctioned off as part of Circuit City's postbankruptcy liquidation. A press release regarding the auction stated, "Although the DIVX system is no longer available, the technology developed by DIVX remains relevant to the areas of compression, distribution, security, usage tracking of movie content, anti-piracy, digital media and watermarking."[109] More pointedly, this press release quoted an executive overseeing the transaction as saying, "Although Circuit City was not able to capitalize on its inventions, the video distribution model it envisioned has become the mainstream."[110]

It is now common for many consumers to "purchase" or "rent" movies without ever fully owning or controlling these video commodities. This can be done through Apple, Amazon, Walmart's Vudu, or any number of similar services. These retailers often charge four to six dollars for these videos, around the same price as DIVX discs once cost. So what is the difference? It is not just a matter of technology or of retailing; what has been normalized is the systematic, simultaneous intertwining of tech, media, and retailing. Brick-and-mortar storefronts for media commodities do remain, but they now compete with the practical *and* virtual storefronts one can access on a computer, tablet, or smart TV. What has become "mainstream," in other words, is the appearance of media retailing in our homes or anywhere there is a screen connected to the internet. The devices themselves are multifunctional, combining media and retail. This pervasion of media retailing across the social landscape has coincided with the industrial incursion of companies defined as "retailers" into the tech and media business sectors. This combination of retail and media industries now appears mainstream too. There appears to be something like a homology, then, between the structure of the media businesses and the practices through which media are shopped for and consumed.

From this vantage, the story of Circuit City and DIVX represents more than just a failed business or platform. With DIVX, Circuit City attempted to redefine itself from being an electronics and media retailer to being a technology distributor and patent licensor that could have been central to the delivery of movies and other media. In this respect, Circuit City sought a mixed industrial identity that anticipated the role that companies like Amazon and Apple currently play in the media industry. Circuit City's failure with DIVX thus reveals some of the technological, industrial, and cultural factors that contemporary multifunctional retailers rely on. The contemporary convergence between media and retail is neither natural nor guaranteed, and the story of Circuit City and DIVX demonstrates the historical contingency of the current industrial situation.

Notes

1 Ben Fritz, Tripp Mickle, and Hannah Karp, "Apple Sets Its Sights on Hollywood with Plans for Original Content," *Wall Street Journal*, 12 Jan. 2017, https://www .wsj.com/articles/apple-sets-its-sights-on-hollywood-with-plans-for-original -content-1484217007.

2 Fritz, Mickle, and Karp, "Apple."

3 Tripp Mickle, "Apple Readies $1 Billion War Chest for Hollywood Programming," *Wall Street Journal*, 16 Aug. 2017, https://www.wsj.com/articles/apple-readies-1 -billion-war-chest-for-hollywood-programming-1502874004.

4 Mickle, "Apple Readies."

5 This was true as of 2005. Paul McDonald, *Video and DVD Industries* (London: BFI, 2008), 143.

6 McDonald, *Video and DVD*, 148–149.

7 Justin Wyatt, *High Concept: Movies and Marketing in Hollywood* (Austin: University of Texas Press, 1994), 70; cited in Jennifer Holt, *Empires of Entertainment: Media Industries and the Politics of Deregulation, 1980–1996* (New Brunswick, N.J.: Rutgers University Press, 2011), 5.

8 Thomas Schatz, "The Return of the Hollywood Studio System," in *Conglomerates and the Media*, ed. Erik Barnow (New York: New Press, 1997), 84; cited in Holt, *Empires of Entertainment*, 5.

9 Derek Johnson, *Media Franchising: Creative License and Collaboration in the Culture Industries* (New York: New York University Press, 2013), 67.

10 Johnson, *Media Franchising*, 68.

11 McDonald, *Video and DVD*, 20–23.

12 McDonald, 33.

13 McDonald, 34.

14 Joshua Greenberg, *From Betamax to Blockbuster: Video Stores and the Invention of Movies on Video* (Cambridge: MIT Press, 2008), 45–48, 63–69.

15 Greenberg, *From Betamax*, 45–48.

16 Greenberg, 20–21; Frederick Wasser, *Veni, Vidi, Video: The Hollywood Empire and the VCR* (Austin: University of Texas Press, 2001), 71.

17 Wasser, *Veni, Vidi, Video*, 88–91.

18 Greenberg, *From Betamax*, 41–42.

19 Wasser, *Veni, Vidi, Video*, 102–103.

20 Barry Monush, ed., *International Television & Video Almanac* (New York: Quigley, 1995), 697.

21 Greenberg, *From Betamax*, 76.

22 McDonald, *Video and DVD*, 140.

23 Wasser, *Veni, Vidi, Video*, 132–135.

24 Daniel Herbert, *Videoland: Movie Culture at the American Video Store* (Berkeley: University of California Press, 2014), 163–166.

25 McDonald, *Video and DVD*, 55.

26 McDonald, 56.

27 McDonald, 145.

28 McDonald, 59–67.

29 Herbert, *Videoland*, 40.

30 McDonald, *Video and DVD*, 143.

31 Herbert, *Videoland*, 41.

32 Herbert, 41.

33 Buzz McClain, "Circuit City Plugs in for the Future," *Video Business*, 23 Feb. 2004, 25.
34 McClain, "Circuit City Plugs."
35 McClain.
36 McClain.
37 Gregory Gilligan, "Circuit City Is Cutting Circles around Competition," *Richmond Times-Dispatch*, 14 June 1993.
38 Gilligan, "Circles around Competition."
39 McClain, "Circuit City Plugs."
40 McClain.
41 McClain.
42 Edmund Andrews, "Struggling for Profits in Electronics," *New York Times*, 10 Sept. 1989.
43 Gilligan, "Circles around Competition."
44 McClain, "Circuit City Plugs"; Gilligan, "Circles around Competition."
45 Gilligan, "Circles around Competition."
46 "Display Ad 91," *Los Angeles Times*, 17 Nov. 1985.
47 Andrews, "Struggling for Profits."
48 Caroline Mayer, "Rapid Growth of Circuit City Sending Waves across Industry," *Washington Post*, 14 Apr. 1986.
49 Andrews, "Struggling for Profits."
50 Ed Christman, "Best Buy, Circuit City a Potent Combo," *Billboard*, 17 June 1995, 80.
51 Gilligan, "Circles around Competition."
52 Christman, "Best Buy."
53 Don Jeffrey, "NARM '94: Sizing Up the Superstores' Impact on Music Retail," *Billboard*, 26 Mar. 1994, N-30.
54 Christman, "Best Buy."
55 Christman.
56 Christman.
57 Ed Christman and Don Jeffrey, "Electronics Webs Confront Troubled Music Depts," *Billboard*, 8 Mar. 1997, 68.
58 Christman, "Best Buy."
59 Gilligan, "Circles around Competition."
60 Gilligan.
61 Ted Shelsby, "Circuit City Shifting Gears," *The Sun* (Baltimore, Md.), 7 Dec. 1993.
62 Shelsby, "Circuit City Shifting Gears."
63 Gregory Gilligan, "All Grown Up, Circuit City Spinoff CarMax Now Stands on Its Own," *Knight Ridder Tribune Business News*, 1 Oct. 2002.
64 Seth Goldstein and Eileen Fitzpatrick, "A Rival Format for DVD Due on Market in '98," *Billboard*, 20 Sept. 1997, 86.
65 Dana Parker, "DVD Doings," *CD-ROM Professional* 9, no. 3 (1996): 13.
66 "The Top Corporate Lawyers," Forbes, Nov. 1995, 146.
67 Lisa Gubernick and Peter Newcomb, "We Loathed Time Sheets," *Forbes*, Dec. 1995, 120.
68 Gubernick and Newcomb, "We Loathed."
69 Gubernick and Newcomb.
70 "DIVX to Be Promoted Soon in Circuit City Stores," *Consumer Electronics*, 22 Sept. 1997.
71 Goldstein and Fitzpatrick, "Rival Format."
72 Bruce Orwall, "A 'Disposable' Video Disk Threatens to Undercut Nascent Market for DVDs," *Wall Street Journal*, 9 Sept. 1997.

73 Gregory Gilligan, "Circuit City Invests $100 Million in Disc Company," *Richmond Times-Dispatch*, 9 Sept. 1997.
74 Junko Yoshida, "Videodisk's Hollywood Connection," *Electronic Engineering Times*, 28 Aug. 1995, 8.
75 Jim McCullaugh, "Playboy Home Video Tenth Anniversary: Sexy Business," *Playboy*, 1 Aug. 1992.
76 Marla Matzer, "Company Town: Start Up Firm Develops Model for DVD Industry," *Los Angeles Times*, 9 Sept. 1997.
77 Matzer, "Company Town."
78 Parker, "DVD Doings."
79 Yoshida, "Videodisk's Hollywood Connection."
80 Matzer, "Company Town."
81 Matzer.
82 Anne Sherber, "Cable, Satellite, Vid Execs Debate Digital TV Options," *Billboard*, 30 Aug. 1997, 83.
83 McDonald, *Video and DVD*, 148.
84 Tom Wolzien, quoted in Matzer, "Company Town."
85 McDonald, *Video and DVD*, 145.
86 Matzer, "Company Town."
87 Matzer.
88 Orwall, "'Disposable' Video Disk."
89 Matzer, "Company Town."
90 Parker, "DVD Doings."
91 Matzer, "Company Town."
92 Matzer.
93 Corey Greenberg, "Divx Is a Four-Letter Word," *Stereo Review*, Jan. 1998, 112.
94 McDonald, *Video and DVD*, 146.
95 Seth Goldstein, "DVD, Divx Stay in Their Own Corners at CES," *Billboard*, 24 Jan. 1998, 93.
96 "Retailers Mixed on DIVX, Some Fearing DVD Sales Fallout," *Consumer Electronics*, 15 Sept. 1997, 1.
97 Orwall, "'Disposable' Video Disk."
98 Stephanie Stoughton, "Circuit City's Slipped Disk; Firm Concedes Defeat, Abandons Divx Technology," *Washington Post*, 17 June 1999.
99 Matzer, "Company Town."
100 "Retailers Mixed."
101 "DIVX to Be Promoted," 1.
102 McDonald, *Video and DVD*, 149.
103 McDonald.
104 Péter Jacsó, "Divx Is Dead—Long Live DVD!," *Information Today*, Sept. 1999, 42.
105 McDonald, *Video and DVD*, 148–149.
106 Kenneth M. Gassman Jr., quoted in Stoughton, "Circuit City's Slipped Disk."
107 Jeffrey Sconce, "Circuit City Unplugged," *World Picture* 2 (Autumn 2008), http://www.worldpicturejournal.com/WP_2/Sconce.html.
108 "Dolby Acquires Anti-piracy Technology Company," *DVD News*, 23 Sept. 2003.
109 "Circuit City—DIVX Patent Portfolio to Be Sold at Auction," *PR Newswire*, 14 July 2011.
110 Gabriel Fried, quoted in "DIVX Patent Portfolio."

2

Amazon, Bookseller

• •

Disruption and Continuity in
Digital Capitalism

EMILY WEST

Amazon.com began as an online book retailer in 1995 not because founder
and CEO Jeff Bezos had a passion to sell books but because books were a logical first product in the earliest days of e-commerce. They were compact and
easy to ship, and the huge variety of titles conformed to the as-yet-uncoined
logic of the "long tail."[1] Starting out as exclusively an online retailer for books,
then moving into CDs and DVDs, Amazon (as it prefers to be called) eventually became "the everything store."[2] Today, bookselling is just one of Amazon's
many business interests (e.g., streaming and cloud services), but it remains a
significant part of its revenue stream. According to one estimate, 7 percent
of Amazon's annual revenue came from books in 2014.[3] Media sales overall,
encompassing more than just books, accounted for 17.6 percent of 2016 revenue according to Amazon.[4] Even as Amazon's business activities proliferate,
books remain important to the company's brand identity and relationship
with consumers and a focus for innovation in e-tailing, technology, and now
brick-and-mortar selling.

To focus on Amazon is to focus on the power of retailing in today's economy, particularly as it relates to the media industries. In the contemporary
marketplace, infrastructures of distribution, including retailing, have much

more influence over what gets produced—and what people actually access in terms of media content—than in the past. Sociologists Edna Bonacich and Jake Wilson have described the historical shift from a "push" system in which manufacturers called the shots for retailers, who were expected to move products, to a "pull" system in which retailers tell manufacturers what they should be supplying and manufacturers attempt to do so "just in time."[5] On-demand printing—one of the businesses Amazon has expanded into—exemplifies this "just-in-time ethos," but accurate and instantly transmittable "point-of-sale" data, as well as anticipatory data of consumer demand such as searches, pre-sales, and social media activity, are also major factors in this overall transformation in retailing.[6]

Amazon could be exhibit A for how the concentrated power of a retailer can transform not just book retailing but the business of publishing itself. Indeed, with the development of the Kindle, which substantially contributed to e-books being 30 percent of the American book market by 2014,[7] Amazon has arguably influenced the very nature of books and reading. While there is certainly evidence for viewing Amazon as a disruptive force in the book market, at a time when tech entrepreneurs are celebrating "disruption" as a productive characteristic of tech companies who have become known for "moving fast and breaking things,"[8] in this chapter, I also place the story of Amazon and bookselling in a longer history of book retailing.

Such contextualizations demonstrate that, in many ways, the story of Amazon and bookselling reflects larger forces transforming retail in general and media retail in particular under digital capitalism. Digital capitalism refers not only to tech giants like Amazon but to how companies of all kinds use digital communication technologies and computing to speed up, rationalize, scale, and reconfigure commerce of all kinds.[9] This includes businesses that ostensibly reside offline, such as brick-and-mortar stores, and those that sell that most important of analog media forms—books. I argue that we should understand Amazon as an emblem of digital capitalism rather than as an exceptional black swan, as it is sometimes characterized. The evidence I offer for this interpretation includes the persistent commodification of media products, including books, much to the chagrin of publishers, authors, and many booksellers; the impact of being a platform business rather than "merely" a retailer; and the transformation of retail space from public, shared, even "democratic" space to personalized, differentiated, even "discriminatory" space. While some of these trends predate Amazon and e-commerce, the envelopment of book retailing within a platform business is a development that is arguably emblematic of the business practices of today's tech giants.

Amazon and Book Retailing:
A History of Commodification vs. Sacralization

It's no secret that Amazon is a much-feared, even hated, behemoth in the book retailing landscape. Headlines such as "Amazon Must Be Stopped" (in *The New Republic*), "Can Anyone Compete with Amazon?," and "Is Amazon Really the Devil?" (in *Publishers' Weekly*) are not uncommon. Amazon.com went online just four years after the internet was open to commercial activity. Less than twenty years later, "Amazon [was] the single biggest book retailer in America: It [sold] 41% of all new books that are sold . . . both e-book and print," according to the Codex Group.[10] Large book chains and independent bookstores alike have struggled in this new environment, with chains in particular closing stores, including, notably, Borders, which was the second-largest bookselling chain in the country until it went out of business in 2011. Independent bookstores took a major hit as well but since 2009 have seen some recovery with growth in the number of stores nationwide.[11]

Beyond the expected heartbreak of a competitive business environment is the animus that Amazon attracts for so clearly treating books, in particular, as merely the means to profitable ends. As just one example of this sentiment, best-selling author James Patterson, upon receiving an award at Book Expo America, said, "Amazon also, as you know, wants to control book selling, book buying, and even book publishing, and that is a national tragedy" because "publishers are not terribly profitable. If those profits are further diminished, publishers will produce less serious literature. It's just a fact of life. And that's one of the reasons why right now, the future of our literature is in danger."[12] In the concern and criticism of Amazon's business practices in bookselling, we see reflected a long-standing cultural anxiety about the relationships among art, culture, and commerce.[13] While books are broadly understood to be subject to market forces, we resist the idea that they are ultimately reducible to them.[14] It is in retail spaces where these tensions come to a head, because in stores, whether in person or online, art and culture are reduced to prices, or commodified.

Given the association of books with culture, education, self-improvement, and community, the tension that book retailers face in attempting to profit from them long predates Amazon's arrival on the scene. Elizabeth Long writes, "If cultural degradation has not followed from increased commercialism, it is nonetheless true that various segments of the literary community have been convinced that it would, ever since the literary marketplace emerged during the eighteenth century."[15] In her history of the American book industry in the twentieth century, Laura J. Miller makes it clear that innovations in book retailing—selling books in stores other than those dedicated to books, the rise of mass-market paperbacks, having bookstore chains in malls, and the arrival of big-box chains—have all been met with consternation because of how they juxtapose the sacred aura of the book with profane commercial imperatives.[16] When the large chain "superstores" for books emerged in the 1990s, "independent booksellers accused the chains of harboring monopolistic designs, and of engaging in unfair competition," and further, were concerned "that they were guided more by profit-and-loss statements than by literary consideration."[17]

Conflicts between book retailers and Amazon have played out in quite similar ways as they have previously in the twentieth century, when new retailing formats also made books cheaper and more accessible to consumers. Certainly, Amazon founder and CEO Jeff Bezos's own instrumental relationship to books as the product that Amazon would first sell is no secret. Bezos's starting point was the insight that the internet was becoming a significant gathering place, where people could be sold to. He apparently considered twenty different product categories, with the intention all along to master one product category before branching into others. He subjected the product list to the following criteria: the product must be familiar, have a large market size, have surmountable competition, a way of accessing a large inventory as well as an online database of products, the ability to out-compete brick-and-mortar stores with discounts, and reasonable shipping costs.[18] Books were the winning product. Less than three years after launching Amazon.com as an online bookstore, Bezos started selling CDs on the site, followed a few months later by DVDs and videos.[19] He announced to the world what his vision had been all along: "Our strategy is to become an electronic commercial destination. When somebody thinks about buying something online, even if it is something we do not carry, we want them to come to us."[20]

Bezos's approach has offended booksellers by using books as "bait" to build an unstoppable e-commerce website. Similar critiques have been levied against Amazon's move into video streaming and television and film production. Amazon's newfound interest in televisual entertainment has been interpreted as merely a cog in its larger bid for retail dominance, given how the Prime Video subscription is "bundled" with the Amazon Prime membership, as well as the broader synergies Amazon enjoys between entertainment properties and retail opportunities.[21]

Amazon has also been roundly criticized for its aggressive pricing of books. There's some irony in chains like Borders and Barnes and Noble suffering at the hands of Amazon's discounting practices, since when they emerged in the 1990s and routinely offered bestsellers at a 30 percent discount, it was independent booksellers crying foul against them.[22] Amazon's tolerance for losing money to gain a competitive advantage has been apparent in its use of loss leaders, which are heavily advertised and discounted products that bring customers into stores. While the major chains—and department stores before them—used bestsellers as loss leaders for decades, Amazon has arguably outplayed them in that game. For example, in 2003, Amazon sold 1.4 million copies of the highly anticipated *Harry Potter and the Order of the Phoenix* at a 40 percent discount with free shipping, from which they earned essentially no profit margin.[23] The following year, Amazon offered a 30 percent discount on *all* books over fifteen dollars, a much more extensive use of discounting than the chain stores had ever offered.[24]

What the chains never saw coming was Amazon's tolerance for delaying profits in order to build their customer base and damage the competition. Amazon didn't post a profit in a quarterly report until 2002[25] and didn't consistently start being profitable until 2015.[26] Although a publicly held company since 1997, the almost limitless vision for the company's future that CEO Jeff Bezos is able to persuade investors of makes them more patient and willing to provide capital for his ventures, with the understanding that profits will eventually be forthcoming. In comparison, for companies like Borders and Barnes and Noble, the scope for expanding into new businesses or markets is understood to be limited.

As early as 1900, American publishers and American booksellers formed trade associations specifically to counter the tendency of some bookstores to sell books at deep discounts, arguing that publishers should be able to set minimum prices for retail.[27] While the associations achieved a great deal of compliance among booksellers who signed agreements to that effect, the department store Macy's was the notable holdout, ultimately resulting in a Supreme Court decision in 1913 in Macy's favor.[28] The idea of "price maintenance" laws waned in and out of favor but by the mid–twentieth century fell more firmly out of favor and was reconceptualized as "price fixing."[29] Therefore, it's not the first time in the history of book retailing that a major player in the market has seen the opportunity in deep discounting that makes it difficult for competitors, particularly independent booksellers, to compete. What is different is Amazon's identity as a tech company and, beyond that, a platform company whose access to data about consumers and competitors, efficiencies across multiple business activities, and ability to raise money to support almost unlimited growth all give it structural advantages not available to other kinds of market actors.

Amazon has also put new pressure on the book market by featuring used books so prominently on the site. While the market for used books is nothing new, historically it has been unusual for a single retail establishment to stock new and used books side-by-side, with some notable exceptions such as the chain Half Price Books and Powell's Books in Portland, Oregon. Both authors and publishers have been ambivalent and, at times, vocally resistant to this practice, as people buying used diverts sales from new books, which produce royalties. Thanks to the United States' first sale doctrine, Amazon can make money on the initial sale of a new book and again when it gets resold used, even though the publisher receives nothing on subsequent sales. Numerous used copies may drive down the price of a new book and create the appearance of a book that no one wants.[30] And of course, as one author has admitted, there are "emotional wounds" in seeing, in this case, an award-winning book being sold used on Amazon for a mere twenty-five cents: "Part of it is sheer vanity, that you think your book would be worth more than that under any circumstances."[31]

Again, the dismay at Amazon's ultracompetitive retailing innovations arguably goes beyond the sour grapes of a disadvantageous business relationship. When it comes to books, these criticisms have unmistakable moral overtones. While we may conceptualize particular books as being somehow resistant to capitalist logics of exchange value by which all products, no matter how distinct in terms of their quality or the labor that went into their production, come to be interchangeable in the market, in fact, books are not immune to these processes of commodification. As more business-minded innovators have entered book retailing, using computing and information technology to maximize efficiency in bookselling and distribution long before Amazon's arrival on the scene, they have typically appealed to consumer sovereignty, implicitly and sometimes explicitly casting as exclusionary and classist the assumptions of those who decry the more commercial aspects of book publishing and retailing.[32]

Like his predecessors among the more commercial book retailers, Amazon CEO Jeff Bezos has sought to make his own moral arguments in favor of more rationalized, scaled, and efficient distribution of books to consumers. By appealing to the principle of consumer sovereignty and to the demands of the rational consumer, Amazon argues for the commercial *and* social good that it produces in the book market. By providing the lowest prices, as well as the ability to instantly compare Amazon with third-party new and used booksellers, Amazon provides the greatest choice for the consumer, the company argues.[33]

There's no doubt that Amazon offers consumers an almost incomprehensibly large selection; as of January 2018, there were 53,455,924 results listed under "Books" on the site, although these may not all be distinct titles and encompass all conditions (new and used), formats (e-book, audiobooks, etc.), and languages. Of course, all these titles are not in Amazon's warehouses; most would be purchased from and shipped by third-party vendors. Since its early days of customizing recommendations based on past purchases and behavior on the website, Amazon has held the sovereignty of the consumer's interests and preferences on a pedestal (known as "customer obsession" in the company),[34] also reflected in the early shift away from providing editorial reviews of books to encouraging consumers to provide product reviews.[35] As Keith Gessen wrote in *Vanity Fair*, in the 1990s, when the chains dominated the market, a single book-buyer (specifically Barnes and Noble's literary fiction buyer) "could make (or break) a book with a large order (or a disappointingly small one)."[36] Although it would be naïve to downplay Amazon's role in shaping what books get promoted and sold today, it's also the case that shelf capacity is no longer limited, and Amazon is much more invested in the consumer response than subjective judgments of what is "good" or beneficial in any social or cultural sense (the company's tolerance for selling controversial and offensive material testifies to that). George Packer summed up this state of affairs nicely in his critical take in the *New Yorker*, writing, "Amazon is good for customers. But is it good for books?"[37]

Packer's question points to the concerns raised by critics, publishers, authors, and many readers about the commodification of books for years. While they are a consumer product that must conform to market pressures in order to succeed, it's also the case that publishers and retailers—or "reluctant capitalists," as Laura J. Miller describes them—have long promoted nonmarket values in their work by cultivating new authors, promoting localism and books for niche audiences, and making space for "serious" literature that may not sell in great numbers but makes a cultural, political, or social contribution. While Amazon's model may bow to consumer sovereignty like never before, with unmatched choice and low prices facilitated by its data-driven, growth-hungry business model, the question remains of what space there is for the nonmarket values that have always been a part of the book business.

The Platformization of Book Retailing and the Consequences of Market Power

As observed by Daniel Herbert in this volume, media retailers are increasingly multifunctional. No longer just the interface that brings consumers and media products together, they are getting involved in media production, distribution, technology, and marketing. This observation is perhaps truer of Amazon than almost any other company. Amazon does a lot more than just sell books to consumers. In the last two decades, it has become an almost completely vertically integrated company when it comes to books, encompassing publishing, printing, and distribution. Amazon has several of its own publishing imprints, including CreateSpace for self-publishing authors.

A major retailer becoming a publisher is not completely unprecedented, as demonstrated by Barnes and Noble, which acquired and developed its own imprints in the 2000s.[38] What is unprecedented is the platformization of the book business. What this means, according to platform theorist Nick Srnicek, is that despite Amazon's apparent business (selling books and online retail), by being a digital intermediary for so many market actors, its primary business is actually acquiring data and then either selling this information to third parties or leveraging it to launch into new businesses.[39] Being a platform, rather than focused on a specific type of business, is what allows Amazon to move quickly into many different products and services, in part because it has so much data available to see where the opportunities are. When we look at the consequences of Amazon's market power, we need to consider the full range of advantages it has as an increasingly vertically and horizontally integrated platform company. This situation is emblematic of the tech giants in digital capitalism while representing a more significant break from past business conditions in the book industry.

Amazon's development of the Kindle and its investment in e-books is an excellent example of how the company uses the various components of its business—personal electronics, digital distribution platforms, and physical distribution of books in record times—to exert unprecedented market dominance. Amazon got into the business of distributing books, not in boxes but electronically, with the 2007 release of its own e-reader, the Kindle. Swimming upstream against the many critics who were skeptical that people would want to read digital books, Amazon released the first commercially successful e-reader—successful due to its wireless connectivity, immediately large selection of e-books, and a lighted screen that is easy on the eyes and well-suited to reading print—and it remains the market leader.[40] Within four years, Amazon was selling more Kindle books than hardcover and paperback books combined, and in 2014, it controlled 65 percent of the U.S. e-book market.[41]

Even as the Kindle starts to lose ground to tablet technology (which Amazon also participates in with its Fire tablet, although well behind Apple's market share with the iPad), Amazon has secured its position as the source for buying e-books, as indicated by a study that found that 40 percent of e-book purchases by iPad owners were from Amazon's Kindle store versus just 29 percent from Apple's own iBookstore.[42] With its purchase of Audible in 2008, Amazon also solidified its position as the source for audiobooks, the fastest-growing sector in digital publishing.[43] What it even means to buy or own a book has, since 2014, been put into question by the Kindle Unlimited subscription service, where for $9.99 per month consumers can access unlimited e-books and audiobooks. Here authors and publishers are paid not by the unit of the book but by the amount of it that people consume via the service.[44]

Amazon's capture of the e-book market due to its early innovation of the Kindle and its strategy of achieving market dominance through aggressive pricing all came together in the Hachette controversy of 2014. In brief, five major publishers, including Hachette (which owns imprints such as Little, Brown and Company and Basic Books), were concerned about Amazon's insistence on pricing e-books at $9.99 or less, recalling previous industry conflicts about book pricing. In 2010, these publishers came to an agreement with Apple's iBookstore to use agency pricing, which meant that publishers were able to set their own prices and Apple would be technically the "sales agent" and not the "retailer."[45] The U.S. Department of Justice went after the agency-pricing agreement on antitrust grounds, and in 2013, the department prevailed in identifying this practice as colluding to fix prices. They required publishers to renegotiate e-book prices with both Apple and Amazon, whereby publishers would have some power to set prices but retailers would retain the right to some discounting.[46] As Hachette was the first publishing group to negotiate with Amazon, when they attempted to play hardball on e-book pricing, Amazon retaliated by substantially slowing down delivery of Hachette books (on the order of weeks instead of days), removing some titles from the site, and removing "presale" buttons on soon-to-be-published books, which are a key tool for ensuring the success of a new book.[47] The controversy hit the headlines, with major authors raising the alarm bells about the (to some) newly apparent power of Amazon to discipline publishers and enforce the business conditions they desired.

The e-book controversy has blown over, at least for now. E-book prices rose with the new negotiations, with Amazon eventually bowing to the "agency lite" pricing, perhaps because the e-book habit had become sufficiently established among consumers and Amazon's dominance as a purveyor of e-books had been solidified. Despite authors' and publishers' fears that their e-books would be consistently selling for just a few dollars or even less, e-book prices have overall risen substantially, shrinking the price gap between physical and e-books.[48] Given the lack of production costs for e-book copies after initial digital formatting, publishers are finding this an increasingly profitable part of their business.[49] Nevertheless, Amazon does still offer monthly sales on e-books at prices ranging from $0.99 to $3.99, including even some bestsellers.

The Hachette controversy highlighted publishers' vulnerability in the face of Amazon's market dominance. Whereas previous retailers could have ill-afforded to not carry the books that people wanted because of the importance of bestsellers to their bottom lines, Amazon is large enough and diversified enough to swallow any such losses. Given the combined importance of pre-sales on Amazon for book publicity, the ability to buy the physical book in a short delivery window on the site for overall sales, and the market dominance of the company's Kindle platform for e-book sales, Amazon leaves publishers with few alternatives in terms of getting their books known and purchased by the public. And as Amazon ventures into publishing (still relatively slowly), the specter of a vertically integrated behemoth that can cherry-pick the best-selling authors from legacy publishers and anticipate audience trends based on all the data available to them is an alarming proposition for many. Today, Amazon's march into every corner of the book business continues with its foray into brick-and-mortar stores.

Amazon Books and the Social Meaning of Retail Space

After establishing itself as the primary force behind bookstore closures across the country, in 2015, Amazon did something few had seen coming—it opened an actual bookstore. By the end of 2017, Amazon Books was already the fifth-largest general bookstore chain in the country, although this was perhaps less a sign of Amazon's rapid expansion (they had thirteen stores in seven states)[50] than the weak state of the bookstore chain market. The locations of Amazon Books so far suggest a somewhat up-scale alternative to Barnes and Noble, with stores appearing in prime retail real estate such as Westfield Century City in Los Angeles, University Village in Seattle, and Legacy Place in Dedham, Massachusetts, where the store resides near an L.L. Bean, Sephora, an Eddie Bauer, a Lululemon, and a massive Whole Foods Market. Amazon Books resembles a hybrid of independent-bookstore scale with many of the features of a chain bookstore, such as a variety of nonbook items for sale, a café, and spaces for customers to read and hang out.

While creating a chain of brick-and-mortar bookstores might seem a retro move for the e-commerce giant, the company's own description of the initiative explains that "Amazon Books integrates the benefits of offline and online shopping to help customers discover books and devices."[51] The sections of the store reflect this integration. There are the conventional genre categories: cooking, children's books, fiction, poetry, science and nature, and self-improvement. And then there are the displays that announce Amazon's deference to consumer preferences and the ability of big data to communicate the will and tastes of consumers: "Books with more than 10,000 Reviews on Amazon.com," "Most wished-for books on Amazon.com," "Highly rated children's books," and "4.8 stars and above." In addition, a couple of displays reference not the massive digital world of consumer responses but the local context, such as "Fiction Favorites in Boston" and "Popular Picks in Legacy Place: Beyond the Bestsellers." Attention to local interests, creating a space for community, and thoughtfully curated selections have been attributed as reasons for the resurgence of independent booksellers over the last decade, and Amazon Books' store design emulates these features.[52]

There's a certain tension in the way that Amazon Books introduces a sense of place and a space for community while simultaneously promoting a highly individualized shopping experience, essentially extending the tailoring that online retailing allows to in-person shopping. While Amazon's approach to brick-and-mortar retailing could be seen as uncharted, it's actually very much in alignment with broader trends in retail, specifically the way that digital communication technologies are driving the repersonalization of retail. Historians have argued that a key development in "modern" consumer culture was the depersonalization of consumption such that buyers and sellers need not be known to each other in order to engage in market exchange.[53] The greater anonymity of retail spaces, exemplified by chain stores and department stores, could be experienced as alienating, but equally, scholars have argued, they could be experienced as democratizing, appearing to liberate consumers from conventional hierarchies and social exclusions.[54] Starting in the nineteenth century, rather than consumers having to ask store employees about prices or negotiate with sellers, prices in shops were clearly displayed; no one need endure the embarrassment of putting an item down after learning the price from a sales associate.[55]

Chain bookstores were criticized precisely for depersonalizing book retailing relative to independent bookstores by emphasizing self-service and, with the rise of the big-box retailers, making the store feel anonymous through its sheer size.[56] Many online retailers, in contrast, have consistently repersonalized shopping, at least in the sense of tailoring the shopping experience for the individual through features such as what appears on the store home page, customized recommendations and special offers, and even what prices are shown. These customizations are based on data the store collects from the consumer's proximate searching activity on the site, previous behaviors and purchases on the site, and personalized data about activity across the web that the store tracks themselves or purchases via third parties.[57] Amazon started customizing the recommendations on their site for individual customers as early as 1996.[58]

Therefore, an actual store like Amazon Books can be understood as in some respect depersonalized, compared to Amazon.com, because customers are exposed to book categories and recommendations that are not tailored to them specifically. On the other hand, Amazon Books is "repersonalized" relative to most retail experiences because prices are not displayed or marked on products (although some books do have the "list price" on the back cover, in tiny print). In Amazon Books, rather than seeing the price listed below the book, most titles have a sentence or two from a positive Amazon consumer review, as well as the number of reviews and stars out of five that the book has received on Amazon.com. Shoppers must scan items with their smartphone to discover the prices, paving the way for more dynamic pricing as well as differential pricing for Amazon Prime members vs. nonmembers. There were numerous signs in the store indicating how to look up prices, and shoppers were helping each other figure out the system (see figure 2.1).

On my visit to Amazon Books in Dedham, Massachusetts, every item I scanned showed a discounted price on my phone (there are a few store scanners available for those who don't have smartphones). I made several purchases, and my receipt showed that I had received 26 percent savings as an Amazon Prime member, very close to the 27 percent in savings that a sign in the store advertised that Prime members had received on average the previous month. Amazon Books, then, in some respects merely extends

FIG. 2.1 A sign in the cookbook aisle at Amazon Books in Dedham, Mass., teaching shoppers how to "Check prices in this store" (photo by author)

the personalized, differentiated relationships consumers have with the retail giant into the brick-and-mortar context.

This hybrid online-offline relationship—made seamless via mobile digital technology—is continuous with ongoing retail trends. Many brick-and-mortar retailers have been coordinating customers' smartphone activities with dynamic elements in the store such as employee interactions, discounts, and smartphone alerts.[59] Amazon has been on the forefront of personalizing shopping online, and now its approach to brick-and-mortar selling puts it squarely at the center of what Turow, McGuigan, and Maris argue is a concerted effort among retailers to acclimate consumers to a "new social imaginary," a way of understanding the world and how it works, that "instantiates social discrimination as normal."[60] While loyalty programs in many supermarkets have reserved certain discounts for loyalty card members since the 1990s, there's been greater transparency in what the discount is, communicated via sticker by the item.[61] At Amazon Books, it's different. Prices are not clearly posted, and it may not be clear to non-Prime shoppers what discounts they are missing. Signing up for a membership that triggers a $119 credit card charge in thirty days (the cost of the annual Prime membership) is the price of getting those mysterious discounts.

Far from being a superstore, Amazon Books locations are modest in size and particularly modest in the number of titles they carry. Because all the books are displayed face out, relatively few titles are stocked. Jia Tolentino writes in the *New Yorker* that the Columbus Circle location she visited in NYC stocked only three thousand titles, paling in comparison to her favorite large indie stores that stock between twenty-five and sixty thousand titles.[62] The shelf in figure 2.2, for example, demonstrates that not only do all book covers face out; they are spaced out for better viewing.

FIG. 2.2 The spacing of the fiction selection by Elena Ferrante at Amazon Books in Dedham, Mass. (photo by author)

The store, in fact, is arranged primarily for "discovery" and not for "search," to apply terms used for online navigation to the offline retail experience. Amazon's director of stores has even described the format as a "mecca for discovery,"[63] arguably in contrast to Amazon's online store experience, which highly rewards "search" but makes "discovery" less likely than browsing in an actual store, much to the ongoing chagrin of publishers attempting to market new books.[64] As Tolentino discovered on her shopping trip, the customer with titles or authors in mind (i.e., doing a search) is bound to be disappointed due to the limited, if highly curated, selection.[65] Similar to Tolentino's observation, I found that most fiction authors had only one book available, with only the very best sellers such as Elena Ferrante, Stephen King, Toni Morrison, and Kazuo Ishiguro warranting three or four titles. If the purpose of Amazon Books is to facilitate discovery that isn't engineered so tightly by personalized recommendation algorithms, then the store design makes sense.

There are some products that Amazon not just sells but produces that do not lend themselves to browsing online as much as books. Amazon Books locations include a significant amount of floor space devoted to Amazon electronics, such as the Kindle, the Fire tablet, the Fire TV Stick, and a variety of "smart home" products that coordinate with Amazon's AI-enabled Echo smart speaker, such as thermostats, lamps, and energy-monitoring electrical plugs. When asked about the company's decision to expand into physical stores, Amazon CFO Brian Olsavsky said, "We think the bookstores . . . are a really great way for customers to engage with our devices and see them, touch them, play with them and become fans."[66] The bookstores, then, are an opportunity for Amazon to have its own showrooms for proprietary personal electronics and compatible products, an area in which the company is at a disadvantage relative to Apple, whose consumer-friendly, aesthetically appealing Apple Stores are famously a destination for consumer pilgrimage.[67] In the Amazon Books at Legacy Place, this part of the store was particularly well staffed so that consumers curious about the electronics could immediately receive information and guidance. Once again, Amazon has used books as the bait that will deliver consumer attention for other lucrative markets. And similar to Prime Video, Amazon is using the stores as a space to convert more shoppers into Prime members, who are known to spend significantly more per year with the company than nonmembers.[68]

Amazon's recent moves into brick-and-mortar retailing, including its 2017 acquisition of Whole Foods Market, reflects a broader integration of online and offline retailing. Just as Walmart and Target have moved into online retail and large brick-and-mortar retailers are using apps to communicate with consumers in their stores in real time, so is Amazon integrating the two but in the opposite direction.

Conclusion: Amazon the Black Swan *and* Bird of a Feather

This volume brings overdue focus to the question of media retailing just as digital capitalism is overturning what have long been considered the fundamentals of retail in the United States. The future of malls and department stores is in question, as almost daily reports of "retail apocalypse" indicate, and retail brands that literally shaped our landscapes and shared spaces are steadily going out of business. Amazon has certainly played a major role in these changes, and the ensuing decline of dedicated media retail spaces—where we encounter cultural materials, both searched for and discovered, and have the chance to observe what others are engaging with even if we're not the intended target market—is part of what is being lost in this shift. Just as digital distribution has promoted "filter bubbles" in news, the shift of book-buying from brick-and-mortar stores to online has facilitated a highly individualized shopping experience for these cultural products, which we have historically conceived of as key to connecting us to each other.

In some ways, Amazon *is* a black swan. It has upended ideas of what a bookstore can be, using its relationships with consumers and infrastructures developed through bookselling to launch countless other businesses. It has upended historic distinctions among printers, publishers, distributors, and retailers. Amazon redefined books and reading through its development of the Kindle, in the process backing into the personal electronics business, which in turn has contributed to the envelopment of the book business into Amazon's larger platform ambitions.

In other ways though, Amazon is very much a bird of a feather flocking with other retailers responding to the challenges and opportunities of digital capitalism. Concern on the part of booksellers and publishers about Amazon's aggressive pricing, power over the market, and extreme deference to consumer preferences is consistent with a long-standing tension between critics of cultural commodification and people who use the latest business tools to expand and rationalize the book business. Amazon Books is part of a broader movement among retailers using digital communication technologies to socialize consumers to a retail experience defined more by differentiation and discrimination than by shared space and consumer experiences held in common. Finally, Amazon's power as a retailing giant over its suppliers is emblematic of an overall shift from a "push" to a "pull" market system, facilitated by high market concentration in retailing in general and retailers' use of digital communication technologies and computing to dictate terms based on data about consumer preferences and behaviors to producers.

Notes

1 Chris Anderson, *The Long Tail: Why the Future of Business Is Selling Less of More* (New York: Hyperion, 2018).

2 Brad Stone, *The Everything Store: Jeff Bezos and the Age of Amazon* (New York: Little, Brown and Company, 2013).

3 George Packer, "Cheap Words," *New Yorker*, 17 Feb. 2014, https://www.newyorker.com/magazine/2014/02/17/cheap-words.

4 Jim Milliot, "Media Sales Rose 7.5% in 2016 at Amazon," *Publisher's Weekly*, 2 Feb. 2017, https://www.publishersweekly.com/pw/by-topic/industry-news/publisher-news/article/72688-media-sales-rose-7-5-in-2016-at-amazon.html.

5 Edna Bonacich and Jake B. Wilson, *Getting the Goods: Ports, Labor, and the Logistics Revolution* (Ithaca, N.Y.: Cornell University Press, 2008), 4–5.

6 Bonacich and Wilson, *Getting the Goods*, 4–5.

7 Jeff Bercovici, "Amazon vs. Book Publishers, by the Numbers," *Forbes*, 10 Feb. 2014, https://www.forbes.com/sites/jeffbercovici/2014/02/10/amazon-vs-book-publishers-by-the-numbers/#463aede44ef9.

8 Jonathan Taplin, *Move Fast and Break Things: How Facebook, Google, and Amazon Cornered Culture and Undermined Democracy* (New York: Little, Brown and Company, 2017).

9 Dan Schiller, *Digital Capitalism: Networking the Global Market System* (Cambridge: MIT Press, 1999), 14–15.

10 Carolyn Kellogg, "Amazon and Hachette: The Dispute in 13 Easy Steps," *Los Angeles Times*, 3 June 2014, http://www.latimes.com/books/jacketcopy/la-et-jc-amazon-and-hachette-explained-20140602-story.html.

11 Carmen Nobel, "How Independent Bookstores Thrived in Spite of Amazon," *Quartz*, 26 Nov. 2017, https://qz.com/1135474/how-independent-bookstores-thrived-in-spite-of-amazon/.

12 Boris Kachka, "James Patterson: 'If Amazon Is the New American Way, Then Maybe It Has to Be Changed,'" *Vulture*, 29 May 2014, http://www.vulture.com/2014/05/james-patterson-calls-out-amazon-at-book-expo.html.

13 Theodor Adorno and Max Horkheimer, "The Culture Industry: Enlightenment as Mass Deception," in *The Cultural Studies Reader*, ed. Simon During (New York: Routledge, 1996), 31–41.

14 Janice A. Radway, *A Feeling for Books: The Book-of-the-Month Club, Literary Taste, and Middle-Class Desire* (Chapel Hill: University of North Carolina Press, 1997), 60.

15 Elizabeth Long, "The Cultural Meaning of Concentration in Publishing," *Book Research Quarterly* 1, no. 4 (1985): 3.

16 Laura J. Miller, *Reluctant Capitalists: Bookselling and the Culture of Consumption* (Chicago: University of Chicago Press, 2006), 3–4.

17 Miller, *Reluctant Capitalists*, 3.

18 Richard L. Brandt, *One Click: Jeff Bezos and the Rise of Amazon.com* (New York: Portfolio, 2011), 46–49.

19 "History & Timeline," *Amazon Press Room*, Dec. 2014, http://phx.corporate-ir.net/phoenix.zhtml?c=176060&p=irol-corporatetimeline.

20 Brandt, *One Click*, 110.

21 Karen Petruska, "Where Information Is Entertainment," in *From Networks to Netflix: A Guide to Changing Channels*, ed. Derek Johnson (New York: Routledge, 2018), 355–364.

22 Miller, *Reluctant Capitalists*, 147.

23 Jim Milliot and Karen Holt, "Media Growth Slows at Amazon," *Publisher's Weekly* 251, no. 31 (2004): 6.

24 Milliot and Holt; Miller and Holt, "Media Growth," 147.

25 "Amazon Posts a Profit," *CNNMoney*, 22 Jan. 2002, http://money.cnn.com/2002/01/22/technology/amazon/.

26 Klint Finley, "Hey Look, Amazon Actually Turned a Profit," *Wired*, 23 July 2015, https://www.wired.com/2015/07/hey-look-amazon-actually%20turned-profit/.

27 Miller, *Reluctant Capitalists*, 153–154.

28 Miller, 154.

29 Miller, 155.

30 David Kirkpatrick, "Online Sales of Used Books Draw Protest," *New York Times*, 10 Apr. 2001, http://www.nytimes.com/2002/04/10/business/online-sales-of-used-books-draw-protest.html; Jim Milliot, "Authors Guild Upset by Amazon Used Books Tactics," *Publisher's Weekly*, 15 Apr. 2002, 15.

31 Kirkpatrick, "Online Sales."

32 Miller, *Reluctant Capitalists*, 54–56, 60; Radway, *Feeling for Books*, 61–65.

33 Milliot, "Authors Guild Upset."

34 John Rossman, *The Amazon Way: 14 Leadership Principles behind the World's Most Disruptive Company* (North Charleston, S.C.: CreateSpace Independent, 2014), 7.

35 Stone, *Everything Store*, 133–134.

36 Keith Gessen, "The War of the Words," *Vanity Fair*, 6 Nov. 2014, https://www.vanityfair.com/news/business/2014/12/amazon-hachette-ebook-publishing.

37 Packer, "Cheap Words."

38 John B. Thompson, *Merchants of Culture: The Publishing Business in the Twenty-First Century* (Malden, Mass.: Polity Press, 2010), 29.

39 Nick Srnicek, *Platform Capitalism* (Malden, Mass.: Polity Press, 2017), 39–46.

40 Stone, *Everything Store*, 252–253.

41 "Amazon.com Now Selling More Kindle Books Than Print Books," *Business Wire*, 19 May 2011, http://phx.corporateir.net/phoenix.zhtml?p=irolnewsArticle&c=176060&ID=1565581; Bercovici, "Amazon."

42 Jim Milliot, "Amazon Ups Its Edge," *Publisher's Weekly*, 24 Jan. 2011, 5–6.

43 Michael Kozlowski, "Global Audiobook Trends and Statistics for 2018," *Good EReader*, 17 Dec. 2017, https://goodereader.com/blog/audiobooks/global-audiobook-trends-and-statistics-for-2018.

44 Brady Dale, "Despite What You Heard, the E-book Market Never Stopped Growing," *Observer*, 18 Jan. 2017, http://observer.com/2017/01/author-earnings-overdrive-amazon-kindle-overdrive-digital-book-world/.

45 Gessen, "War of the Words."

46 Gessen.

47 Kellogg, "Amazon and Hachette."

48 Michael Hiltzik, "No, Ebooks Aren't Dying—but Their Quest to Dominate the Reading World Has Hit a Speed Bump," *Los Angeles Times*, 1 May 2017, http://www.latimes.com/business/hiltzik/la-fi-hiltzik-ebooks-20170501-story.html.

49 Gessen, "War of the Words."

50 Jim Milliot, "Amazon Books Will Be the Nation's Fifth-Largest Bookstore Chain," *Publisher's Weekly*, 1 June 2017, 6.

51 "Amazon.com Announces Third-Quarter Sales Up 34% to $43.7 Billion," *Business Wire*, 26 Oct. 2017, http://phx.corporate-ir.net/phoenix.zhtml?c=97664&p=irol-reportsother.

52 Nobel, "Independent Bookstores."

53 Douglas J. Goodman and Mirelle Cohen, *Consumer Culture: A Reference Handbook* (Santa Barbara, Calif.: ABC-CLIO, 2004), 14–17.

54 Jason P. Chambers, "Equal in Every Way: African Americans, Consumption, and Materialism from Reconstruction to the Civil Rights Movement," *Advertising & Society Review* 7, no. 1 (2006), DOI: 10.1353/asr.2006.0017; Josh Lauer, "The Good Consumer: Credit Reporting and the Invention of Financial Identity in the United States," *Enterprise & Society* 11, no. 4 (2010): 691–692.

55 Goodman and Cohen, *Consumer Culture*, 17–18.

56 Miller, *Reluctant Capitalists*, 5.

57 Joseph Turow, *The Daily You: How the New Advertising Industry Is Defining Your Identity and Your Worth* (New Haven, Conn.: Yale University Press, 2011), 139–140.

58 Stone, *Everything Store*, 51–52.

59 Joseph Turow, Lee McGuigan, and Elena R. Maris, "Making Data Mining a Natural Part of Life: Physical Retailing, Customer Surveillance and the 21st Century Social Imaginary," *European Journal of Communication* 18, no. 4–5 (2015): 472.

60 Turow, McGuigan, and Maris, "Making Data Mining," 464.

61 Joseph Turow, *The Aisles Have Eyes: How Retailers Track Your Shopping, Strip Your Privacy, and Define Your Power* (New Haven, Conn.: Yale University Press, 2017), 82–83.

62 Jia Tolentino, "Amazon's Brick-and-Mortar Bookstores Are Not Built for People Who Actually Read," *New Yorker*, 30 May 2017, https://www.newyorker.com/culture/cultural-comment/amazons-brick-and-mortar-bookstores-are-not-built-for-people-who-actually-read.

63 Nat Levy, "Amazon's New Seattle-Area Bookstore Shows How Its First Major Brick-and-Mortar Concept Has Evolved," *Geekwire*, 25 Aug. 2017, https://www.geekwire.com/2017/amazons-new-seattle-area-bookstore-shows-first-major-retail-concept-evolved/.

64 Gessen, "War of the Words."

65 Tolentino, "Amazon's Brick-and-Mortar Bookstores."

66 Milliot, "Media Sales Rose."

67 Pamela N. Danziger, "3 Things Retailers Need to Learn from Apple about the Experience Economy," *Forbes*, 13 Dec. 2017, https://www.forbes.com/sites/pamdanziger/2017/12/13/three-things-retailers-need-to-learn-from-apple-about-the-experience-economy/#741bf7181307.

68 Clare O'Connor, "Walmart and Target Being Crowded Out Online by Amazon Prime," *Forbes*, 6 Apr. 2015, http://www.forbes.com/sites/clareoconnor/2015/04/06/walmart-and-target-being-crowded-out-online-by-amazon-prime.

3

The First Sale Doctrine and U.S. Media Retail

• •

GREGORY STEIRER

When we as consumers buy a new video game from a retail store in the United States, we take for granted a number of things: that we can play the game for as long as we like, in our home or (if we are a student) in our dorm room, alone or with friends; we can give it as a present to a family member, lend it to a friend, or swap it with a classmate; and we can also sell it on eBay or even trade the game to a retail store like GameStop for credit toward the cost of another game. That we can do all these things seems so obvious that we rarely ask ourselves why we can do them; indeed, our right to do these things seems such a logical corollary to the idea of property itself that the better question might strike us as being why we would *not* be able to do them. Media studies scholarship has traditionally approached consumer ownership from a similar perspective, taking for granted as the natural state of affairs consumers' right to do more or less what they like with their purchased goods, save for reproducing them (or in the case of films, publicly exhibiting them). Admittedly, this is in part because, as the introduction to this collection notes, media studies as a discipline has tended not to be particularly interested in media retail or consumer goods, but it also reflects the inherent tendency of institutionalized legal structures to recede from view, obscuring from the social beings that inhabit them the man-made rules and processes that underlie what appears to be natural. Which is to say that our right to lend or sell the media goods we own is not in fact natural at all; it is the result of a specific, historically contingent legal principle called "the first sale doctrine" (or sometimes "the exhaustion doctrine").

This chapter aims to denaturalize the various rights that accompany the ownership of a media good in the United States by offering a brief but comprehensive account of the first sale doctrine as it has functioned from the late-nineteenth century to the present day, with particular emphasis on the economic reasoning that has underlain the doctrine. Because the first sale doctrine applies not only to consumers but also to retailers, it has exerted a tremendous but often unrecognized influence on the evolution of most forms of media distribution in the United States. Accordingly, I argue in this chapter that the doctrine, despite efforts by virtually every media industry to constrain or abrogate it, has shaped—and continues to shape—basic taken-for-granted features of media consumption and media retail and that it has done so in a manner designed to serve the interests of neither consumers/retailers nor formal rights holders but rather free-market capitalism itself. The "portrait" of media retail I put forth here is thus intended not only to denaturalize the United States' current system of media retail but also to interrogate the complex economic reasoning employed by U.S. courts and legislators in their development and application of the first sale doctrine.

This chapter consists of three sections. The first section provides a definition of the first sale doctrine and a brief account of its origin. The second offers an analysis of the doctrine's economic function, with particular attention paid to its effects on both retail markets and consumers. And the third provides three important examples of attempts by media publishers and technology firms to weaken or circumvent the doctrine. Before we proceed, however, a brief comment is in order regarding this chapter's focus on the United States. Because the United States' legal system and mode of lawmaking differ from that of other nations, the manner in which the first sale doctrine developed historically within the United States has no direct parallel to that of the doctrine's development in other nations. Despite these differing histories, however, the first sale doctrine nevertheless functions today in most countries very much as it does in the United States. In part, this is a result of globalization and the formalization of transnational markets via trading pacts and integrated markets, both of which have necessitated the international standardization of intellectual property law. Although I focus here on the United States, my analysis of the first sale doctrine, with respect to both its function and the economic values it represents, is thus broadly applicable to media retail everywhere.

What the First Sale Doctrine Is

Rooted in both statute and common law, the first sale doctrine revolves around a relatively simple proscription: once initial copyright or patent holders have sold a copy of a good they created, they are barred from using copyright or patent law to exert any control over what the purchaser does with that copy save for enforcing the laws' general prohibition against reproduction (as well as, for copyrighted works, public exhibition). Expressed in even simpler terms, after its first sale, the copyrighted or patented good becomes no different from any other kind of consumer good. The purchaser can resell it, give it away, destroy it, repurpose it, and so on.

As this definition makes clear, the first sale doctrine should not be understood as pertaining exclusively to a purchaser's right to distribute or dispose of purchased goods; it can also govern the right to use such goods. As U.S. Supreme Court Justice John Roberts explained in the court's recent opinion for *Lexmark v. Impression Products*, "The purchaser and all subsequent owners are free to use or resell the product just like any other item of personal property, without fear of an infringement lawsuit."[1] When dealing with copyrighted (as opposed to patented) goods, however, judges and legal scholars have tended to employ a narrower understanding of the doctrine, which restricts its purview to the right of distribution/disposition.[2] The emphasis on distribution is in part the result of the language employed by the Copyright Act of 1976, but it is also an effect of what was until fairly recently the technological impossibility for a copyright holder to monitor how a media good is used or to enforce restrictions on that use.[3] Now that digital media goods have rendered such monitoring and enforcement possible, however, legal scholars such as Ariel Katz have begun to apply the broader definition to copyrighted goods as well, arguing that the first sale doctrine prohibits (or was intended to prohibit) "post-sale restraints" of any kind on both patented and copyrighted goods alike.[4]

What kinds of goods are protected under the first sale doctrine? Technically, it applies only to goods for which a valid copyright or patent has been issued: to media goods consisting of written words, images, or music and to "technological" goods making use of original inventions or procedures. In practice, however, virtually every good today makes use of copyrighted material, whether that be a picture on a box, an instruction booklet, or a decorative design. For this reason, the first sale doctrine actually covers a large swathe of all retail products. Indeed, two important legal cases at the end of the twentieth century involving the doctrine revolved around hair-care products, the labels on which were protected by copyright.[5] That the first sale doctrine only applies to copyrighted and patented goods is a function of it technically operating as a limited revocation of the exclusive right to distribution granted to creators by intellectual property law.[6] For those few goods that contain no intellectual property at all, the first sale doctrine is thus unnecessary: such goods enter the world already free from postsale restraints.

Note also that the right to use or distribute a purchase free from postsale restraint is enjoyed by all purchasers, regardless of whether they be consumers or retailers. In contrast to much media studies and social science scholarship, which treats consumers and retailers as separate classes of economic actors, the law treats them as identical. To some extent, this is because legal thinking with respect to property rights is rooted in the principle of universality: the subject of the law is conceived abstractly so that his or her social position or self-identity is made irrelevant. There is yet another reason, however, for the first sale doctrine's refusal to differentiate between kinds of purchasers, and that is that most American citizens at different times in their lives occupy the positions of both consumer and retailer, purchaser and seller. Indeed, today, online sites such as eBay, which hail visitors simultaneously as potential buyers and sellers, tend even to normalize individuals' identification with both sides of commercial exchange.

How the First Sale Doctrine Has Shaped Media Retail and Distribution

In many respects, the form that media retail has taken in the United States is the direct result of the first sale doctrine. If the doctrine had never existed, media retail would look very different today (assuming no other bodies of law came to serve its function). The most immediate difference would be in how media goods are priced. Under the doctrine, intellectual property holders are barred from stipulating as a term of sale that their product must be resold at or above a particular price. Usually called "resale price maintenance," such stipulations have also been historically subject to antitrust considerations, as they are generally believed to have anticompetitive effects that are harmful to consumers. Were the first sale doctrine not to exist, retailers might thus be prevented from competing with each other on price. Warner Bros. could legally require, for example, that *Batman* Blu-ray discs be sold at the same price by every retailer. In such a world, there would be no need for consumers to comparison shop, as there would be no "deals" to find.

In addition to its effect on pricing, the first sale doctrine has impacted the current system of media retail by providing legal authority to individuals and companies to sell lawfully acquired media goods without permission from or any form of legal relationship with the rights holders. Sales of such goods (which are often but not always "used" goods) are typically called "secondary" sales. Such sales take place when a student sells his or her textbooks back to a university bookstore, when a collector sells a rare comic on eBay, when a gaming store sells trading cards that it has removed from sealed packs, or when an individual sells a collection of letters to an archive. As this short list of examples suggests, the secondary markets that have resulted from the first sale doctrine serve a wide variety of economic and social functions. Not only do they generate substantial economic activity and reduce ownership costs for consumers; they also help circulate media goods that are no longer (or never were) available in primary retail markets: out-of-print books, discontinued video games, original comic book artwork, and so on.

Thanks to secondary markets, consumers can also experiment with new kinds of products, selling them to others if they end up not liking them or their interests change and also purchasing them at "used" prices that are typically lower than that of prices for the same good in the primary market. Indeed, secondary markets not only exhibit supply-and-demand pricing the way that primary markets do; they also enable a natural form of "versioning," whereby different kinds of consumers elect to pay different prices for the same product.[7] A low-income college student, for example, could choose to pay a low price for a poor-condition novel missing its dust jacket and filled with marginalia, whereas a well-off collector could choose to pay a high price for the same book in perfect condition. Such versioning serves an important social role by helping ensure that consumers of different means have access to media goods. It also has a spill-over effect on primary-market pricing, as primary-market retailers find themselves exposed to competition from sellers of both new and used products: if retailers price new products too high, would-be purchasers may elect to buy "used" versions on the secondary market instead.

Despite the downward pressure they exert on primary-market prices, secondary markets do not guarantee low prices forever: once the primary market's supply of a good is exhausted, continued high demand may result in prices on the secondary market that are even *higher* than they were in the primary market. In this respect, the first sale doctrine also enables "inflated" prices and "price gouging"—although most business and economics scholars argue that "high" prices of this kind are beneficial to consumers in the aggregate, as they ensure that goods of limited supply are efficiently allocated to those who derive the most value from them.

Finally, by severely restricting top-down control of media distribution, the first sale doctrine also enables a wide variety of informal or "grassroot" distribution pathways, which in turn generate new kinds of social identities and communities. Comic book collectors, *Yu-Gi-Oh!* card players, James Joyce scholars, retro-gamers, *Star Trek* fans, and hip-hop DJs are just a few of the distinct identities that have developed thanks to the affordances of the first sale doctrine. As media studies scholarship has long emphasized, such identities, although grounded in consumption, tend to give rise to and develop out of distinct social networks, most of which exhibit a bottom-up, rhizomatic, or "organic" structure. In a world without the first sale doctrine, these networks—were they still to exist—would be produced and controlled by the original rights holders and would thus lack much of the variability, idiosyncrasy, and multiplicity that we typically associate with genuine communities. What, for example, would a local comic book convention look like in a world where attendees cannot buy, sell, trade, or obtain autographs without the permission of each book's copyright holder? What would comic book consumption even *mean* in such a world? If distribution is, as Ramon Lobato has suggested, "the ground upon which reception occurs," then the first sale doctrine has been vital in ensuring that the ground remains open and contested and that rights holders remain limited in their ability to dictate what and how media *mean*.[8]

As the earlier paragraphs demonstrate, the first sale doctrine seems to provide a number of benefits to society as a whole and to media consumers in particular. The doctrine is not, however, immune from criticism. Most of this criticism revolves around the interactions between the doctrine and other principles and bodies of law and would thus take us far beyond the scope of this chapter. The general thrust of the criticism can be summarized, however, by observing that the first sale doctrine is an extraordinarily blunt tool for regulating markets. This bluntness is most notable in the doctrine's almost complete disregard for context. As legal scholar Herbert Hovenkamp explains, "Enforcement of the post-sale restraint is denied automatically, with no consideration of the restraint's purpose or effect. This means that market power, competitive effects and implications for innovation are all irrelevant."[9] Although such disregard for context results, at least theoretically, in a more predictable legal order, it also risks undermining competition and, in some cases, interferes with noneconomic policy goals.

Let us take, for example, the first sale doctrine's proscription against resale price maintenance. The oldest—and most influential—defense of price maintenance argues that uncontrolled price-cutting can result in long-term anti-competitive effects that are harmful to consumers. Price maintenance, in this theory, works to prevent or ameliorate the effects of price-cutting, which in primary-market retail has tended over time to lead to highly concentrated markets made up of only a few highly capitalized retailers. As Judge Gary Bartlett complained in his dissent in *Straus v. American Publishers Association*—one of the many early twentieth-century cases to revolve around price maintenance for books—the practice by big department stores of setting prices at or below costs not only results in the bankruptcy of small, specialized retailers but also causes "great damage to manufacturers, producers and wholesale dealers in loss of customers who have been driven into insolvency."[10] Although U.S. courts and lawmakers have nevertheless almost universally held that the lower prices consumers receive more than make up for the long-term decrease in competition, consumers themselves (as well as local governments and social activists) have regularly disagreed. The difficulties of the American bookstore as a result of price-cutting by Amazon, for example, have elicited both concern and regret from a wide range of readers, authors, and publishers. Other countries, such as France and Japan, deeming a diverse retail market for books essential to a robust public sphere, have accordingly sought to protect consumers' long-term interests by authorizing various forms of intranational resale price maintenance for books.

Unfortunately, because the price maintenance that has been authorized for books is often minimal in scope and duration (usually applying only to new books and lasting only for a short period after first publication) and because many book retailers rely heavily upon British and American imports, the impact of price maintenance on national book industries has been difficult for economists and policy analysts to gauge and agree upon.[11] Indeed, given the lack of clear evidence justifying price maintenance for books, the laws that support it may serve more of a symbolic than an economic function. Because used books and imported books are usually not subject to price maintenance, such laws might also be inadvertently shifting book sales to secondary and import markets, thus harming the primary national market the laws are designed to protect. Japan's *saihan seido* system—which is one of the world's few resale price maintenance systems to include other media besides books (specifically recorded music, newspapers, and magazines)—has been extremely controversial for these reasons and has required restrictive import laws in order to remain effective for the recorded music market.[12]

Industry Efforts to Circumvent the First Sale Doctrine

Because the first sale doctrine works so effectively—and indeed, unsubtly—to limit copyright and patent holders' control over their work, media publishers and technology companies have repeatedly attempted to contravene or invalidate it. At times, these attempts have been motivated by genuine market problems caused by new technology. For the most part, however, they have fought against the doctrine in order to benefit themselves, typically by way of decreased competition, higher profits (usually via higher prices), and increased control over how their products are used. Legal scholars Aaron Perzanowski and Jason Schultz thus argue that twenty-first-century rights holders increasingly "see exhaustion [i.e., the first sale doctrine] and, by extension, personal property rights as an unfortunate legal loophole to be closed at the first opportunity."[13] Although I agree that copyright holders are by and large (at least when it comes to their own property) opposed to the first sale doctrine, I also recognize that the complex nature of media markets sometimes renders the question of cui bono difficult to answer. Which is to say that what benefits rights holders does not always harm consumers/retailers. For this reason, the analyses provided in the following sections try as much as possible to avoid framing any party as "good" or "bad"; instead, they seek to demonstrate the complexity of the first sale doctrine as it applies to actual industrial practice.

Bobbs-Merrill Co. v. Straus

Often identified as the common-law origin of the first sale doctrine, *Bobbs-Merrill Co. v. Straus* represents the first concerted attempt by an entire industry to contravene the law's prohibition on postsale distribution restraints. The details of the case are usually presented as so: In 1904, the Bobbs-Merrill Company published a novel titled *The Castaway*, which it copyrighted in its own name. Within each book, the publisher printed below the copyright notice two sentences indicating that "the price of this book at retail is one dollar net. No dealer is licensed to sell it at a less price, and a sale at a less price will be treated as an infringement of the copyright."[14] Isidor Straus and Nathan Straus, owners of Macy's department store, proceeded to violate the restriction by selling copies for eighty-nine cents. Bobbs-Merrill Co. quickly filed suit in New York for copyright infringement. In 1908, the case was heard by the U.S. Supreme Court, which, affirming the ruling of the appeals court, held that copyright does not include "the right to impose, by notice, such as is disclosed in this case, a limitation at which the book shall be sold at retail by future purchasers, with whom there is not privity of contract."[15]

Beyond its role in codifying the common law's approach to postsale restraints, *Bobbs-Merrill Co. v. Straus* is important for three reasons. First, the action of the publisher represents one of the earliest attempts by a copyright holder to attach to a retail good a notice restricting the rights of the purchaser. Although the Supreme Court's ruling ostensibly invalidated such notices, copyright holders were subsequently able to rely on the confusion caused by the application of copyright law to commercial software in the 1970s in order to reintroduce such notices for digital media, and (as I will discuss later in this section) today, restrictive notices represent a common—and, with some very important exceptions, legal—means of depriving digital-media purchasers of the rights that usually accompany ownership.

Second, the court's ruling indicates that the problem, legally speaking, was not so much the postsale restraint itself but the issue of privity: if the notice had been held to be enforceable, it would have subjected to the terms of a contractual obligation third parties who had not agreed to the contract in question. The parties to the contract printed inside Bobbs-Merrill Co.'s books presumably included the Bobbs-Merrill Co. and those booksellers and wholesalers to whom they directly sold the books, but they did not include the Strauses nor the wholesalers from whom the Strauses originally acquired their copies of *The Castaway*. There existed, in other words, no *privity* of contract between Bobbs-Merrill Co. and the Strauses. Had there been privity, however—for example, if the publisher had sold its books directly to the Strauses on the condition that they charge at least one dollar per book—then the postsale restraint *would have been* enforceable but only against the

Strauses (and not their customers) and only as a matter of contract violation, not copyright law.

Finally, the Bobbs-Merrill Co.'s attempts to require resale price maintenance must be understood as part of a collective effort by U.S. publishers and booksellers to control the market for new books. From this perspective, the lawsuit was less about the specific actions of the publisher and retailer with respect to *The Castaway* and more about the book industry's attempts to establish a cartel designed to reduce retail competition. Indeed, the appeals court, in finding for Straus, based its decision in large part on the illegality of the industrial combination under federal antitrust law:

> It also follows and is found as a fact that such notice was put in such books . . . not because the complainant reserved or intended to reserve to itself any interest in said books containing such printed notices, nor because it merely licensed or intended to license the purchasers thereof . . . to use or sell such books in a certain way . . . but as an attempt by complainant, as a member of said American Publishers' Association, to enforce as against this defendant the rules of such associations and combination fixing prices, in an effort to maintain them. It is part of a scheme, and the right of the complainant to maintain this action depends on the validity of that scheme or combination.[16]

The scheme itself was subsequently found illegal in *Straus and Straus v. American Publishers' Association*.[17] Although the antitrust dimensions of *Bobbs-Merrill Co. v. Straus* have been routinely ignored in recent accounts of the case, they provide a useful reminder that what is at stake with the first sale doctrine is not just the right of consumers to fully own their purchases but also the competitive structure of entire retail industries.

The Rental Record Amendment

Beginning in the 1980s, a small number of American retailers and entrepreneurs began to experiment with a new form of music store: the record rental shop. Although sometimes offering records for sale, these shops generated revenue primarily by renting vinyl records to consumers at prices ranging from one to two dollars per day, an amount substantially lower than the typical sale price for a new or used record. Rentals of records and other media had always been legal under the first sale doctrine, but until the 1980s, there had been little interest in the business model by retailers—nor, would it seem, much natural demand from consumers. The advent of the cassette tape, however, changed the underlying economics of rentals by enabling consumers to record their own copies of rented music.

That record rental was legal under the first sale doctrine was indisputable; the question facing lawmakers in the 1980s was whether it should be made illegal. Representatives for record labels, songwriters, recording artists, and traditional retailers argued that it was bad for the industry as a whole while also being ethically indefensible. In a joint statement delivered before a congressional subcommittee in 1983, the National Association of Recording Merchandisers, the Recording Industry Association of America, and a host of other trade organizations attacked record rentals as "fundamentally unfair": "For the minimal cost of buying one album, a shop can enjoy substantial revenues from renting a record time and again. The rental shop does not contribute anything to the creation or production of the music, yet it enjoys the fruits of the copyright owners' labors."[18] As an example of the damage that record rentals might inflict on the industry, industry representatives pointed to Japan, where wide-scale institutionalization of record rentals appeared to have resulted in both decreased album sales and higher album prices.[19]

Defenders of record rentals disputed the industry's arguments, in part by suggesting that consumers as a whole would benefit from cheaper access to recordings. Their primary defense, however, was that abrogation of the first sale doctrine for music rentals would constitute a dangerous curtailing of consumer/retailer rights. Marlow Cook, a representative for the Audio Recording Rights Coalition, for example, suggested that a law proposing to require rental shops to obtain rental licenses from copyright holders was in fact a back-end means of forcing upon retailers anticompetitive arrangements such as resale price maintenance.[20]

The argument on behalf of rentals, however, suffered a fatal flaw, and that is that the majority of record rental shops seemed to have in fact utilized rentals as a means of bypassing copyright proscriptions against unauthorized reproduction. Many provided free blank cassette tapes with rentals, while some—such as Ma and Pa's Rental Records in Palatine, Illinois—advertised their service using scare quotes: "'Rent' Your Favorite Album for $2.50 and Get a Ampex Cassette Free."[21] Others employed advertising language that could have been introduced in court as evidence of contributory infringement. Hampton Record and Rental, for example, promised consumers that they would "never, ever buy another record!!," while Dudeff's Record Rentals coyly explained, "Now, we won't tell you HOW best to enjoy these albums, but, we figure, if you're smart enough to come to Dudeff's in the first place, you're smart enough to figure that one out for yourself."[22]

In the end, the music industry won, and with the passage of the Record Rental Amendment in 1984, music recordings were exempted from the first sale doctrine with regards to renting, leasing, or lending for commercial gain.[23] Although rental shops could, in theory, remain open by obtaining rental authorization from relevant copyright holders, the cost of obtaining such authorization rendered the rental market economically unviable.

This account of the history of record rentals in the United States reveals two important aspects of the first sale doctrine. First, although the doctrine generally functions to protect consumers, consumers do not all share the same values and economic interests; as a result, the "protections" provided by the doctrine can also sometimes inflict harm. Traditional music retailers, for example, stood to suffer from the competition of rentals, while record collectors—judging by the example of Japan—stood to face higher prices. Although there is no logical reason to prefer traditional retailers to rental shops or collectors to renters, there is also no reason to prefer the latter. We should thus be careful not to ascribe a superior value to every market formation or distribution network developing "organically" under the first sale doctrine. A market in which some elements of the first sale doctrine are inoperative will not necessarily provide less value than a market in which all are operative.

Second, the fate of record rentals demonstrates the degree to which the effects of the first sale doctrine vary depending on the specific conditions surrounding any given market or industry. In the case of the record industry, Congress found sufficient evidence to believe that the doctrine was being used to facilitate what appeared to be a form of large-scale copyright infringement. They based this reasoning on two observations: (1) music recordings, unlike other media goods, tend to be repeatedly reused by consumers, and (2) rental shops had appeared only after the introduction of affordable home recording devices. Lawmakers could thus identify little reason for a consumer to rent a record for a single day other than to copy it. Were, however, the media good in question to have been something other than music recordings and were consumers not to have had easy access to home recording technology, the effects of the rental right provided by the first sale doctrine would thus have likely been judged differently. Indeed, in the case of *video rentals*, which American shops began offering in the 1970s, neither of the conditions pertaining to records appeared to be operative: consumers typically watched movies once, and they typically lacked the means (or desire) to copy rentals. Accordingly, when asked by the film industry to ban video rentals, the same lawmakers that banned record rentals refused, and video rental shops quickly developed into an integral part of the broader film industry.[24]

The Digital Media Good

Over the last decade, copyright holders, partnering with technology companies, have made available for purchase by consumers a myriad of new digital versions of familiar physical retail products. Like their physical counterparts, these digital versions are sold by retailers to consumers for a one-time fee;

the consumer then "owns" the product, which resides as a persistent file on the consumer's own device, as a file stored remotely on the retailer's network, or both. Examples of these products include music tracks available for purchase on iTunes, Kindle e-books available through Amazon, PS4 video games available from the PlayStation Store, and films available on Walmart's Vudu. Although this category of media good, which industry analysts sometimes label *electronic sell-through* (EST), represents only a fraction of consumer spending on media—much more of which is spent on physical goods, one-time access rights, and subscription services—the category is nevertheless financially important to copyright holders and is one with which many American consumers engage. A host of stakeholders have thus wondered, Does the first sale doctrine apply to such goods?

With regards to postsale distribution, the answer is complicated but unambiguous. As the U.S. Copyright Office concluded in 2001, after a thorough review of the impact of copyright law on electronic commerce, "[It] is not a question of whether the [first sale] provision applies to works in digital forms—it does."[25] Just as the sale of a physical media good exhausts the copyright holder's right to control the distribution of that good, so too does the sale of a digital media good. As the copyright office went on to note, however, the catch is that the sale of a digital media good—again, like that of a physical media good—*does not* exhaust the copyright holder's exclusive right to make copies of that good.[26] This means that despite the protection provided consumers by the first sale doctrine, they can in practice almost never legally distribute the digital media goods they own, since doing so would require that they make and transfer copies of the original files. In the recent *Capitol Records v. Redigi*, the court, citing a series of rulings regarding peer-to-peer software, ascribes the result to the "laws of physics": "It is simply impossible that the same 'material object' can be transferred over the Internet."[27]

At first glance, the reasoning employed by both the copyright office and the courts seems to put the interests of copyright holders above those of digital media consumers. The former is granted increased control over its intellectual property while the latter is denied the ostensibly "natural" rights that traditionally accompany the purchase of a media good. In truth, however, in regards to digital media goods, U.S. legal institutions are much less concerned with the interests of any one kind of market participant than they are with the long-term viability of the market itself, the existence of which they view as substantially benefitting stakeholders of all kinds as well as society as a whole. The abrogation of the postsale distribution right for digital media goods is thus ultimately meant to protect the EST market—and other kinds of media markets as well—by proscribing the unlicensed distribution of media goods over the internet. Were the first sale doctrine's distribution right made practically (rather than just theoretically) applicable to digital media, the unique "physics" of digital media goods would risk destroying the markets for these goods: "pirate" sites like The Pirate Bay would become legal, and consumers would be able to access virtually any media file over the internet without paying for it. A world in which digital media goods are effectively free would clearly benefit consumers in the short term; in the long term, however, these same consumers would almost certainly suffer from a vastly reduced supply of new content, as professional media producers—no longer reliably able to monetize the media they produce—found themselves unable to earn sufficient revenue to cover the costs for producing the media in the first place. That consumers (not to mention producers and retailers) would ultimately be *worse off* in such a world, is, of course, a matter of opinion, and indeed there may well be much to recommend a world in which substantially less media content is produced. From the perspective of the U.S. legal system, however, rooted as it is in the principles of classical economics, a world without functional markets for media is a fundamentally impoverished one—for rights holders *and* consumers—and the invalidation of consumers' rights to lawfully distribute legally acquired digital media is a small price to pay to keep these markets functioning. Given how fundamental this view of markets is to the U.S. legal system (and indeed to most modern legal systems), the question of whether the first sale doctrine holds for *the distribution* of digital media goods can be regarded as more or less settled ("yes in theory, but no in practice") and unlikely to change.

The question remains, however, whether copyright holders have the legal right to restrain purchasers of digital media goods from *other kinds* of postsale use besides distribution. Can a copyright holder, in other words, employ an end-user license agreement (sometimes called a terms-of-service agreement) to impose conditions of use upon a purchaser of a digital media good? As with the question of distribution, the answer is clearly "yes"; what is less clear is whether the enforcement of such restrictions falls under copyright law or contract law. If the former, infringement suits could be filed in federal court and could seek statutory damages, which can be very high; if the latter, suits could only be filed in state court and could seek only actual damages, which can be very low. The construal of infringements as contract violations would thus make postsale restraints for digital media goods so complex and expensive to enforce in courts that lawsuits would simply not be filed. Although common law on this question is not yet settled, under the conditions laid out in the Ninth Circuit's ruling in *MDY Industries, LLC v. Blizzard Entertainment, Inc.*, most postsale restraints on use would probably be considered as falling under contract law.[28] Whatever the question's ultimate answer, however, postsale restraints on the use of digital media goods will almost certainly remain common, since such restraints are not dependent upon courts alone for their enforcement. As Lawrence Lessig and other scholars have observed, they can also be enforced by software code itself so that, for example, a Kindle e-book can be programmed to prevent itself from being used in ways that violate Amazon's terms of service.[29]

Ultimately, media publishers and technology companies seem to have succeeded in invalidating the first sale doctrine for digital media goods. The world of digital media retail in the United States thus looks very different from that of physical media retail. Consumers of digital media goods face numerous usage restrictions, secondary markets do not exist, and competition on price is minimal or nonexistent (depending on the media good in question). Were electronic-sell-through markets consumers' only means of access to media, these changes would represent a massive transfer of power from consumers/ retailers to copyright holders. The existence of so many other means of access, however, has rendered their impact relatively minor. Indeed, rights holders' success in invalidating the first sale doctrine for digital media goods appears to have been somewhat self-defeating, as the comparatively low-value proposition for these goods has helped ensure that they remain a marginal form of media consumption in comparison with physical media goods and subscription services.[30] The U.S. media market as a whole has in fact developed over the last decade in such a way that a digital first sale doctrine would probably not make much of a difference to consumers today. The example of Re-Digi, a service allowing consumers to buy and trade "used" iTunes purchases, is instructive in this regard. Although a New York district court ruled that the first sale doctrine provided no defense for Re-Digi's violation of Capitol Records' copyrights, the current structure of the digital music market suggests that Re-Digi's service was doomed anyway.[31] In a world of cheap music streaming via Spotify, Apple Music, and other services, there would appear to be little rationale for a secondary market for iTunes music purchases.

Conclusion

As the earlier examples demonstrate, the first sale doctrine is neither natural nor inevitable; it is rather the product of courts and legislators and reflects a number of complex considerations regarding markets, competition, and the public good. Despite this complexity, however, lawmakers have consistently understood the doctrine's purpose as that of helping ensure efficient, well-functioning, and relatively open markets for copyrighted and patented goods. In this respect, the doctrine functions to subordinate the interests of *both* owners and consumers/retailers of intellectual property to the interests of "the market" itself. When U.S. courts and legislators have scaled back the doctrine—as they have for both music recordings and digital media goods— their intention has thus been not to harm consumers or to benefit rights holders but rather to ensure that well-functioning markets continue to exist for copyrighted and patented goods.

Whether lawmakers have achieved this goal is, of course, an open question. We might, for instance, see lawmakers' acceptance of digital rights management systems as *inhibiting* the development of an open market for digital media goods; on the other hand, given the wide-scale prevalence of internet piracy (which, in its apparent imperviousness to legal efforts to squelch it, functions in many ways as a de facto first sale doctrine for media goods), we might also see courts' revocation of the first sale doctrine for digital media goods as a rearguard effort to *support* the function of such a market. Whatever the case, we should also recognize that the first sale doctrine is but one aspect of a much larger regulatory regime; as such, how it functions in practice is substantially shaped by other laws pertaining to intellectual property. The safe harbor provision of the Digital Millennium Copyright Act, for example, exempts online service providers such as Google/YouTube from legal liability for the content posted by users; as a result, rights holders find it difficult to prevent the unauthorized distribution of media goods even on legal websites and online platforms.[32] The safe harbor provision has thus rendered toothless in some important respects copyright law's proscription of postsale distribution for digital media goods.

We also might question the value of open markets themselves. To be sure, the first sale doctrine, in keeping with its roots in neoclassical economic reasoning, holds as a matter of faith the notion that open markets are inherently beneficial. As I have tried to demonstrate throughout this chapter, however, the question of who benefits from open markets in media goods is so complex and context-dependent that, when analyzing markets and the legal infrastructure that supports them, we are in fact better off rejecting all-or-nothing notions of "benefit" and "harm" entirely. Some consumers, some retailers, some media producers, and some media distributors may benefit in some contexts from the particular kinds of open market produced by the first sale doctrine, while other stakeholders from these same categories may not. In its creation of "winners" and "losers," the first sale doctrine thus resembles capitalism itself, and we would not be wrong in seeing the doctrine's historical development in terms of the institutionalization of classical-economic, "free-market" principles. Indeed, in recent decades, the U.S. Supreme Court has even expanded the doctrine's purview to include imported goods as well as domestic, thereby depriving domestic producers of a powerful tool for segmenting the American market from that of the rest of the world.[33] The first sale doctrine thus provides a strong counterargument to complaints that corporate rights holders have effectively captured U.S. intellectual property law in the twenty-first century. With respect to retail media goods at least, the doctrine continues to serve the interests not of rights holders—nor even of consumers/retailers—but rather of open markets themselves, and, barring a radical change in the world's economic order, it is likely to continue to do so for the foreseeable future.[34]

Notes

1 Impression Products, Inc. v. Lexmark International, Inc., 17 S. Ct. 1523, 1529 (2017).
2 See, for example, Quality King Distributors, Inc. v. L'Anza Research Int'l, Inc., 523 U.S. 135, 152 (1998).
3 17 U.S.C. §109(a). Previous versions of the statue expressed the entitlement in slightly broader terms. Cf. Pub. L. 80–281, 61 Stat. 652, §27 and Pub. L. 60–349, 35 Stat.1075, §41. Unlike copyright law, patent law does not contain a statutory codification of the first sale doctrine.
4 Ariel Katz, "The First Sale Doctrine and the Economics of Post-sale Restraints," *Brigham Young University Law Review* 2014, no. 1 (2014): 55–142.
5 Sebastian Intl., Inc. v. Consumer Contracts, Ltd., 846 F.2d 1093; *Quality King Distributors, Inc.*, 523 U.S. 135.
6 17 U.S.C. §106(3); 35 U.S.C. §271(a)
7 Carl Shapiro and Hal Varian, "Versioning: The Smart Way to Sell Information," *Harvard Business Review*, Nov./Dec. 1998, 106–114.
8 Ramon Lobato, *Shadow Economies of Cinema: Mapping Informal Film Distribution* (London: Palgrave Macmillan, 2012), 15.
9 Herbert Hovenkamp, "Post-sale Restraints and Competitive Harm: The First Sale Doctrine in Perspective," *NYU Annual Survey of American Law* 66 (2011): 487, 541.
10 Straus v. American Publishers' Ass'n, 177 N.Y. 473, 493 (Bartlett, G., dissenting).
11 See, for example, Warnaby and Upton, "Are Books Different?," *International Journal of Retail & Distribution Management* 22, no. 4 (1994): 13–19; George Bittlingmayer, "Resale Price Maintenance in the Book Trade with an Application to Germany," *Journal of Institutional and Theoretical Economics* 144, no. 5 (1988): 789–812.
12 See "Saihan Seido—Japan's Resale Price Maintenance System," *NipPop*, 5 Feb. 2005, http://nippop.com/features/Saihan_Seido___Japan_s_Resale_Price_Maintenance_System.
13 Aaron Perzanowski and Jason Schultz, *The End of Ownership: Personal Property in the Digital Economy* (London: MIT Press, 2016), 32–33.
14 Bobbs-Merrill Co. v. Straus, 210 U.S. 339, 341 (1908).
15 Bobbs-Merrill Co. v. Straus, 210 U.S. 350.
16 Bobbs-Merrill Co. v. Straus, 139 F. 155, 178 (1905).
17 Straus & Straus v. American Publishers' Ass'n, 231 U.S. 222 (1913).
18 U.S. Congress, House Committee on the Judiciary, *Hearings on H.R. 1027, H.R. 1029, and S. 32*, 6 Oct. 1983. 98th Cong. 1st and 2nd sessions (Washington, DC: GPO, 1985), 19.
19 U.S. Congress, *Hearings*, 33–35.
20 U.S. Congress, 123.
21 U.S. Congress, 24.
22 U.S. Congress, 29, 30.
23 Pub. L. No. 98–450, 98 Stat. 1727 (1984).
24 See Frederick Wasser, *Veni, Vidi, Video: The Hollywood Empire and the VCR* (Austin: University of Texas Press, 2001), 110–116.
25 U.S. Copyright Office, DMCA Section 104 Report 20, 78 (2001).
26 U.S. Copyright Office, 79–80.
27 Capitol Records, LLC v. ReDigi Inc., 934 F. Supp. 2d 640, 649 (2013).
28 MDY Indus., LLC v. Blizzard Entm't, Inc., 629 F.3d 928, 939–943 (2010).
29 Lawrence Lessig, *Code Version 2.0* (New York: Basic, 2006).

30 Gregory Steirer, "Clouded Visions: UltraViolet and the Future of Digital Distribution," *Television & New Media* 16, no. 2 (Feb. 2015): 184–189.

31 Capitol Records v. ReDigi Inc., 934 F. Supp. 2d 640, 654–657 (2013).

32 17 U.S.C. §512.

33 See Quality King Distributors, Inc. v. L'Anza Research Int'l, Inc., 523 U.S. 135; Kirt-
saeng v. John Wiley & Sons, Inc., 568 U.S. 519 (2013).

34 This chapter has been made possible in part by funding from the National Endowment for the Humanities (NEH). Any views, findings, or conclusions expressed
herein do not necessarily represent those of the NEH.

4

Game Retail and Crowdfunding

●●●●●●●●●●●●●●●●●●●●●●

HEIKKI TYNI AND OLLI SOTAMAA

In June 2015, over seventy-three thousand fans came together on the online crowdfunding platform Kickstarter to fund the development of a digital game called *Yooka-Laylee* (Playtonic Games, 2017). A spiritual successor to and a revival of the 3-D platformer genre popular during the Nintendo 64 era, *Yooka-Laylee* is an example of a high-profile crowdfunding campaign that enticed a significant consumer base to directly interact with an independent game studio and "prebuy" a game that, at the time, had neither been developed nor received the backing of a big publisher to guarantee its release. As such, this case illustrates how current game industry business models are intimately tied to participatory forms of media consumption. It also shows how online platforms that facilitate alternative funding schemes contest traditional ideas concerning the game commodity and its retail, necessitating new and more nuanced ways of understanding the relationship between buying and selling goods.

This chapter focuses on the relationship between digital games and crowdfunding. Crowdfunding a game means collecting relatively small monetary contributions from a relatively large online crowd to fund the development of the game. The reward for this is typically the complete game when it is finished, making the funder a preorder customer of sorts. Recent research on the digitalization of retailing identifies transformations along several different fronts: retailing exchanges, the nature of retail offerings, settings and places of retail, and actors who participate in retailing.[1] The contemporary global game industry, defined by the advent of popular new gaming platforms, digital distribution services, and free-to-play models, exemplifies many of these transformations. In the context of this chapter, crowdfunding is considered as a special case of media retail that has both similarities and differences to other forms of retail. In academia, the crowdfunding of games has been described in a few seminal articles.[2] The topic of game retail has been researched before but only in passing and not from the perspective of crowdfunding. Considering the relationship of game retail and crowdfunding, this chapter breaks new ground in offering a unique perspective on both areas.

Within the past four decades, digital games have grown to an industry with an annual revenue of around $100 billion.[3] The evolution of video game retail has been characterized by a constant flow of new technologies and quickly emerging changes within the marketplace. In recent years, game studios worldwide have shifted from providing discrete offerings toward establishing ongoing relationships with their players. In other words, the days of digital games as "fire-and-forget" commodities seem to be numbered, as games are increasingly bought and sold as ongoing services that are routinely patched, updated, expanded, and modified.[4] This does not necessarily mean that the significance of retail is decreasing. It is, however, clear that incorporating service aspects to retail challenges us to rethink the nature, duration, and actors of media retail.

It has been argued that the contemporary media environment is defined by more complex relations between corporate media and grassroots participatory culture.[5] Many of the prospects attached to this new participatory culture were only a short while ago considered downright utopic but are now becoming a reality. This realizing potential has both good and not-so-good consequences: users have more power to shape and customize the products and services they are offered, but at the same time, marketing pressures drive cultural producers to aggressively fight for customer attention. Within game studies, this has resulted in calls for more attention to the push-pull dynamic between the industry and the players[6] and the blurring boundaries between people who develop games and those who play them.[7] Consequently, this chapter focuses more closely on the blurring of consumer purchases and retail salesmanship. In our reading, crowdfunding offers a "retailization" of development, underlining how media production in general and game development in particular play an important role in the study of emerging forms of retail.

When examining the relationship between media retail and crowdfunding, games offer a particularly apt topic of inquiry. Digital games have played a key role on leading crowdfunding platforms like Kickstarter and Indiegogo, popularizing new features and funding schemes (such as stretch goals, add-ons, and gamified campaigns) that are currently considered mainstream crowdfunding practices.[8] Studying them will provide new information about game retail while also helping us better understand the dynamics of crowdfunding and its relation to conventional business models for media. In terms of method and data, this chapter draws from several approaches and data sets. Starting from the beginning of 2015, the authors have followed several different game crowdfunding campaigns as long-term case studies.[9] Case study analysis is supplemented with an online survey of crowdfunding backers conducted in the fall of 2016[10] and an ongoing interview study. The thematic interviews cover crowdfunding project creators, intermediaries who offer them services, and Kickstarter staff.

The chapter first gives a concise overview of the history and the current-day conditions of video game retail. It then describes the general characteristics of game crowdfunding, after which crowdfunding is discussed from the perspectives of preordering games, retailing crowdfunded games, and crowdfunding as a form of "retail spectacle." Finally, it is argued that games crowdfunding represents a unique case of "retailization" of consumption in which the backer-customers become agents of retail, exemplifying the emerging, hybrid forms of more participatory retail cultures.

Video Game Retail

The beginning of the modern video game industry is often associated with such early commercial games as *Computer Space* (1971) and *Pong* (1972) and the advent of the Magnavox Odyssey (1972). However, the roots of electronic gaming and the business around them can be tracked back at least to the industrial revolutions of the nineteenth and early twentieth century and the early coin-op machines and penny arcades.[11] Many of the early coin-operated video games were in fact manufactured by the companies responsible for the earlier coin-op amusements. Already the early game arcade business had a relatively clear division of labor: (1) manufacturers produced the machines, (2) distributors purchased them from manufacturers and then sold them to operators, (3) machine operators—normally also responsible for repair and maintenance—placed the machines in locations ranging from bars and bowling alleys to dedicated game arcades, and (4) location owners paid the costs of powering the video game machines on a day-to-day basis.[12] The income from the machines was normally divided equally between the machine operator and the location owner—the actors closest to the consumer. The very media form of commercial video games was closely intertwined with the commodity form: the early arcade games were designed to persuade players to insert quarter after quarter and therefore had no end.[13]

During the 1980s, Nintendo and Sega, especially, popularized what we now call the "traditional game industry," in terms of both the value chain and game retail. This video game value chain consisted of (1) platform holders who provide and control the game consoles; (2) publishers who fund game productions; (3) developers who build games; (4) distributors, typically for each major market area; and (5) retailers who sell the games and consoles to consumers (Johns, 2006). A developer working in this environment needs to negotiate deals with the other parties or, more typically, make a deal with a publisher who will then handle the interaction with the other value chain actors. Often monetary connections tie the value chain parties together on different levels; for example, publishers may also pay licensing fees to platform holders, and different parties jointly monetize marketing efforts. Finally, each party takes its share from the retail price of a game sold. Traditionally, only 10–15 percent is collected by the developer, and the retailer retains around 30–35 percent of the video game retail value.[14]

Market research company Newzoo estimated the global game industry revenues to be more than $100 billion in 2017.[15] At the same time, GameStop, the largest video game retail outlet that operates more than seven thousand retail stores worldwide, reached global sales of only around $3 billion.[16] The business of traditional retailers, ranging from merchants such as Walmart, Best Buy, and Toys "R" Us to independent brick-and-mortar retail stores has been challenged by rental options, mail subscription services, and kiosk rental services like RedBox.[17] The most significant transformations to retail are, however, provoked by digital distribution services. In 2010, studies indicated that digital distribution had only marginally affected traditional retail sales.[18] Five years later, however, it was estimated that retail-based game sales covered almost 30 percent of the annual global sales.[19] By 2016, the size of the digital distribution sector in the United States had risen to 56 percent of the total digital games market.[20] In the Asia-Pacific region, responsible for 47 percent of total global game revenues,[21] the share is expected to be even higher.

Today, each industry segment has its own digital distribution platforms. The console game segment, responsible for the largest share of the game industry revenues until the late 2000s, is controlled by the console manufacturers' online marketplaces including the PlayStation Store (Sony), Xbox Live Marketplace (Microsoft), and Nintendo eShop (Nintendo). At the same time, with annual revenues of around $3.5. billion, the Steam platform owned by Valve Corporation is expected to govern up to 75 percent of the PC market space for downloadable games.[22] Similarly, revenues from other related sectors such as free-to-play MMOs (massively multiplayer online games), social gaming, and PC downloadable content seem to be steadily growing.[23] The most rapid growth is identified in the mobile gaming sector, reported to account already for almost one-third of the global games market.[24] The mobile games market is dominated by the Apple App Store (iOS) and Google Play Store (Android) that both publish hundreds of new games every day.

Within digital distribution services, the platform owner has adopted a role very similar to the retailer. Platform owners typically take around 30 percent of the retail value of the game[25] and practically cut out the traditional retailers from the equation. At the same time, the rest of the pot, up to 70 percent, is reserved for the developer. It is easy to see why the new model attracts many game developers. It has made it very easy, almost for anyone, to launch a game commercially, and the game developer needs only to negotiate with the platform holder, who also controls the access to the digital storefront. While it is up to the game developer to decide whether they want to use additional funds—for example, for promotion or for hiring a dedicated publisher—they are normally able to secure a significantly improved profit margin when compared to the previous publisher-driven model.

Digital distribution and physical game retail intertwine in both direct and indirect ways. Besides selling new game copies, retail stores also benefit from secondhand sales of physical game commodities. In fact, selling a secondhand copy of a game is more lucrative for a retail store than selling a new game, as developers, publishers, and platform holders do not get a revenue share from a used game.[26] Consecutively, publishers and platform holders use various incentives to encourage customers to buy games through digital distribution, where games largely cannot be resold. Another area that highlights the same conflict of interests is preordering. To combat secondhand sales, preordering of new games is now aggressively encouraged by publishers in various ways. A sizeable section of gameplay might, for example, be cut from an upcoming title, to be introduced as exclusive downloadable content for those who preordered the game. At the same time—due to the continued importance of the largest retail chains in selling the biggest games—game studios often provide retailers like GameStop and Walmart with chain-exclusive preorder content, which the retailers then use to combat other stores, both physical and digital.[27] Additionally, GameStop has recently announced that it is starting to publish games itself,[28] reflecting the drastic measures the world's largest video game retail chain is taking in order to keep itself integrated in the digital game value chain.

Crowdfunding Games

To crowdfund a game means that there is a project creator (a game developer) who publicly presents a prototype or a design document of a game online, typically on a crowdfunding platform, to collect relatively small monetary contributions from a relatively large online crowd to fund the development of the game. In almost every case, the people who donate to the campaign, the "backers," are offered the complete game as a reward as soon as it is finished. Typically, the project creator creates a pitch video in which they describe the game they would like to make, the skills and assets that prove they can actually execute the plan, and possible concept art, alpha footage, or a prototype of the early version of the game.

Funding is based on a tiered system, where each funding tier offers increasing rewards. With game campaigns, the lowest reward tier is typically set at ten to twenty dollars, offering a digital download of the game when it is eventually ready—a sum that is mostly in line with the average cost of a new game on Steam. At the same time, higher reward tiers might offer a physical game copy, a soundtrack, signed artwork, and so on.[29] In most cases, backers can also donate a sum below the lowest tier, which still gives them access to project updates—which can be backer exclusive—and allows them to be listed as backers on the platform site. Project creators get to keep everything they receive on top of their minimum goal and, typically, gradually rising "stretch goals" are used to describe how the project will use the extra funds should any be collected. In most cases, stretch goals expand and flesh out the game in various ways. Additionally, many campaigns sell add-on content that is not included in the reward tiers. However, pledging for that content still raises the overall funding of the project—and therefore adds to the momentum that most projects strive toward.

On Kickstarter, the top of the campaign page is reserved for the pitch video, which therefore is the first site element the user will see. In general platform instructions, project creators are told that campaigns with a pitch video succeed significantly more often; subsequently, almost all campaigns have one nowadays. Next to the video, the page displays the progress and the goal of the campaign, the backer count, the remaining campaign time, and a highlighted "Back this project" button. Underneath this button, there is also a smaller "Remind me" button that lets registered users be notified about the campaign when there are only two days left. After the campaign has closed, the "Back this campaign" button is typically replaced with a suitable new button, such as "Follow the development," linking to a development blog; "Late-pledge this project," linking to a separate preorder site; or "Buy it now," linking to a digital storefront if the game is already released.

A typical Kickstarter page displays the items that the campaign aims to sell—or presell—as packaged reward tiers, used to tempt interested backers in a couple of different ways. Reward tiers are presented on the side panel of the page, with the cheapest tier on the top and the possible additional options getting gradually more expensive when scrolling down the page. Projects sometimes also offer reward tiers that are limited in number or time—for example, small batches of "Early Bird" tiers that are cheaper versions of the regular tiers. The lower parts of the campaign page offer more information on the project—featuring stylized graphics made specifically for the project, such as artwork, details on game mechanics, short profiles on team members, links to possible demo versions, testimonials, and so on. It is also a common practice to display any possible stretch goals as a list that highlights the already unlocked content prominently while displaying one or more upcoming stretch goals as the next goal to beat. It is also quite typical to tease further upcoming stretch goal content with shadowed graphics. The highly successful campaign of *Bloodstained* (ArtPlay, 2018), for example, displayed the stretch goal progress as a stylized pixel-graphics castle that grew in size with the campaign, with stretch goals "moving" through the castle and a cellar trapdoor all the way to the dungeons. All this no doubt made following the campaign progress a much more enjoyable experience.

Crowdfunding as Preordering?

In terms of selling games, crowdfunding is primarily about preordering, as the game has not been made when the money is collected. Some campaigns—such as *Fear Effect Sedna* (Sushee, 2018), another project aimed at reviving a past game series—even label one or more reward tiers directly as a "Pre-order." Kickstarter also gives creators the option to allow the public to preview their page prior to the campaign start; this might be significant for getting last-minute feedback on the campaign but also to give backers a heads-up on limited preorder content, for example. The similarities between regular preordering and crowdfunding are also reflected in the attitudes of the backers. In their interview study, Elizabeth Gerber and Julie Hui found out that many backers "refer to the transaction as 'buying' and 'getting,' suggesting that crowdfunding shares some elements with the consumer experience."[30] Furthermore, in an online user survey conducted by the authors, three-quarters of the respondents reported to at least somewhat agree that crowdfunding a product is like preordering it, whereas roughly two-thirds agreed that crowdfunding a product is the same as buying that product. With crowdfunded board games, a campaign might also be openly labeled as funding a print run of a completed or slightly updated game. Furthermore, some board-gaming campaigns offer additional high-level reward tiers that are directed to retailers interested in reselling the game (e.g., "Retailer tier—Get 10 copies of the game for a small discount").

This preorder form that the crowdfunding model adopts has direct consequences. First, the used games market is of little consequence to crowdfunding campaigns. A developer who successfully manages to collect funding from the crowd for their game has complete control over its sales in the prerelease stage. Second, if the game is offered as a physical copy during the campaign, the crowdfunding model allows the developer to produce the exact number of copies with no need to worry about stock surplus.

This focus on preordering positions crowdfunding as a perfect example of what James Newman has called a "culture of obsolescence" that perpetually foregrounds innovation, upgrade, and previewing, prevalent within the wider industry of digital games.[31] For him, the modern digital games business relies on planned obsolescence: the industry is built around the notion that games have short lifespans and they are retired quickly to clear room for the next coming-soon title.[32] In a sense, the crowdfunding model takes this "just around the corner," "coming soon" feeling to an extremity. Arguably, it is precisely this feeling that drives many backers to fund games that are still to be realized—"vaporware." In this preexisting, predefined stage, these games are full of possibilities. After years of completely hopeless and unheard fan campaigning, a crowdfunding campaign for *Shenmue 3* (Ys Net, 2018) appeared seemingly from nowhere and quickly became the highest-funded digital game on Kickstarter. While it very well might one day turn out to be yet another disappointing sequel, the crowdfunding campaign for *Shenmue 3* virtually fulfilled everybody's hopes and dreams of a perfect conclusion for the *Shenmue* franchise. Here, digital games, crowdfunding, and the emphasis on anticipation curl around each other.

While the optimism toward the positive outcome of a popular game crowdfunding project no doubt relates to several factors, arguably much of it is to do with the backers' perception of being able to influence the development of the game one way or the other—if not as an individual, then as a community that deserves to be heard. In our survey, almost three-quarters of respondents at least somewhat agreed that "participating in a crowdfunding campaign feels like taking part in the product's development." Two out of three respondents agreed that backing a campaign offered the respondent ways to influence the development of the crowdfunded product. Further, over half of the respondents agreed that in backing a crowdfunding campaign, they *wanted* to influence the product's development. Newman highlights how some preorder schemes give the customers the possibility of playing games prior to release—as beta releases—and how this makes the player-customers more than that: they become a part of the development team.[33] Newman writes, "The pleasures of engaging with [the game] in its unfinished state derive from being both a player and playtester, fan and de facto developer."[34]

Whereas with the traditional games industry, the "culture of obsolescence" stymies compatibility between old platforms and new software,[35] games crowdfunding offers one of the most direct channels to address this problem. It can be argued that the crowdfunding model liberates consumer-users from such corporate programming and allows them to concentrate on substantial projects created more by their peers than the faceless entertainment industry. Here, at its best, the "compatibility with redundant, superseded platforms and software" is restored and support continued.[36] Almost all the survey respondents agreed that they want to support independent development. When Newman argues that "by paying now and playing later, [preordering player-customers] are literally buying into the future of videogames," he might as well be talking about (the idealistic nature of) crowdfunding as a perfect channel for small, independent game developers striving to release themselves from the oppressive publishers.[37]

Retailing Crowdfunded Games

Many factors, including the cost of development and the expected profits from the game sales, affect the selling of games in the crowdfunding model. The majority of crowdfunded digital games are released in a digital-only form because of the easiness and availability of digital distribution compared to the challenges of physical production. A smaller percentage of games are released as physical copies, although some of these are only a very limited run through small, specialized publishing houses and perhaps only in one of the key markets (the United States, Europe, and Japan).[38] Furthermore, the funding and production of games using the crowdfunding model can affect the actual form of the game in different ways.

Both traditionally sold games and crowdfunded games often offer expensive collector's editions that are reported to be a small, limited printing only. Many crowdfunding projects, however, state that besides this campaign-exclusive physical release, there will be no general release in the physical retail channels. During the development phase, this stance might be reevaluated— for example, if the project has generated a lot of positive interest among the player community and press—and the developer may partner with a publisher to bring out a physical release. *Yooka-Laylee*, for example, was not supposed to get a physical release, but over a year into the development process, Playtonic announced that a publisher, Team 17, would be bringing the game into retail stores after all. Furthermore, of the seventy-three thousand–plus *Yooka-Laylee* backers, roughly six thousand fans chose to get one of the more expensive physical editions that were offered during the campaign, and 625 fans pledged as much as £340 to get a "retro-themed physical package complete with classic box, SIGNED manual and an exclusive *Yooka-Laylee* N64 cartridge with built-in 64GB flash drive."[39]

Because the majority of crowdfunded digital games are being released through digital distribution only, a physical release for a game might be considered a specialty or luxury good. As with *Yooka-Laylee*, higher reward tiers many times offer campaign-exclusive versions of the game. Using *Gears of War 3* (Microsoft Studios, 2011) as an example, Newman highlights preorder schemes where exclusive content, such as special items and access to the beta version of the game, is offered: "The lure, exclusivity and distinctiveness of these unlockables which are available only through the beta access granted by the pre-order process and which are portioned out (and subsequently revoked) over particular periods, work to create a sense of urgency in the pre-order transaction that belies the *prima facie* fact that there remain [many months] until the game is released."[40]

For Newman, access necessitates preordering. Similar arguments can certainly be applied to crowdfunding projects: offers promoting exclusivity grab backers' attention. Three out of four respondents in our survey agreed at least partially that "I sometimes fear that I will miss out on a good offer unless I back a campaign." Higher-tier campaign versions of crowdfunded games often become collectible rarities, as they typically are not available elsewhere after the campaign.

It has been argued that a crowdfunding campaign acts as a good indication of postlaunch demand.[41] Thus it follows that a highly successful crowdfunding campaign is an indication of high postlaunch demand. However, this has not always been the case; despite highly successful campaigns, *Mighty No. 9* (Comcept, 2016) and the OUYA game console did poorly on the postlaunch marketplace. Examples like these might be explained by poor execution of the products and the negative prelaunch reviews reflecting this—a situation that becomes even more possible due to crowdfunding backers usually receiving their products prior to general launch. *Mighty No. 9*, for example, was hampered by a problematic production period and delays—something that greatly irritated backers already before they had even received the game. Poor postlaunch success might also be an indication of the crucial core audience buying the crowdfunded product already in the campaign phase, leaving too few interested consumers to buy the game from retail channels.

From Game Retail to Spectacle Retail

One of the differences between retailing through crowdfunding and retail via brick-and-mortar or digital storefronts is the collective nature of the crowdfunding campaign experience. On the comments section of a popular crowdfunding campaign, whenever yet another stretch goal is close to being reached, a communal feeling of enthusiasm can be witnessed and is often contagious. In a polemic blog post about crowdfunding, Ian Bogost argued that we often do not even really want what we are funding—instead, backing a project is like "buying a ticket on the ride, reserving a front-row seat to the process . . . [f]or the experience of watching it succeed beyond expectations or to fail dramatically."[42] Perhaps acknowledging this feeling of spectacle as an important part of campaign momentum, Kickstarter now offers "Kickstarter Live": an option for the creators to include platform-supported live streaming onto their project site—to discuss the latest stretch goals, for example. Here, the project creator has a possibility to appear as a "show host" or even a celebrity who every night appears on the familiar channel to advertise, inform, answer questions, and build community. As such, popular crowdfunding campaigns can be turned into shared spectacles that concentrate and celebrate the upcoming product.

Giving regular updates is a necessary part of successful campaigns,[43] and the pressure to provide live updates almost every day nicely highlights the heavy emphasis that well-planned crowdfunding projects now put on promotion during the campaign phase. In some cases, this might even affect the retail form of the product; it is easier to create new reveals and ongoing buzz with fragmented products—that is, gradually revealing new components and features. For example, many miniature board games such as *Conan* (Monolith, 2016) and *Zombicide: Black Plague* (CoolMiniOrNot, 2016) have been very successful on Kickstarter; an established strategy for these kinds of games is to expand the initial base game with new, campaign-exclusive miniatures, one by one, that once "unlocked" are free for all backers. As with preorder offers that offer exclusive DLC (downloadable content) levels to a game, a question arises whether these components and features were originally a part of the core game and were removed from it only to allow this kind of piecemeal sales strategy.

Continuing on the same note, Bogost compared crowdfunding to television shopping channels.[44] Typically, products are presented as special, campaign-exclusive offers that are available only for a short time, and often, both in crowdfunding and on shopping channels, there are special tie-in products that you can get as free "throw-in gifts"—but only if you "act fast!" As with crowdfunding, television shopping channel product demonstrations are often presented in front of an audience that gives applause and sets the tone, with the goal of convincing the viewer that "this truly is an especially good offer!" However, unlike the shopping channel, crowdfunding campaigns are speaking to an enthusiast audience that is specifically there because of their excitement for that particular product. As such, the negative connotation one might attach to shopping channel retail is largely absent within a backer community.

Backers as Agents of Retail

Crowdfunding backers are overwhelmingly people who have come together to support a campaign toward which they are very amicable or even enthusiastic. Many backers visit an open campaign page several times during a campaign and take part in the general (often enthusiastic) discussion surrounding the project. This has various consequences. First, existing backers often try to help in welcoming new backers and offering answers to frequently asked questions. Second, as most projects use stretch goals (i.e., the more money that is collected, the more content every backer gets), community members might get organized to entice new backers to join in. Third, members also sometimes persuade existing backers to raise their pledge or let themselves be persuaded to do the same. During the campaign of *Conan* (Monolith, 2016), a miniature board game, new backers had endless questions about issues such as shipping, payments, and release dates. This soon resulted in existing backers addressing many of these questions for newcomers, substituting for Monolith's community manager when he was not available. Furthermore, backers openly discussed whether to spend more money on the project, or "up their pledge," to help reach upcoming stretch goals quicker. Many backers raised their pledge gradually as new stretch goals and optional add-ons were revealed, eventually declaring that they would go "all in"—that is, getting all the content there was to get (costing roughly $650, in contrast to the $90 asked for the base game).

Identifying this predisposition of the backers to aid in the sales process, it is now a common practice among crowdfunding campaigns to ask the existing backer community to spread the word in their social media channels, with the shared understanding that the more backers and collected funds there are, the more content everybody gets. Moreover, some crowdfunding campaigns, such as *Bloodstained*, *Exploding Kittens* (The Oatmeal, 2015), and *BATTLETECH* (Harebrained Schemes, 2018), have introduced special backer community "achievements." With *Bloodstained*, the community could earn achievements when different social media channels used by the campaign attracted a certain number of followers, when enough fan art was posted on Tumblr, when the campaign site was shared enough times, and so on. A certain amount of unlocked achievements would then yield bonuses for the campaign, such as wallpapers, new in-game costumes, and "silly" cheat codes for the game. Almost all the achievements were unlocked, and the strategy no doubt worked to great effect in both harnessing the fan community to spread the word (i.e., viral marketing) and getting fans enthusiastically engaged with the campaign.

Blurring the lines between producers and customers, creators of crowdfunding projects are often talented but "regular" people. Most game developers who choose to utilize crowdfunding are independent creators working alone or in small teams of one to five. They might be working from their homes and profess their fandom toward the same objects of admiration as the backers. However, Heikki Tyni describes how removing other value chain actors such as retailers and publishers from the production network can simply result in the developer having to take care of these tasks themselves, including various methods of trying to directly sell the product to customers.[45] Outsourcing functions of retail to backers might be invaluable and sometimes the only way to succeed. When project creators address the concerns of the backers—for example, through project community forums—they meet them on a peer-to-peer level, providing access that is perceived as extremely valuable in modern marketing. One of the central ways to create long-term brand loyalty in contemporary social network markets is through social influence—for example, getting a customer to recommend a product to a friend. Here, game development, game retail, and fan communities create new hybrid relationships exemplifying new, participatory forms of media consumption that aid in the selling of the game on producers' behalf.

Conclusions

As stated at the beginning of this chapter, we believe that studying the ways in which new participatory forms of interaction affect the media retail environment will help us better understand the logic of media and game culture more broadly. Crowdfunding is obviously not the only recent development challenging our notions of media retail. At the same time, many of the observations made in this chapter resonate with the wider transformation toward a service-based game industry model in which the nature of retail exchanges and the roles reserved for key actors, from developers to players, get significantly reevaluated.

Based on this study, crowdfunding actively works to decentralize some of the existing models of retail. At the same time, as game retail is moving away from the traditional stores, different phases in the production and distribution of video games adopt the characteristics of retail. First, crowdsourcing offers a *retailization of game development*. Instead of only focusing on delivering the game, the development team activities are now connected to the crowdfunding campaign that ultimately determines the sale of the product. Simultaneously, as the retailers and publishers are removed from the picture, game developers are asked to master many tasks traditionally associated with the retailers. Second, crowdfunding also results in the *retailization of consumption*: the campaigns rely heavily on the active role of consumers, reinventing backers as agents of retail who try to convince others to invest their money in the campaign they have backed.

Overall, it is relevant to ask what kind of games come out of this crowdfunding model. Arguing for more research focus on the economic models underlying digital games, Sebastian Deterding asks "how particular economic conditions enable, constrain, shape and support particular aesthetic forms of games."[46] As a production logic, the crowdfunding model has a clear set of characteristics, many of which shape the games produced through it. First, the model necessitates that the game idea is presold to a large enough crowd of customers before it can be made. This might mean, for example, choosing a concept that is known to be popular over an eccentric art game. Second, the project creators need to open up the production for cocreative participation by the backer community, which might both result in changes in the final game and encourage game concepts that support small outside contributions. Third, for feedback on development, crowdfunding creators largely rely on amateurs—that is, the backer community—instead of professionals, such as a publisher. Finally, the pressure created by the expected transparency of crowdfunding projects and the backer community to finish the game within an acceptable time frame might result in games being increasingly released in unfinished forms (as opposed to negotiating more time with a publisher).

All in all, crowdfunding troubles the tendency of studying media retail in isolation from the creative sphere of production. As the most intriguing transformations appear to spawn from the interplay between retail and other phases in the life cycle of a game, it is difficult to argue for keeping these domains of research apart from each other.

Notes

1 Johan Hagberg, Malin Sundstrom, and Niklas Egels-Zandén, "The Digitalization of Retailing: An Exploratory Framework," *International Journal of Retail & Distribution Management* 44, no. 7 (2016): 694–712.

2 Heikki Tyni, "Double Duty: Crowdfunding and the Evolving Game Production Network," *Games and Culture* (2017); Anthony N. Smith, "The Backer–Developer Connection: Exploring Crowdfunding's Influence on Video Game Production," *New Media and Society* 17, no. 2 (2014): 198–214; Antonio José Planells, "Video Games and the Crowdfunding Ideology: From the Gamer-buyer to the Prosumer-investor," *Journal of Consumer Culture* 17, no. 3 (2015): 620–638.

3 "Global Games Market Report 2017," *Newzoo*, 2017, https://newzoo.com/insights/trend-reports/newzoo-global-games-market-report-2017-light-version/.

4 Tim Chang, "Gaming Will Save Us All," *Communications of the ACM* 53, no. 3 (Mar. 2010): 22–24; Olli Sotamaa and Tero Karppi, eds., *Games as Services—Final Report*, TRIM Research Reports 2, University of Tampere, Finland, http://tampub.uta.fi/bitstream/handle/10024/65772/978-951-44-8167-3.pdf.

   Instead of buying the new *Call of Duty*, playing it, and moving on, games such as *World of Warcraft* can be seen as passports to persistent virtual worlds that are treated as services by the developers and maintained and updated for years and years.

5 Henry Jenkins, *Convergence Culture: Where Old and New Media Collide* (New York: New York University Press, 2006).

6 Mia Consalvo, *Cheating: Gaining Advantage in Videogames* (Cambridge: MIT Press, 2007).

7 Olli Sotamaa, *The Player's Game: Towards Understanding Player Production among Computer Game Cultures* (PhD diss., University of Tampere, 2009).

8 L. Crane, interview with author, 10 Dec. 2015.

9 All the case study campaigns use Kickstarter (www.kickstarter.com), currently the most popular crowdfunding platform for game projects. Consecutively, this examination is limited to that platform.

10 The survey was conducted by researchers from the University of Tampere Game Research Lab, and it was open from 30 September to 15 November 2016 on SurveyGizmo.com. The link to the survey was shared on popular social media networks and in the comments sections of over twenty crowdfunding projects. After disqualified entries were removed, the dataset includes answers from altogether 426 crowdfunding campaign backers.

11 Erkki Huhtamo, "Slots of Fun, Slots of Trouble: Toward an Archaeology of Electronic Gaming," in *Handbook of Computer Games Studies*, eds. Joost Raessens and Jeffrey Goldstein (Cambridge: MIT Press, 2005), 3–21.

12 Carly A. Kocurek, "Coin-Drop Capitalism: Economic Lessons from the Video Game Arcade," in *Before the Crash: An Anthology of Early Video Game History*, ed. Mark J. P. Wolf (Detroit, Mich.: Wayne State University Press, 2012), 195.

13 Julian Kücklich, *Insert Credit to Continue: Narrative and Commodity Form in Video Games* (unpublished manuscript, 2010).

14 Tracy Fullerton, Christopher Swain, and Steven Hoffman, *Game Design Workshop: Designing, Prototyping, and Playtesting Games* (New York: CMP, 2004); Jennifer Johns, "Video Game Production Networks: Value Capture, Power Relations and Embeddedness," *Journal of Economic Geography* 6, no. 2 (2006):151–180.

15 "Global Games Market."

16 "GameStop Reports Sales and Earnings for Fiscal 2016 and Provides 2017 Outlook," *GlobalNewswire*, 23 Mar. 2017, https://globenewswire.com/news-release/2017/03/23/943762/0/en/GameStop-Reports-Sales-and-Earnings-for-Fiscal-2016-and-Provides-2017-Outlook.html.

17 Randy Nichols, *The Video Game Business* (London: British Film Institute, 2014), 106–108.

18 Nichols, *Video Game Business*, 106.

19 *Global Games Market Research 2015* (New York: SuperData Research, 2015).

20 Aphra Kerr, *Global Games: Production, Circulation and Policy in the Networked Era* (New York: Routledge, 2017), 36.

21 "Global Games Market."

22 Matthew Handrahan, "Steam Paid Revenue Flat in 2016 despite Escalating Releases—Steam Spy," *Gamesindustry*, 6 Jan. 2017, http://www.gamesindustry.biz/articles/2017-01-06-steam-paid-game-revenue-flat-in-2016-despite-escalating-releases-steam-spy.

23 *Global Games Market Research*.

24 *Global Games Market Research*.

25 Kerr, *Global Games*.

26 This practice has been criticized for directly driving the cost of retail game copies up. James Brightman, "Pre-owned Increases Cost of Games, Cannibalizes Industry, Says Dyack," *Gamesindustry*, 27 Mar. 2012, http://www.gamesindustry.biz/articles/2012-03-27-pre-owned-increases-cost-of-games-cannibalizes-industry-says-dyack.

27 In most cases, these exclusives later become available for all to purchase—for example, through a "Game of the Year" edition released half a year to a year later that collects all the scattered content in the same package.

28 Mike Williams, "GameStop Becomes a Publisher with GameTrust," *USgamer*, 18 Apr. 2016, http://www.usgamer.net/articles/gamestop-becomes-a-publisher-with-gametrust.

29 A constantly updated list by the authors tracking crowdfunded games released on Steam indicates that the average lowest cost for getting the game for projects using U.S. dollars is $14.94 (based on 260 games).

30 Elizabeth Gerber and Julie Hui, "Crowdfunding: Motivations and Deterrents for Participation," *ACM Transactions on Computer-Human Interaction* 20 (2013): 14.

31 James Newman, *Best Before: Videogames, Supersession and Obsolescence* (Abingdon, Va.: Routledge, 2012), 68.

32 Newman, *Best Before*, 68.

33 Newman, 68–69.

34 Newman, 69.

35 Newman.

36 Newman, 11. See, for example, *Pier Solar and the Great Architects* (WaterMelon, 2010), which is a homebrew game released for Sega Genesis in 2010 and for Sega Dreamcast in 2015 (the latter via a crowdfunding campaign). Physical Dreamcast game discs were printed and shipped to backers.

37 Newman, *Best Before*, 68–69.

38 A constantly updated list by the authors tracking crowdfunded games released on Steam indicates that 79 games out of (total) 333 have received a physical release. Thirty-three of these are identified as a limited release.

39 *Yooka-Laylee* Kickstarter campaign page, 2015, https://www.kickstarter.com/projects/playtonic/yooka-laylee-a-3d-platformer-rare-vival.

40 Newman, *Best Before*, 72.

41 Paul Belleflamme, Thomas Lambert, and Armin Schwienbacher, "Crowdfunding: Tapping the Right Crowd," *Journal of Business Venturing* 29, no. 5 (2014): 585–609.

42 Ian Bogost, "Kickstarter: Crowdfunding Platform or Reality Show?," *Fast Company*, 18 July 2012, http://www.fastcompany.com/1843007/kickstarter-crowdfunding-platform-or-reality-show.

43 Ethan Mollick, "The Dynamics of Crowdfunding: An Exploratory Study," *Journal of Business Venturing* 29, no. 1 (2014): 1–16.

44 Bogost, "Kickstarter."

45 Tyni, "Double Duty."

46 Sebastian Deterding, "Toward Economic Platform Studies" (presentation, Twelfth Annual Game Research Lab Spring Seminar, "Money and Games," Tampere, Finland, 18–19 Apr. 2016).

5

The App Store

• • • • • • • • • • • • • • • • • • • •

Female Consumers, Shopping, and Digital Culture

ELIZABETH AFFUSO

Since Apple introduced the iPhone in 2007, app-based retail media has expanded rapidly. In recent years, some apps have begun to function as both media products and retail stores. Taking advantage of the click-through shopping experiences pioneered by iTunes, Amazon, and Pinterest, individual entertainment franchises and star brands have developed apps that work as retail stores selling products that are conventionally branded and also curated tie-ins. The rise of celebrity apps coincides with the increased merger of content with advertising in media and points to a move toward lifestyle as a core component of contemporary celebrity. Celebrity apps thus function as lifestyle boutiques that merge media content with retail experiences that are always open and always at your fingertips.

This chapter examines the development and impact of celebrity retail apps within the media business. I explore the architecture and use of these apps to demonstrate how they function as curated retail experiences. This chapter also addresses the subscription model in place—relating it to predecessors in magazines and streaming media—to look at exclusivity as a sales tactic. I begin with an analysis of entrepreneurial celebrity to establish the moment in celebrity culture that encourages this push toward app-based economies and then pursue a technical and economic analysis of apps and mobile shopping to establish the structures and frames of app-based retail. Finally, I analyze the Kardashian/Jenner apps as a case study of celebrity apps connected to one entrepreneurial celebrity brand to examine how entrepreneurial celebrity and digital retailing practices converge. Through their skilled cultivation and deployment of these apps, the Kardashians are particularly emblematic of this new convergent form of celebrity and retailing, showing how retail can become a site that sells not only products but also the lifestyles of celebrity brands.

Using formal and textual analysis of the apps and related advertising and social media discourse, this chapter argues that new ideas about celebrity and branding, along with increased precarity in celebrity economies and the continued embrace of neoliberal economic principles, have pushed celebrities into this technolandscape. I focus particularly on the way that these retail spaces target female consumers and question what these new forms of shopping mean for media retail overall. I am interested in assessing the implications of branded apps for contemporary media retail practices, especially in spaces where retail merges seamlessly with entertainment, while deploying celebrity apps as a frame to explore larger issues related to femininity, celebrity, interactivity, and shopping in contemporary media cultures.

Entrepreneurial Celebrity and the Politics of App Shopping

The rising influence of reality television stars and microcelebrity brands have contributed to a shift toward "entrepreneurial celebrity" within celebrity culture more broadly. Entrepreneurial celebrities are those who seek out brand extensions within the retail sector, most typically shops, restaurants, books, or beauty and fashion lines. Entrepreneurial celebrity used to be looked down upon, but this has changed dramatically in the last twenty years. Many factors contribute to this change, including the rise of internet and reality television stars, who make money in less conventional ways. Both celebrities and fans appear more comfortable with the idea of self-branding. Female celebrities succeed particularly well in this entrepreneurial vein, in part because many of the entrepreneurial opportunities fall into traditionally feminized spaces such as beauty and fashion. This switch to self-branding, along with postrecessionary changes in attitudes toward money, make people less skeptical of maximizing monetary potential. Female celebrities especially benefit as fashion and beauty industries move away from hiring models as spokespeople for brands toward celebrities. This shift places film and television stars in ad campaigns, in the front row at runway shows, and in branded attire on red carpets. Examples of this type of fashion-branded partnership include Kristen Stewart's partnership with Chanel, Jennifer Lawrence's with Dior, and Emma Stone's with Louis Vuitton. These relationships can benefit both parties, as fashion and beauty labels get stars as spokespeople, while stars get dressed or made up by the brand that they front.

These partnerships also provide consistent sources of revenue for stars who struggle in contemporary celebrity culture. The precarity of conventional star models makes additional revenue streams not only desirable but also necessary for many celebrities. Conventional forms of entertainment no longer provide the clear revenue streams that they once did due to the way that streaming media has impacted the syndication market and the DVD sales industry, specifically by reducing the residuals that actors rely on to make additional revenue, especially during lean periods. Such stars increasingly look to retail as a result. In this context, apps are part of a larger move to diversify celebrity brands. These new revenue streams expand the retail potential of media texts and conflate media texts with retail experiences in significant ways. As advertising becomes less visible and more seamlessly integrated into media texts, we see the increased development of media designed explicitly to sell products and not the other way around. Nonnarrative models in television, such as reality and lifestyle programming, are uniquely well suited for these types of additional revenue streams, as these shows are often predicated on the building of a personal brand.

Retail tie-ins are nothing new, but the degree to which they are an acceptable and even encouraged strategy is. We have moved beyond a collaborative line sold in a retail partnership à la Mary Kate and Ashley Olsen for Walmart, Jennifer Lopez for Kohl's, or Victoria Beckham for Target into a world where running a direct-to-consumer store via a lifestyle website or mobile app (or both) is a desirable way of making money for stars. In this new model of entrepreneurial celebrity, stars effectively act as the shopkeepers in a multichannel retail experience. Joseph Turow notes that in contemporary retail cultures, a "multichannel shopper" who uses the website, the mobile app, and the physical store is the most desirable for merchants.[1] This multichannel retail model can be overlaid onto the celebrity model, where stars play to multichannel fans who will follow them from television, movies, or albums to social media and apps. Stars like the Kardashians/Jenners, Gwyneth Paltrow, and Taylor Swift all represent this multichannel celebrity model, and their apps clearly embody the direct sales strategy of contemporary celebrity.

These new models of brand diversification can have gendered associations and meanings. They take part in a larger system of business strategies that Alyxandra Vesey has defined as "postfeminist entrepreneurialism," which are, "business strategies for female recording artists representing themselves as workers and capitalist subjects through the endorsement of mass-produced, hegemonically feminine consumer products that exploit individual brands to engender affective registers of proximity and empowerment for female consumers."[2] While Vesey's analysis is focused on perfume lines associated with female recording artists such as Nicki Minaj and Jennifer Lopez, the concept of "postfeminist entrepreneurialism" can be extended to female celebrities across media. A key part of postfeminist discourse is that women "are agentically 'choosing' to participate and find pleasure for ourselves in the same consumer-driven, hyperfeminine, glamorized body projects long used to construct us as passive spectacles for the male gaze," as Mary Celeste Kearney has noted.[3] All the entrepreneurial celebrity brands discussed in this chapter fall into the vein of women choosing to both disseminate and consume hyperfeminized aesthetic practices.

This entrepreneurialism is shared by not just movie, television, and pop stars but also microcelebrity and influencer brands. Celebrity apps rely on sharing economies of influence to produce desire, reflecting larger systemic changes in how desire is created in contemporary culture. Whereas magazines once held great sway over producing consumer desire for female audiences, we now see that position shifting toward influencer brands as the source of desire in such spaces as Instagram and YouTube. Influencers and influencer brands typically peddle lifestyles by showcasing elements such as diet, exercise, fashion, home, and family to show followers how to live a perfectly aestheticized life. Whereas historically socialites attained this position via familial status and disseminated influence through channels such as *Vogue*, *Vanity Fair*, and *Town and Country*, influencers today can come from any background, provided that they can use social media to showcase an idealized lifestyle. Influencers primarily make their money via product placements, appearance fees, and endorsements. Influencer brands provide a multitude of new retail experiences, whether click-through shopping on Pinterest, Instagram sales, or apps.[4] The models of economic exchange that exist among celebrities, microcelebrities, and regular users is especially important in digital culture because the profitability and uses of these sectors are still developing, leading to the emergence of entrepreneurial opportunities for personal brands open to tech-savvy engagement.

Celebrity App Economics

Outside the app-based retail sphere, many successful entrepreneurial brands fall into areas where female celebrities have historically been considered expert, such as parenting, diet, beauty, and fitness. This model can be seen in Jessica Alba's Honest Company, a brand of affordable eco-friendly baby and beauty products sold in major retailers such as Target and Amazon, which was launched in 2011 and is valued at $1 billion at the time of this writing.[5] At the same time, Alba's company has two apps that function as retail stores— *The Honest Company* and *Honest Beauty*—indicating how some stars use app models in tandem with classic models of celebrity entrepreneurism. Gwyneth Paltrow's Goop operates at the higher end of the wellness- and health-themed celebrity brand; it started as a lifestyle blog in 2008 and has grown into a private-label fashion and beauty brand, wellness summit, and brick-and-mortar business. At this point, it is possible that many consumers are bigger fans of Goop than of Paltrow's Oscar-winning acting career. Brands like Goop operate as part of a new iteration of retail, which relies on lifestyle bloggers and social network users to curate experiences and fetishize particular products. Goop has the *G. Spotting* app, which is less of a store than an ad for other stores, restaurants, and even cities that are part of the Goop-branded lifestyle. The travel app functions as a sort of mobile city guidebook, complete with a mapping functionality that takes advantage of the geo-locational features of mobile use with sections on restaurants, shops, activities, culture, hotels, bars, and health and beauty. The *G. Spotting* app provides a way to map these products in the digital and physical spaces in which they exist.

While Alba and Paltrow primarily use their apps as mobile extensions of their brands, other celebrity apps seamlessly bridge shopping, entertainment, and social media. A host of companies partner with celebrities to create such apps. Two of the most prolific and successful are Whalerock Industries and Glu Mobile. Whalerock, which creates the popular Kimojis and the increasingly successful Kardashian/Jenner apps, was founded in 2014 by Lloyd Braun, a media industry veteran with previous experience at Yahoo and ABC. Glu Mobile, a Silicon Valley–based brand, made celebrity-driven mobile games such as *Katy Perry: Pop, Nicki Minaj: The Empire*, and most successfully *Kim Kardashian: Hollywood*. Glu expanded its app offerings away from mobile games and toward celebrity lifestyle apps with the 2017 launch of Taylor Swift's app *The Swift Life*.[6] The titling of the app as *The Swift Life* also speaks to the ways that these apps conflate retail and lifestyle.

Retail spaces have long been a source of entertainment spectacle, and shopping for leisure has been an important aspect of modernity. Early department stores provided shoppers with entertainment value as much as they offered material goods. Similarly, the development of the shopping mall in the mid–twentieth century created a place that was about the spectatorial experience of retail as much as shopping itself.[7] As Marita Sturken and Lisa Cartwright have noted, "It has been argued that people derived their sense of their place in the world and their self image at least in part through their purchase and use of commodities which seemed to give meaning to their lives in the absence of the meaning derived from a closer knit community."[8] Here, Sturken and Cartwright point toward the development of consumer culture along with increasing urbanism and isolation at the turn of the twentieth century. This idea is becoming more relevant today, as social fragmentation has only intensified in a society now characterized by what psychologist Sherry Turkle calls being "alone together."[9] If city shop windows encouraged practices of mobile looking, apps take that one step further by turning everything into a mobile practice, whether the body is actually mobile or not, through new mobile screen technologies. And as Sturken and Cartwright have noted, "Today consumption continues to be thought of as both a form of leisure and pleasure and as a form of therapy."[10] Within celebrity apps, this conflation of leisure, pleasure, and therapy is further exacerbated by the coding of retail with issues of lifestyle and wellness and the commingling of retail with the affective economies of socially networked spaces.

As Anne Friedberg argues, "In contemporary culture, the marketing of 'commodity-experiences' has almost surpassed the marketing of goods."[11] This conception of retail as entertainment, as distraction, and as respite from busy life extends into app-based forms. If the development of the department store was directly linked to the standardization of the working week and rising mechanization at the turn of the twentieth century, then the app-based retail landscape appears strongly linked to the twenty-first-century neoliberal workforce and its logics.[12] The "always on" logic and structure of apps contributes to this neoliberal, 24/7 economy. As Jonathan Crary writes of that 24/7 work, "Of course, no individual can ever be shopping, gaming, working, blogging, downloading, or texting 24/7. However, since no moment, place, or situation now exists in which one can *not* shop, consume, or exploit networked resources, there is a relentless incursion of the non-time of 24/7 into every aspect of social or personal life."[13]

Retail has—via the app-based experience—adapted to the logics of 24/7 work by providing a sense that commodities and media content can be easily disseminated, absorbed, and most important, purchased anytime and anywhere. Shopping no longer requires being available during shopping hours, but rather shopping adapts to your hours in the palm of your hand. As Sherry Turkle describes networked culture, "The global reach of connectivity can make the most isolated outpost into a center of learning and economic activity."[14]

App-based shopping combines conventional retail models with models from the sharing economy of digital culture. In the media industry, this sharing or spread of content "relies as much (or more) on their circulation by the audience as it does on their commercial distribution, [and] that spreadability is determined by process of social appraisal rather than technical or creative wizardry and on the active participation of engaged audiences," as Henry Jenkins, Joshua Green, and Sam Ford have argued.[15] Celebrity retail apps, along with sites like Instagram and Pinterest, represent models for monetizing women's lifestyle sharing economies at the same time that they perpetuate heteronormative ideologies that place women as shoppers. Apps work via brand partnerships to sell items that either are branded content of the stars or are curated objects that relate to the stars' brands, turning the stars into lifestyle curators for app users. The development of the iPhone in 2007 and the opening of the app store to outside developers created opportunities for a multitude of types of businesses, including media and celebrity industries, to generate new forms of revenue.

Apps provide a customizable experience for mobile life, providing entertainment and convenience-based services at your fingertips. The post-iPhone mobile marketplace thrives on a customizable experience with apps providing much of the customization and functionality to turn the phone into a dynamic tool of entertainment and retail consumption via games, lifestyle content, and shopping. Scholars Jeremy Wade Morris and Sarah Murray have referred to apps as "mundane software," noting that "mundane is ultimately a flexible yet useful qualifier for a particular iteration of the software commodity that is marked by its ubiquity, its discardability, and its increasing incorporation into the rhythms, routines, and rituals of daily life through smaller, more mobile devices."[16] This notion of incorporation into quotidian rituals is also noted by Ethan Tussey in his book *The Procrastination Economy: The Big Business of Downtime*. Here Tussey argues that "the procrastination economy creates a mobile day part around our in-between moments. The content and programming of the procrastination economy similarly mediate the tension between productivity and entertainment by fashioning a subject position for those who are waiting, procrastinating, and/or killing time. Media companies create content, apps, and services based on the idea that we look at our phones to fill liminal moments."[17]

Smartphone users expect their devices to be tools of organization, of mobility, and of entertainment, aggregating all parts of their lives onto these devices. The on-the-go-ness of these apps also means that purchases are made impulsively, while multitasking in many cases. Mobile shopping and mobile gaming both thrive on the at-your-fingertips impulse purchase. The whole app is effectively the checkout line at a conventional store, but instead of gum and bottled water, you get media content.

Apps are relatively easy and inexpensive to develop and provide revenue via downloads, subscriptions, and in-app purchases, transforming retail products themselves into immaterial commodities. These in-app purchases may offer conventional retail products, as you would find in the Amazon or Target apps, but they can also offer microtransactions, through which one exchanges real or in-game currency for exclusive content. These microtransactions are typically priced between $0.99–$4.99, making them inexpensive enough to support impulse buying. My use of the term "App Store" in the title of this chapter is twofold in that it refers to the App Store on your phone where apps are sold and downloaded from, which is a retail store in itself, but also to the idea that the individual apps themselves are stores. If we equate this with brick-and-mortar retail, then platforms like the App Store are the mall and the apps are the individual stores. As in a mall, the stores are paying the mall a price to be there—in this case, a revenue-sharing model. Apps are "beholden to a revenue split with the retailers—usually around 30% of an app's retail price—and any use of in-app transactions must be done through the store (thus giving the retailers a cut of micro-transactions as well)," as Jeremy Wade Morris and Evan Elkins have pointed out.[18] The microtransactional nature and constant updating of app content encourage longer-term relationships with the software by enticing consumers to constantly check in (encouraged by the push-notification functionalities of the smartphone). This longer-term relationship demands that users make apps a part of their daily routine to avoid missing content or losing status.

The subscription model is pervasive in the digital media economy and has impacted the conventional retailing of media, as evidenced by Netflix, Hulu, and Spotify among others. We can also see examples where the subscription model is paired with a combination of lifestyle and media retailing, such as the combination of Amazon Prime and Prime Video. This reliance on subscription models for entertainment marks a shift from the retailing of goods and services to commodities as intangible objects. In keeping with this, many apps are free to download, with some content available for free but with the vast majority of content situated behind paywalls in the form of subscriptions, microtransactions, or some combination thereof. This type of app is known as freemium within the app community, as they are free at the point of entry but paywall premium content. As with magazines, gym memberships, streaming services, or other forms of subscription content, apps are priced low and renew automatically, often creating a set-it-and-forget-it revenue stream. The subscriptions provide a base-level revenue stream that makes the apps big business even before advertising or click-through shopping revenue comes in.

The placement of apps on the phone also allows app developers to take advantage of their geolocational and statistical functions, generating information about where and for how long users participated in the app experience. These data about shopping, location, and lifestyle practices can be used to sell items in an even more specific way and currently help retailers provide a customized retail experience for individual consumers, such as location-specific specials, coupons based on previous buying, and aisle-mapping information based on your location in a store. Companies promote these economic and convenience-oriented benefits to consumers to overcome privacy concerns, which Joseph Turow has documented in *The Aisles Have Eyes*. Privacy concerns are minimal on the part of brands because users are opting into information sharing, and this exchange of information is fundamentally changing the nature of retail. Many apps default location settings to "Always" or "While Using the App," relying on users to self-police their privacy. This tracking data provides additional revenue streams for the apps and app companies because it can be sold. As with much of digital culture, what is actually for sale is the data of the user; the content is merely there to drive data collection.

Consequently, these retail apps create an increasingly customized, narrowcast shopping experience. This is much less about the mass-market retail store—the department or big-box store appealing to all audiences—and is much more aligned with other trends that we see in retail pushing toward a narrowcast experience. The redistribution of stores in malls around clusters—shoe stores, teen stores, and fast fashion—so consumers no longer have to walk the mall, evokes this new digital model.[19] This physical redesign mimics the web- and app-based shopping experiences where like goods are clustered in a search for easy comparison. In the culture of 24/7 convenience, consumers no longer want to waste time discovering things but rather want to have the options that most interest them curated either by the stores themselves or by like-minded peers in sharing spaces like Pinterest or Instagram.

Keeping up with the Kapitalism: A Kardashian App Case Study

The Kardashians and their family of brands thrive especially well within this culture of multichannel retail, mobile shopping, and influencer celebrity. The Kardashians have been entrepreneurial and used retail as a core part of their cultural identity since the opening of DASH—their first retail store—in 2006, the year before the debut of *Keeping Up with The Kardashians*. In the early seasons of that show, along with spin-off series like *Kourtney and Kim Take Miami*, *Kourtney and Khloé Take the Hamptons*, and *DASH Dolls*, much of the show functioned as day-to-day drama about running an ever-expanding retail business. Notably, the iPhone and *Keeping Up with The Kardashians* premiered the same year, and few celebrities have been better at tapping into the rapidly expanding mobile shopping market than the Kardashians. The family's capacity for making money within digital culture appears endless, whether it's on personal blogs, Twitter, Instagram, Snapchat, mobile games, or apps. According to *Forbes*, the family collectively earned $122.5 million in 2016.[20] With their multichannel approach, they have created a model of digital retail that points to the greater multichannel, transmedia strategies that the media business needs to survive in digital culture.

Although the initial spectacle of *Keeping Up with the Kardashians* was predicated on a sex tape, the brand itself is centered on a modern family narrative. As executive producer Ryan Seacrest has said of the family, "At its foundation, it was an aspirational, Hollywood reality version of *The Brady Bunch*. They were unvarnished and that honesty and irreverence resonated."[21] Yet even amid this "authentic" family narrative, the female body remains the primary product for sale. This is seen in Kardashian product lines such as Kardashian

Beauty at ULTA, Kylie Cosmetics, Kim Kardashian's KKW Beauty Contouring Kits, and on spin-off shows like *Revenge Body with Khloé Kardashian*. As Laurie Ouellette has noted of reality television and its appeal to audiences, it "does not dupe passive TV viewers, as much as it presents resources (advice, demonstrations, examples, motivational strategies, product endorsements) for achieving a model of personhood that requires active investment and participation."[22] These are products designed to achieve the "model of personhood" that Ouellette describes and also to position this model as something that can be achieved via the act of consumption. This focus extends from the television shows and product lines into the mobile apps, which serve as a centralized place for how-to instruction and purchases to achieve these goals. The content of all five of the Kardashian/Jenner apps and their retail products overall place the women firmly within the discourse of postfeminist commodity production in that what is being sold are the exact tools of femininity so commonly ascribed to the patriarchy but here placed within the empowerment logic of a women-owned brand.

Each of the apps features specific categories that are associated with the star brands of the individual sisters. Khloé Kardashian's app, with her brand focus on body transformation, offers topics such as "The 9 Songs I Just Added to my Gym Playlist," "Watch: My Trainer's Next Level Ab Workout," and "Homemade Healthy Chips." Meanwhile, Kourtney Kardashian's focus on health and natural motherhood manifests in topics like "Healthy Breakfast Ideas for Kids," "Make My Detox Water," and "My All Natural Skin Saver." Kendall Jenner's position as a fashion model points toward a fashion-forward brand, which is embodied in her app via stories like "Shop My Sneaker Closet," "Sexy+Chic: Sheer Tops," and "Get My 60s Headband Look." Some of these features provide clear click-through shopping experiences, while others provide tips for how to gain the Kardashian lifestyle through recipes or tutorials. These features also provide access to the Kardashians' team of experts, such as trainers, makeup artists, and hairdressers.

Kim Kardashian and Kylie Jenner, fronting the direct-to-consumer makeup lines KKW Beauty and Kylie Cosmetics, respectively, have the most concrete branded lines outside of the show, and their apps reflect this, veering more closely to conventional retail stores. In Kylie Jenner's app, this manifests as features such as "The Kylie Shop: Shop the Brights Collection Now!," "Shop the Selfie: Moto Babe," and "How to Throw a *Life of Kylie* Viewing Party." For Kim Kardashian, whose brand is the strongest, the app provides additional paywalls to unlock more content than is available for the standard subscription fee. This is most clearly on display in the $0.99 makeup tutorials that allow you to learn how to get contouring tips from Kim herself. Here, the Kardashian family deftly monetizes something that appears for free in other spaces—in this case, YouTube makeup tutorial videos. At the time of this writing, there are 1.07 million Kim Kardashian makeup tutorials on YouTube, and it was just a matter of time before the family found a way to make this another part of their business enterprise. The in-app tutorials also represent a clear example of the ways that influencers and microcelebrities—such as YouTube makeup tutorialists—impact the content of mainstream celebrity brands.

These apps resemble reality television to the extent that their content functions as advertisement. As Diane Negra and Maria Pramaggiore have noted, the Kardashian women are well aware of "the program's role as a launching pad for their endorsement endeavors."[23] The mobile apps function in the same way. The rise of reality television tracks onto the decline of conventional broadcasting methods in favor of time-shifted ones that feature ad-skipping or ad-minimizing functions. Part of the appeal of these shows for the business—in addition to their cheaper production schedules and nonunion labor—is in their capacity to render a lot of product onscreen, thus making up for the advertising gap.

The apps also create value through a sense of exclusivity, specifically by offering subscriber-exclusive content. This is a classic retail branding strategy, which seeks to reward customers that prove their loyalty with products or access available only to the most dedicated. Even though anyone can download the Kardashian apps, most of the content on them is only available to subscribers—it is "locked," in the parlance of the Kardashian/Jenner apps. This subscription model makes users feel like they belong to an exclusive club. The Kardashians and other celebrities rely on brand loyalty to maintain success across a wide array of properties in a diversified brand. The apps allow them to aggregate these properties in one place, pitched as content to a loyal audience.

At the same time, this loyalty comes at the price not just of the products pitched and sold but also of the app itself. It is a club environment, like Costco, where you buy into the perks. In this case, the perk is access to the Kardashian life. In the apps, loyalty comes in the form of microtransactions. At $2.99 monthly via autopay through the App Store, these loyalty programs are cheap enough to not feel like real spending—a requirement in the postrecession economy. Consumers would be less likely to spend money on these apps if they were priced at $35.88 per year. The psychological math makes $2.99 per month more palpable and a small-enough amount not to merit canceling the autopay when taking stock of your finances.

At this pricing structure, the apps provide a base-level revenue stream that is significant, with Kardashian/Jenner apps producing $32 million in subscription revenue in 2015 alone.[24] The apps also provide a launchpad for the Kardashians' more conventionally branded businesses. In the case of Kylie Jenner, the app becomes an entry point for her $450 million a year cosmetics business, Kylie Cosmetics. With its best-selling lip kits and Kyshadow, Kylie Cosmetics operates on a model of false scarcity, so app subscribers get early access to information about product drops in exchange for their brand loyalty. The Kardashian empire is built on a multichannel strategy that prompts shoppers to move back and forth between different sales channels, whether brick-and-mortar stores like DASH, web-based ones like Kylie Cosmetics, or mobile-based ones like the apps. The apps provide a seamless way to link loyal shoppers into the multichannel retail experience while also gathering large amounts of personal information about the likes, interests, and habits of subscribers to produce more specific products and content for Kardashian fans. Loyalty comes at a cost for the consumer in terms of the data analytics that they are providing to the company in question. Here the company is not a conventional retail store like Target, Macy's, or Nordstrom—nor is it a major e-retailer like Amazon—but rather a celebrity brand.

Affective Entertainment and Multichannel Celebrity

If we think about digital culture as an economy thriving on affective responses—likes, shares, and comments—then much of the content of celebrity apps targeted at female audience members is about self-transformation and self-improvement. As Ouellette has noted of reality television, "Human capital in a more quotidian sense can also be cultivated with the assistance of a cadre of consultants and experts who help ordinary people to increase their worth through wardrobe upgrades, plastic surgery, fitness programs, boot camps, interventions, life coaching, tough love, lifestyle instruction, and other methods."[25] Reality television logic extends into the apps, which put these consultants at users' fingertips. The Kardashian brands overall—and the apps in particular—promise to teach ordinary audience members how to increase their worth by giving access to instructional information or branded products that will enable audience members to have smoother skin, fitter bodies, and more ageless faces. Stardom is not the goal so much as developing a personal brand regardless of profession or ambition—the ultimate postfeminist, neoliberal ideal. The apps provide access to interactive resources to achieve the "model of personhood" that the Kardashian empire embodies. This can be seen as one that privileges beauty and consumption but also as a successful women-owned, women-run brand.

Celebrity apps perform forms of simulated shopping that we see exploding in postrecession culture. The *Hollywood Reporter* has referred to this same period of time in which the Kardashians became the epitome of American—if not global—celebrity as "The Kardashian Decade."[26] This is classic star studies logic; as Richard Dyer describes, "Stars matter because they act out aspects of life that matter to us; and performers get to be stars when what they act out matters to enough people."[27] In a postrecession climate, the Kardashians provided a spectacle of constantly escalating consumption and in the apps provide the tools to mimic this consumption at a variety of price points from DIY to luxury. Starting the run of the show in the Jenner family home—modest by Kardashian standards—and then moving over the course of the series into more lavish homes, combined with the development of their brand from a single DASH store into a multichannel retail empire, the spectacle of improving consumption is part of the appeal for audience members. This is especially true for fans who may be facing increasingly uncertain times personally but can live vicariously through the sisters and their good fortune. The spectacle of consumption reverberates widely in contemporary culture from conventional entertainments such as television shows to digital culture, where popular You-Tube genres like unboxing and haul videos seek to perform consumption. This performance of shopping provides the affective experience of retail even for those who cannot afford to purchase. Websites and apps combine to provide in-home, digital shopping as a form of entertainment to consumers who may not have the time or the resources to shop themselves. This extends the ideas of shopping as entertainment, as spectacle, as therapy, and as leisure-time activity. As with window shopping, digital forms of shopping and consumption provide an entertainment spectacle of retail that creates pleasure in looking and is an important part of the retail experience. Media like the Kardashian apps create spaces where the pleasure in looking becomes a digital entertainment merging seamlessly with other more conventional forms of entertainment.

What Swift, Paltrow, and the Kardashian/Jenners are selling is a lifestyle supported through a multichannel media empire. The media are sometimes classic media objects like pop songs, music videos, video games, movies, and television, but they are also increasingly designed to sell a celebrity lifestyle above all else. As traditional and reality television stardom alike become increasingly financially tenuous, stars need to develop business models that enable them to keep multiple revenue streams open. In this 24/7 climate, app stores put these revenue streams right at the audience's fingertips.

Notes

1 Joseph Turow, *The Aisles Have Eyes: How Retailers Track Your Shopping, Strip Your Privacy, and Define Your Power* (New Haven, Conn.: Yale University Press, 2017), 146.
2 Alyxandra Vesey, "Putting Her on the Shelf," *Feminist Media Studies* 15, no. 6 (2015): 994.
3 Mary Celeste Kearney, "Sparkle: Luminosity and Post-Girl Power Media," *Journal of Media and Cultural Studies* 29, no. 2 (2015): 265.
4 For more on microcelebrity, see Alice Marwick, "Instafame: Luxury Selfies in the Attention Economy," *Public Culture* 27, no. 1 (2015): 137–160.
5 Kia Kokalitcheva, "Jessica Alba's Honest Company Is Reportedly in Talks to Sell to Unilever," *Fortune*, 16 Sept. 2016, http://fortune.com/2016/09/15/honest-company -unilever-rumor/.

6   For an analysis of the Glu Mobile games, see Alison Harvey, "The Fame Game: Working Your Way Up the Celebrity Ladder in *Kim Kardashian: Hollywood*," *Games and Culture* 13, no. 7 (2018): 652–670; and Jessalynn Keller and Alison Harvey, "*Kendall and Kylie*: Girl Affects, Celebrity, and Digital Gaming in Millennial Girl Culture," in *Appified*, eds. Jeremy Wade Morris and Sarah Murray (Ann Arbor: University of Michigan Press, 2018).

7   For more about the history of shopping, see Anne Friedberg, *Window Shopping: Cinema and the Postmodern* (Berkeley: University of California Press, 1994); and Marita Sturken and Lisa Cartwright, *Practices of Looking: An Introduction to Visual Culture* (Oxford: Oxford University Press, 2001).

8   Sturken and Cartwright, *Practices of Looking*, 193.

9   Sherry Turkle, *Alone Together: Why We Expect More from Technology and Less from Each Other* (New York: Basic, 2011).

10 Sturken and Cartwright, *Practices of Looking*, 197.

11 Friedberg, *Window Shopping*, 115.

12 David Harvey writes, "Neoliberalism is in the first instance a theory of political economic practices that proposes that human well-being can best be advanced by liberating individual entrepreneurial freedoms and skills with an institutional framework characterized by strong private property rights, free markets, and free trade." *A Brief History of Neoliberalism* (Oxford: Oxford University Press, 2007), 2.

13 Jonathan Crary, *24/7: Late Capitalism and the Ends of Sleep* (London: Verso, 2013), 30.

14 Turkle, *Alone Together*, 152.

15 Henry Jenkins, Sam Ford, and Joshua Green, *Spreadable Media: Creating Value and Meaning in a Networked Culture* (New York: New York University Press, 2013), 195.

16 Jeremy Wade Morris and Sarah Murray, introduction to *Appified*, eds. Jeremy Wade Morris and Sara Murray (Ann Arbor: University of Michigan Press, 2018), 17.

17 Ethan Tussey, *The Procrastination Economy: The Big Business of Downtime* (New York: New York University Press, 2018), 29.

18 Jeremy Wade Morris and Evan Elkins, "There's a History for That: Apps and Mundane Software as Commodity," *Fibreculture Journal* 25 (2015): 72.

19 Aaron Schrank, "Brick and Mortar Stores Are Dying, but Not at This Mall," *Marketplace*, 8 June 2017, https://www.marketplace.org/2017/06/08/business/how-one-california-mall-changing-and-thriving.

20 Natalie Robhemed, "Top Earning Reality Stars 2016: Kardashians, Jenners Combine for $122.5 Million," *Forbes*, 6 Nov. 2016, https://www.forbes.com/sites/natalierobehmed/2016/11/16/top-earning-reality-stars-2016-kardashians-jenners-combine-for-122-5-million/#16b7a6dd274d.

21 Leslie Baron, "The Kardashian Decade: How a Sex Tape Led to a Billion Dollar Brand," *Hollywood Reporter*, 16 Aug. 2017, http://www.hollywoodreporter.com/features/kardashian-decade-how-a-sex-tape-led-a-billion-dollar-brand-1029592.

22 Laurie Ouellette, "Enterprising Selves: Reality Television and Human Capital," in *Making Media Work: Cultures of Management in the Entertainment Industries*, eds. Derek Johnson, Derek Kompare, and Avi Santo (New York: New York University Press, 2014), 92.

23 Maria Pramaggiore and Diane Negra, "Keeping Up with the Aspirations: Commercial Family Values and the Kardashian Brand," in *Reality Gendervision: Sexuality and Gender on Transatlantic Reality Television*, ed. Brenda Weber (Durham, N.C.: Duke University Press, 2014), 83.

24 Nathan McAlone, "The Kardashian and Jenner Apps Are Already on Pace to Make an Insane $32 Million per Year," *Business Insider*, 16 Sept. 2015, http://www.businessinsider.com/kardashian-jenner-apps-on-pace-to-make-32-million-this-year-2015-9.

25 Ouellette, "Enterprising Selves," 92.

26 Baron, "Kardashian Decade."

27 Richard Dyer, *Heavenly Bodies: Film Stars and Society* (London: Routledge, 2004), 17.

Part II

Media and the Politics of Constructing Retail Space

• •

6

Shelf Flow

• •

Spatial Logics, Product Categorizations, and Media Brands at Retail

AVI SANTO

Raymond Williams's influence on media studies is unmistakable. His concept of *flow* pushed scholars to analyze how the arrangement of programming segments, advertising, and station identifications worked together to produce meaning for viewers, whose experience of watching television—particularly commercial television—Williams argued was not reserved to individual programs but was experienced as "'an evening's viewing' . . . in some ways planned, by providers and then by viewers, *as a whole* . . . planned in discernible sequences which . . . override particular program units . . . though the items may be various the television experience has in some important ways unified them."[1] Williams's contention was that networks often carefully crafted flow to produce intentional fuzziness between programming and commercials as well as to yield overarching thematic connections across clusters of programs.

Contemporary shelf slotting and visual merchandising practices at retail share quite a bit in common with Williams's observations about broadcast television in the mid-1970s. Simply put, items are not arranged randomly on store shelves. Rather, they are subject to economic, aesthetic, and cultural logics and imaginings of how the consumer relates to products based on where they are located in the store, on the shelf, and what their neighboring products are. But the meanings that merchandise takes on in relation to its shelf mates cannot fully be controlled by retailers or brand owners. While in part this is because shopper agency cannot fully be accounted for, my focus is largely on exploring how competing industrial logics and objectives generate what John Fiske calls "fracturing forces" that defy "unitary meaning or a unified viewing subject."[2] Mimi White suggests that such fracturing forces create "a system that promotes interpretation among the continuities *and discontinuities* of the segments that comprise flow."[3] I argue that shelving incongruities generate possible intertextual readings for shoppers both based on how objects are shelved alongside others in distinct store areas and also by structuring absences that call attention to gaps in the ways products circulate.

While flow offers a conceptual approach to studying the meanings formed around any and all products shelved at retail, these arrangements and incongruities are particularly meaningful for media brands. In this essay, I look to adapt Williams's work on television flow to the study of how character and entertainment merchandise positioning at retail affects how brand stories are conveyed to consumers. I do so primarily by analyzing how Spider-Man and Wonder Woman products were displayed at Target during the summer of 2017, which coincided with the release of the *Spider-Man: Homecoming* and *Wonder Woman* motion pictures. Following Stuart Hall,[4] I contend that retail environments serve as sites where consent and resistance toward normative hegemonic constructions of gender, age, and other identity categories regularly play out.

In applying William's conception of television flow to retail spaces, I want to stipulate that I am not conflating these environments nor suggesting that retail's organizational logics have in any way been influenced by television's scheduling practices. A few other caveats are also needed: first, merchandise on store shelves is constantly rearranged as new products arrive and old ones are cleared out, so my analysis of Spider-Man's and Wonder Woman's shelf lives at Target is really just a snapshot. Indeed, Wonder Woman–related toy merchandise changed locations from my first store visit on July 2 to my second visit on August 14 (these changes can offer insights into how retailers and brand owners [re]imagine consumer investment in particular products). Second, as the dates I've provided suggest, I first visited Target a full month after *Wonder Woman* was released in U.S. theaters (though only three days before *Spider-Man: Homecoming*'s release). Most film-related merchandise arrives in stores at least six weeks prior to a theatrical release. While I am unable to discuss how *Wonder Woman* was promoted at Target leading up to its premiere and how product assortment and arrangement shaped expectations for the film, my analysis will offer insight into how retail shapes a sense of a franchise's long-term impact and sustainability through product carryover and placement beyond the initial promotional window. Third, my shelving analysis is necessarily partial, based on only a couple of visits to a single Target location in Norfolk, Virginia. While all Targets adapt a centralized floor plan and retail planogram (diagrams indicating where merchandise should be placed on shelves), individual stores often deviate from the map they are provided because of uneven access to products or local variations in consumer behavior or simply because employees vary in their investment in following detailed instructions. Finally, though most retailers subdivide their spaces according to consumer, product, and brand categories, store layouts differ depending on the brand identity that retailers seek to convey to customers. While beyond the scope of this essay, it is important to note that some of the same merchandise was carried at Toys "R" Us and Hot Topic but displayed in very different ways. Simply put, products take on very different meanings in different retail environments. I contend that the ways that merchandise is presented on shelves offer important insights into the strategies driving retailer and brand owner efforts to connect their respective—and interwoven—brands to manufacture consumer desires.

In what follows, I explore three concentric layers at Target that capture how shelving is designed to organize the experience of shopping but also potentially disrupts the manufacturing of brand and consumer stories through these same planned layouts. I first explore Target's overall store design, wherein I discuss how the store's organization is both meaningful and vexing for media brands like Spider-Man, followed by the organization of its toy section, and lastly an exploration of one row in that section—namely, the "character toys" row where *Wonder Woman* merchandise was shelved. I then step beyond the toy aisles to assess how the shelving of Wonder Woman toys interacted with other Wonder Woman–branded items at Target to generate possible intertextual meanings across the store.

Store Design

Target stores have thirty-two separate departments, ranging from automotive and bedding to groceries and toys. These departments provide multiple possible sites of encounter with branded merchandise in a wide range of product categories. For example, at the time of my first visit, Spider-Man-themed merchandise could be found in twenty separate store sections from kitchenware, sporting goods, and school supplies to bathroom accessories, bedding, and infant, toddler, boy's, men's, girl's, and women's clothing and shoes and intimate apparel, not to mention electronics, entertainment, and toys. Thus Marvel-Disney was guaranteed consumer encounters with the Spider-Man brand throughout the store, even if shoppers actively avoided the toy aisle. This contributed to an understanding of the character's value as exceeding any particular item Spider-Man adorned, transforming the hero into a lifestyle brand whose ubiquity and style allows it to add form to a variety of functional household items that shoppers might be seeking.

Indeed, for media brands, the potential sprawl of merchandise across big-box retail sites like Target can prove quite valuable—and not strictly in the economic sense. Typically appearing on retail shelves six weeks in advance of a tentpole film release, merchandise serves as an important promotional vehicle that is "considered part of building the excitement and hype for a movie."[5] The more merchandise spread across the store, the more opportunity to build anticipation for the film and to encourage the perception that it is already popular given the ubiquity of that merchandise.

In the contemporary transmedia environment, however, these items serve a greater purpose than mere promotion for a film or even as extensions of it; they also participate in teaching consumers how to recognize migratory cues essential for following media franchises across platforms as well as for differentiating between various iterations of a property. Geoffrey Long argues that all transmedia properties make use of hermeneutic codes (questions raised within a narrative), negative capability (strategic narrative gaps that audiences desire to fill in), and migratory cues ("a signal towards another medium—the means through which various narrative paths are marked by an author and located by a user through activation patterns") to guide audiences across multiple media platforms.[6] While merchandise can occasionally raise questions and fill in narrative gaps related to transmedia story worlds, I contend that more often, media-branded products utilize migratory cues to signal toward other merchandise and raise questions about the shared usability of these items for consumers seeking to express their personal and community narratives through them. In this sense, the hermeneutic codes operationalized by media-branded merchandise often link consumers with media franchises by raising questions like "How does a Spider-Man toothbrush allow its owner to express some aspect of their personality in relation to the character?" and "How will a Spider-Man toothbrush holder encourage a love for oral hygiene matching its owner's love for the character?" and, of course, "How can one own one item without the other?" This final question hints at the ways negative capability works with merchandise, wherein items are rarely presented as stand-alone fare (though they are typically sold separately) but rather as parts of sets. Negative capability works to help consumers identify gaps that might be filled in by other merchandise (i.e., "What should be placed inside a Spider-Man backpack?" "Perhaps a Spider-Man pencil case?" "And maybe that needs to house a set of Spider-Man pencils and erasers?"). Migratory cues often direct shoppers to complementary items that can be used to fill in these gaps.

These cues are often embedded in package designs drawn from the film that connect myriad products together, implying relationships between them that shoppers can choose to explore. Package design is an important tool that manufacturers use to help products stand out on shelves.[7] Unsurprisingly, consumer product divisions for entertainment conglomerates often insist that multiple licensees utilize the same package design to ensure coherence across branded merchandise.[8] This approach ensures not only that shoppers will spot *Spider-Man Homecoming* products on a shelf but also that they will begin to recognize the package design across different store sections. Even if shoppers don't end up buying any of these items, the practice of recognizing these cues across multiple and seemingly unrelated store sections can help prepare consumers to follow a franchise from outpost to outpost. Meanwhile, differences in packaging between *Homecoming*, *Ultimate*, and other iterations of the Spider-Man brand erect porous boundaries that alert (some) consumers to differences amid franchise outposts while also encouraging curiosity about how the character and/or story world has been rendered differently in each iteration by purposely making certain iconic elements—like Spider-Man swinging into action—recurrent across different package designs. The process of teaching consumers to recognize and differentiate among franchise outposts is potentially aided by store layouts that disperse and embed items amid multiple similar products, requiring shoppers to be observant.

As Christopher Byrne notes, "Increasingly, a movie is seen as an event in the life of a character brand,"[9] but for a franchise to flourish, products featuring media brands must circulate continuously and in forms that encourage habitual rather than rarified usages. Media brands utilize the placement of merchandise in multiple store sections to signal to shoppers the scope of a franchise, its imagined audiences, and perhaps most importantly, its "ordinariness" (without sacrificing the brand's ability to also seem special). This is a tricky balance to strike, but when a media brand is able to branch out beyond the expected site(s) for its merchandise, it conveys its specialness precisely by demonstrating its ability to cross over into mundane and routine areas of consumer activity. In so doing, it also suggests that the brand has a broader appeal beyond a specific demographic or fan base. When Spider-Man toothbrushes sit alongside *Star Wars*– and Batman-branded equivalents, it supposedly places the franchise amid a select group of properties that are perceived as both iconic and part of a common cultural lexicon.

For this to work, however, it requires the absence of other franchises in these same sections. Shoppers will not only notice recurrent characters and franchises, but they will also recognize absences of particular media brands within lifestyle categories (especially if they happen to be searching for them). Media-branded merchandise may be absent from store shelves for a wide range of reasons, including competition over limited shelf space coupled with retail conservatism over testing out new stock when sales for existing products remain consistent.[10] Typically, the failure to expand beyond expected store sections coincides with "shop talk," or "the discursive construction of retail as a nexus of brand and consumer interactions," that sets limits on the appeal of a particular brand among imagined shoppers.[11] For example, despite box-office success, *Moana* (2015) was characterized by industry experts as having limited merchandising appeal because the character was perceived to have minimal role-play capabilities and to lack iconic outfits, accessories, and identifiable antagonists.[12] This belief pervaded despite *Moana* toys nearly cracking the top fifty in retail sales in 2016.[13] Though unspoken, these rationalizations are likely informed by an implicit bias against nonwhite characters and story worlds as merchandisable. After all, Moana seems very much a character with recognizable outfits, accessories, and antagonists; they just happen to be non-European. While the lack of Moana toothbrushes and dishes at Target was almost entirely the result of industry insiders lacking faith in the property's broader appeal, which limited the scope of its licensing program, the message implicitly conveyed to Target shoppers was that *Moana* is not a property with staying power regardless of its success in theaters and on toy shelves.

This perception is potentially exacerbated by the way that certain media brands remain on store shelves well beyond their theatrical release while others disappear quickly. As I discuss later, the extended shelf life of a property is often dependent on payments made to retailers by manufacturers and brand owners. Yet the perception for many shoppers is that certain properties are simply more popular than others. Tying all this back to flow and White's assertion that audiences notice continuities as well as discontinuities, it might be argued that the dispersal—or lack thereof—of a range of media-branded products within retail spaces can influence how shoppers invest in a property's cultural resonance, as they are likely to form impressions based on the expected, unexpected, and absent sites for such merchandise across the store. The dispersal—or lack thereof—also offers insights into how media owners and retailers perceive a property's potential resonance with different consumers at varying levels of lifestyle integration. As such, it should be noted that *Wonder Woman* (*WW*) was not as well represented as *Spider-Man* across Target's different sections.

Target's need to fill a lot of different product categories created an opportunity for Marvel-Disney's consumer products division to insert Spider-Man into almost every imaginable room in the house and every conceivable childhood activity (some adult ones as well), but this type of sprawl also meant that the company could not fully control how the Spider-Man lifestyle-brand story was laid out for consumers: Spider-Man toothbrushes were stacked next to *Star Wars* and Batman toothbrushes, not the Spider-Man toothbrush holder stocked in a different section of the store; Spider-Man backpacks were featured in luggage, not school supplies, where they might have complemented Spider-Man-branded erasers and pencil sharpeners.

This is not to suggest, however, that Target's store layout wasn't designed to take shoppers on "common sense" journeys throughout the store that affirmed and normalized certain identity categories. Claus Ebster and Marion Gaurus suggest that store planners should take a page from urban planning and conceptualize the store as if it were a city with distinct paths, edges, landmarks, nodes, and districts that segregate shoppers into distinct consumer categories, usually by gender and age.[14] Many retailers employ a vertical matrix that organizes the store first according to consumer categories and then assigns each of those groups product categories that stereotypically align with their perceived roles/identities and finally highlight select brands as representative of the symbiotic tastes shared by retailers and their imagined consumer base.

This Consumer-Product-Brand (CPB) category matrix is an important site of synchronicity, negotiation, and frustration between brand owners and retailers. In many instances, their shared interests in organizing products and brands according to demographic categories are perfectly aligned—Hollywood is similarly not immune to dissecting film and television audiences according to age and gender—but demographics at retail aren't necessarily applicable across all product lines. In a 2012 interview, Melissa Segal, head of global licensing at the Jim Henson Company, complained, "We have a property that's kind of tween and kitschy called *Cyclops*, and we're doing a lot of gifty product . . . and someone we were meeting with said, 'But there is no tween gift aisle at retailer X. It's easier in home furnishings, or there's not that place at retail.'"[15] Segal also lamented that many Jim Henson properties like *Sid the Science Kid* and *Dinosaur Train* appeal to both boys and girls, but retailers still require that products featuring those brands conform to gendered expectations in order to determine their aisle placement.

Target's CPB schema segregates both officially and unofficially by gender and age categories. Items stereotypically intended for men line the back wall of the store: men's clothing, followed by electronics, home entertainment, luggage, and seasonal items like patio furniture and barbeques. The toy section at Target is located across from the electronics and home entertainment sections. To its right are the outdoors, camping, and sporting goods sections, though there are no demarcations indicating where one section ends and the next begins. While the toy section contains items for both boys and girls, as does the outdoors and sporting goods section, and there is nothing inherently masculine or feminine about a television screen, a long history of gendering leisure technologies meant for public and private usage privileges male consumer desires in these sections. Indeed, former global general manager for DreamWorks Animation franchises Rick Rekedal claims that the retail toy buyer might as well be the retail boy buyer because of the ways stores typically privilege that category in stocking toy shelves.[16]

In turning my attention to analyzing how Target's toy section was organized, its masculinized location cannot be overlooked, not because the toy section was overly invested in boys' play culture but because its placement linked childhood with manly pursuits (and vice versa) while cordoning it off from feminized domestic chores. In turn, the children's section became associated with manly discourses of leisure, mobility, indulgence, and fun that could appeal to all shoppers.

Toying Around

There are eleven aisles and twenty-one rows in Target's toy section (each aisle has two parallel rows, except the first; moving left to right, left-facing rows are designated "A" and right-facing rows "B"). On first glance, Target's toy section appears to be a microcosm of the larger store. Following the CPB model, it is organized first according to age and gender categories, then according to certain types of toy products, and finally according to particular brands, which often encapsulate an entire product category. Row 1B houses educational toys for toddlers primarily by Fisher-Price. At the opposing end, row 11B displays Nerf-branded air and water guns. These items have historically been marketed to boys age eight and up. The aisle immediately following marks the beginning of Target's outdoor sports and camping section. Before proceeding, it is necessary to address an important caveat to my claims about Target's gendered toy aisles, which is the retailer's recent promise to eliminate signage and other signifiers that differentiate boys' toys from girls.[17] While there was no overt gender labeling, a confluence of paratexts (i.e., things that prepare shoppers for their encounter with a given product) from product mix and labeling to displays and packaging made it difficult to not interpret aisles according to gender.[18] Brand owners who continue to be invested in gendering playthings produce many of these paratexts, even as Target has supposedly backed away from such overt categorization (though it likely benefits the retailer to appear socially progressive without needing to change how products are actually organized on its shelves). Take, for example, row 4A, which features the Disney Princess line along with merchandise for *Elena of Avalon*, *Frozen*, and *Moana*. Though there is no sign indicating that this row is for girls, a combination of language used in identifying the row for shoppers (the row is literally titled "Disney Princesses") as well as in labeling toys on that row "fashion dolls"—accompanied by a large, 3-D banner jettisoning out from the top of the middle shelf featuring Ariel from *The Little Mermaid*, Rapunzel from *Enchanted*, and an interpolative slogan that reads, "Dream Big, Princess"—eliminate any confusion as to the intended audience for these products. This certainly conforms to Ken Parker's observation that "a successful display captures the consumer, enticing them with representations of their dreams, aspirations and desires . . . or at least who the visual merchandisers think they should be."[19]

As the prior example also intimates, there was slippage between product and brand categories when it came to designating rows. While some rows were identified according to types of toys—row 10B, "Toy Vehicles and Playsets," or row 7A, "Building Sets and Magnetic Kits"—others were named for the brand that occupied nearly all the real estate on that row. Row 4A was for Disney Princesses, 4B was the Barbie row, and rows 7B and 8A were simply called "LEGO." LEGO products actually occupied almost three full rows at Target, as three-quarters of the items found on the "Building Sets and Magnetic Kits" row were also by LEGO, though Target placed only DUPLO, LEGO Juniors, and girl-themed sets including DC Super Hero Girls (DCSHG) sets featuring Wonder Woman on that row, once again segregating by gender even within the same aisle while replicating the association between girls' play culture and juvenility.

Clearly, while certain brands stood in for larger product categories at Target, manufacturers also had strong stakes in claiming and coordinating shelf space. What appeared on the surface to be a midsized selection of brands and products was in fact dominated by fewer than ten manufacturers (Hasbro, Mattel, LEGO, MGA Entertainment, SpinMaster, Jakks Pacific, Playmates, Moose Toys, and Just Play) claiming 80 percent of the toy section. Hasbro had products featured in seven of eleven aisles and had a single row all to itself for Nerf products. Mattel toys were also found on seven of eleven aisles, and it had two exclusive rows devoted to Fisher-Price and Barbie products.

Such shelf allocations are not accidental; nor are they natural byproducts of the size of these manufacturers. Ellen Seiter noted in the 1990s that the consolidation of retail has made the industry more risk averse in its product selection, privileging established manufacturers with mass-production and low-price-point capabilities as well as recognizable brands with built-in marketing through film and television content.[20] Indeed, retail's consolidation has led manufacturers like Hasbro and Mattel to reconceive their business models and position themselves as full-fledged entertainment companies. Similarly, it has led brand owners in the entertainment industry to reduce the number of licensees they are willing to engage, focusing primarily on major players with the ability to guarantee shelf placement at retail. Through this mutually beneficial arrangement, companies like Disney and Hasbro are able to leverage their combined brands to persuade retailers that there is minimal risk of products failing to sell, but they do so largely by expanding existing franchises and toy lines rather than introducing new ones.

One of the primary reasons Target sees companies like Hasbro and Disney as less risky is because of the slotting fees these companies often fork over. Though not widely publicized outside these industries, it is common practice for retailers to demand that manufacturers pay additional costs for a range of in-store "perks," among them the mere ability to get their products placed on shelves. Often decisions on what products to carry are based less on consumer demand or buyer instincts regarding product quality, functionality, appeal, or originality than on who is able to meet these payment guarantees—a process that clearly benefits larger operations with deeper pockets.[21] In 2000, slotting fees were estimated to net retailers $9 billion annually and cost manufacturers and brand owners between $5,000 and $25,000 per store to introduce a single new product onto its shelves.[22] In 2013, it was estimated that a national rollout would cost manufacturers an average of $2.5 million in slotting fees per product.[23] Where retailers have claimed that such fees are necessary mechanisms for managing scarce shelf space, incentivizing manufacturers to put forward innovative in-demand products in order to recoup expenses, critics argue that such fees produce barriers for new manufacturers and brand owners seeking to enter the market, stifle innovation, and often amount to "extortion."[24]

Beyond the cover charge for entry, brand owners and manufacturers pay retailers for shelf optimization, which can include everything from the product's proximity to the eye level of its imagined consumer; its proximity to the edge of an aisle, which increases its degree of visibility to shoppers walking by; and its proximity—or not—to like items. Of course, the degree of control that brand owners and manufacturers have over aisle allotment is mitigated by the ways that retailers conceptualize product categories, which in turn transforms the brand story being told. While Disney and Warner Bros. may wish to keep their character toys separate and pay slotting fees to do so, Target's stock keeping unit (SKU) system at least partially determines their proximity to one another.

Where in the Store Is Wonder Woman?

Merchandise for the *Wonder Woman* film was a subject of concern among fans and industry analysts even before it was due to hit store shelves. There was concern over a lack of merchandise as compared with other superhero franchises[25] and a lack of marketing for said merchandise.[26] There was concern over licensing miscues that potentially undermined *WW*'s pseudofeminist girl-power message, like branded diet bars and lingerie (neither of which were sold at Target),[27] and there was concern over who the intended audience for this merchandise might be.[28] Warner Brothers seemed caught off guard by the film's success and had to adjust its marketing strategy to make *Wonder Woman* a larger lure for the forthcoming *Justice League* (*JL*) film.[29] These factors contributed to Wonder Woman's shelf presence at Target.

Wonder Woman–branded toys at Target could be found on three different aisles: She was featured as part of Mattel's DC Super Hero Girls in row 6A, which largely stocked fashion dolls intended for tween girls (see Tussey and Bak's chapter in this volume). *WW* merchandise from the 2017 blockbuster was stocked in row 8B: "Character Toys." A third smattering of Wonder Woman–themed merchandise was located in the LEGO aisle in row 7A, where she was included as part of two DCSHG sets and one *WW* set. Wonder Woman's immediate LEGO shelf mates were Disney's *Frozen* and *Moana*, not *LEGO Batman* sets stocked on the opposite end of the opposing row. The majority of my analysis will focus on *WW* merchandise on the "Character Toys" row, but it is worth noting that the LEGO aisle was the only place in the entire store where both *WW* and DCSHG shared shelf space.

WW's presence on the character row certainly introduced a playable female-centric superhero story to boys who wandered down that aisle, though it is unclear whether her limited visibility was sufficient to invite girls to that same space. Still it is unlikely that Warner Brothers or Target actively intended to challenge the relationship between action toys and boys' play culture by including the character on this row. Rather, I contend that it was most likely a byproduct of efforts to continue organizing products by brand and consumer categories. Target's CPB model constructs associations between certain types of consumers, products, and brands, with superhero-themed toys based on film franchises occupying a space in the toy section traditionally directed toward boys. Similarly, given the narrative threading between *Batman v Superman*, *Wonder Woman*, and the *Justice League* film installments, it seems reasonable to assume that Warner Brothers wanted *WW* toys stocked alongside other DCEU (DC Extended Universe) properties. Still *WW*'s presence alongside Batman action figures, costumes, and toy weaponry produced unexpected interconnections between these two socially constructed realms, which both challenged and reinforced gender norms.

Upon my first visit to Target on July 2, a mere five weeks after the film's initial release, when *WW* was still the number-three-ranked movie in the United States, I was surprised to find *WW* toys stocked at the back of the character toys row, where they were out of customer sight (they could not be seen from the main shopping pathway; shoppers had to venture onto the actual aisle to spot *WW* toys). In total there were seven different *WW* toys featured in this section: three nine-inch figures (Diana in her Wonder Woman costume, in her Amazonian armor, and love interest Steve Trevor); three twelve-inch figures (a Diana Prince doll dressed in a blue party dress with accompanying hidden sword, a battle-ready doll with swinging arm motion and shield, and a two-pack of Diana with a horse); and finally, a costume pack featuring a tiara and bracelets. The section looked fully rummaged through. Six of the fifteen hanging hooks were empty. The lack of stock likely belies a conservative approach to ordering unproven products common among retail buyers. Byrne asserts, "Typically buyers won't get punished for not buying something.

If it's a hit, they can always sign on later. . . . On the other hand, taking a big position on a product that doesn't produce can saddle retailers with inventory that negatively affects profitability."[30] According to Thomas Lee, Target often walks a fine line when it comes to maintaining a lean inventory in order to avoid putting unsold items on clearance, turning over merchandise an average of only 6.4 times per year as compared to Walmart's 8.3, with the downside being a higher rate of out-of-stock items.[31] Yet the choice to keep empty hooks on its shelves rather than consolidate remaining *WW* products gave shoppers the impression that there was high demand for *WW* toys rather than a short supply. While barren shelves also induce potential disappointment and frustration at the lack of available stock, this is a risk that Lee suggests Target is willing to take, since it believes shoppers will simply purchase alternate merchandise. For media properties, however, uncertainty about access to products can undermine consumer investment in the property as a lifestyle brand.

WW merchandise was shelved alongside clearance items for *Justice League Action*, *Batman Unlimited*, and *Batman v. Superman*, which made the property seem even further on the decline, despite its box-office success. Tellingly, the clearance items were still more expensive than their equivalent *WW* toys. A Batman mask was on clearance for $11.99, while a *WW* costume was priced at $9.99. These shelving practices made *WW* merchandise seem simultaneously obsolete and a poor bargain in comparison with her male superhero counterparts.

Additionally, despite their side-by-side shelf placement and their equivalent action orientation, Target's product labeling system identified *WW* dolls as "deluxe fashion figures," while Batman dolls were listed as merely "deluxe figures." The additional "fashion" descriptor borrowed from language typically used on girl-centric doll aisles and likely was encouraged by Mattel, which specializes in this type of doll (the Mattel website also lists these figures as "fashion dolls"), but placed alongside male counterparts on the character toy row, it both limited *WW*'s versatility and called attention to the asymmetry between very similar toys. If "fashion" could be interpreted as a euphemism for "girl's toy," the absence of an equivalent signifier for Batman or Superman dolls affirmed how patriarchy's power resides in its invisibility and "obviousness," as something ultimately more desirable for its lack of limitations rather than for any specific qualities directly attributed to it.

When I returned to Target on August 14, *WW* toys were still housed on the same row, but they had been upgraded to a position near the front of the aisle entrance. *WW* toys were now sandwiched in between *JL* playthings and *Teenage Mutant Ninja Turtles* dolls and sets. The move was partly motivated by the advanced release of *JL* merchandise several months before the film. Studio executives had begun to recognize that *WW*'s box-office success could be leveraged in promoting *JL*, as evidenced by the inclusion of more *Wonder Woman* clips in the second full-length trailer for the film released on July 22. But as has often been the case with many science fiction ensemble films featuring strong female protagonists (see Rey and *Star Wars: The Force Awakens* or Black Widow and *The Avengers*),[32] Warner Bros. and Mattel had underrepresented Wonder Woman in advanced merchandise, thus making the leftover *WW* toys an important bridge between these franchise installments. None of the new *JL* toys at Target featured Wonder Woman, though every other core member of the team and the main villain were represented. Though *WW* toys were intended to compensate for the lack of *JL* equivalents, their placement alongside the latter actually seemed to reveal Wonder Woman's peripheral status within the DCEU. Differences in packaging, in the quantity of stocked materials (there were only four leftover varieties of *WW* toys, and the largest stockpile was Steve Trevor figures), and in how these items were displayed—*WW* toys occupied one vertical column at the far edge of the DCEU toys, whereas *JL* occupied four horizontal and vertical columns—all marked Wonder Woman merchandise as "different" from those of her colleagues. While her toys had been reclaimed from the clearance rack, they were clearly marked as older models in comparison with the newly arrived *Justice League* merchandise. Though this was most certainly not Warner Brothers', Mattel's, or Target's intention, shelving practices seem to have revealed underlying gender anxieties about how to market the DCEU even as they apparently embraced a more ambiguous strategy for courting fans.

This anxiety played out well beyond the character toys aisle at Target. Wonder Woman merchandise elsewhere at Target seemed to largely eschew the *WW* film. One reason likely stems from the strategy Target employed in presenting *WW* toys. As Rekedal explained, the toy section is often the gateway to establishing a wider product mix and broader presence in the rest of the store.[33] Because toy aisles are still organized according to gender, product extensions across the store often follow similar gendered pathways. *WW* toys posed somewhat of a problem because they were housed on a row typically used to measure boys' investments in particular franchises. To extend that particular iteration of the brand into other parts of the store risked escalating confusion over its consumer categorization, especially in sections of the store where age categories superseded gender. For example, kids' toothbrushes at Target, which are housed on a row dedicated to oral hygiene, feature a range of branded products that in theory could appeal to both boys and girls. But prior coding of Elsa or Spider-Man as directed at different groups of kids based on where their toy products are shelved (and how these properties are generally marketed by their parent company) help guide children and parents toward normative gender associations. *WW*-branded toothbrushes, which did not exist, would have offered a more ambiguous CPB association.

And yet, even in areas of the store where gender categories dominate, such as clothing, *WW* merchandise was absent. Suggesting uncertainty about whom the film was intended to reach, there were no T-shirts—a staple of film-related merchandise—in either the boys'/men's or the girls'/women's sections. *WW*'s absence from these lifestyle and household product categories reduced the property's iconicity and value as a cultural resource for shoppers who were likely to recognize discontinuities in Wonder Woman's flow across store aisles as compared with other "equivalent" characters just as much as they were bound to notice how well traveled Spider-Man was.

With the exception of a handful of Funko bobbleheads toward the back wall of the home entertainment section, there was no other official *WW* merchandise available in the store. There were, however, numerous other Wonder Woman–branded items unrelated to the film to be found in diverse sections of Target. There were several items connected to the pretween DCSHG series, ranging from girls' T-shirts, pajamas, socks, and underwear to backpacks and lunch bags. There was also a range of Wonder Woman products that featured retro 1970s-style branding including women's underwear, curtains, plush blankets, and beach towels. With a lack of overt migratory cues directing shoppers to locate *WW*-themed merchandise, it follows that those seeking Wonder Woman–branded products would have begun to use these other iterations of the character to fill in both narrative gaps and unfulfilled consumer expectations, in turn producing unintended readings across store sections, product categories, and franchise outposts.

Conclusion

In this essay, I've provided a cultural map of a prominent retail space that demonstrates how store design and shelving practices attempt to manage shopping experiences but also produce complex, contradictory, and confusing discourses about the relationships among consumers, products, and brands. I've suggested that Williams's ideas about television's flow can offer insights on how to analyze the organization of CPB categories at the macro (store) and micro (rows) levels. Much as Williams argued that flow shapes our experience of watching television beyond isolated programs, retail spaces are designed to create shopping experiences that tie together myriad categories of consumption. At the same time, the very rationales for how television schedules and store spaces are organized are also what can lead to unanticipated intertextual meanings that potentially disrupt the intended messaging. This is because the socioeconomic structures and product(ion) categorization that guide scheduling and shelving practices cannot fully account for the idiosyncrasies of actual content inserted into these time and shelf slots. The variables for flow are precisely that content is ever changing while the organizing principles are slower to adapt. This is certainly true of retail spaces, where merchandise is regularly rearranged. While planograms and other visual merchandising guides can offer formulaic strategies for displaying merchandise, they remain oblivious to the ways that particular brands and/or packaging will produce differentiated meanings when placed alongside one another in store sections/rows already laden with consumer expectations. And of course, store design and shelving strategies can only generate structured environments for shoppers to navigate; they cannot dictate the ways that people actually traverse such spaces nor account for the varying degrees of knowledge or investment that consumers bring with them into retail environments about particular media brands, which will inevitably impact the types of intertextual connections they make, the migratory cues they pick up on, and their willingness to look past or read into particular organizational schemas. Further investigations into how actual shoppers read store layouts and shelving strategies in relation to particular media brands are still needed to test flow's adaptability to retail spaces.

Notes

1 Raymond Williams, *Television: Technology and Cultural Form* (London: Routledge, 2003), 93, 96.
2 John Fiske, *Television Culture* (London: Methuen, 1987), 105.
3 Mimi White, "Flows and Other Close Encounters with TV," in *Planet TV*, eds. Lisa Parks and Shanti Kumar (New York: New York University Press, 2003), 6 (emphasis added).
4 Stuart Hall, "Notes on Deconstructing 'the Popular,'" in *People's History and Socialist Theory*, ed. Raphael Samuel (London: Routledge, 1981), 227–240.
5 Christopher Byrne, *A Profile of the United States Toy Industry: Serious Fun* (New York: Business Expert Press, 2013), 33.
6 Geoffrey Long, *Transmedia Storytelling: Business, Aesthetics and Production at the Jim Henson Company* (MS thesis, Massachusetts Institute of Technology, 2007), 59.
7 Ted Minini, "How Packaging Can Become the Ultimate Storyteller for Brands," *Design Force*, Apr. 2014, http://www.designforceinc.com/packaging-as-ultimate -storyteller-for-brands.
8 Minini, "Packaging."
9 Byrne, *Profile*, 32.
10 Byrne, 126.
11 Avi Santo, "Retail Tales and Tribulations: Transmedia Brands, Consumer Products, and the Significance of Shop Talk," *Cinema Journal* 58, no. 2 (Spring 2019): 115–141.
12 Sarah Whitten, "'Moana' Sails at the Box Office, but Faces Choppy Waters Navigating to *Frozen*'s Success," *CNBC*, 21 Dec. 2016, https://www.cnbc.com/2016/12/21/ disneys-moana-has-one-pitfall-its-not-frozen.html.
13 Whitten, "'Moana' Sails."
14 Claus Ebster and Marion Gaurus, *Store Design and Visual Merchandising: Creating Store Space That Encourages Buying* (New York: Business Expert Press, 2011).
15 Melissa Segal, interview with the author, 11 July 2012.
16 Rick Rekedal, interview with the author, 14 July 2012.

17 Rebecca Hains, "Target Will Stop Labeling Toys for Boys or for Girls. Good," *Washington Post*, 13 Aug. 2015, https://www.washingtonpost.com/posteverything/wp/2015/08/13/target-will-stop-selling-toys-for-boys-or-for-girls-good/?noredirect=on&utm_term=.40e1e40646d4.

18 Jonathan Gray, *Show Sold Separately: Promos, Spoilers, and Other Media Paratexts* (New York: New York University Press, 2010).

19 Ken Parker, "Sign Consumption in the 19th-Century Department Store: An Examination of Visual Merchandising in the Grand Emporiums (1846–1900)," *Journal of Sociology* 39, no. 4 (2003): 353–354.

20 Ellen Seiter, *Sold Separately: Parents and Children in Consumer Culture* (New Brunswick, N.J.: Rutgers University Press, 1995).

21 Willian L. Wilkie, Debra M. Desrochers, and Gregory T. Gundiach, "Marketing Research and Public Policy: The Case of Slotting Fees," *Journal of Public Policy & Marketing* 21, no. 2 (Fall 2002): 275–288.

22 Jack O'Dwyer, "Battle for Store Shelf and Media Space Fought with $$," *O'Dwyer's*, 13 Apr. 2015, http://www.odwyerpr.com/story/public/4409/2015-04-13/battle-for-store-shelf-media-space-fought-with.html.

23 O'Dwyer, "Battle."

24 Wilkie, Desrochers, and Gundiach, "Marketing Research."

25 Rob Leane, "Wonder Woman, and the Merchandise Problem," *Den of Geek*, 24 May 2017, http://www.denofgeek.com/us/movies/wonder-woman/265162/wonder-woman-and-the-merchandise-problem.

26 Yohana Desta, "What's Going on with Wonder Woman?," *Vanity Fair*, 28 Apr. 2017, https://www.vanityfair.com/hollywood/2017/04/wonder-woman-marketing.

27 Jenavieve Hatch, "'Wonder Woman' Partnered with Think Thin in Tone-Deaf Branding Move," *Huffington Post*, 5 May 2017, https://www.huffingtonpost.com/entry/wonder-woman-partnered-with-think-thin-in-tone-deaf-branding-move_us_590c7de4e4b0104c734e3c26.

28 Richard Gottlieb, "Wonder Woman; What's Selling," *Global Toy News*, 15 June 2017, http://www.globaltoynews.com/2017/06/wonder-woman-whats-selling.html.

29 Eric Weiss, "The DCEU Has a Problem—Everybody Likes Wonder Woman," *Polygon*, 17 June 2017, https://www.polygon.com/2017/6/17/15821584/wonder-woman-justice-league.

30 Byrne, *Profile*, 127.

31 Thomas Lee, "Target Walks Fine Line on Stocking Stores; Some Shoppers Frustrated," *Star Tribune*, 16 Dec. 2013, http://www.startribune.com/target-walks-fine-line-on-stocking-stores-some-shoppers-frustrated/235963911/.

32 Suzanne Scott, "#Wheresrey?: Toys, Spoilers, and the Gender Politics of Franchise Paratexts," *Critical Studies in Media Communication* 34, no. 2 (2017): 138–147.

33 Rekedal, interview with the author, 14 July 2012.

7

Get Your Cape On

•••••••••••••••••••••

Target's Invitation to the DC Universe

ETHAN TUSSEY AND MEREDITH BAK

Despite the success of Christopher Nolan's *Dark Knight* trilogy, DC Comics watched as the narratively interconnected films of their rival Marvel increased the revenue expectations for superhero franchises. From 2008 to 2016, Marvel films nearly doubled the box-office revenue of the DC films released by parent company Warner Bros. Entertainment.[1] Much of this success was due to sheer volume, as Marvel released twelve films to DC's seven films in that span. Clearly, DC needed to diversify its superhero offerings. Warner Bros. president Kevin Tsujihara admitted as much in October 2013, stating, "We need to get a Wonder Woman on the big screen or TV," explaining that the lack of DC superhero franchises beyond Superman and Batman was a "missed opportunity."[2] Marvel's films had broader audience appeal, while DC films concentrated on pleasing a core group of male fans. This strategy had ensured that the films succeeded at the box office but had also earned the series a negative reputation with critics for being a joyless slog of "hypermasculinity."[3] Recognizing these challenges, DC Comics sought to redirect the tone of their flagship film franchise by appealing to female consumers, embracing characters like Wonder Woman that, as Charlotte Howell argues, had otherwise been perceived within the industry as "tricky" because her feminist roots were considered a hard sell to the perceived male-dominated comic book fandom.[4]

Yet as much as the *Wonder Woman* film found commercial success, equally significant efforts occurred in the retail context outside the theatrical market. Derek Johnson has deemed "licensing and creative partnerships across industry lines" the more "risk-averse" strategy for expanding the popularity of a media franchise.[5] This is especially true for franchises with a primarily male fandom looking to attract more female fans. Johnson notes that this was the case for Lucasfilm's HerUniverse apparel and Major League Baseball's line of clothing designed by Alyssa Milano.[6] In these cases, female fandom finds a retail niche while the franchise as a whole maintains its normative ideologies. Given this context, the development and launch of the toy line for DC Super Hero Girls (DCSHG) reveal how retail partnerships inform corporate understanding of female superhero fans and influence efforts to make a brand appear less "hyper-masculine." Toys like DCSHG have proven to be a fruitful object of study for media scholars, particularly for those that want to understand their influential role in media franchising. Marsha Kinder, Mary Celeste Kearney, and Joy Van Fuqua each demonstrate how the production of toys shapes the ways that consumers play within media franchises (typically in ways that reaffirm traditional gender assumptions).[7] While DCSHG echoed these dynamics, the stakes were amplified as DC was using the toy line to learn to address female fans in advance of introducing female superheroes like Wonder Woman to the valuable cinematic extensions of their brand. Suzanne Scott argues that toys have become an important testing ground "used to make sense of the audience."[8] The lessons learned are crucial to the company's relationship with young female superhero fans because, as Ellen Seiter asserts, children "provide an opportunity to inculcate brand loyalty at an early age, thus ensuring future markets."[9]

The launch of the DCSHG toy line was an example of a "corporate performance" in which media companies demonstrate an awareness of an existing subculture to display an affinity for a target demographic while maintaining maximum continuity with existing business practices.[10] Warner Bros. made their goals public with a press release describing DCSHG as an effort to introduce a new generation of girls to the female heroes of the DC universe.[11] The setting for this introduction was the toy aisles of Target, as DC signed a temporary exclusive retail deal with the big-box chain. The experience of discovering these characters in the toy aisle was orchestrated by the creative collaboration between Target, toy manufacturer Mattel, and rights holder Warner Bros. / DC to package a franchise for new audiences—in this case, a young female demographic. The deployment of short online video content in the space of YouTube also situated DCSHG within a lineage of television promotion for toy lines like *My Little Pony*, *Rainbow Brite*, *Strawberry Shortcake*, *Transformers*, and *He-Man: Masters of the Universe* long critiqued as "program-length commercials."[12] Considering this alliance between toy and media industries, we argue that DCSHG's appeal to "empower" girls is produced not only through the toys' design and web series narrative but through the combined efforts of manufacturer, license holder, and retailer. Unlike previous research on the relationship between manufacturer and licenser, we emphasize the importance of the retail context and sociopolitical world of the point of purchase. Nick Couldry and Anna McCarthy's work on "MediaSpace" reveals "the ways that media forms shape and are shaped by the experience of social space" because "the politics of media images and economies are not separate from the politics of space."[13] Moreover, Avi Santo argues that the relationship between media industries and retailers are increasingly important because "merchandise constitutes one of the key components through which media industries have redefined their relationship with fan culture and have sought to define fandom not only in consumerist terms but also within existing frameworks for consumer product extension: namely the reconstitution of fandom as a lifestyle category rather than a communal experience."[14] Following these examples, our analysis considers how the development of DCSHG for Target deploys site-specific lifestyle branding strategies as a solution to the "tricky" problem of developing female superheroes.

Retailers play an important role in the process of franchise-building by promoting and providing visibility to products such as toys and apparel and by carrying brands that mutually reinforce their own corporate identities. While DCSHG is in many ways similar to other toy lines designed to "empower" young girls, its exclusive launch at Target in the spring of 2016 both built upon and contributed to the retail giant's own corporate image. Target's prominence in public relations materials for DCSHG offers assurances that the toy line matches their constructed dedication to progressive gender politics. The following analysis considers industry promotion to argue that this material positions the franchise as "empowering" for young girls by emphasizing the postfeminist values of "girl power" and individual consumer choice. We also look to research in journals on retail to identify the strategies that inform the arrangement of toys at the point of sale. John T. Caldwell has argued that examining industry beliefs about craft and the audience can lead to insights about the creative process as well as the narratives that organize corporate understanding about their own brands.[15] Following Caldwell's call, we contend that Target's role as a partner in the merchandising of DCSHG marketing—from the design of the characters to the arrangement of the display—reveals how female empowerment is defined in the toy aisle.

The "Target" Market for DCSHG

The experience of discovering DCSHG in the toy aisle of Target has the potential to make a lasting impression on a new generation of superhero fans.

David Buckingham and Julian Sefton-Green have demonstrated with *Poké-mon* that media franchises "offer different kinds of appeal—and different levels of complexity—for different age groups."[16] Wide ranges of products permit fans to engage aspirationally, grow up with a brand, or "regress" through nostalgia.[17] DCSHG aims to provide the kind of brand pedagogy Buckingham and Sefton-Green describe by serving as an introduction to these characters for a new generation while also evoking the cultural memories of parents that grew up with earlier depictions of Batgirl, Catwoman, and Wonder Woman.

Beyond the brand identifications of consumers, however, the DCSHG toy line is unique both for what it conveys about gendered play and for the spatial politics of Target. Scholarship in the fields of retail and brand management has long maintained a "brand extension theory" that argues that there is "an image transfer between store brands and the retailer brand."[18] A number of messages are conveyed to consumers via this image transfer, including the retailer's brand values, reputation, and social responsibility.[19] Retail scholars have shown that "consumers not only pay attention to the traditional marketing program of the stores (products, prices, services offered, etc.) but also to how retail stores are executing their marketing plans within the greater societal network."[20] As Melissa Aronczyk argues, brand managers can leverage the dynamic relationships among various product extensions at particular historical moments to signal affinity with broader cultural attitudes.[21]

In the initial press release for the DCSHG collection, DC president Diane Nelson and Scott Nygaard, senior vice president of merchandising at Target, stressed two things about the toys: first, they were an opportunity to "introduce a new generation" to these female heroes, and second, the series would offer girls the opportunity to "envision themselves as strong, powerful and connected beings at the center of their own superhero story."[22] These values and priorities are conveyed via the physical design of the store displays.[23] When the toys first appeared at Target, they were given special "endcap" placement across their 1,800 U.S. locations. Endcaps are featured retail spaces that convey importance, timeliness, and novelty to consumers. Merchandisers covet this store placement, reportedly willing to spend nearly half their promotional budgets to secure these locations in stores.[24] As a Target exclusive, DCSHG had endcap placement similar to other Target-exclusive brands such as C9 by Champion, Aldo's A+ collection, and the Lilly Pulitzer line.[25] Endcaps are like in-store advertisements that convey the retailer's endorsement and distinguish products from the rest of the offerings in the aisles.

Essentially, endcap placement aligns DCSHG with Target's brand. Target is characterized by its spokespeople as dedicated to "high-end,"[26] "artisanal,"[27] "multicultural"[28] products that "appeal to its upper-middle class demographic."[29] This approach is exemplified by Target's numerous partnerships with a range of boutique businesses and designers aimed at "making great design accessible to all."[30] Socioeconomically, Target has a more affluent and younger clientele than Walmart, supporting a different set of brand values to be expressed through its endcap placements.[31] These brand values include issues of gender construction. DC's decision to partner with Target capitalizes on the store's recent positive press over its move to eliminate gender labels in their toy and bedding aisles in August 2015, following a viral campaign initiated by Ohio mother Abi Bechtel lampooning the retail giant's gendered signage.[32] In response to these social media efforts, Target relabeled in-store signage in the kids' bedding and toy sections and promised neutral-toned shelf backing.[33]

Target's embrace of gender-neutral labeling corresponds with branding changes that have occurred at the retailer in response to slowing growth in the middle years of the 2010s. Ashley Rodriguez of *Advertising Age* reports that Target has transitioned from a general retailer to one specializing in "four core areas where the brand can stand out: style, including home, apparel and other products; baby, encompassing clothes and gear; kids' clothes and toys; and wellness."[34] As part of these four strategic emphases, toys carry particular value to the project of courting a middle-class progressive clientele through an alignment with the politics of gender equality. Rodriguez further characterizes its "exclusive" partnerships as an effort to reach "fresh customers" and attract "trendy" demographics.[35] While conservative critics complained that the removal of "clear gender markers might be 'confusing' to children,"[36] supporters took to social media to applaud Target's decision and to "troll" the retailer's critics.[37] While other retailers like Walmart and Toys "R" Us removed gender labels from toy aisles before Target, their decisions were framed more as practical solutions for space-saving rather than as politically oriented: "For instance, Walmart tries to maximize its space by putting two to three categories in one aisle."[38] Conversely, Target positioned its decision as part of the politics of its branding.

Adding to the perception of Target as a progressively oriented retailer was the company's response to anti-LGBT legislation (signed into effect during the exclusive partnership window for DCSHG). Responding to restrictive public restroom legislation in North Carolina, Target announced a policy allowing patrons to use restrooms and fitting rooms of their choice via a news release entitled "Continuing to Stand for Inclusivity."[39] Although Target ultimately compromised with those who objected to this move, undertaking a $20 million project to install single-occupancy restrooms in many of its stores,[40] its initial statement "to stand with inclusivity" crafted a corporate identity around issues of gender inclusivity and diversity in which the DCSHG line would appear to be a natural fit.

Mattel's limited-time exclusive partnership with Target and the endcap placement of DCSHG products can thus be read within this larger discussion surrounding gendered marketing during its initial appearance at the retailer in 2016. DCSHG's placement on endcaps reinforced the specific brand narratives that Target sought to cultivate. Although it would ultimately gain access to the toy line after Target's window of exclusivity had ended, Walmart placed DCSHG in the girl's toy aisle as simply another offering in a competitive marketplace for that gendered product category. By comparison, the spatial neutrality of the endcaps where DCSHG toys had been placed at Target reinforced the retailer's politically branded decision to remove labeling from toy aisles.[41] Endcap placement both features the DCSHG line and exempts it from the traditionally labeled toy aisles, thus aligning the toys with Target's own progressive image.

The Center of the "Planogram"

Toy displays are meticulously organized around "planograms," proprietary audience-tested arrangements of merchandise. Target refers to the design of its planograms as the "secret sauce" that distinguishes its appeal to its customers from its competitors.[42] These planograms ensure the uniformity of merchandise arrangement across Target locations and manage industry assumptions about consumer psychology. Research from Proctor and Gamble, for instance, claims that customers make purchasing decisions within the first three to seven seconds of noticing products on a store shelf.[43] Similar research argues that the spatial positioning of products informs a number of assumptions about the price and popularity of the items.[44] Tests of different kinds of display schemas reveal that center placement (at the eye-line of the average adult) increases consumers' perception of the value of the product.[45] Yet that center placement is also understood to be a draw for surrounding items and accessories that consumers will be more likely to try if they are intrigued by the centered product.[46] Such a radial arrangement allows retailers to display merchandise as connected constellations, privileging centrally placed items but providing an array of peripheral products to invite return visits and future purchases.

Costumes are at the center of Target's DCSHG endcaps (figures 7.1 and 7.2). Associated with traditionally gendered "dress up" play, the costumes command attention and are consistent with the claim that the toy line will allow girls to put themselves in the middle of their own superhero stories. They also evoke the theme song of the web series, "Get Your Cape On!," which at once positions girls as active and empowered but simultaneously focuses on costuming and fashion. The costumes hang from the top of the display—eliminating the need for external packaging—and take on the appearance of clothes hanging in a closet. Their placement directs children's eyes upward, inviting young consumers to embody an aspirational stance as they imagine dressing like the superhero of their choice. Rows of action figures flank the costumes at adult eye-level, while

FIGS. 7.1 AND 7.2. Original Target displays for DC Super Hero Girls (photos by Devan Hartung and Jordan Mixon)

the line's distinct "action dolls" are presented below, at what is assumed to be children's eye-level. While internally the planogram for DCSHG is labeled as "for girls," and DC specifically developed the toy line as an invitation to girls to engage with the superhero brand, the combination of types of toys in the same planogram distinguishes DCSHG as a brand that offers girls a variety of ways to play.[47]

This retail logic of centrality within connected constellations of products provides a productive means to reflect on the politics of DCSHG as well as gendered marketing in media franchising more broadly. Historically, when traditionally male-skewing media franchises have tried to incorporate female fans, they fall back on postfeminist frames of empowerment and choice that ultimately partition female fandom as separate but equal.[48] The consideration of how to design and frame the DCSHG line is a marked departure from earlier attempts to merchandise the same intellectual properties. An early 1970s line of eight-inch figures marketed as the Super Gals was produced by toy company Mego as part of the company's "World's Greatest Super Heroes" line. The "gals," which included Wonder Woman, Supergirl, Batgirl, and Catwoman, accompanied a series of eight male superheroes from both Marvel and DC and were billed in promotional materials as "the female companions of the super-heroes."[49]

Unlike this earlier attempt, which separates and places female heroes alongside their male counterparts, DCSHG's distinguishes itself by placing them at the center of the property and offering access through a range of play forms. To distinguish the figures from earlier efforts, the press release for DCSHG boasted "the first-ever 6-inch action figure designed for girls" in addition to noting other novel elements, such as the "first 12-inch collection of action dolls featuring strong, athletic bodies that stand on their own in heroic poses; and first-ever action role-play toys for girls."[50] While the range of DCSHG costumes allows girls to take on the roles of their favorite heroes, the figures' articulated bodies and the distinct new format of the action doll—a hard plastic–molded, articulated twelve-inch figure with styleable hair—materially reflect the brand's ethos of action and girls' empowerment: like any strong, empowered girl should, the toys stand independently and are mobile and dynamic.

DCSHG's distinct product range aims to enable a variety of play practices for girls and reflects a broader industry shift away from the "pinkification" of girls' toys. In 2014, Julie Kerwin organized a crowdfunding campaign to create a line of action figures featuring female superheroes called IAmElemental. Kerwin described the mission behind her efforts to create toys that "allow girls (and boys) to envision themselves as strong, powerful and connected beings at the center of a story of their own making."[51] DC president Diane Nelson used nearly identical language when describing DCSHG, claiming the toys allowed children to "envision themselves as strong, powerful and connected beings at the center of their own superhero story."[52] As interindustry exchanges that organize consensus across the retail, branding and toy industries,[53] these very similar publicity statements reflect shifting expectations around the themes and aesthetics of girls' playthings. Only a year prior to the launch of DCSHG, Mattel introduced a line of superhero-themed Barbie dolls called Barbie Princess Power whose visual characteristics, such as her eye mask and wings, bore a striking resemblance to the earlier independent IAmElemental line. Meant to aid flagging Barbie sales,[54] Mattel designed the line with input from a survey of nearly 2,500 girls aged three to ten, ultimately combining the icons and themes of princesses and superheroes to give Barbie a pink costume with a tiara and a purple cape. Joy Van Fuqua points to the pink "color-code" of girl toys as evidence of an industrial logic that undermines the progressive messages of female superheroes such as the Powerpuff Girls by equating "consumerism and girlishness."[55]

DCSHG aimed to counter this industrial logic in ways that resonated in retail spaces. As Nelson explained in interviews, "We have golds, greens, and reds that really pop on aisles that are full of pink. The characters wear practical uniforms instead of swimsuits and high heels."[56] In one harrowing promotional tale meant to affirm this new strategy at the launch of the toy line at New York Comic Con 2015, the creators of DCSHG explained that they considered changing Wonder Woman's clothing from her traditional primary colors to a pink outfit but were told by a focus group of young girls to retain their classic costumes.[57] Tania Missad of Mattel reported that the girls "wanted classic, recognizable superheroes. They wanted authenticity."[58] In the case of Wonder Woman, Warner Bros. even dramatized the costume incident in two episodes of the DCSHG web series, "Crazy Quiltin" and "Designing Disaster" (see figure 7.3). In it, Wonder Woman herself questions her choice of outfit, wanting to meet the requirements set by her teacher that she must design a supersuit that displays "creativity, craftsmanship, and practicality." After struggling to save the day in platform heels, a pink cape, and an audacious *W* tiara, she returns to her classic look, affirming her choice by stating that it was "time for me to be me."

This industry story, later narrativized in the web series, distances the brand from the extreme femininity characterized by the color pink and other Mattel brands like Barbie and equates the superheroes' original aesthetics with "authenticity." Moreover, within the physical space of Target, those costumes with their "authentic" aesthetics serve as a hub for a wide range of "empowering" play products. In this way, product design, the variety of toy offerings, and their retail placement in Target all coordinate to challenge the pinkified code of previous merchandise. Simultaneously, however, the toys, which invite girls to identify with particular characters and choose how they wish to play, exemplify what Sarah Banet-Weiser calls "postfeminism's emphasis on choice

FIG. 7.3 Wonder Woman tries a new costume in "Designing Disaster" (screen capture)

and individualism, authorized by consumer media culture,"[59] thereby offering choices within the limiting framework of consumption. The radial transmedia design and in-store arrangement of DCSHG toys thus offer multiple pathways to and through the brand, which purport to validate girls' individual play preferences (in terms of both character identification and play types), though all such choices are predicated upon economic consumption.[60]

In this sense, DCSHG reflects many of the arguments made by Kristen Warner regarding "plastic representation."[61] Examining the politics of casting and racial diversity, Warner writes, "Paltry gains generate an easy workaround for the executive suites whereby hiring racially diverse actors becomes an easy substitute for developing new complex characters. The results of such choices can feel—in an affective sense—artificial, or more to the point, like plastic."[62] She continues, "Plastic representation uses the wonder that comes from seeing characters on screen who serve as visual identifiers for specific demographics in order to flatten the expectations to desire anything more." Plasticity is an apt metaphor for toy analysis, given its malleable nature, capable of adapting and transforming to conform to particular consumer interests. In the toy aisles, such forms of representation can spatially and aesthetically signal political or cultural commitments, such as DCSHG's apparent rejection of girls' pink culture in favor of heritage-inspired authenticity. Beneath that plastic surface, however, retailers, toy manufacturers, and IP (intellectual property) holders still imagined kids in distinctly gendered terms.

From Exclusivity to Exclusion

DCSHG's endcap placement and planogram centrality only defined the toy line during the initial three-month window when the toys were a Target Exclusive. After this, DCSHG toys were removed from endcaps and placed within the toy aisles at Target and across a number of other retail stores, reabsorbed into the conventional logic of gendered toy displays. In a downtown Chicago Target in March of 2017, for example, DCSHG toys were displayed in predictable gendered groupings. The franchise's LEGO sets, for instance, were placed along a prominently pink and purple aisle alongside product lines conventionally aimed at girls, including LEGO Friends, LEGO Disney Princesses, and LEGO Elves. Notably, the analogous DC and Marvel Super Hero LEGO sets were found across the aisle, surrounded by lines that were aimed at boys or gender-neutral, such as the LEGO Juniors and Creator lines. Similarly, DCSHG action figures were found not among other action figures but in an aisle with other figures and fashion dolls aimed at girls, such as the *Powerpuff Girls*, *Trolls*, Ever After High, *Project MC²*, *Miraculous Ladybug*, and Shibajuku brands. Such display practices would seem to undercut the progressive message on the surface of toy lines like DCSHG by effectively grouping toys by gender (indeed, the appearance of DCSHG action dolls alongside similar toys created for Netflix's *Project MC²* and Nickelodeon's *Mysticons* effectively created a store section that could be labeled as "empowering girls' toys").

Given this return to form, and the gender divisions that come with it, it is important to recognize the effect of exclusive partnerships in framing customers' initial encounters with brands and as a crucial moment of meaning making for brand managers and creative workers. DCSHG was a Target-exclusive brand from March to July of 2016.[63] Exclusive deals are not unusual for entertainment brands, but they took on new importance as media companies recovered from the recession.[64] These partnerships give retailers popular brands for a limited time, creating a sense of urgency and heightening their investment in providing support at launch to establish a strong brand impression for the product during the exclusive licensing window. Warner Bros. consumer products executive Brad Globe notes that "retail now really requires these (merchandise) events. You want to get the consumers' attention when they walk into the store."[65] An exclusive partnership transforms a toy launch into an event that creates an association with the retailer and takes advantage of the advertising efforts in weekly newspaper circulars and television advertisements. At the same time, these exclusive retail events can work to overshadow the marketing for competing products. While Benjamin Klein and Kevin M. Murphy contend that exclusivity can facilitate retail competition over products, Hans Zenger argues that the enhanced support that exclusive deals give to larger manufacturers (like Mattel) can make it harder for smaller companies to find distribution.[66] The partnership between DC / Warner Bros., Mattel, and Target was a strategic move that made DCSHG's brand of girl empowerment more visible than those of competitors such as IAmElemental, which is primarily sold by independent toy shops, with few major retail outlets. Target's market dominance and promotional push during the exclusive window generated the appearance that the DCSHG line was leading the way in the industry's attempt to rethink marketing for girls.

The exclusive partnership with DCSHG also helped combat the bad publicity generated for Target, manufacturer Hasbro, and studio Disney surrounding the marketing of *Star Wars: The Force Awakens* in 2015. While the narrative of the movie centered on the heroine, Rey, much of the toy marketing—including exclusive products carried by Target that became particular focuses of social media critique—did not include the character. Hasbro and Target appeared to have reverted to the toy industry wisdom that boys would not play with female characters. They considered *Star Wars* a male brand despite hopes by the director of the film that the series would be more inclusive and cater to the franchise's female fans.[67] Against the #WheresRey controversy of late 2015, the arrival of DCSHG in early 2016 seemed to offer a new kind of exclusive partnership to redress this previous exclusion with the promise of retail centrality.

Conclusion

While the experience of discovering DCSHG at Target during the exclusive partnership window was different than encountering the brand in other contexts, Target's partnership with DC and Mattel supported the construction of a progressive, empowering brand identity aimed at refiguring the role of female consumers within the superhero franchise's constellation of products. Jayson Quearry has argued that the reliance on postfeminist empowerment is a strategy that helps producers fit female characters within the larger DC universe, as it equalizes these superheroes' physicality across gender while maintaining market differentiation through markers of essential femininity.[68]

In this context, DC Comics has come to realize that there is a lucrative female market for comic products in an industry that had once been the domain of males. DC comic books entered a new age of branding in 2015 under the heading "DC You," aimed at cultivating a reputation for diversity and progressive political themes.[69] During this rebrand, then-president of DC Entertainment Diane Nelson was given oversight of Warner Bros. consumer products, and CEO Kevin Tsujihara explained that the move made sense because so much of Warner Bros.' consumer products efforts were being driven by licenses for DC characters and story lines.[70] Nelson was already overseeing all of DC's storytelling efforts (comics, films, and television) and subscribed to the belief that there does not need to be "creative crossover" between the stories being told in these separate mediums.[71] These decisions to diversify DC's intellectual properties meant tailoring character depictions and story lines for diverse target demographics, yet Nelson also expressed a renewed commitment to interaction across every business at Warner Bros.[72] So while each version of the DC characters may be unique, the lessons learned about packaging the franchise for consumers are widely shared. For example, the character designs for the *Wonder Woman* film toy line are different from the designs of DCSHG, but they include DCSHG-style "action dolls" that "can be positioned in heroic action poses while holding such iconic Wonder Woman accessories as her sword, bow and arrow, shield, and her iconic lasso."[73] While these dolls "stand on their own" like DCSHG figures, they also come with an evening gown and several costumes typical of toys targeted at girls.

The lessons learned in the toy aisles of Target thus contribute to DC's newfound knowledge of how to appeal to more diverse audiences inclusive of girls and women. Additionally, the success of DCSHG both financially and critically (it earned Mattel a Toy of the Year Award in the action-figure category by the Toy Industry Association and contributed to a stock-price increase for the toy manufacturer) has also informed its competitors.[74] Disney subsequently launched the *Force of Destiny* web series and line of *Star Wars* toys, modeled after DCSHG, as an attempt to make amends for earlier controversies. The forerunner of DCSHG, IAmElemental, received a television contract with the Jim Henson Company following the success of the toy line it inspired.[75] Given these implications, the relationships between Target, Mattel, and Warner Bros. / DC must be understood as essential to this process. DC became party to Target's retail politics and progressive lifestyle branding while benefiting from Mattel's attempt to move past earlier failures like Princess Power Barbie. Thanks to these lessons, children encountering these toys in the aisles of Target will see themes of postfeminist empowerment—however limited— increasingly centered in the product constellations of major media franchises presented at retail.

Notes

1 Aaron Gunderson, "Marvel vs. DC Movie Ratings Box Office Battle," *Reviews.org*, 18 Apr. 2018, https://www.reviews.org/marvel-vs-dc/.

2 Jonathan Handel, "Warner Bros.' Kevin Tsujihara Talks *Gravity* J.K. Rowling and Tentpole Strategy," *Hollywood Reporter*, 5 Oct. 2013, https://www .hollywoodreporter.com/news/warner-bros-kevin-tsujihara-talks-643556.

3 Ann Hornaday, "'Batman v Superman' Is So Desperate to Be Taken Seriously, It Forgets to Have Fun," *Washington Post*, 23 Mar. 2016, https://www.washingtonpost .com/goingoutguide/movies/batman-v-superman-is-so-desperate-to-be-taken -seriously-it-forgets-to-have-fun/2016/03/23/3fb28f10-f0f5-11e5-a61f-e9c95c06edca _story.html?utm_term=.1bcedbeb55e6.

4 Charlotte E. Howell, "'Tricky' Connotations: Wonder Woman as DC's Brand Disruptor," *Cinema Journal* 55, no. 1 (Fall 2015): 141–149.

5 Derek Johnson, *Media Franchising: Creative License and Collaboration in the Culture Industries* (New York: New York University Press, 2013), 69.

6 Derek Johnson, "May the Force Be with Katie: Pink Media Franchising and the Postfeminist Politics of HerUniverse," *Feminist Media Studies* 14, no. 6 (2014): 895–911.

7 Joy Van Fuqua, "What Are Those Little Girls Made Of? The Powerpuff Girls and Consumer Culture," in *Prime Time Animation: Television Animation and American Culture*, eds. Carol A. Stabile and Mark Harrison (New York: Routledge, 2003), 205–219; Mary Celeste Kearney, "Sparkle: Luminosity and Post-Girl Power Media," *Continuum* 29, no. 2 (Mar. 2015): 263–273; Marsha Kinder, *Playing with Power in Movies, Television, and Video Games: From Muppet Babies to Teenage Mutant Ninja Turtles* (Berkeley: University of California Press, 1991).

8 Suzanne Scott, "#Wheresrey?: Toys, Spoilers, and the Gender Politics of Franchise Paratexts," *Critical Studies in Media Communication* 34, no. 2 (2017): 139.

9 Ellen Seiter, *Sold Separately: Parents and Children in Consumer Culture* (New Brunswick, N.J.: Rutgers University Press, 1995), 103.

10 John Caldwell, "Critical Industrial Practice: Branding, Repurposing, and the Migratory Patterns of Industrial Texts," *Television & New Media* 7, no. 2 (2006): 123.

11 "Warner Bros. Consumer Products and DC Entertainment, in Partnership with Mattel, Join Forces with Target to Create a Powerful National Retail Program for DC Super Hero Girls," *Business Wire*, 9 Feb. 2016, https://www.businesswire .com/news/home/20160209006419/en/Warner-Bros.-Consumer-Products-DC -Entertainment-Partnership.

12 Marsha Kinder, *Playing with Power*, 40.

13 Nick Couldry and Anna McCarthy, introduction to *MediaSpace: Place, Scale and Culture in a Media Age* (London: Routledge, 2004), 2.

14 Avi Santo, "Fans and Merchandise," in *The Routledge Companion to Media Fandom*, eds. Melissa A. Click and Suzanne Scott (New York: Routledge, 2017), 329.

15 John T. Caldwell, *Production Culture: Industrial Reflexivity and Critical Practice in Film and Television* (Durham, N.C.: Duke University Press, 2008), 35.

16 David Buckingham and Julian Sefton-Green, "Gotta Catch 'Em All: Structure, Agency and Pedagogy in Children's Media Culture," *Media, Culture & Society* 25, no. 3 (1 May 2003): 379–399, 382.

17 Buckingham and Sefton-Green, "Gotta Catch 'Em All."

18 Florence Kremer and Catherine Viot, "How Store Brands Build Retailer Brand Image," *International Journal of Retail & Distribution Management* 40, no. 7 (2012): 529.

19 Grete Birtwistle, Ian Clarke, and Paul Freathy, "Store Image in the UK Fashion Sector: Consumer versus Retailer Perceptions," *International Review of Retail, Distribution and Consumer Research* 9, no. 1 (Jan. 1999): 1–16; Shruti Gupta and Julie Pirsch, "The Influence of a Retailer's Corporate Social Responsibility Program on Re-conceptualizing Store Image," *Journal of Retailing and Consumer Services* 15, no. 6 (2008): 516–526.

20 Gupta and Pirsch, "Influence," 522.

21 Melissa Aronczyk, "Portal or Police? The Limits of Promotional," *Critical Studies in Media Communication* 34, no. 2 (2017): 111–119.

22 "Warner Bros. Consumer Products."

23 Paul Richardson, Arun K. Jain, and Alan Dick, "The Influence of Store Aesthetics on Evaluation of Private Label Brands," *Journal of Product and Brand Management* 5, no. 1 (1996): 19; Colleen Collins-Dodd and Tara Lindley, "Store Brands and Retail Differentiation: The Influence of Store Image and Store Brand Attitude on Store Own Brand Perceptions," *Journal of Retailing and Consumer Services* 10, no. 6 (2003): 345–352; Janjaap Semeijn, Allard C. R. van Riel, and A. Beatriz Ambrosini, "Consumer Evaluations of Store Brands: Effects of Store Image and Product Attributes," *Journal of Retailing and Consumer Services* 11, no. 4 (2004): 247–258.

24 Xavier Drèze, Stephen J. Hoch, and Mary E. Pur, "Shelf Management and Space Elasticity," *Journal of Retailing* 70, no. 4 (1994): 302.

25 Ashley Rodriguez, "The Minneapolis Retailer That Once Defined Contemporary Chi Is Bidding to Regain That Image by Doubling Down on Design That Is Both Fab and Functional," *Advertising Age*, 24 Aug. 2015, 18.

26 Natalie Zmuda, "Walmart, Target, Kmart, Kohl's: Leading 50 Years of Retail Revolution," *Advertising Age*, 19 Mar. 2012, 2.

27 Rodriguez, "Minneapolis Retailer."

28 Kavita Kumar, "More Skin in the Game for Doll Diversity," *Star Tribune*, 11 Dec. 2016, http://www.startribune.com/multicultural-dolls-a-hit-for-target-and-other-retailers/405687726/.

29 "Target Corp in Retailing (USA)," *Euromonitor International*, 1 Mar. 2017, http://www.euromonitor.com/target-corp-in-retailing/report.

30 "Target Partners with 17 Leading Better-for-You Brands to Launch Exclusive 'Made to Matter' Product C," *Target Corporate*, 9 Apr. 2014, http://corporate.target.com/press/releases/2014/04/target-partners-with-17-leading-better-for-you-bra; "Target Unveils New Design Partnership Program," *Target Corporate*, 13 Jan. 2012,

http://corporate.target.com/press/releases/2012/01/target-unveils-new-design
-partnership-221743.

31 Matt Carmichael, "The Demographics of Retail," *Advertising Age*, 19 Mar. 2012,
http://adage.com/article/adagestat/demographics-retail/233399/.

32 Abi Bechtel, "Target Finally Listened to My Viral Tweet about Boys' and Girls'
Toys," *Time*, 12 Aug. 2015, http://time.com/3991166/target-viral-tweet-about-boys
-and-girls-toys/.

33 "What's in Store: Moving Away from Gender-Based Signs," *Target Corporate*,
7 Aug. 2015, https://corporate.target.com/article/2015/08/gender-based-signs
-corporate.

34 Rodriguez, "Minneapolis Retailer."

35 Rodriguez.

36 Schuyler Velasco, "Barbie Ad Stars a Boy for the First Time: The End of Gendered
Toys?," *Christian Science Monitor*, 17 Nov. 2015, https://www.csmonitor.com/
Business/2015/1117/Barbie-ad-stars-a-boy-for-the-first-time.-The-end-of-gendered
-toys.

37 Tim Nudd, "Target Loved the Guy Who Trolled Its Haters, Judging by This Genius
Facebook Post," *Ad Week*, 14 Aug. 2015, http://www.adweek.com/creativity/target
-loved-guy-who-trolled-its-haters-judging-genius-facebook-post-166408/.

38 Samantha Masunaga, "Target Plays Catch-up in Removing Gender Based Toy
Labels," *Los Angeles Times*, 10 Aug. 2015, http://www.latimes.com/business/la-fi
-target-gender-labeling-20150810-story.html.

39 "Continuing to Stand for Inclusivity," *Target Corporate*, 19 Apr. 2016, https://
corporate.target.com/article/2016/04/target-stands-inclusivity.

40 Sarah Halzack, "Target to Spend $20 Million on Single-Stall Bathrooms after
Backlash to Its Restroom Policy," *Washington Post*, 17 Aug. 2016, https://www
.washingtonpost.com/news/business/wp/2016/08/17/target-hit-some-turbulence
-this-summer/?utm_term=.4caf5ad98120.

41 Of nine stories about the controversy over gender-neutral toy aisles appearing in the
New York Times, Washington Post, Canadian Business, Boston Globe, and *Christian
Science Monitor*, only one noted that Walmart also removed gender labels from
toy aisles. See Velasco, "Barbie Ad"; Erica Weisgram, "Now That Target Won't
Label Toys by Gender, Some Alternatives," *New York Times*, 17 Aug. 2015, https://
parenting.blogs.nytimes.com/2015/08/17/truth-in-signage-in-the-toy-aisle-after
-target-removes-gender-labels-whats-next/; Hiroko Tabuchi, "A Tiara? No Thanks,"
New York Times, 29 Oct. 2015, https://www.nytimes.com/2015/10/28/business/
sweeping-away-gender-specific-toys-and-labels.html; Claire Cain Miller, "Boys and
Girls, Constrained by Toys and Costumes," *New York Times*, 31 Oct. 2015, https://
www.nytimes.com/2015/10/31/upshot/boys-and-girls-constrained-by-toys-and
-costumes.html; Yanan Wang, "Boy Actor Prominently Featured in Commercial for
Designer Barbie Doll," *Washington Post*, 17 Nov. 2015, https://www.washingtonpost
.com/news/morning-mix/wp/2015/11/17/boy-actor-prominently-featured-in
-commercial-for-designer-barbie-doll/?utm_term=.3d0188714e33; Rebecca Hains,
"Princess Leia Is a General Now. But Why Isn't She in More Toy Stores?," *Washington Post*, 18 Nov. 2015, https://www.washingtonpost.com/posteverything/wp/
2015/11/17/turning-princess-leia-into-a-general-isnt-a-feminist-move/?utm_term=
.55d209b0f198; Rebecca Hains, "Why Boys Should Play with Dolls," *Boston Globe*,
22 Nov. 2015, https://www.bostonglobe.com/magazine/2015/11/17/why-boys
-should-play-with-dolls/aujIqanxzYdW10Xjn9VhoN/story.html; Sarah Halzack,

"Toying with Changes in Gender Marketing," *Washington Post*, 6 Dec. 2015. "What We Learned in 2015," *Canadian Business*, Jan. 2016, 45.

42 Lee Henderson, Target Communications, interview with the authors, 16 May 2017.

43 Ana Valenzuela and Priya Raghubir, "Product 'Position'-ing: Implications of Vertical and Horizontal Shelf Space Placement," in *AP—Asia-Pacific Advances in Consumer Research*, eds. Sridhar Samu, Rajiv Vaidyanathan, and Dipankar Chakravarti (Duluth, Minn.: Association for Consumer Research, 2009), 22–23.

44 Valenzuela and Raghubir, "Product 'Position'-Ing," 22–23.

45 Valenzuela and Raghubir.

46 Valenzuela and Raghubir.

47 A former Target employee that assembled the DCSHG's display confirmed that the planogram said "for girls."

48 Derek Johnson, "May the Force," 895–911.

49 "The 1974 (75) Film Strip Catalog," *MEGO Museum*, 12 May 2018, http://www.megomuseum.com/catalog/inserts/strips.shtml.

50 "Warner Bros. Consumer Products."

51 Julie Kerwin, "The IAmElemental Journey," *IamElemental*, 2018, http://www.iamelemental.com/iamelemental-toy-company-story/.

52 "Warner Bros. Consumer Products."

53 John T. Caldwell, "Cultures of Production: Studying Industry's Deep Texts, Reflexive Rituals, and Managed Self-Disclosures," in *Media Industries: History, Theory, and Method*, eds. Jennifer Holt and Alisa Perren (Malden, Mass.: Wiley-Blackwell, 2009), 202.

54 Erin McKelle, "'Barbie in Princess Power' Superhero Doll Aims to Break Down Gender Barriers . . . Kinda," *Bustle*, 13 Feb. 2015, https://www.bustle.com/articles/64024-barbie-in-princess-power-superhero-doll-aims-to-break-down-gender-barriers-kinda; Lindsay Whipp, "Heroic Effort as Barbie Changes Her Shoes but Not Her Career," *Financial Times*, 21 Aug. 2015, https://www.ft.com/content/39b242fe-45ec-11e5-af2f-4d6e0e5eda22.

55 Van Fuqua, "Consumer Culture," 214.

56 Dinah Eng, "Meet the DC Exec Turning Girl Superheroes into a 'Billion-Dollar Brand,'" *Fortune*, 23 May 2016, https://fortune.com/2016/05/23/dc-super-hero-girls-diane-nelson/.

57 Corrina Lawson, "DC Super Hero Girls: This Time, They Asked Us," *GeekMom*, 15 Oct. 2015, https://geekmom.com/2015/10/dc-superhero-girls/.

58 Lawson, "DC Super Hero Girls."

59 Sarah Banet-Weiser, "Postfeminism and Popular Feminism," *Feminist Media Histories* 4, no. 2 (2018): 154.

60 Banet-Weiser, "Postfeminism," 155.

61 Kristen Warner, "In the Time of Plastic Representation," *Film Quarterly* 71, no. 2 (Winter 2017), https://filmquarterly.org/2017/12/04/in-the-time-of-plastic-representation/.

62 Warner, "Plastic Representation."

63 "Target to Debut 'DC Super Hero Girls,'" *License Global*, 10 Feb. 2016, https://www.licenseglobal.com/toys-games/target-debut-dc-super-hero-girls.

64 Marc Graser, "H'wood Shelf-Help Plan; Retail Add-ons Buying, Promote Pics," *Variety*, 21 Mar. 2011, https://www.thefreelibrary.com/H%27wood+shelf-help+plan%3A+retail+add-ons+boost+buying%2C+promote+pics-a0252847558.

65 Graser, "H'wood Shelf-Help Plan."

66 Hans Wenger, "When Does Exclusive Dealing Intensify Competition for Distribution—Comment on Klein and Murphy," *Antitrust Law Journal* 77, no. 1 (2010): 205–212.

67 Ross A. Lincoln, "J.J. Abrams Explains His 'Star Wars Boy Thing' Comment," *Deadline*, 4 Dec. 2015, http://deadline.com/2015/12/jj-abrams-explains-boys-thing -star-wars-comment-misunderstood-1201653533/.

68 Jayson Quearry, "Look in the Sky! It's a Feminist! It's a Postfeminist! No, It's Super-girl!: How a Network-Shift Altered Supergirl's Production Practices" (term paper, Georgia State University, 2017).

69 Aja Romano, "DC Comics Steps Up its Diversity Efforts with 'DC You' Lineup," *Daily Dot*, 9 July 2015, https://www.dailydot.com/parsec/dan-didio-emphasizes -diversity-in-dc-you-lineup-sdcc/.

70 Dave McNary, "Diane Nelson Expands Role to Warner Bros. Consumer Prod-ucts as Brad Globe Steps Down," *Variety*, 28 Aug. 2015, http://variety.com/2015/ film/news/diane-nelson-warner-bros-consumer-products-brad-globe-steps-down -1201580831/.

71 Cynthia Littleton, "DC Boss Diane Nelson Talks Super Hero Strategy vs Marvel at Variety Summit," *Variety*, 16 Sept. 2015, http://variety.com/2015/biz/news/dc-diane -nelson-batman-vs-superman-marvel-flash-arrow-1201595124/.

72 Littleton, "DC Boss."

73 "WBCP and DCE Reveal Global Licensing and Merchandising Program for First-ever Motion Picture of *Wonder Woman*," *Warner Bros.*, 31 Mar. 2017, https:// www.warnerbros.com/studio/news/wbcp-and-dce-reveal-global-licensing-and -merchandising-program-first-ever-motion-picture.

74 "Mattel Wins Toy of the Year Award for DC Super Hero Girls (™) in the Action Figure Category," *Mattel Newsroom*, 21 Feb. 2017, https://news.mattel.com/news/ mattel-wins-toy-of-the-year-award-for-dc-super-hero-girls-tm-in-the-action-figure -category; R. Chandrasekaran, "Mattel Not Toying around with Its Turnaround Effort," *Benzinga*, 10 Oct. 2016, https://www.benzinga.com/analyst-ratings/analyst -color/16/10/8546406/mattel-not-toying-around-with-its-turnaround-effort.

75 "The Jim Henson Company to Develop Kids Series Based on IAmElemental's Female Action Figures," *PRNewswire*, 7 Nov. 2017, http://www.prnewswire .com/news-releases/the-jim-henson-company-to-develop-kids-series-based-on -iamelementals-female-action-figures-300550904.html.

8

Shop, Makeover, Love

• •

Transformative Paratexts
and Aspirational Fandom for
Female-Driven Franchises

COURTNEY BRANNON DONOGHUE

In Warner Bros.' *Wonder Woman*, a pivotal scene occurs in London after Steve Trevor and Diana (a.k.a. Wonder Woman) leave Themyscira, the island of the Amazons. Before beginning a mission to the frontline of World War I, Trevor and his secretary, Etta Candy, take Diana shopping at an upscale department store in an effort to disguise the Amazonian princess. Diana is visibly uncomfortable trying on the restrictively elaborate dresses of the modern woman.[1] Diana's awkward first experience in a retail space as a consumer follows a familiar cinematic transformation. From *Pretty Woman* (1990) to *The Devil Wears Prada* (2006), the glamorous makeover is a well-trodden journey where a female character's development and fulfillment results from her male counterpart's Pygmalion-like creation of the feminine ideal. The fashion montage reflects a common trajectory for the out-of-place female character where shopping transforms a (wonder) woman into the pretty woman.

For female audiences, the transformative promise of the Hollywood makeover trope often extends into a film's licensed merchandise through participation in the shopping economies. As Avi Santo examines in his chapter in this collection, a wide variety of merchandise from T-shirts and blankets to figurines and makeup appeared in brick-and-mortar and online stores to promote the Warner Bros. film. Women and girls of all ages gain access to the iconic superhero in different spaces. Product tie-ins historically have operated as a central marketing strategy for the major studios as generations of kids have carried lunch boxes to school or dressed as their favorite characters.[2] While much attention has been given to the product tie-ins of male-driven franchises like the Marvel Cinematic Universe or Lucasfilm's *Star Wars*, this chapter offers a different perspective on studio merchandising, retail spaces, and audience engagement. I discuss conglomerate Hollywood media franchising practices, using *Star Wars* and *Wonder Woman* merchandising as specific examples of normatively gendered paratextual spaces that traditionally targeted boys and men. In comparison, I consider the mobilization of unconventional retail strategies for two successful female-driven films—Universal's *Fifty Shades of Grey* (2015) and Sony's *Eat Pray Love* (2010)—where the merchandised appeals to girls and women were ingrained into marketing from the beginning. Against the backdrop of a growing postfeminist empowerment industry, I examine the relationships among these media properties, marketing strategies, and retail spaces for gendered franchising and the long tail of distribution.

Through its paratextual function, merchandising creates a meaningful extension of the film's narrative for audiences. Jonathan Gray identifies the role of paratexts—promotional materials, video games, podcasts, merchandise, and so on—as crucial to contemporary media production and consumption. Beyond their monetary value, "paratexts are not simply add-ons, spinoffs, and also-rans: they create texts, they manage them, and they fill them with many of the meanings that we associate with them."[3] Paratexts create a multitude of meanings working to fill gaps for female fan engagement. In the case of recent female-driven studio films, licensed product tie-ins frame audience participation through a postfeminist lens of empowerment consumerism and aspirational transformation.[4] Rosalind Gill identifies postfeminism as a "sensibility"—one that frames individualism, personal choice, and consumerism as the sites of transformation and fulfillment for the contemporary woman.[5] This ideological turn toward regulating the neoliberal self is what Andi Zeisler calls "marketplace feminism," or the selling of postfeminist empowerment to the female consumer.[6] Product tie-ins and merchandising for female-driven films routinely function as paratexts representing not only the gendered nature of media franchising but also postfeminist logic grounded in a particular iteration of marketplace feminism for largely straight, white, cisgendered women.

In this chapter, I am interested in exploring product tie-ins of female-driven films as paratexts and what they reveal about studio marketing practices and imagined fan participation within the space of media retail. I combine on-site observation inside Target, Walmart, and CVS stores located in Metro Detroit and Dallas–Fort Worth (as well as their online retail components) along with trade and popular press analysis through a feminist media industry studies lens.[7] Earlier feminist media studies literature often explores the narrative transformation of female characters in retail spaces within the film narrative through makeovers and shopping. However, I consider how this postfeminist logic extends beyond the screen into the marketing of female-driven films. I offer a paratextual analysis of specific product tie-ins and merchandising strategies in everyday retails spaces—brick-and-mortar stores, broadcast shopping networks, and online sites.

Whether prayer beads or sex toys, product tie-ins and retail marketing campaigns embody an industry investment in marketplace feminism and individual empowerment as aligning the female fan paratextual experience with shopping. Paratexts for recent female-driven films map onto the imperatives of personal growth and empowerment through market feminism. In the process, consumers have the ability to participate in these transformative narratives through retail. In turn, along with the consumer, retail spaces are themselves transformed. Specific gendered product tie-ins structure audience-member experiences through a transformative process of spiritual, emotional, and/or sexual awakening for mostly white female consumers. And it is this transformation, through a postfeminist, neoliberal lens, that in turn reinforces normative views of female audiences as good consumers and their audience value as reflecting what I call aspirational fandom.

The Female Empowerment Marketplace

Hollywood's recent female-driven films share commonalities with the tradition of "chick lit" and "chick flicks"—genres of books and films exploring the struggles and triumphs of the modern single working woman. The plucky protagonists of these stories embody postfeminist narratives of personal agency and individual discipline for achieving idealized love, sex, money, and professional success. Most notably, 1990s heroines Bridget Jones (*Bridget Jones's Diary*) and Carrie Bradshaw (*Sex and the City*) serve as mediated sites for understanding how grounded postfeminist ideals are invested in "economic discourses of aspirational, niche-market Western societies" and largely white heteronormative standards of beauty.[8] In contrast to feminism critiquing power structures in order to imagine wide-scale systemic change, Yvonne Tasker and Diane Negra suggest that "postfeminist culture enacts fantasies of regeneration and transformation that also speak to a desire for change."[9] As this chapter argues, a number of female-driven films are deeply rooted in the postfeminist project to liberate white womanhood through neoliberal consumption.

Significantly, these transformation fantasies mirror a growing feminist discourse that speaks to female professionals in technology, business, creative sectors, and beyond. An empowerment industry has emerged in the United States, selling the power of individualism and the promise of transformation to a new generation of mostly white, upper-class, educated female professionals. An array of books, conferences, podcasts, websites, TED Talks, and professional networks advise women on how to advance in the workplace and find happiness in their professional and personal lives.[10] Two examples best illustrate this path of the empowered female professional as neoliberal consumer. First, Facebook's COO and former Google vice president Sheryl Sandberg's best-selling book *Lean In: Women, Work, and the Will to Lead* (2013) shares professional strategies from her experience working in male-dominated Silicon Valley.[11] By placing the onus on individual female workers to break the barriers holding back career advancement, *Lean In* has been widely criticized as "trickle-down feminism" that ignores larger systemic barriers like industrywide discrimination, wage gaps, and intersectional issues of race, sexuality, and class.[12] Sandberg developed a Lean In industry through local Lean In Circles, speaking engagements, and conferences. Second, in the best-selling self-help memoir *The Happiness Project* (2009), writer Gretchen Rubin creates a month-by-month plan to make changes in all areas of her NYC life from decluttering to parenting. Rubin built a motivational franchise encompassing a series of personal journals, coloring books, mugs, lectures, and a weekly podcast for inspiring fans to make daily life changes.[13]

Lean In and *The Happiness Project* extend into merchandising empires selling an accessible package for circulating their charismatic leaders' post-feminist messages. In promoting female empowerment, women's summits or career guidebooks do offer networking and support communities for women on a large scale. Yet Sandberg and Rubin's you-can-have-it-all personas create motivational franchises deeply rooted in what Andi Zeisler calls "marketplace feminism." Zeisler asserts, "Marketplace feminism prioritizes individuals. The wingwoman of neo-liberalism, marketplace feminism's focus is on casting systemic issues as personal ones and cheerily dispensing commercial fixes for them."[14] These retail spaces sell a specific commercial product—a roadmap to personal or professional change through self-monitoring, improvement, and consumerism that mirrors Hollywood's branded product tie-ins for targeting female audiences.

Female Paratext Spaces in Male-Driven Franchises

Since the 1990s, technological, structural, and economic convergence have transformed Hollywood studio organization and practices—namely, the concentration of ownership and increased investment in licensing intellectual property and cross-media franchises.[15] The major studios have become even more dependent on big-budget media franchises that must extend across multiple conglomerate divisions (film, television, gaming, publishing, music, etc.), with an ever-growing-longer tail of distribution (theatrical, subscription VOD [video on demand], transactional VOD, DVD, television, etc.), and increased the importance of international markets. Individual studios only make around a dozen big-budget projects each year, so the financial and creative stakes are high in an effort to mitigate risk against a failed property release or expansion.[16] Growing prints and advertising (P&A) budgets as well as licensed product tie-ins function as a promotional strategy to offset a studio's financial risk. Significantly, a major strategy for branding and marketing these massive story worlds includes merchandising partnerships. This form of saturated marketing evolved from the era of New Hollywood blockbusters like *Jaws* and *Star Wars*.[17]

By the 2010s, products that advertise the latest tentpole film occupy prime real estate across promotional and retail spaces from fast-food containers and big-box store shelves to magazine shelves and social media campaigns. In an industrial moment when investing in known intellectual properties and expanding distribution windows are vital practices for the major studios, marketing and merchandising efforts offer an illuminating space to explore studio priorities and current tensions surrounding female-driven content and audiences. Female-driven films—or what I define as female-led stories produced by and/or marketed to women—are often discounted as niche or a limited market in relation to the more expensive franchising practice of male-driven action, sci-fi/fantasy, or superhero movies.[18]

A recent cycle of commercially successful female-driven projects—*Mad Max: Fury Road, Twilight, Fifty Shades of Grey*, and more recently, *Wonder Woman* and *Girl's Trip*—directly contradicts traditional studio logic about the viability of female-driven content.[19] Yet old logic persists as strong female theatrical attendance continues to be viewed as an exception or anomaly. An industrywide perception of women as less valuable than other audiences marginalizes female-driven content and fan engagement. Devaluation stems from two central industry myths: (1) women don't go to the movies, and (2) female-led films can't open.[20] And in turn, this lore impacts every process from how films are developed to how they are distributed.[21] Even as theatrical data contradict this narrative—women make up 52 percent of the audience—female moviegoers routinely are underserved by studios who prioritize eighteen- to thirty-four-year-old men.[22]

At times, industry efforts to address female audiences range from misunderstood to highly contentious, as the recent *Star Wars* and *Wonder Woman* conventional marketing approaches illustrate. Months before the highly anticipated

2015 premiere of *Star Wars: Episode VII—The Force Awakens*, frustrated fans took to Twitter, resulting in the hashtag movement #WheresRey. Fans criticized a wave of toys released across brick-and-mortar and online retailers excluding the film's central female character, Rey (Daisy Ridley). Hasbro, who carries the license for official *Star Wars* merchandise, reactively announced months later a new line of products prominently featuring the female protagonist, from figurines to lightsabers, in response to the film's record-breaking opening weekend and fan pushback.[23] Yet the controversy continued into 2016 as Rey was left out of a *Star Wars* Monopoly game due to "insufficient interest"—or what Suzanne Scott identifies as the corporate strategy of paratextual scapegoating.[24] Fans returned to social media to call out the franchise's underserved—and often ignored—female fandom in a cinematic and paratextual universe traditionally imagined for men. As Scott contends, #WheresRey illustrates how "paratexts function to codify gendered franchising discourses, even in the midst of a franchise's attempt to adopt more progressive representational strategies and acknowledge the diversity of its audience."[25] *The Force Awakens* (and the 2017 follow-up *Star Wars: Episode VIII—The Last Jedi*) features a more diverse cast with women and/or characters of color in lead roles, as compared to previous installments. However, only after *The Force Awakens* had proven theatrical bankability and consistent fan pushback did Hasbro "course correct" by releasing an array of Rey toys for *The Last Jedi*.

Largely segregated in the toy aisles of Target or Walmart, female characters' visibility on retail shelves reveals more than Hasbro's history of gendering product tie-ins for major media franchises toward male audiences.[26] The example of Rey calls attention to the systemic and systematic erasure of female paratextual participation and product tie-ins from masculinized cinematic spaces. This is not the first time Hasbro has downplayed or left out major female characters from media franchise toy sets—similar criticisms followed the absence of Gamora (*Guardians of the Galaxy*) and Black Widow (*The Avengers*) from licensed merchandise lines.[27] It is arguable that female characters' absence is more a reflection of a strategically gendered marketing practice than oversight. The message is clear: no girls allowed in these paratextual spaces.

"Pink franchising" is a common industry approach to licensed merchandising for female fandom, particularly for story worlds and brands traditionally represented and marketed by the studios to so-called fanboys. Derek Johnson identifies a similar contradictory logic with the development of the *Star Wars* spin-off franchise HerUniverse, a line of apparel advertised on the official site as "fashion for every fangirl." He asserts, "Entities like Lucasfilm—and its licensed partners in franchising media properties like *Star Wars*—continue to position *Star Wars* and its consumers in relation to normative ideologies of gender and sexuality, even while claiming to empower the lifestyle choices of marginalized consumers."[28]

HerUniverse includes clothing, accessories, and home décor from Marvel, DC Comics, Disney, and *Star Wars* properties and provides space in the paratextual universe for female fans in normatively gendered ways. This strategy to extend the *Star Wars* experience with female-friendly product tie-ins parallels the CoverGirl makeup line released for *The Force Awakens*. Designed by makeup artist Pat McGrath, the limited-edition makeup collections feature dark eye crayons and metallic lipsticks aimed to capture sci-fi industrial glamour. *Allure* magazine published a guide for creating stylized looks with CoverGirl's Star Wars line. The collection's marketing campaign—"Light Side / Dark Side. Which side are you on?"—offered a range of character-inspired looks from the dark apprentice and stormtrooper to Jedi and droid.[29] For example, ten mascara formulas featured "iconic Star Wars quotes," including "There has been an awakening" and "Indeed you are powerful."[30] Significantly, almost every single movie line is spoken by one male character to another in the face of battle or struggle. Removed from the context of the film's narrative and into cosmetic cosplay, each mascara's name reads more as a generic postfeminist mantra bringing strength and transformation with each swipe of the brush over lashes. As Scott suggests, "When merchandise aimed at female fans does appear, these paratexts routinely function as heterosexist attempts to hail them as postfeminist consumer subjects, rather than acknowledging them as a part of the franchise's preexisting fan demographic."[31] Where formerly little space existed for female sites of play, beauty-product paratexts imagine gendered participation as simultaneously connected and disconnected to the *Star Wars* canonical universe.

A shift in the uneven feminized marketing from Rey's early merchandise exclusion to later inclusion by *The Last Jedi* coincides with Warner Bros.' *Wonder Woman* empowerment campaign. On the one hand, in contrast to the findings of Avi Santo's research as detailed in his chapter of this collection, a range of cross-generational apparel, home décor, toys, and so on specifically targeting female fans appeared widely in retail spaces. On the other hand, Diana's image continued to adorn an array of adult beauty and health products from MAC makeup sets to branded razors reflecting a conventional pink franchising approach toward the traditionally male-dominated superhero genre. The array of merchandise featured Wonder Woman from Warner Bros.' DC Extended Universe (DCEU) and the DC comic book version. A handful of licensed health-conscious products appeared that were tied directly to the film's release—namely, Pinkberry, Diet Dr. Pepper, and thinkThin. This contrasts with the broader deals with snack-food companies for other films in the DCEU franchise—*Batman v Superman*'s with General Mills or *Suicide Squad*'s with Doritos.[32] Fans criticized not only the disproportionately small number of corporate partnerships *Wonder Woman* secured versus numerous deals for the male-driven studio films but also the focus on gendered consumer products promoting weight loss.

One highly publicized tie-in was thinkThin, a health-food company marketing protein mixes and bars to women. Special in-store displays of diet bars prominently appeared across U.S. big-box stores in the summer of 2017. In announcing the partnership, thinkThin's president stated, "No one epitomizes the thinkThin lifestyle better than Wonder Woman," and praised the bars for giving women "the everyday strength they need to power through the day."[33] The thinkThin partnership heavily integrated social media participation. The company's Instagram account launched a #thinkWonderWoman campaign encouraging female fans to post selfies holding powerful poses and determined faces with thinkThin bars.

Diana, the epitome of the Amazonian warrior as feminist power, became the face of diet bars. As Rosalind Gill and Christina Scharff assert, "The autonomous, calculating, self-regulating subject of neoliberalism bears a strong resemblance to the active, freely choosing, self-reinventing subject of postfeminism."[34] Similar to the *Star Wars* CoverGirl makeup line, branded diet bars are deeply rooted in the promise of neoliberal consumption offering female empowerment with each calorie-controlled bite. Nowhere is it clearer how female consumption and participation in cinematic and paratextual spaces is controlled and regulated based on postfeminist ideals of individual will and the power of transformation.

In response, thinkThin received a wave of backlash in the press and social media coverage criticizing the diet-bar campaign as tone deaf and body shaming (see figure 8.1). As one *Glamour* magazine writer argues, "We don't need yet another example of young women being told their bodies aren't good enough. On its own, thinkThin may be a fine product. With the princess of Themyscira surrounding it, it feels like a directive."[35] This message of consumer weight loss strikingly contradicts the body shaming Gal Gadot experienced during preproduction. After the 2013 casting announcement of Gadot in the lead role, the Israeli actress came under intense scrutiny for being too thin for the role.[36] In turn, Gadot underwent an intense strength training regime to bulk up for the film, similar to her male superhero counterparts. Press coverage highlighted how this diet and exercise regime transformed Gadot into a more "acceptable" Wonder Woman.

This self-regulation extends into the retail spaces I observed. Instead of being integrated among other diet or supplement bars along the store shelves, the branded thinkThin bars were featured in a stand-alone display positioned in high-traffic areas around the health-food aisle. Adorned in Amazonian armor with sword and shield in hand and positioned for battle, Diana's thin figure fiercely covers the prominent display. In many ways, the thinkThin campaign celebrates the physical strength and commitment to change associated with the journey of both Diana (the character) and Gadot (the actress) as empowering. The directive for fans is clear: think thin (but not too thin) for a better you.

FIG. 8.1 Example of Twitter criticism of think-Thin *Wonder Woman* product tie-ins (screen capture)

As Johnson argues, "While the logics of 'pink' media franchising have increasingly affirmed the participation of girls and women in cultural arenas that more generally privilege men and boys, that participation has been regulated, remade, and reshaped to fit within, more so than trouble, traditional norms of gender, sexuality, age, and race"[37] In these two product examples from *Star Wars* and *Wonder Woman*, female engagement reflects a regulated paratextual experience offering female fans the limited experience of a makeover, whether through cosmetics or weight loss. Franchised merchandising lines steeped in marketplace feminist rhetoric gesture toward gendered barriers and promoting access to masculine franchised cinematic spaces but in conventionally superficial and normative ways.

The Transformative Power of Paratexts

The examples of *Star Wars* and *Wonder Woman* illustrate how targeted merchandising makes a space of cultural engagement for female audiences that industry lore traditionally designates "for" men. In contrast, for genres aimed overtly at women relying on romantic development and self-discovery, Universal's *Fifty Shades of Grey* and Sony's *Eat Pray Love* paratexts offer a different experience of transformation for the female consumer.[38] Both films stem from female-authored source materials, feature female protagonists, and target female demographics. In embodying a postfeminist sensibility of change and transformation, product tie-ins promise an accessible path to empowerment and personal improvement from ordinary, everyday retail spaces—brick-and-mortar stores, online sites, and broadcast shopping networks.[39]

In 2012, Universal Pictures entered a bidding war to option the best-selling erotica book series *Fifty Shades of Grey* by E. L. James that originally began as *Twilight* fan fiction, minus the vampires.[40] The trilogy follows inexperienced Seattle college graduate Anastasia Steele's romantic entanglement with tortured billionaire businessman Christian Grey. The so-called ladyporn books are known for sex scenes detailing the couple's BDSM (bondage, discipline, sadism, masochism) and dominant-submissive relationship. Starring Jamie Dornan and Dakota Johnson, Universal and its sibling company Focus Features gave the film a targeted 2015 Valentine's Day release date. Despite middling critical reviews, the first film installment became the studio's fourth-biggest theatrical opening weekend in a year, with strong box-office performances by female-driven releases *Trainwreck*, *Mad Max: Fury Road*, and *Pitch Perfect 2*.

In an audience study of *Fifty Shades*, Melissa A. Click explores the books' popularity with female fans. Framed within a postfeminist context, she argues the trilogy's "appeal is rooted in women's use of the series' recurrent themes of fantasy, romance, and sex to make sense of the sexualized cultural environment in which they are immersed."[41] Specifically, Click observed in her discussions with readers, many twenty- to thirtysomething, white, and single, how the books became a way to reflect upon their own sexual and relationship experiences. The allure of *Fifty Shades* was more than sex. Female readers engaged with the process of seduction and romance, which I suggest parallels Universal's marketing and merchandising strategy.

The marketing campaign around *Fifty Shades* framed the film as romantic coupling through erotica, whereas merchandising focused on the exploration of pleasure for female fans. Official licensing ranged from *Fifty Shades*–branded wines to deals with Audi, Calvin Klein, and Revlon.[42] Many of these partnerships integrate romantic seduction with Grey's luxury lifestyle into the paratextual experience, particularly as sexual experimentation drives Ana's maturation, confidence, and eventual wedded coupling with Christian. On one end, the Vermont Teddy Bear Company features the official *Fifty Shades of Grey* bear in a suit holding handcuffs and a blindfold. Including candy and adult-sized blindfolds, the online retailer describes the bear's "smoldering eyes, gray suit, satin tie, mask and handcuffs. She can't help but submit to loving him."[43] The company's popular "Bear-grams" are available for celebrating birthdays, holidays, and other special occasions. In promoting the Universal property, the *Fifty Shades* bear distinctively stands out as a departure from the company's brand selling whimsical gifts.

On another end, the British online retailer Lovehoney began manufacturing and selling a line of *Fifty Shades of Grey* sex toys known as the Official Pleasure Collection in 2012. As part of the marketing campaign leading up to the film's 2015 release, Target began to carry items from this collection in their online and physical stores. In contrast to Lovehoney's extensive licensed sextoy line available directly through their site based on the book series, Target only sold a handful of offerings—"Yours and Mine" blindfolds, "vibrating love rings," lubricant, and massage oils. Target discretely located the line of branded products in the sexual health area despite the retailer having carried vibrators advertised as "personal massagers or vibes" since 2012.[44]

When Target began stocking *Fifty Shades* products leading up to the film's 2015 theatrical release, the news went viral. For example, one image of the pleasure collection from an Oklahoma Target store mocked the display of the sex toys next to children's toothbrushes and circulated widely on Twitter. In response to an *Entertainment Weekly* inquiry, the company explained the intended retail strategy for this product line: "We directed stores to place the display on a back cap (which means the back of an aisle, not the main aisle facing part) in the adult health area of the store."[45] The reality of Target's efforts to integrate the *Fifty Shades* collection into their conventional health retail space illustrates the challenges of broader corporate communication and retail consistency across the more than 1,800 U.S. brick-and-mortar locations. It also suggests how movie merchandising offering a departure from normative female consumption seems to disrupt retailing boundaries of the "family-friendly" big-box store. Female fandom as coupled role-playing and submission is then available with the click of an online purchase or a trip to the neighborhood Target. Whether branded wine or sex toys, *Fifty Shades* products offer access to an extraordinary paratextual engagement within an ordinary marketplace that often defies conventional retail strategies. What results is a transformation in the relationships among female fan engagement, retailers, and licensed merchandising for female-driven films by creating new spaces for fantasy and pleasure.

Based on the 2006 best-selling memoir, *Eat Pray Love* offers a different experience of personal awakening and self-discovery. The story follows Elizabeth Gilbert as she leaves an unhappy marriage and spends a year traveling to Italy, India, and Indonesia on a journey of middle-aged self-discovery. In the 2010 Sony film, Julia Roberts portrays the author as she enjoys pasta and language lessons in Italy, works and meditates in an Indian ashram, and helps a local community and falls in love in Indonesia. The transnational voyage parallels her postdivorce personal struggles, where Roberts's Gilbert works to let go of the past. The book's success launched the author as a sought-after inspirational speaker with lucrative licensed merchandising deals.

In anticipation of the film's August release, Sony partnered with the Home Shopping Network (HSN). Described as a "complete take over" of the broadcast shopping channel, seventy-two hours of exclusive programming targeted HSN's thirty- to fifty-year-old middle- to upper-middle-class demographic. Sony negotiated 10 to 15 percent of sales from products that incorporated the *Eat Pray Love* brand, reportedly a departure from conventional studio marketing.[46] With each day dedicated to selling products from one of the three countries in *Eat Pray Love*, viewers could purchase a professional-style pasta maker to recreate the film's prominent Italian cuisine or $350 prayer beads similar to the ones Gilbert carries in India during her meditation practice.[47]

Founded in 1982 and bought by competitor QVC in 2017, HSN is a broadcast network selling consumer products and lifestyle brands from its headquarters in St. Petersburg, Florida. The cable network features a variety of home goods, health and beauty products, clothing, and jewelry sold by a cast of regular hosts. Broadcast as timed segments, specific themed products or merchandising lines flow from one into another throughout the twenty-four-hour programming schedule. HSN relies on creating an event, a specific retail experience where the jewelry, clothing, or home goods are only available for a limited time. Reminiscent of an infomercial, the network's hosts create a sense of urgency through their sales presentation ("time is running out" or "only a limited number available"), which is accentuated by on-screen graphics of a timer counting down the end of the product presentation and number of remaining items left. Consumers place orders with an HSN representative by phone or online, whereas a few callers are given the opportunity each segment to speak directly with the hosts live on-air.

HSN's chief executive called the weekend of *Eat Pray Love* a "wrap-around experience" and "immersive event."[48] The network interspersed film footage into the segments to seamlessly promote the upcoming theatrical release and the paratextual products. During the India-themed broadcast, an organic cotton T-shirt adorned with "Search for Everything" and a large lotus flower was available for $34.90. The product description on HSN's website read, "What are you looking for? Wherever your quest takes you, get there in comfort and style." Related to the traces of Buddhist philosophy scattered throughout Gilbert's story, the lotus flower is a symbol of renewal and rebirth. A common thread runs through many of these products targeted at the network's disproportionately female audience, one of a cleansing and transformative spiritual journey, particularly as loosely connected to Western white women's fascination with Eastern philosophy and religious practices.

In her discussion of Hollywood travel romances like *Eat Pray Love* and *Under the Tuscan Sun*, Kendra Marston suggests that international travel for both films' middle-aged female protagonists "operate[s] as empowering, affective extensions of the melancholic white self, with the pseudosymbiotic fusion of person and places allowing for a philosophical and spiritual 'transcendence' over neoliberal feminism's consumer capitalist logic."[49] Roberts's Gilbert aims to transcend this logic through her cinematic journey by leaving behind material, consumerist trappings and the confining demands of professional and domestic labor. Yet the film's paratexts commodify and reify female personal growth within a consumer marketplace disguised as aspirational empowerment.

Paratexts for *Eat Pray Love* and *Fifty Shades of Grey* share a common entry point for female fan engagement employing the spiritual, emotional, and/or sexually transformative experiences of the protagonists. Yet there is a disconnect across these paratextual experiences between these tangible products and their intangible promise of individual transformation. Jia Tolentino points to branded corporate feminism, as "this version of empowerment can be actively disempowering: It's a series of objects and experiences you can purchase while the conditions determining who can access and accumulate power stay the same."[50] First, across the array of licensed merchandise, who is the desirable female audience and who is left out? Women of color are routinely invisible or marginalized from these paratextual spaces. Upwardly mobile, white female professionals with the luxury of time and disposable income serve as the imagined fandom. Supposedly accessible across everyday retail spaces, empowerment consumption often preferences cisgendered straight white, Western women and, in turn, Hollywood's imagined version of the "desirable" female consumer. Second, what exactly is promised in this exchange is also significant. Marketplace feminism operates on not only the economic value of a good or service but also the symbolic value of transformation for discovering the aspirational self. As Gill and Scharff contend, "To a much greater extent than men, women are regulated to work on and transform the self, to regulate every aspect of their conduct, and to present all their actions as freely chosen. Could it be that neoliberalism is always already gendered, and that women are constructed as its ideal subject?"[51]

Through Ana and Elizabeth's journeys, this process of commodification sells a dream of the idealized self as the good-girl neoliberal consumer with free market choice. In reality, this form of female fandom as endless self-improvement spills gendered work into everyday spaces from the office to shopping aisles. Even inside women's fantasy spaces, there is still work to be done.

Conclusion

Conglomerate Hollywood's relationship to female-driven content reflects a larger conflicting perception of female audiences and their participation in a moment when the industry is openly struggling with gender equity and sexist work cultures from the development process to the writer's room.[52] Even as Ava DuVernay becomes the third woman—and notably, first African American woman—to direct a feature budgeted more than $100 million with Disney's *A Wrinkle in Time* (2018), long-held industry lore still associates female-driven films with economic risk and niche audiences.[53] Driven by an increased dependence on intellectual property and convergence practices, Hollywood studios rely heavily on product tie-ins and licensed merchandising to maximize ever-increasing distribution windows. As a female studio screenwriter told me in an interview, "Marketing is so expensive. Your average movie's marketing budget is between $30 and $50 million. So you're talking a huge amount of money,

[and] they want all the marketing shortcuts they can get . . . we have increasing amounts of content. To break through the noise, you have to be everywhere."[54]

Production budgets for female-driven projects are comparatively smaller, with scaled-down marketing resources relative to larger male-driven tentpoles. To "break through the noise" with female-driven content and audiences, studios still rely on conventional notions of female fan engagement wrapped in the flimsy paper packaging of postfeminist empowerment.

Product tie-ins from *Wonder Woman* diet bars in Target to *Eat Pray Love* prayer scarves on HSN represent a journey for the female fan—a path for improving her body, her relationship, and her spiritual growth. In many ways, Hollywood feminized paratexts mirror conventional character development in the romantic comedy and makeover film—where women seek transformative love, success, and fulfillment in under two hours—with the empowerment promised by marketplace feminism. As Johnson describes pink media franchising, "Postfeminism finds significant tools for commodifying new forms and marketplaces of consumer identity, while using those identities to mark what culture is 'right' or 'wrong' for whom."[55] For the female neoliberal consumer, the line between work and leisure is always already blurred.[56] Even in feminized spaces of fantasy and pleasure, women are still expected to invest their time and labor inward toward self-improvement and self-regulation. These sensibilities continue to embody how the major studios value and target female fans as acceptable consumers through their paratextual experience. And the transformative experience of buying female-targeted merchandise is an illustrative site for examining how female fan participation and retail spaces are simultaneously being reimagined.

As Hollywood's partnerships with retailers expand to reflect shifts in developing and releasing female-driven content, it will be vital to interrogate how the relationship between studio production and distribution cultures and licensed merchandising continue to shape female paratextual experiences beyond traditional exhibition spaces. Examining merchandising campaigns within a variety of retail spaces allows us to complicate the path from production to circulation as nonlinear and geographically decentralized. Utilizing a feminist lens to study media industry practices offers an opportunity to rethink scholarly conversations where studio practices, retail environments, and audience work intersect along gendered lines.

Notes

1 Ashley Elaine York, "From Chick Flicks to Millennial Blockbusters: Spinning Female-Driven Narratives into Franchises," *Journal of Popular Culture* 43, no. 1 (2010): 3–25; Suzanne Ferriss, "Fashioning Femininity in the Makeover Flick," in *Chick Flicks: Contemporary Women at the Movies*, eds. Suzanne Ferriss and Mallory Young (New York: Routledge, 2008), 41–57.

2 Jonathan Gray, *Show Sold Separately: Promos, Spoilers, and Other Media Paratexts* (New York: New York University Press, 2010); Avi Santo, "Batman versus the Green Hornet: The Merchandisable TV Text and the Paradox of Licensing in the Classical Network Era," *Cinema Journal* 49, no. 2 (Winter 2010): 63–85.

3 Gray, *Show Sold Separately*, 6.

4 Angela McRobbie, "Post-Feminism and Popular Culture," *Feminist Media Studies* 4, no. 3 (2004): 255–264; Yvonne Tasker and Diane Negra, "Introduction: Feminist Politics and Postfeminist Culture," in *Interrogating Postfeminism: Gender and the Politics of Popular Culture*, eds. Yvonne Tasker and Diane Negra (Durham, N.C.: Duke University Press, 2007), 1–26.

5 Rosalind Gill, "Postfeminist Media Culture: Elements of a Sensibility," *European Journal of Cultural Studies* 10, no. 2 (2007): 147–166.

6 Andi Zeisler, *We Were Feminists Once: From Riot Grrrl to CoverGirl®, the Buying and Selling of a Political Movement* (New York: PublicAffairs, 2016).

7 Timothy Havens, Amanda D. Lotz, and Serra Tinic, "Critical Media Industry Studies: A Research Approach," *Communication, Culture and Critique* 2 (2009): 234–253.

8 Havens, Lotz, and Tinic, "Critical Media Industry," 7.

9 Tasker and Negra, "Introduction," 22.

10 Sheelah Kolhatkar, "The Feel-Good Female Solidarity Machine," *Bloomberg*, 4 Feb. 2016, https://www.bloomberg.com/features/2016-feel-good-female-solidarity -machine/.

11 Sheryl Sandberg, *Lean In: Women, Work, and the Will to Lead* (New York: Alfred A. Knopf, 2016).

12 Elaine Blair, "Anne-Marie Slaughter's Unfinished Business," *New York Times*, 23 Sept. 2015, https://www.nytimes.com/2015/09/27/books/review/anne-marie -slaughters-unfinished-business-women-men-work-family.html.

13 Gretchen Rubin, *The Happiness Project* (New York: HarperCollins, 2009); Gretchen Rubin, *Happier at Home* (New York: Crown Archetype, 2012).

14 Zeisler, *We Were Feminists*, 255.

15 Henry Jenkins, *Convergence Culture: Where Old and New Media Collide* (New York: New York University Press, 2006); Jennifer Holt, *Empires of Entertainment: Media Industries and the Politics of Deregulation, 1980–1996* (New Brunswick, N.J.: Rutgers University Press, 2011).

16 Tino Balio, *Hollywood in the New Millennium* (London: BFI Press, 2013); Courtney Brannon Donoghue, *Localising Hollywood* (London: BFI Press, 2017); Derek Johnson, *Media Franchising: Creative License and Collaboration in the Culture Industries* (New York: New York University Press, 2013).

17 Thomas Schatz, "The New Hollywood," in *Film Theory Goes to the Movies*, eds. Jim Collins, Hilary Radner, and Ava Preacher Collins (New York: Routledge, 1993), 8–36; Justin Wyatt, *High Concept: Movies and Marketing in Hollywood* (Austin: University of Texas Press, 1994).

18 Diane Negra, "Quality Postfeminism? Sex and the Single Girl on HBO," *Genders* 39 (2004), https://www.atria.nl/ezines/IAV_606661/IAV_606661_2010_52/ g39_negra.html; Diane Negra, "Failing Women: Hollywood and Its Chick Flick Audience," *Velvet Light Trap* 64 (Fall 2009): 91–92.

19 Bob Mondello, "This Year, Women (and Girls) Rule the Big Screen," *All Things Considered*, 8 June 2015, https://www.npr.org/2015/06/08/412919488/this-year -women-and-girls-rule-the-big-screen; Breeanna Hare, "Yes, Hollywood, Women

Do Go to Movies," *CNN Entertainment*, 4 Dec. 2009, http://www.cnn.com/2009/SHOWBIZ/Movies/12/04/women.audience.box.office/.

20 Hare, "Yes, Hollywood"; Rachel Montpelier, "MPAA Report 2016: 52% of Movie Audiences Are Women and Other Takeaways," *Women and Hollywood*, 24 Mar. 2016, https://blog.womenandhollywood.com/mpaa-report-2016-52-of-movie-audiences-are-women-other-takeaways-12320da989b4; Lindy West, "Most Moviegoers Are Women, Even Though Movies Treat Women like Garbage," *Jezebel*, 26 Mar. 2014, https://jezebel.com/most-moviegoers-are-women-even-though-movies-treat-wom-1552165358; Hermione Hoby, "*Wonder Woman* Director Patty Jenkins: 'People Really Thought That Only Men Loved Action Movies,'" *Guardian*, 26 May 2017, https://www.theguardian.com/film/2017/may/26/wonder-woman-director-patty-jenkins-people-really-thought-that-only-men-loved-action-movies.

21 Ricardo Lopez, "Despite Dollars in Diversity, Hollywood Still Averse to Making Inclusive Films," *Variety*, 2017, http://variety.com/2017/film/news/diversity-box-office-winners-hollywood-1202603438/; Manohla Dargis, "Women in the Seats but Not behind the Camera," *New York Times*, 10 Dec. 2009, http://www.nytimes.com/2009/12/13/movies/13dargis.html.

22 Melissa Silverstein, "MPAA Data Shows That Women Are Still the Majority of Moviegoers," *IndieWire*, 26 Mar. 2014, http://www.indiewire.com/2014/03/mpaa-data-shows-that-women-are-still-the-majority-of-moviegoers-207223/; Montpelier, "MPAA Report"; Steven Zeitchik, "Hollywood's Box-Office Woes: Is the Industry Aiming Too Narrowly at Men?," *Los Angeles Times*, 18 July 2017, http://www.latimes.com/entertainment/movies/la-et-mn-box-office-women-20170718-story,amp.html.

23 Suzanne Scott, "#Wheresrey?: Toys, Spoilers, and the Gender Politics of Franchise Paratexts," *Critical Studies in Media Communication* 34, no. 2 (2017): 138–147; Caroline Framke, "#WheresRey and the Big *Star Wars* Toy Controversy, Explained," *Vox*, 9 Jan. 2016, https://www.vox.com/2016/1/7/10726296/wheres-rey-star-wars-monopoly; Leah Libresco, "#WheresRey? The *Star Wars* Heroine Is Featured in Fewer Toys Than All the New Dudes," *FiveThirtyEight*, 11 Jan. 2016, https://fivethirtyeight.com/features/wheresrey-the-star-wars-heroine-is-featured-in-fewer-toys-than-all-the-new-dudes/.

24 Hoai-Tran Bui, "Despite Promises, Rey Will Be Left Out of *Star Wars* Monopoly Due to 'Insufficient Interest,'" *SlashFilm*, 13 July 2017, http://www.slashfilm.com/despite-promises-rey-will-be-left-out-of-star-wars-monopoly-due-to-insufficient-interest/.

25 Scott, "#Wheresrey?," 139.

26 Derek Johnson, "May the Force Be with Katie: Pink Media Franchising and the Postfeminist Politics of HerUniverse," *Feminist Media Studies* 14, no. 6 (2014): 895–911.

27 Clare O'Connor, "After Outcry, Disney Launches New Rey Toys for *Star Wars* Fans," *Forbes*, 12 Jan. 2016, https://www.forbes.com/sites/clareoconnor/2016/01/12/after-outcry-disney-launches-new-rey-toys-for-star-wars-fans/#60d808887927; Gavia Baker-Whitelaw, "Why Is Gamora Missing from *Guardians of the Galaxy* Merchandise?," *Daily Dot*, 6 Apr. 2014, https://www.dailydot.com/parsec/fans-notice-lack-of-gamora-merchandise/; Donna Dickens, "Disney Unveils *Age of Ultron* Merchandise, Black Widow Conspicuously Absent," *Uproxx*, 20 Apr. 2015, http://uproxx.com/hitfix/disney-excludes-black-widow-from-age-of-ultron-merchandise/.

28 Johnson, "May the Force," 896.
29 Bahar Niramwalla, "CoverGirl *Star Wars* Limited Edition Makeup Collection Looks," *Beauty Desk*, 10 Sept. 2015, http://beautydesk.com/covergirl-star-wars -makeup-collection-looks/.
30 Sophia Panych, "Exclusive: See the Entire CoverGirl x *Star Wars* Collection!," *Allure*, 12 Aug. 2015, https://www.allure.com/gallery/covergirl-star-wars-collection.
31 Scott, "#Wheresrey?," 142.
32 Sabrina Rojas Weiss, "*Wonder Woman* Is Not Getting the Sort of Love (or Budget) That It Deserves," *Refinery 29*, 6 May 2017, http://www.refinery29.com/2017/05/ 153283/wonder-woman-product-tie-in-thinkthin.
33 Rebekah Marcarelli, "ThinkThin Partners with Warner Bros. Pictures *Wonder Woman*," *Winsight Grocery Business*, 25 Apr. 2017, http://www.groceryheadquarters .com/Whats-New/ThinkThin-Partners-with-Warner-Bros-Pictures-Wonder -Woman/; "Women's Most Desired Super Powers Revealed in thinkThin® National Survey," *PR Newswire*, 27 Apr. 2017, https://www.prnewswire.com/news-releases/ womens-most-desired-super-powers-revealed-in-thinkthin-national-survey -300446935.html.
34 Rosalind Gill and Christina Scharff, introduction to *New Femininities*, eds. Rosalind Gill and Christina Scharff (London: Palgrave Macmillan, 2011), 7.
35 Leah Cornish, "Apparently *Wonder Woman* Wants You to 'Think Thin,'" *Glamour*, 4 May 2017, https://www.glamour.com/story/wonder-woman-think-thin; Jenavieve Hatch, "*Wonder Woman* Partnered with Think Thin in Tone-Deaf Branding Move," *Huffington Post*, 5 May 2017, https://www.hufingtonpost.com/ entry/wonder-woman-partnered-with-think-thin-in-tone-deaf-branding-move_us _590c7de4e4b0104c734e3c26.
36 Julie Miller, "*Wonder Woman* Actress Gal Gadot Responds to 'Too-Skinny' Criticism," *Vanity Fair*, 26 Dec. 2013, https://www.vanityfair.com/hollywood/2013/12/ gal-gadot-wonder-woman-skinny-criticism.
37 Johnson, "May the Force," 907.
38 The 2015 *Fifty Shades of Grey* film is part of a three-part series based on the books including *Fifty Shades Darker* (2017) and *Fifty Shades Freed* (2018). My discussion focuses on the first film's theatrical release and merchandising.
39 Gill, "Postfeminist Media Culture," 149.
40 Julie Bosman, "Universal Acquires Movie Rights to Trilogy of Erotic Novels," *New York Times*, 26 Mar. 2012, https://mediadecoder.blogs.nytimes.com/2012/03/26/ universal-acquires-movie-rights-to-trilogy-of-erotic-novels/.
41 Melissa A. Click, "*Fifty Shades* of Postfeminism: Contextualizing Readers' Reflections on the Erotic Romance Series," in *Cupcakes, Pinterest, and Ladyporn: Feminized Popular Culture in the Early Twenty-First Century*, ed. Elana Levine (Chicago: University of Illinois Press, 2015), 17.
42 Marc Graser, "*Fifty Shades of Grey* Wasn't Too Spicy for Audi Partnership," *Variety*, 10 Apr. 2015, http://variety.com/2015/film/news/fifty-shades-of-grey-audi -1201468646/.
43 "'15' Fifty Shades of Grey Bear," *Vermont Teddy Bear Company*, 2017, https://www .vermontteddybear.com/15-fifty-shades-of-grey-bear.
44 Although big-box discount stores long carried lubricants and birth control, by 2012, Target, CVS, Walgreens, Kroger, and other nationwide chains had all expanded their sexual-health product offerings; Sharon Jayson, "Many Chain Stores Now Add a Toy Aisle for Adults," *USA Today*, 30 May 2012, https://usatoday30.usatoday

.com/news/health/wellness/story/2012-05-29/vibrators-and-sex-toys-sales/
55289424/1.

45 James Hibberd, "*Fifty Shades* Sex Toys Hit Target," *Entertainment Weekly*, 5 Feb.
2015, http://www.ew.com/article/2015/02/05/fifty-shades-sex-toys-now-target/.

46 Lauren Streib, "*Eat Pray Love*: How Much Did It Make?," *Daily Beast*, 16 Aug.
2010, https://www.thedailybeast.com/eat-pray-love-how-much-did-it-make.

47 Marc Graser, "How HSN Is Helping Hollywood Sell Its Movies," *Variety*, 6 July
2010, http://variety.com/2010/film/news/how-hsn-is-helping-hollywood-sell-its
-movies-1118021377/.

48 Jeannine Stein, "Eat, Pray, Love—and Shop," *Los Angeles Times*, 15 Aug. 2010,
http://articles.latimes.com/2010/aug/15/image/la-ig-eatpraylove-20100815.

49 Kendra Marston, "The World Is Her Oyster: Negotiating Contemporary White
Womanhood in Hollywood's Tourist Spaces," *Cinema Journal* 55, no. 4 (Summer
2016): 26.

50 Jia Tolentino, "How 'Empowerment' Became Something for Women to Buy," *New
York Times*, 12 Apr. 2016, https://www.nytimes.com/2016/04/17/magazine/how
-empowerment-became-something-for-women-to-buy.html?_r=0.

51 Gill and Scharff, introduction, 7.

52 Cara Buckley, "Powerful Hollywood Women Unveil Anti-harassment Action Plan,"
New York Times, 1 Jan. 2018, https://www.nytimes.com/2018/01/01/movies/times
-up-hollywood-women-sexual-harassment.html?_r=0.

53 Katy Chevigny, "Can She Pull It Off? (or, How to Hire Women Directors)," *Filmmaker Magazine*, 17 Feb. 2016, http://filmmakermagazine.com/97378-can-she-pull
-it-off-or-how-to-hire-women-directors/#.WniJGpM-e9s.

54 Female studio screenwriter, phone interview by author, 2 Aug. 2017.

55 Johnson, "May the Force," 908.

56 Tasker and Negra, "Introduction," 3.

9

Female Treble

● ●

Gender, Record Retail, and a
Play for Space

TIM J. ANDERSON

> It's that place where your dreams meet the
> listener. That's where the final connection
> was made. That audience you dreamt of is
> walking through the door right now, and
> you can stand there and watch that hap-
> pen. There are your listeners. You know,
> the place also served as a kind of a lost
> boys club. So if you were a young musi-
> cian and you came into town and you
> didn't know what to do, the first thing
> you did was you went to Tower Records.
> —Bruce Springsteen

The popular music industry is rife with masculine myths that extend across
genres into the most pedestrian realms of North American retail, privileging the identities and tastes of men in the "dream" space of music shopping.
This essay draws upon evidence in both trade and general periodical literature to both make that case and underscore numerous attempts to connect

alternatively to female consumers. Those recent experiments to make record retail spaces more attractive to female shoppers rewrite narratives about what it means to be included in music fandom and reshape the public formation of cultural standards and canons. Indeed, music is a social act, and to take music seriously means that we must address its consumption. Just as modes of production and performance affect musical meanings, the mode through which music is received is fundamental to understanding its social position and perception—and retail is a significant site for that initial reception. A record producer's imagination of audiences and audiences' imaginations of those musicians on the record are essential elements in the communicative act of recording, no matter how asynchronic the contact between music, musician, and audiences may be. Just as social are the multiple logistical maneuvers necessary to place a record in front of a listener. Indeed, Will Straw argues that the examination of the material cultures and practices surrounding music allows researchers "to examine the material supports which enable music to assume its social and cultural existence."[1] As one of these material supports, music retail is always a significant site for analysis for cultural material arrangements designed to influence both exchange and important moments of reception.

To investigate the material support of retail and the way that it creates a social context for gendering the strategies and practices of buying music, this chapter will examine three interrelated phenomena. First, it will examine the construction of the mythologized record store as a space of masculine privilege and toxicity. Second, it will discuss the negotiated participation of women in this retail context. Finally, it will explore the construction of alternative spaces of retail consumption for women based on different social values and practices. Altogether, the chapter reveals music retail as a powerful but also dynamic force in the material construction of music's social and cultural existence.

Masculinized Retail

In a career built on creating and cultivating myths of American masculinity, Springsteen's quote about the Tower Records retail space as a kind of "lost boys club" should not be overlooked: in the annals of record retail, there is no more important chain in U.S. history than Tower Records. Discussing how he and his bandmates imagined the long-ago-folded-yet-still-famous Tower store on Los Angeles's Sunset Strip as a special destination, Springsteen explains in *All Things Must Pass*, Colin Hanks's 2015 documentary about the rise and fall of the retail chain, that visiting the store in the 1970s was a special thrill. Tower Records had not yet made their East Coast expansion, yet the vast holdings of each Tower store had become legendary to musicians and record collectors throughout the United States. "There was the thrill of being surrounded by music—80 percent of it is a complete mystery to you," Springsteen explains.

Sir Elton John claims in the same film that "without any exaggeration, I spent more money in Tower Records than any other human being." The store with its vast collection was John's "music center": "Tower Records had everything. Those people knew their stuff. They were really on their ball. I mean, they just weren't employees and they happened to work at music stores. They were devoted to music, and that's what I loved about the Tower. I talk about music with them. They could say, 'Hey, have you heard this?' And, eh, it was, it was just like they were like friends. I knew the guys in the store pretty well because I was so, you know, a regular."

For many aspiring musicians, working at Tower Records was a dream job. As Dave Grohl of Foo Fighters and Nirvana fame put it, "I love music, and I only wanted to work at Tower Records and be surrounded by these cool people and all this cool music. I just, I just imagine that everybody that worked at Tower was an aficionado."

As devoted as these stars were, Tower and other records stores were resolutely masculine. As Dave Grohl noted, "Every music store, whether it was a place to go buy drum sticks or a place to go buy records, [included] total snobs." This snobbery supported a darker, more chauvinistic atmosphere where young men were allowed to never grow up. In Tower's case, this was encouraged by the store's owner and founder, Russ Solomon, who maintained "a music environment" that did not enforce any dress code.[2] Tower institutionalized a kind of Peter Pandom of "dress styles, language styles, words and music." As Solomon remembers, "It was the most natural thing in the world that the people behind the counter should look like the people who are on the other side buying."[3] Indeed, Hanks's documentary highlights the retailer's purposeful continual pubescence while underscoring the retailer's culture of chauvinist arrogance in imagining the people on the other side of the counter as men. In one praise-filled review of the documentary appearing in *Jezebel*, a blog dedicated to understanding popular culture aimed at women readers, Julianne Escobedo Shepherd notes that she thought the film was "great" and recommended it as it underscored how Tower nurtured "the snooty, condescending-to-women, male record store clerk."[4] Escobedo Shepherd points out that this is corroborated in the documentary by Heidi Colter, one of Tower's first female employees. Applying for a job in the early 1960s at Tower's Sacramento record store on Watt Avenue, Colter was told by a manager that they "weren't hiring girls that year because they'd already had one and she hadn't worked out." Instead, she took a position at Tower's adjacent bookstore, which hired her and a few other women. Colter eventually advanced to become the vice president of operations at Tower Books, but her comments and those of others in the documentary validate "the snotty record store dude trope," where young men dominate the retail space through condescension and the prioritization of collectors, who almost always were men.[5]

One of the reasons that Escobedo Shepherd's review is particularly sensitive to this issue is that she had spent years working as both a record-store clerk and music critic where she sensed that many of these "lost boys" tended to cling to a "territorial and almost paranoid ownership over music knowledge." While Escobedo Shepherd's male coworkers treated her well, her male customers nevertheless continually questioned her knowledge. Another one of Escobedo Shepherd's female colleagues had worked at a record store where she often recounted "all the various and familiar ways she was accosted or condescended to by male customers." Escobedo Shepherd's colleague noted that these ranged from being dismissed by men who believed that "she didn't know the records she was selling" to being hit on while trapped behind the register.[6] Even as record stores such as Tower's have shuttered by the thousands, a toxic masculine record-store culture remains. For example, in a 2017 blog post, Chicago-based writer Lorena Cupcake interviewed "a cross section of folks in Chicago's vinyl community" and emerged with a variety of generic "horror stories." First and foremost was "sexism among the shelves." From men who ignore or talk down to their girlfriends when in the store to ignoring female clerks, male customers consistently took liberties that female customers never did. One anonymous source that had worked at stores since the 1990s noted that "there's a lot of harassment for female or female-read employees, for sure. Not different from any other retail environment, really, but it can be so intense in record stores because of the fetishization/minimization of women who know about music."[7]

Women in public, both as professionals and consumers, are routinely subjected to being hit upon, harassed, and threatened. Just like men, women consume music, and it would only make sense that building a market free of sexism would be financially beneficial. However, many record retailers have often seen this atmosphere as a necessary element because of a chicken-or-the-egg dilemma, unwittingly generating and currying sexist behavior because of the persistent imagination of their consumer base as unrelentingly male. For many, this image of the record store as a space dominated by men motivated to search madly for sonic obscurities and that-which-was-once-considered-trash-that-has-transformed-into treasure is best depicted in Nick Hornby's novel, *High Fidelity*. Throughout the novel, protagonist Rob Fleming runs his independent record store with two other male employees and confesses that his shop has always been dependent on a special form of clientele, the young male collector: "I get by because of the people who make a special effort to shop here Saturdays—young men, always young men, with John Lennon specs and leather jackets and armfuls of square carrier bags—and because of the mail order: I advertise in the back of glossy rock magazines, and letters from young men, always young men, in Manchester and Glasgow and Ottawa, young men who seem to spend a disproportionate amount of their time looking for deleted Smiths singles and 'ORIGINAL NOT RE-RELEASED' underlined Frank Zappa albums. They're as close to being mad as makes no difference."[8]

Historical data have often reproduced this male record-collector stereotype. For example, a 1985 survey about the record-purchasing power of twenty-four- to thirty-five-year-old "yuppies" revealed that 40 percent of record buyers were women. However, once the demographic reached an over-thirty-five threshold, nearly 70 percent of the survey's respondents were men.[9] Twelve years later, a 1997 study by Strategic Record Research of ten thousand consumers clarified that men and women bought records in different spaces. As the study showed, "the largest percentage of males [shopped at] Tower (61.9% men, 38.1% women), while the leading music merchant for women [was] Target (70.2% women, 29.8% men)."[10] And in 2016, the *Guardian* surveyed You-Gov data on vinyl record purchases and observed numerous stores in Britain to conclude that "lonely, middle-aged men love vinyl."[11]

Female Music Consumers

Nevertheless, none of these claims prove that women do not consume equivalent if not greater amounts of recorded music. By contrast, in 1997, the then-VP of market research for Sony Music Distribution, Linda Ury Greenberg, suggested that while the initial sale of CDs in the early to mid-1980s was driven by males, as the decade progressed, "women became more comfortable with [the new format], and the numbers evened out." Greenberg underscored that "the proportional increase in female music purchasers [corresponded] to the growth in country music, which appeals to many women."[12] While the genre of country music may be more accommodating for women buyers, in some cases a substantial difference in format saw women occasionally overtake their male counterparts in terms of consumption. In 2014, *Buzzfeed* cited research to report that 53 percent of those legally downloading music and 52 percent of those purchasing CDs were women.[13]

These differences remind us that there is no reason that the consumption of recorded music should be so stridently gendered as masculine. Indeed, what is intrinsic to records and other media goods such as films, television shows, and more is that they are "experiential goods" that can never be completely commoditized and cannot be fully determined until the moment they are experienced/used. Production, reproduction, distribution, storage, authentication, and purchase can all contribute to a record's differentiation across its lifespan, each substantially affecting its received valuation. Used records with specific markings of provenance can and often do trump issues of fidelity and convenience in the marketplace. Experiential goods also rely on forms of publicity that expose potential consumers to a variety of experiences that enable their exchange and consumption. To provide fans a taste of the good, recorded music appears in radio playlists, film soundtracks, video games, and so on, while records are also placed in front of critics, both formally and informally, to generate word-of-mouth comments that spread throughout select social networks. Because social networks are fundamental to the marketplace success of every media good produced, issues of race, class, and gender are often determinant forces in how the composition of the record will be produced, distributed, and consumed. This is particularly evident surrounding the issues of genre that organize the business and social world of music around discussions of authenticity and community.[14]

Take, for example, one of the most scathing examinations of the masculinized aspects of music consumption ever written: Germaine Greer's article on classical music consumption titled "Why Don't Women Buy CDs?" Written for the September 1994 edition of *BBC Music Magazine*, Greer draws from research showing that both record companies and retailers in the early 1990s understood that the gap between female and male classical CD buyers in the United Kingdom was significant. The HMV chain found that 64 percent of its classical customers were male, while Virgin Retail showed another sixty/forty split between men and women. EMI Classics surveyed four thousand members of the general U.K. population and found that the largest proportion of women buyers, 40 percent, appeared in a consumer segment referred to as "strugglers." The sixteen- to thirty-five-year-old strugglers who only occasionally bought classical records composed only 15 percent of the consumer population. However, while the consumer segment of "collectors" represented an even smaller 5 percent of the population, they were the most dedicated consumers. These collectors were overwhelmingly male, thirty-five and older, "middle class and residents of south-east England." The HMV finding echoed the results of a similar survey taken by the classical record collector magazine *Gramophone*. The magazine's six thousand respondents confirmed the HMV's image of the collector. The *Gramophone* collector was older, solidly middle class, and male. As Greer noted, *Gramophone* reported that "the average age of the readers was 53, average UK income was £27,670, 47% of them had 250 or more CDs in their collections—and 95.5% of them were men."[15]

These numbers did not surprise Greer. Throughout her life as a listener and buyer of classical records, Greer had observed that the great majority of classical collectors were men. Furthermore, those men, according to Greer, seemed to be more animated by a completist desire and a sense of control than any actual passion for music. "The men I know who have whole walls of shelved CDs do buy every version of every symphony or sonata principally in order to own it," Greer claimed.[16] According to Greer, this need for control through ownership supported some less-than-noble behaviors: "Male CD collectors will ask each other if they have the latest Chilingirian or the rarest Michaelangeli pirate in much the same way that dogs sniff each other's bottoms."[17] Responding to Greer,

David Lister published a column in the *Independent* in which he claimed that "the CD collection oft proclaims the man" and that when men enter a room for a party, they "will always finger through the CD collection, something a woman never does." Furthermore, "Women even manage to miss out on the pleasure of purchase. In record shops they know what they want and go straight to it. Or they ask the assistant where it is. Never do they spend a happy hour or more browsing through the CDs, seeing what the new CD collecting is one of the last invisible bonding activities for men: a club without walls, a way of sharing a passion. Until women appreciate that, they will never fully appreciate music."[18]

Greer's essay preemptively counters by explaining that unlike middle-class men, middle-class women have the same allotment of neither free time nor money. As such, the push to spend significant amounts of time and money in record shops and collect deep catalogs of music is impractical for most women. For Greer, most women "are not prepared to invest their lesser earnings in such an illusion of power." Instead, "the quintessential female leisure purchase is chocolate."[19]

Greer's article does not argue that women do not buy records. Instead, it is that they consume differently and that there are nowhere as many female classical collectors as male. This collector aspect of record consumption both transcends genres and impacts record retail. While there have been and continue to be a few record shops that specialize in specific genres, it is more common than not that record retailers offer a range of genres in order to sell to a more general public. This balancing of the desires of collectors, fans, and everyday consumers is part of the retail tightrope that most record stores walk. On the one hand, they have had to carry the most popular records to cater to a general public while catering to those who are in the search of catalog and more obscure fare. For catalog stores such as Virgin, HMV, or Tower, popularity depended historically on the fact that both the collector and once-in-while consumer could use the space as a kind of one-stop shop for all the in-print records they may be interested in. Much like a bookstore would characteristically stock a variety of genres and publishers so that a science-fiction fan would rub shoulders with an enthusiast of romance novels, this meant the catalog store had to carry goods from a variety of genres and labels. As such, popular music assets would be placed in the same space as jazz and classical. While these genres would often be physically separated, how they were managed and displayed were often more alike than not. Bestsellers received the best sightlines, and staff would often encourage repeat buyers to invest in specific canons of recordings and artists. While genres had different modes of production and distribution, the goal of record retailers remained the same: sell the largest number of units with the widest margins possible by maintaining a balance of appeal between those who repeatedly purchase unpopular items and those who occasionally purchase the most popular goods.

Indeed, this is one of the reasons that Greer's feminist criticism of classical record collectors can be made of collectors of other genres when it comes to record retail: record collectors of all sorts, whether they be pop, country, jazz, or classical in their orientation, have long been imbricated in a set of underinvestigated retail practices that inform their collective habits. Take, for example, collectors who search for unpopular or rare records. Because collectors demand these goods, retail practices have produced specific hierarchies and values to address a record's origin, age, and authenticity. These not only affect marketplace values but critical ones as well. Compilation albums are often defined as bad objects in opposition to these collector tastes. Indeed, while compilations have always found purchase in catalogs and mom-and-pop stores, these kinds of products have found their success in supermarkets, coffee shops, and television, embracing commerciality and convenience at the perceived expense of collectible issues such as authenticity and scarcity. Unlike core repertoire and rare albums with "deep cut" tracks, compilations of all sorts suffer under the suspicion of compromised artistic integrity. Although greatest-hits compilations can be cheap and easy ways for performers to meet their contractual obligation with publishing labels, collectors scoff at their highly commercial market positioning as low-pressure, mass-appeal entry points for casual buyers and new listeners. Furthermore, commercial compilations invite comparisons to amateur mixtapes. While Lister points out that collectors consume differently from women who are more likely to engage with compilations,[20] Greer extols the virtues of the compilation, particularly the mixtape: "Giving compilation tapes strengthens networking. The message is 'these things please me and, because we are true friends, they will give you pleasure, too.'"[21] Greer further notes that the exchange of a mixtape compilation is not only social but also a copyright violation made to satisfy an affective economy of underserved needs. Compilations represent the corporatization of this social practice by contrast. Finally, Greer notes that "women tend to buy compilations . . . because of pragmatism rather than ignorance." She adds that "women are not embarrassed to buy a 'best of . . .' album, whereas male 'strugglers' would want to maintain a façade of expertise by buying core repertoire albums."[22]

Market emphasis on this small niche of collectors also stands in contrast to relative gender equity in the audience for recording artists' concert tours. For example, in 2014, the research company Live Analytics in conjunction with the research firm Bovitz confirmed that of the 11.5 percent of Americans that did attend a live music event in 2013, 49 percent were men and 51 percent women.[23] In fact, as part of the debate centering around who was buying classical records in the 1990s, one *New York Times* reporter noted that "among those who call themselves lovers of classical music, women are more likely to attend live performances, while men outnumber women when it comes to buying music."[24] As the 1994 director of EMI Classics, Roger Lewis, explained with regards to the sale of classical music records, it wasn't "a male/female problem." Instead, EMI Classics viewed the market based on segments in which "certain types of product do appeal more to one sex than the other."[25]

Alternative Retail Spaces

Indeed, one of those products was the compilation—and in new retail contexts, it could serve industry efforts to create new material supports for music consumption. Appearing the same year as Germaine Greer's essay, a 1994 *New York Times* article titled "For Musical Appreciation, Sexes Go Their Own Ways" claimed not only that the classical compilation was a hit with women buyers but also that in some cases, sales could come from an unexpected space: the U.S.-based lingerie chain Victoria's Secret. Marketed by Victoria's Secret, the "Classics by Request" series was a set of romance-themed compilations of classical music that consumers could purchase through the chain's mail-order catalogs and retail stores. As the *Times* reported, the Victoria's Secret series claimed "five of the 10 classical records that have sold more than a million copies."[26] Steve Murphy, an executive at EMI's classical label Angel Records, noted the irony in the fact that existing record retail standard-bearers were being outflanked by an intimate clothier. Indeed, Joseph V. Micallef, the then-chairman of the Classical Committee at the National Association of Recording Merchandisers, claimed that "the success of Victoria's Secret [hinted] at an enormous market untapped."[27] Victoria's Secret understood the power that offering a point-of-sale compilation record could have for a store's bottom line. In 2001, the *New York Times* reported that "sales managers [at Victoria's Secret] had only to slip the disc into the store player, and soon women were picking up bras, panties and Beethoven."[28]

By 2001, Victoria's Secret had sold fifteen million CDs, so other retailers followed suit, offering their own music compilations. One company in particular, Rock River Communications, produced CD compilations for other lifestyle and clothing retailers such as Pottery Barn, The Gap, Eddie Bauer, Polo / Ralph Lauren, Restoration Hardware, Structure, Williams Sonoma, and Lane Bryant. Led by Billy Straus, River Rock specialized in "mixes of sentimental favorites or jazz classics or one-hit wonders [that were] concocted to convey the image of the stores that sell them." Combining trusted retail brands with compilations to be played in store, Straus saw his company as assisting in "streamlining the music buying process." These discs were designed for people who "have jobs and maybe have families, the reality is they don't have two hours to go hang out at Tower Records."[29] In other words, these compilations were designed and sold in spaces focused on middle-class domesticated adults, with the attendant feminine gender norms ascribed in abundance to goods such as interior decoration and fashion.

For these stores, records are ancillary rather than primary goods that also act as acoustic ambassadors. Just as a friend's mixtape is filled with musical suggestions that come from a trusted source, these lifestyle brands leveraged their brand reputations to sell these compilation albums. Unlike the record shop that relies on a behind-the-counter expert, this model uses the significant and long-standing affective investments made by these brands to promise an extension of the consumer lifestyles on offer. These compilations were often played in these lifestyle stores to provide not only background music but also a risk-reduction strategy for listeners who were considering their purchase. Purposely nonintimidating, these records also offered relatively low price points, expert curation, and gestures of affectionate association to extend specific retailers' brand aesthetics into customers' lifestyles. Both retail compilations and mixtapes are curations created to make connections, develop trust, and build bonds. Of course, while Greer claims that compilation tapes strengthen friendships, the bonds made between the compilation and the retailer aimed to build market allegiances.

Throughout the 1990s and 2000s, these compilation records were also developed with the understanding that most older women do not buy music in record stores. As such, these collections provided an alternative mode of music consumption within more feminized shopping contexts. For example, writing in 1996 for *Billboard*'s "Classical Keeping Score" column, Heidi Waleson highlighted the gift of curation offered by RCA Victor and *Family Circle* magazine in their CD series. With the magazine and the label both part of Bertelsmann's media holdings, both collaborated to market "the Family Circle Collection, a midprice ($9.99) CD series targeted specifically at the magazine's 27 million readers." As the author noted, the magazine's readers represented 25 percent of all American women. The median age of the reader was forty-five with a median family income of less than $40,000 per year, with 65 percent of these readers being married. The first ten titles released in August 1996 included "Weekday Soothers," "Dinner Specials" (that included recipes), and "Best Ever Piano Favorites," with liner notes drawn from *Family Circle* editorial content.[30] The intent of the series was to add music to the lives of female *Family Circle* readers too intimidated to choose classical music in the traditional manner. As Lisa Cooperstein, then-director of books and licensing for *Family Circle*, who codeveloped the series with then-marketing consultant for BMG classics Deborah Morgan, noted, the compilation acted as a gift that fit the ethos of *Family Circle* magazine: "The goal of the magazine is to create happier, better, simpler lives for women. It's all about simplifying complex issues—such as walking into a record store and not knowing whether to choose Beethoven or Vivaldi. These women want music and to have their children exposed to it, but they aren't that educated about music. These compilations do it for them."[31] RCA promoted this material with spots on *CBS This Morning*, *Oprah*, and *Martha Stewart's Living*; organized events in U.S. malls; placed their products in one-stop mass-market shopping outlets such as Walmart; and pushed "to get the series into grocery and drug outlets that carry the magazine but have not traditionally carried music."[32]

While these compilations extended retail lifestyles based in the imagination of feminine commercial desires, the limitations of their market frameworks have long been a source of feminist criticism. This criticism has the potential to reshape retail practices. In 1995, for example, Carolynn Schmitt and her then-boyfriend, Tim Jackson, opened the independent record store Adult Crash in the East Village of Manhattan with purposeful attention paid to the production of gender in their retail space. Schmitt admitted that she stocked Adult Crash with clothing as well as records because "record stores are usually so male oriented, I thought it would help to make the girls come in and look at records." As Mr. Jackson noted, "We both have feminine sensibilities, especially after shopping at one record store after another and being intimidated by a real male atmosphere. This is a real conscious effort to stay away from all that."[33] To be sure, stores like Adult Crash have proved to be the exception rather than the rule.

As a result, women continue to seek out other contexts for music consumption—particularly online. Laura Barton hypothesized in the *Guardian* that surveys showing that women were a major consumer of MP3s were partially due to the fact that "buying music online means they can circumnavigate the emporia":

> Entering a record store is something akin to going into a very expensive clothing or furniture shop populated by tiresomely obsequious staff. Only here, as they hover among the rows of vinyl inquiring as to whether you are "looking for anything in particular," the implication is not that you cannot afford their wares, more that you, lady, do not deserve to buy them. Yes, somewhere in the set of their mouths and the arch of their brows is the unspoken question, "You do realise we don't stock James Blunt, don't you?" ... The implication is that although women may like records, they do not, cannot, must not like them as much as men.[34]

This emergence of a new set of online spaces—which began with legally dubious file-sharing forums such as Napster and eventually morphed into online stores and streaming sites—radically shifted the retail context. As the 2000s proceeded, record stores continued to shutter, sales of records slumped, and the popular music economy transformed into one that is now based on services such as Spotify, YouTube, and so on. In response to a 2006 *New York Times* article about the swift collapse of record retail that followed, Emily Jo Schnipper of Palo Alto, California, wrote to the editor to explain, "As a 21-year-old obsessive CD buyer, I was not shocked about the plight of record stores. More women than men download digital music, but your photos of browsers, all men, is an accurate depiction of many stores. I'm not suggesting to paint them pink, but catering to a wider clientele may aid their survival."[35]

Conclusion

The collapse of brick-and-mortar record retail in the early twenty-first century has provided those record retailers with a chance for a new future. Indeed, the sales of millions of compilations at Victoria's Secret or Pottery Barns throughout the United States prove that differing social contexts can mobilize both different musical products and purchasers. Will Straw argues that the many uses of music in everyday life and various "material configurations" invite researchers and investors to study music's many "contexts of sociability."[36] While Straw highlights "places of night-time congregation," retail has always generated specific social contexts of exchange that, as retailers have often realized, can be racialized, classed, and gendered. This recognition has supported a number of interventions on behalf of small business owners and musicians participating in the postrecessionary resurgence of vinyl record retail.[37] As the format once thought to be outdated has seen a substantial comeback, affordable and stylish turntables meet with the willingness of fashion and supermarket spaces such as the U.K.'s Sainsbury chain to carry vinyl records.[38] Others have pointed to the celebration of Record Store Day, an event begun in 2007 at the nadir of physical record retail, as an event that has helped spur new interest in record collecting. Five years into the annual event, there seemed to be a sense of growth, with one survey commissioned by the cofounder of the event revealing that "that 70% of vinyl shoppers were under age 34, and half were women."[39] At least one storeowner in Tampa, Florida, credited Record Store Day with diversifying the typical record-buying crowd. Co-owner of Mojo Boos and Records Melanie Cade explained that she used to sell records at record collector shows, and "it was just a bunch of older men." With Record Store Day, Cade explained, "you started seeing more diversity in terms of age. I've seen people from all walks of life. We have way more women, and young women, collecting records now than we used to at all."[40]

Many record retailers in the English-speaking world realize that they must transform to meet the demands of female consumers. In 2014, *Billboard* reported that while Amazon was the biggest retailer of vinyl records at 12.3 percent market share, Urban Outfitters, the multinational clothing and housewares retailer, claimed second with an 8.1 percent market share.[41] While a fashion-based retailer may seem like an unlikely space to purchase records, perhaps more unlikely has been the willingness of traditional self-service record retailers to change. As more women have entered these self-service record stores, they have taken to social media to openly challenge traditional record retail when it harbors sexist practices that other, less traditionally masculine spaces of retail do not. For example, in 2016, English singer-songwriter Kate Nash took to Twitter to explain the offense she found in how one record shop housed a category labeled "Females of all description" that conflated products by independent rock artists Florence and the Machine with records from distinctly different genres such as "Reggae/Tamla/Rap etc." Nash succinctly posted a photo of the offending bin with the comment "This kinda sh** drives me insane. The genre 'females of all description' is not a music genre. It's sexist."[42] Celebrating the tenth annual Record Store Day, Nash "urged young girls to embrace record shops as a way of 'discovering their identity.'" Later becoming an ambassador for the industry's most significant non-Christmas-season day of sales, the singer noted that her love of punk was developed "as a teenager browsing vinyl in charity shops and at Spitalfields Market in central London." For Nash, girls "deserve" to be included in these spaces because record shopping "is a way of discovering their identity and music, and give[s] you a sense of power."[43]

In her article titled "Forget High Fidelity: How Women Are Reclaiming Record Stores," Sian Gardiner identifies and discusses how more women were both buying and selling vinyl and, as a result, "staking their claim in this traditionally male space."[44] Gardiner's interviewees claimed progress, but they also noted that they still had a long way to go in making record retail more gender equitable by hiring more women clerks and paying attention to those clues that alienate women buyers. Yet the progress has been substantial. One of Gardiner's subjects was Carrie Colliton, the co-organizer of Record Store Day, who recalled witnessing in 2016 an exchange in North Carolina where "a black teenage girl walked up to the counter to buy her metal record, and asked the clerk what time they were opening on Record Store Day."[45] For Colliton, moments like these, where a young woman breaks "practically every stereotype about women, music and record stores there is," were exciting because they made the fact of "more and more women and teenage girls, coming in and shopping for themselves" less exceptional.[46] Perhaps most significantly, in April 2018, reports began to circulate around a project involving writers Veronica West and Sarah Kucserka, production company Midnight Radio, and ABC Signature Studios to create a *High Fidelity* television series about a woman who runs a record store.[47] Across all these developments, the cultural politics of record retail are under significant pressure to change.

Notes

1 Will Straw, "Music and Material Culture," in *The Cultural Study of Music: A Critical Introduction*, eds. Martin Clayton, Trevor Herbert, and Richard Middleton (New York: Routledge, 2012), 229.

2 Solomon reportedly snipped off the ties of any employee or businessman who would dare wear one in any of his retail spaces or corporate headquarters.

3 Andrea Domanick, "Sex, Drugs, and (Selling) Rock and Roll: Tower Records Founder Russ Solomon Has No Regrets," *Noisey*, 16 Oct. 2015, https://noisey.vice.com/en_ca/article/rjxv93/tower-records-russ-solomon-all-things-must-pass-documentary.

4 Julianne Escobedo Shepherd, "Tower Records Doc Confirms There's Historical Precedent for Condescending Male Record Store Clerks," *Muse*, 12 May 2016, https://themuse.jezebel.com/tower-records-doc-confirms-theres-historical-precedent-1776328380.

5 Escobedo Shepherd, "Tower Records."

6 Escobedo Shepherd.

7 Lorena Cupcake, "These Are the Most Annoying Habits of Record Store Shoppers," *Vinyl Me, Please*, 20 June 2017, http://www.vinylmeplease.com/magazine/these-are-most-annoying-habits-record-store-shoppers.

8 Nick Hornby, *High Fidelity* (New York: Riverhead, 1995); Will Straw relates a similar invisibility for women in the popular imagination of record retail. By the end of production on *Vinyl* (2000), a documentary on record collecting, director Alan Zweig admitted to Will Straw that only five of his one hundred interview subjects were women: "[Zweig] had tried (he claimed, convincingly) to find more female collectors, following up on every lead and making certain that his search was well publicized, but had met with no success." See Will Straw, "Sizing up Record Collections: Gender and Connoisseurship in Rock Music Culture," in *Sexing the Groove: Popular Music and Gender*, ed. Sheila Whitely (New York: Routledge, 1997), 4.

9 Mike Shalett, "On Target," *Billboard*, 20 July 1985, 18.

10 Don Jeffrey, "Buycycles: An Analysis of Consumer Purchasing Trends," *Billboard*, 4 Oct. 1997, 77.

11 Harriet Gibsone, "Vinyl Destination: Who Is Actually Buying Records?," *Guardian*, 12 Aug. 2016, https://www.theguardian.com/music/2016/aug/12/vinyl-destination-who-is-actually-buying-records.

12 Don Jeffrey, "Music-Buying Habits Detailed in RIAA Study," *Billboard*, 19 Apr. 1997, 103.

13 Reggie Ugwu, "Who Buys Music Anymore? A Statistical Inquiry: What the Music Consumer Looks like Today versus 10 Years Ago," *Buzzfeed*, 17 Sept. 2014, https://www.buzzfeed.com/reggieugwu/who-buys-music-anymore-a-statistical-inquiry?utm_term=.wc5Jv9eqB3#.bww3VKgJ1k. Outside North America, a 1966 governmental survey indicated that West Germans spent "around $150,000,000 annually for records" and that women bought more records than men in a disproportionate manner as women made up 52.8 percent of the West German population but bought "about 60 percent of all phonograph records." See "A Swinging Record-Buying Bonn Spends 150 Mil Yearly," *Billboard*, 3 Sept. 1966, 34.

14 Keith Negus, *Music Genres and Corporate Cultures* (New York: Routledge, 1999).

15 Germaine Greer, "Why Don't Women Buy CDs?," *BBC Music Magazine* (Sept. 1994), 36–37.

16 Greer, "Why?," 35.

17 Greer, 36.

18 David Lister, "It's True, We're All Obsessed with Our Discs," *Independent*, 3 Oct. 1994, https://www.independent.co.uk/voices/its-true-were-all-obsessed-with-our-discs-1440571.html.

19 Greer, "Why?," 36.

20 Lister, "It's True."

21 Greer, "Why?," 36.

22 Greer, 36–37.

23 "U.S. Live Event Attendance Study," *Live Analytics*, 17 Nov. 2014, https://www
.slideshare.net/LiveAnalytics/us-live-event-attendance-study.

24 Diana Jean Schemo, "For Musical Appreciation, Sexes Go Their Own Ways," *New
York Times*, 15 Nov. 1994.

25 Greer, "Why?," 37.

26 Schemo, "For Musical Appreciation."

27 Schemo.

28 Julie Flaherty, "Music to a Retailer's Ears; Sorry. Springsteen Won't Be Playing at
Pottery Barn Today," *New York Times*, 4 July 2001.

29 Flaherty, "Music."

30 Heidi Waleson, "Classical Keeping Score: Family Circle Has Music in Mind for Its
Female Readers via RCA Victor Series," *Billboard*, 21 Sept. 1996, 38. Waleson noted
that the series was intended to continue for five years and would also include more
future titles such as "Weekend Starter" and "Music for a Bad Hair Day."

31 Waleson, "Classical Keeping Score."

32 Waleson.

33 Gia Kourlas, "Herenow; A Record Shop Where Customers Rival the Collection,"
New York Times, 1 Jan. 1995.

34 Laura Barton, "G2: Shortcuts: I'll Do the Funky Gibbon on My Own Terms,"
Guardian, 16 May 2006, 2.

35 Emily Jo Schnipper, letter to the editor, "For Men Only," *New York Times*, 30 July 2006.

36 Straw, "Music and Material Culture," 232.

37 Hannah Ellis-Petersen, "Record Sales: Vinyl Hits 25-Year High," *Guardian*, 2 Jan.
2017, https://www.theguardian.com/music/2017/jan/03/record-sales-vinyl-hits-25
-year-high-and-outstrips-streaming.

38 Sian Gardiner, "Forget High Fidelity: How Women Are Reclaiming Record Stores,"
MixMag, 6 Mar. 2017, http://mixmag.net/feature/forget-high-fidelity.

39 Marco R. della Cava, "Reason to Celebrate on Record Store Day; Special Releases
Will Only Help Sales Surge," *USA Today*, 12 Apr. 2012.

40 Jay Cridlin, "Surge in Vinyl Popularity Keeps Store in Groove," *Tampa Bay Times*,
23 Apr. 2017.

41 Ed Christman, "Urban Outfitters Doesn't Sell the Most Vinyl," *Billboard*, 29 Sept.
2014, https://www.billboard.com/articles/6266616/urban-outfitters-doesnt-sell
-most-vinyl.

42 Nicola Oakley, "'Sexist' Labelling in Record Store Prompts Angry Rant from Singer
Kate Nash," *Mirror*, 29 Aug. 2016, https://www.mirror.co.uk/3am/celebrity-news/
sexist-labelling-record-store-prompts-8729612.

43 Joe Nersessian, "Kate Nash: Record Stores Can Help Young Girls Discover
Their Identity," Independent.ie, 22 Apr. 2017, https://www.independent.ie/
entertainment/kate-nash-record-stores-can-help-young-girls-discover-their-identity
-35644565.html.

44 Gardiner, "Forget High Fidelity."

45 Gardiner.

46 Gardiner.

47 Kristie Rohwedder, "A 'High Fidelity' TV Series with a Female Lead Might Happen and It's an Exciting Twist on the 2000s Film," *Bustle*, 6 Apr. 2018, https://
www.bustle.com/p/a-high-fidelity-tv-series-with-a-female-lead-might-happen-its
-exciting-twist-on-the-2000s-film-8712181.

10

"It's Not Just Commerce, It's Community"

• •

Erotic Media and the Feminist
Sex-Toy Store Revolution

LYNN COMELLA

Located in a former wig shop in the heart of downtown Oakland, California, Feelmore Adult Gallery is not your typical sex shop. Owner Nenna Joiner, who opened the business in 2011, told the interior designer she worked with that she wanted the store to feel like a jazz lounge: cool, comfortable, and classy.[1] Erotic art hangs on the walls, colorful vibrators sit on the shelves, and hard-to-find collectibles and memorabilia, from old *Playboy* magazines to vintage condom ads, are prominently displayed on sturdy tables that take up most of the retail space. Part art gallery, part adult store, and part community resource center, it is an easy place to lose oneself.

A Las Vegas native who grew up in a retail family, Joiner moved to the San Francisco Bay Area in the early 1990s. Soon afterward, her aunt, who had worked for the San Francisco AIDS Project, gave her a copy of the *Good Vibrations Guide to Sex* and suggested that she pay a visit to the legendary sex-toy retailer. "I went down there and loved it," Joiner recounted. "But what really brought me to the idea of opening a store of my own is that every time I went there, I wouldn't see anything that really represented me. All the empowered images were of white women. Being a black female, I wondered, 'Where are we?'"[2]

As Joiner's interest in the adult industry grew, she recognized that there was a need in the African American community for more diverse sexual images and resources. She decided to start a business that could deliver what she thought was missing from other, predominantly white, women-run sex shops.

Joiner developed a business plan, researched Oakland's zoning ordinances, and began looking for a commercial space, a process that took about five years. She quickly discovered that banks were unwilling to lend money to an adult-oriented business because it was perceived as too risky, and many landlords were wary of leasing her a space because they did not want to be associated with the stigma of an adult store.

Despite these setbacks, Joiner would not be deterred. While she waited for the pieces of her business plan to fall into place, she began selling sex toys and adult DVDs out of the trunk of her car. She also took a class with the Queer Women of Color Media Arts Project and began making queer pornography, an endeavor that would later earn her two Feminist Porn Awards. And perhaps most fortuitously—and entirely by happenstance—she met fellow Oakland resident Joani Blank, the sex educator and therapist who founded Good Vibrations in 1977. Blank became a friend and mentor, even loaning Joiner the last bit of money she needed to open her store.

Feelmore Adult Gallery is part of a long line of woman- and queer-run sex-toy shops whose owners see their businesses as being about much more than simply making money and turning a profit. Since the early 1970s, with the founding of Eve's Garden in New York City in 1974 and, several years later, Good Vibrations in San Francisco in 1977, feminist entrepreneurs have challenged the idea of business as usual within the historically male-dominated adult industry, reimagining in the process who sex shops are for and what kinds of spaces they can be.[3] Businesses such as Good Vibrations, Feelmore, and others are committed to providing customers with accurate sexual information and quality products, as well as catering to individuals—women, queer folks, and gender-nonconforming people of all ages and walks of life—that are frequently overlooked or altogether ignored by the mainstream commercial sex industry.

For some of these businesses, the question of whether or not to carry erotic media was at first a vexing one. Although early feminist sex-store pioneers distanced their businesses from pornography as a way to differentiate them from more conventional adult stores, by the mid-1980s, with the rise of adult video, they began to expand their retail missions to incorporate erotic videos into their product mix, becoming hubs of distribution for sexually explicit media geared toward women and couples. By the late 1990s, conversations on the sex-shop floor between customers and sales staff were providing inspiration for a new wave of feminist and queer pornographers, some of whom would go on to start production companies of their own.[4] Good Vibrations eventually began producing its own erotic media to fill what it saw as representational gaps in the larger sexual marketplace.[5] Drawing on the visual language employed by feminist and queer pornographers, Good Vibrations used "sexually explicit imagery to contest and complicate dominant representations of gender, sexuality, race, ethnicity, class, ability, age, body types and other identity markers."[6] This practice would continue with Nenna Joiner, whose foray into making pornography featuring queer women of color was not only a stepping stone for her to learn more about the adult industry but a deliberate intervention into the predominantly white world of sex-positive entrepreneurship and cultural production.[7]

Feminist sex-toy stores have historically played an important role in helping customers navigate what was for many the illicit yet fascinating world of erotic videos. They did this by producing a larger cultural and commercial context—what I refer to as a sex-positive ecosystem—that supported and, indeed, encouraged the production and consumption of sexual media geared toward marginalized audiences. And yet, at the same time, these businesses were shaped and sometimes constrained by the perspectives of their predominantly white, college-educated, middle- to upper-middle-class, and sometimes, although not always, queer-identified owners. As a black lesbian filmmaker and business owner, Nenna Joiner challenged the dominant paradigm of sex-positive capitalism by putting black sexuality at the center of her media making and retail operation, treating it not as an afterthought but as a fundamental organizing principle of her commercial mission and brand.

The Making of a Market

In 1977, sex therapist and educator Joani Blank opened the Good Vibrations retail store in the heart of San Francisco's Mission District neighborhood. After years of working with women and couples in a therapeutic milieu, Blank realized that there needed to be a sex shop for people who hated sex shops: a place where women in particular could get the products they wanted without the feeling of distaste—or the experience of harassment—that often accompanied their visits to more conventional adult stores. Although she did not know it at the time, Good Vibrations would become the standard-bearer for a new kind of sex store that brought the techniques of sex therapy and the language of sex education into a retail environment, inspiring future generations of feminist and queer entrepreneurs to follow in her footsteps.[8]

From the get-go, Blank was determined to avoid the look and trappings of a typical adult store, with its highly sexualized aura and "seamy" appearance. Drawing upon highly gendered codes of middle-class sexual respectability, she created a welcoming and homey environment, one that was intentionally unerotic, in the hope of appealing to female shoppers who might otherwise never consider venturing into one of "those places." Blank displayed products outside of their bulky and often sexist packaging and encouraged customers to pick items up and turn them on so they could feel the strength of their vibration. She thumbed her nose at selling lingerie, because she felt it perpetuated sexual stereotypes. She also refused to carry pornography.

By the mid-1970s, feminist opposition to pornography was intensifying in certain corners of the women's movement. Sexuality, to paraphrase film scholar Linda Williams, was increasingly on/scene and its growing presence and accessibility were causing concern.[9] It was on television and newsstands and in private clubs and XXX-rated movie theaters. In this era of porno chic, the idea that pornography was a tool of patriarchal oppression was gaining traction.[10] By the end of the decade, calls for legal remedies to mitigate what some feminists saw as its harmful effects were becoming louder.[11]

Blank, for her part, insisted that she was not an antipornography feminist. Rather, her decision to not carry pornography was rooted in the fact that she personally was not a fan and simply figured that other women were similarly turned off. She also felt that pornography was a sex-shop cliché and worried that carrying it would undermine the alternative, women-friendly retail vibe that she and her staff were working so hard to cultivate.[12]

Her concerns were not entirely misplaced. Writing in 1985, media scholars Chuck Kleinhans and Julia Lesage noted that "porn bookstores, magazine racks, and theaters stand as a visual expression of male dominance of public space. . . . Commercial pornography is men's turf. It not only obsessively repeats male sexual fantasies, often misogynist, it also reinforces more generalized male heterosexual privilege to express and define sexuality."[13] Given this landscape, Blank's reluctance to carry pornography made sense. For her, a feminist reclamation of sex-toy stores involved upending the dominant codes and conventions that had long defined these businesses, replacing them instead with new representational strategies and retail norms.

Blank's attitude toward pornography slowly began to change when, in the early 1980s, she hired Susie Bright to work on the sales floor at Good Vibrations. Precocious and witty, Bright was not yet the nationally known author and trailblazer "Susie Sexpert."

In 1984, several years after she began working at Good Vibrations, Bright helped start *On Our Backs* (*OOB*), a groundbreaking sex magazine for the "adventurous lesbian." *OOB* featured pictorials of lesbians with dildos and strap-ons, dyke leather daddies and their femmes, threesomes, vibrators, and public sex. With its sexual imagery and erotic fiction, the magazine offered an unapologetic counterpoint to antipornography feminist discourses, reclaiming lesbian lust as an act of cultural defiance. The publication was revered by many and despised by others. Some feminist and gay and lesbian bookstores refused to carry it, and a few that did found their magazine racks vandalized by angry patrons.[14]

During this time, Bright also began penning a regular column about pornography for *Penthouse Forum*, and her interest in and knowledge about erotic film eventually found its way to Good Vibrations. "VHS was exploding," she told me. "Movies are like stories. They are just like books. It's education; it's entertainment. I thought of Good Vibrations as being part of the cultural conversation and expansion around sex, so not having movies was sort of like saying we don't use forks."[15]

In *Smutty Little Movies*, media historian Peter Alilunas argues that the VHS (Video Home System) revolution was a game changer for the pornography industry in more ways than one. Home video "all but decimated the traditional adult theater circuit, permanently changed the industry, and altered the cultural landscape."[16] As home video became dominant, new opportunities for previously marginalized producers and audiences emerged, challenging the hegemony of heterosexual male pleasures. The combination of privacy, availability, and technology, according to Alilunas, "created the possibility to rethink the presentation of sexuality that, in some cases, embraced an unabashed celebration of women's pleasure."[17]

Candida Royalle, a former adult performer turned director, was one of the first women to imagine a new audience for pornography. She recognized that the private viewing pleasures afforded by home video meant that "women could now sneak a peek in the safety of their own domains and couples could enjoy them privately, rather than sitting among questionable guys in raincoats, in dark seedy theaters with sticky floors."[18] All that women needed were movies created with them in mind. But what might porn for women look like and how might it be different from what already existed?

In 1984, Royalle founded Femme Productions, with the goal of making a different kind of pornography. As Royalle would later note, "I wanted to make films that made people feel good about their sexuality and about who they are as sexual beings. I wanted to make films that say we all have a right to pleasure, and that women, especially, have a right to our own pleasure."[19]

The biggest challenge Royalle faced was finding distributors that would carry her films. This was not simply because she was a woman making pornography—there were other women who were already behind the camera when she started making her movies. Rather, she was a woman making a different kind of pornography: "It wasn't the typical box cover with the blonde, big-boobed babe. Instead, it was always a loving couple. It just had a different set of markers . . . the whole presentation was different, and my price was a little higher because it was higher quality."[20]

Royalle realized that she would have to up her game if her movies stood any chance of reaching consumers. A consummate marketer, she decided to use her best asset: herself. An appearance on the *Phil Donahue Show* and articles in nationally circulating magazines helped put Femme on the map, and sales soon followed.

The success of Royalle's movies was an early indicator of the shift toward what at the time was a very nascent but growing women's market for sex toys and pornography. By the mid-1980s, female entrepreneurs and consumers had begun placing new demands on the larger adult industry. Good Vibrations, for example, began offering warranties and sending defective merchandise back to manufacturers, making it clear that they were not going to stand behind shoddy products that stopped working after one use. In time, manufacturers and content producers bought into the idea that when it came to women, they were dealing with a sophisticated consumer class that expected more from the products they were purchasing.

Good Vibrations was among the first businesses to begin selling Candida Royalle's films. According to Royalle, the company opened "their doors to the idea that women wanted their own products and things aimed at them … knowing that there was already this tiny little space carved out where I could place my stuff gave me encouragement. And the fact that they showed support, that they carried my products, spoke well of them and reviewed them highly was very important. I think we really worked hand-in-hand."[21]

Good Vibrations and other feminist retailers became important hubs of distribution for all kinds of products that other, more conventional adult stores were not interested in carrying. Over time, a sex-positive synergy developed between feminist retailers and cultural producers who worked together to ensure that a quality selection of erotic videos, books, and sex toys made it into the hands of consumers. As I have argued elsewhere, this synergy is not ancillary to the history of feminist pornography and the growth of the women's market but a fundamental part of the broader commercial context that helped position feminist pornography as a form of discursive intervention and cultural critique.[22]

Feminist Retailer as Media Producer

In 1989, as the adult video market continued to grow, Good Vibrations finally began carrying a small collection of erotic videos that had been carefully selected by Susie Bright. In putting the collection together, Bright looked for movies that reflected the best of what the pornography industry had to offer. This included films that featured women who genuinely appeared to be enjoying themselves and didn't look as if they were faking orgasms. She also chose movies with good scripts that were free from gender and racial stereotypes. Good Vibrations staff wrote their own descriptions of films and removed the videos from their often-tawdry box covers, putting them in blank ones instead so customers—especially those who were new to the world of erotic videos—would not be turned off by "cheesy" or deceptive boxes that had little to do with what the film inside was actually about.

Despite occasional skirmishes among staff about the video collection, all kinds of people rented and purchased porn from Good Vibrations. It quickly became a hub of distribution for films that were not readily available at many other video stores; it also became a source of well-regarded information for customers who wanted to take a peek inside the world of adult video but were unsure where to begin or what to watch. As Cathy Winks wrote in the introduction to *The Good Vibrations Guide: Adult Videos*, "It didn't take long for us to realize that we were providing a completely unique service for a grateful and enthusiastic audience. Good Vibrations was in the right place at the right time to represent the erotic tastes of consumers largely ignored by the mainstream adult industry: women, male/female couples and lesbians. Whether our customers were novices with next to no prior exposure to porn, or experienced 'connoisseurs,' they appreciated our efforts to sift through the thousands of erotic videos released every year in search of the cream of the crop."[23]

It remained the case, however, that Good Vibrations was limited in terms of what it could carry based on what was being made. In an effort to bring more diverse sexual imagery to customers, Good Vibrations eventually decided to throw its hat into the ring and, in 2001, founded a video production subsidiary called Sexpositive Productions (SPP). According to Carol Queen, Good Vibrations' longtime staff sexologist, SPP was a way for the company "to address the fact that we saw far too few good porn movies featuring bisexual characters and plots, big women performers, diversity, and various kinds of [explicit education]—all things that customers constantly asked us for. . . . We wanted to address these absences . . . and find new—better, more respectful, more realistic—ways to represent otherwise underrepresented groups of people."[24]

Between 2001 and 2003, SPP produced five films, including *Slide Bi Me*, a bisexual romp that was nominated for a Gay Adult Video News Award, and *Please Don't Stop: Lesbian Tips for Giving and Getting It*, which featured an all-women-of-color cast. Rave reviews notwithstanding, the life span of SPP was short. By the time SPP finally got off the ground, other companies, such as San Francisco–based lesbian porn producer SIR Video, had begun making the kind of representationally diverse and body-positive videos that Good Vibrations staff had long wanted to make. But more than this, according to Queen, the economics of the endeavor were never quite right. Alternative porn such as the kind SPP was making was expensive to produce and did not have the mass appeal that other, more mainstream types of pornography had. Selling the volume needed to make money was an ongoing challenge. The rise of internet pornography, moreover, also cut into sales and curtailed the company's ability to sustain the project.[25]

Through SPP and Good Releasing, another video production company that Good Vibrations founded in 2009, Good Vibrations took pornography and made it its own, showing that it did not have to wait for others to make the kind of diverse sexual imagery its staff and customers wanted to see. This included funding and producing a number of erotic films by up-and-coming Bay Area filmmakers, including Nenna Joiner's first movie, *Tight Spaces*.

The Feelmore Experience

Nenna Joiner attributes her interest in sex to watching cable television as a kid. Her parents and grandparents worked long hours, and to fill her time after school, she often watched adult channels that most parents, she conceded, "would forbid their children from watching."[26] She got her first taste of sex from the Playboy channel, and when she eventually got a phone in her room, she began calling 1-800 numbers. "Those first visual impressions of sexual encounters stuck in my head and even today I recognize porn as my first teacher when it came to understanding heterosexual sex."[27] One question nagged at her though: Where were all the black and brown women and men?

Years later, around 2004, Joiner had an epiphany: she wanted to be part of the adult industry. In an effort to learn more about the industry, she began attending the annual AVN Adult Entertainment Expo in Las Vegas, applied for part-time jobs at sex shops around the Bay Area—with no luck—and started selling adult DVDs that she had purchased online at local nightclubs. She was trying to figure out where in the industry that she, as a black entrepreneur, could have the biggest impact. She realized that what she really wanted to do was open a brick-and-mortar store in which sex toys were just one part of a larger, community-oriented enterprise.

While Joiner waited for her store to become a reality, she began shooting pornography. Her uncle just happened to own his own media production company, and she became his gopher, eventually working her way up to production assistant and sound engineer. She learned how to edit and how to create stories that conveyed emotion. She put out a casting call on Facebook and interviewed dozens of people who expressed interest in being part of her films. Joiner asked them why they wanted to perform in porn and what type of content they thought was missing from pornography. What were their desires and how might she bring them to life?[28]

Making pornography featuring queer women of color gave Joiner a voice and a platform that she used to amplify her vision and promote her new store. In 2011, shortly after Feelmore opened, she won a Feminist Porn Award (FPA) for her first film, *Tight Spaces*, taking home the trophy for "Most Deliciously Diverse Cast." The following year, *Hella Brown*, which featured an all-black cast and screened at the Berlin Porn Festival, won another FPA for "Hottest

Dyke Film." Every nomination and award kept Joiner and her retail business in the media spotlight.[29]

Joiner's films were just one part of her broader efforts to address the kinds of absences she saw in the larger adult industry, from pornography to sex toys to adult retail businesses. "People always ask, 'Why a sex store?'" Joiner told me. "I just thought Oakland was really lacking. I could've taken my money and done other things with it, but I saw a need. Sometimes I think you really need to look around your community and see what the true need is."[30]

Joiner wanted to make her business different than other sex shops, including those owned by women. That meant reaching out to people who might never visit a sexually oriented business. Connecting with them sometimes involved going out into the community and talking directly to underrepresented groups—clients at a methadone clinic or an AIDS organization, for example—about everything from love and codependency to consensual sexual touch. This type of outreach did not necessarily translate into sales, but it was important to Joiner that she be a visible face of black business ownership in the Oakland community.

Joiner realized early on that getting people through Feelmore's doors did not always involve leading with sex; rather, it was about creating a comfortable, welcoming environment that could, ideally, transcend sex: "You don't just throw lube and dildos at this community, especially for communities that have never seen that."[31] In an effort to appeal to a wider set of community interests and concerns, Feelmore hosted comedy nights and partnered with Walgreens to give flu shots. Joiner organized a workshop featuring a psychologist and a financial planner. "How can you think about sex if you've just lost your job and you are financially stressed?" she asked.

Joiner discovered that many people who might otherwise be apprehensive about stepping into a sex shop could be sold on the vintage aspects of the store, from its rare books to its selection of vintage vinyl. These items allowed customers to engage with the space in ways that did not necessarily involve purchasing a sex toy. Joiner once watched an older couple dance in the middle of her store while music featuring jazz singer Sarah Vaughan played in the background. Another time, a mother and her adult daughter came in, and the younger woman, after seeing the vintage copies of *Oui* magazine, talked about the *Oui* T-shirt that her mother used to wear when she was growing up. "People remember where they were," Joiner said. "So when people come in [and see the collectibles], they talk about where they were. It's part of their history."[32]

This approach, which involves catering to what Joiner describes as a sense of "nostalgic inclusion," is one way that she attempts to create a distinctly Feelmore experience that is about more than just sex. According to Joiner, "One of the things I hear from people is that they are so happy that I have these magazines. The guys will say, 'Dude, look what this woman looks like and she is real.' They are picking up magazines, the *Playboy* and the *Penthouse*, not for the women, but for the ads. They are looking at the old shoes, the old stereo systems, the old cars and looking at how great the old ad work was. Now, sexuality is less intimidating."[33]

Finding ways to make sexuality—and by extension, her business—more inviting to the communities that she most wants to reach is an ongoing experiment for Joiner. As an adult business owner, she knows what it is like to negotiate the stigma that comes from running a sexually oriented business and is aware of just how scary, shameful, and threatening sex can be for many people. Navigating stigma can be even more complicated for people of color whose sexuality is simultaneously defined and constrained by enduring stereotypes, such as the myth of hypersexuality and black sexual deviance.[34] Carrying vintage media is just one strategy among many that Joiner uses to help ease curious yet tentative customers into a space that can be unfamiliar to some and off-putting to others.

Conclusion

Just blocks from Feelmore in downtown Oakland is a billboard with an image of a black hand holding a small vibrator. This is the Bullet. It is about two inches tall, runs on batteries, and is designed for pleasure. Alongside the image are the words "Our Bullets Don't Hurt."

Nenna Joiner created Feelmore's "Our Bullets Don't Hurt" marketing campaign following the shooting of Michael Brown in Ferguson, Missouri. In the wake of the decision to not indict the white police officer who shot Brown, an unarmed black man, protests erupted, including in Oakland. As Joiner stood on the sidewalk outside of her store, watching police officers in riot gear marching in formation past her business, she grew frustrated. She was frustrated with racism, frustrated with gun violence, and frustrated with a police presence that unfairly targeted black communities. "Our bullets don't hurt," she called out to the officers as they walked by. In that moment, a new, community-oriented marketing campaign was born.[35]

Joiner's contributions to the adult industry as an African American lesbian filmmaker and adult retailer build upon and extend decades of work by feminist and queer entrepreneurs to change the business of pleasure by making it more inclusive. The differences in her approach, however, are notable. For most feminist retailers and pornographers that came before her, including Joani Blank and Candida Royalle, gender was their primary entry point for challenging the representational absences that shaped the larger adult industry. They created retail spaces with women in mind and pornography geared toward female viewers; they pushed manufacturers to develop packaging that was softer and less overtly sexualized and generated marketing campaigns that led with sex education rather than titillation in an effort to appeal to women by underscoring what made their businesses different from more conventional ones.

These were tremendously important cultural interventions, and yet the idea of being "for women" was often narrowly defined and frequently overlooked differences among women based on race, age, social class, and ability. In the absence of a robust intersectional framework, the idealized female sexual consumer was often imagined to be a white, middle-class, and presumably heterosexual woman.

This is not to say that questions of diversity and inclusion did not matter to sex-positive feminist entrepreneurs; they most certainly did. But it took a conscious effort and commitment on the part of white feminist retailers and media makers to address the ways in which sexuality and, by extension, their businesses were racialized and take steps to diversify their content, packaging, marketing campaigns, and sales staff. While some made concerted efforts to do this, not everyone was comfortable moving beyond their personal experiences and frames of reference.[36]

Nenna Joiner is positioned outside the white hegemony that defines—and very often limits—how race and inclusivity are discussed within the adult industry. For Joiner, these things are not afterthoughts but an essential part of how she thinks about her business and its mission of radical inclusivity. As feminist historian Mireille Miller-Young notes, "Just as black feminists have challenged the mainstream feminist movement to be accountable to race, class, and nation . . . black women bring a special insight to feminist pornography."[37] They also bring important insights to the feminist sex-toy retailing movement, pushing sex-positive entrepreneurs and cultural producers to expand how they imagine and speak to the relationship between race and sexuality, commerce and community, and erotic media and adult retailing.

Notes

1 Nenna Joiner, *Never Let the Odds Stop You* (Oakland, Calif.: Nenna Feelmore, 2015), 4.

2 Nenna Joiner, interview with author, 14 July 2008.

3 For a detailed discussion about the history of feminist sex-toy stores and the women who pioneered them, see Lynn Comella, *Vibrator Nation: How Feminist Sex-Toy Stores Changed the Business of Pleasure* (Durham, N.C.: Duke University Press, 2017).

4 See Shar Rednour and Jackie Strano, "Steamy, Hot, and Political: Creating Radical Dyke Porn," in *New Views on Pornography: Sexuality, Politics, and the Law*, eds. Lynn Comella and Shira Tarrant (Santa Barbara, Calif.: Praeger, 2015), 165–177.

5 Carol Queen, "Good Vibrations, Women, and Porn: A History," in *New Views on Pornography: Sexuality, Politics, and the Law*, eds. Lynn Comella and Shira Tarrant (Santa Barbara, Calif.: Praeger, 2015), 179–190.

6 Constance Penley, Celine Parrenas Shimizu, Mireille Miller-Young, and Tristan Taormino, "Introduction: The Politics of Producing Pleasure," in *The Feminist Porn Book: The Politics of Producing Pleasure*, eds. Tristan Taormino, Celine Parrenas Shimizu, Constance Penley, and Mireille Miller-Young (New York: Feminist Press, 2013), 9.

7 There are a growing number of important books that engage with the subject of black female sexuality, representation, desire, and labor in the pornography industry, including Mireille Miller-Young, *A Taste for Brown Sugar: Black Women in Pornography* (Durham, N.C.: Duke University Press, 2014); Ariane Cruz, *The Color of Kink: Black Women, BDSM, and Pornography* (New York: New York University Press, 2016); and Jennifer Nash, *The Black Body in Ecstasy: Reading Race, Reading Pornography* (Durham, N.C.: Duke University Press, 2014).

8 Comella, *Vibrator Nation*.

9 Linda Williams uses the term *on/scenity* to describe "the gesture by which a culture brings on to its public arena the very organs, acts, bodies, pleasure, that have been designated ob/scene and kept literally off-scene." Linda Williams, ed., *Porn Studies* (Durham, N.C.: Duke University Press, 2004), 3.

10 For a far-reaching discussion regarding pornography and sexual representation in the 1970s, see Carolyn Bronstein and Whitney Strub, eds., *Porno Chic and the Sex Wars: American Sexual Representation in the 1970s* (Amherst: University of Massachusetts Press, 2016).

11 For a comprehensive history of the feminist antipornography movement, see Carolyn Bronstein, *Battling Pornography: The American Feminist Anti-Pornography Movement, 1976–1986* (Cambridge: Cambridge University Press, 2011).

12 Joani Blank, interview with author, 9 Dec. 2015.

13 Chuck Kleinhans and Julia Lesage, "The Politics of Sexual Representation," *Jump Cut* 30 (Mar. 1985), https://www.ejumpcut.org/archive/onlinessays/JC30folder/PoliticsSexRep.html.

14 Lisa Troshinsky, "Vandals Target Lesbian Erotica Magazine," *Washington Blade*, 23 Mar. 1990.

15 Susie Bright, telephone interview with author, 18 June 2010.

16 Peter Alilunas, *Smutty Little Movies: The Creation and Regulation of Adult Videos* (Oakland: University of California Press, 2016), 6.

17 Alilunas, *Smutty Little Movies*, 117.

18 Candida Royalle, "What's a Nice Girl like You . . . ," in *The Feminist Porn Book: The Politics of Producing Pleasure*, eds. Tristan Taormino, Celine Parrenas Shimizu, Constance Penley, and Mireille Miller-Young (New York: Feminist Press, 2013), 63.

19 Candida Royalle, "Porn in the USA," *Social Text* 37 (Winter 1993): 23.

20 Candida Royalle, telephone interview with author, 7 Nov. 2001.

21 Royalle, telephone interview.

22 See Lynn Comella, "From Text to Context: Feminist Porn and the Making of a Market," in *The Feminist Porn Book: The Politics of Producing Pleasure*, eds. Tristan Taormino, Celine Parrenas Shimizu, Constance Penley, and Mireille Miller-Young (New York: Feminist Press, 2013), 79–93.

23 Cathy Winks, *The Good Vibrations Guide: Adult Videos* (San Francisco: Down There Press, 1998), vii.

24 Queen, "Good Vibrations," 186.

25 Queen, 187.

26 Joiner, *Never Let the Odds*, 22.

27 Joiner.

28 Mireille Miller-Young, "Community Sex Work: A Conversation with Nenna Feel-more Joiner," in *Queer Sex Work*, eds. Mary Laing, Katy Pilcher, and Nicola Smith (London: Routledge, 2015), 172.

29 The Feminist Porn Awards were founded in 2006 by Toronto-based feminist retailer Good For Her. The awards were a way to recognize and celebrate adult filmmakers who were producing nonfetishizing movies featuring people of color, transgender performers, and queer folks. The final year the awards took place was 2015. For more about its history, see http://www.feministpornawards.com/blog/the-feminist-porn-awards-how-did-it-all-start/.

30 Nenna Joiner, interview with author, 16 Sept. 2011.

31 Joiner, interview, 2011.

32 Joiner, interview, 2011.

33 Joiner, interview, 2011.

34 See Miller-Young, *Taste for Brown Sugar*.

35 "Feelmore Adult Gallery," *YouTube*, 29 Apr. 2017, https://www.youtube.com/watch?v=OBaoPGoQw3E.

36 Candida Royalle, for example, discussed the fact that she was criticized for not crossing boundaries of race and class in her films or doing more to represent lesbian sexuality. She conceded that she felt she was not the right person to do this, because as a white heterosexual woman, these were not her experiences. See Royalle, "Porn in the USA," 27–28.

37 Mireille Miller-Young, "Interventions: The Deviant and Defiant Art of Black Women Porn Directors," in *The Feminist Porn Book: The Politics of Producing Pleasure*, eds. Tristan Taormino, Celine Parrenas Shimizu, Constance Penley, and Mireille Miller-Young (New York: Feminist Press, 2013), 118.

Part III

Practices and Participation in Media Retail Communities

●●●●●●●●●●●●●●●●●●●●●●●

11

Comic Book Stores
as Sites of Struggle

● ● ● ● ● ● ● ● ● ● ● ● ● ● ● ● ● ● ● ●

BENJAMIN WOO AND

NASREEN RAJANI

At the 2017 New York Comic Con (NYCC), Marvel Comics invited retailers to a panel where three editors and a writer would unveil the company's plans for the coming year. It turned into a tense standoff between the industry's largest publisher and their primary customers—the owners and managers of comic book stores. When one of Marvel's representatives boasted about sold-out titles, they were met with heckles from the audience, and retailers aired grievances with a range of Marvel policies during the question-and-answer period. However, "things got weird" when a questioner pivoted from the economics of lenticular covers to recent changes in the Marvel Universe: as reported by comics journalists, "He complained about Captain America being black, Thor being a woman and Iceman being gay. . . . 'Why don't you make new characters? Don't make changes to the old characters that we love.' This was met with a smattering of applause." As momentum built behind this sentiment, Marvel's representatives intervened to end the panel.[1] This incident crystallizes some of what is unusual about comic book stores as a media retail institution.

By definition, cultural intermediaries stand in between producers and consumers, working to shape the circulation of both media goods and discourses about them,[2] but in the field of American comic books, both publics are remarkably dependent on comic book stores. Whereas purchasers of books, recorded music, or home video releases might seek out particular, obscure titles at a specialty store, they are not the main way that books, albums, or movies are sold, and it is hard to imagine executives from a major Hollywood studio or one of the big three record labels putting themselves in a position to be hectored by the managers of independent video or record stores. Notwithstanding comics' increased availability through trade bookstores and digital portals like Comixology, retailers exert such influence because local comic shops remain central to the economy of comics culture. Most remain independent businesses: there are no big-box comic book stores, and individual retailers rely on their own horse sense about product lines and audiences without recourse to sophisticated market research or even much in the way of their own promotion, which (such as it is) remains in the hands of publishers and distributors. But comic book stores are also culturally loaded spaces for their patrons. They grew out of fannish collecting practices—with young entrepreneurs often pillaging their personal collections for capital or stock—and have been shaped by fannish *doxa*. For decades, they have served as material, spatial anchors for the culture of comic book fans. "New comic day" is a media ritual, bringing devoted readers and collectors into their local store to browse, discuss, and maybe even purchase some of the week's offerings. In few other popular media industries are the cultures and economies of production, circulation, and reception so entangled, and all these threads run through your local comic shop, or "LCS."

Comic shops have become key sites of struggle over efforts to make comics culture more inviting to audiences outside of what has been, for some time, its imagined core demographic of middle-aged white men. Neither the comic book industry nor fan communities oriented to its products are monolithic, but we want to explore how struggles over diversity—both *whether* and *how* best to achieve it—play out in local, independent comic book stores. For some "introverted" retailers, new audiences or new products that are intended to serve underrepresented consumers appear as a threat to the comics culture they spent their careers nurturing; to "extroverts," they are the only hope for survival in an increasingly competitive entertainment market.[3] Both groups find supporters and detractors among creatives, publishers, and different constituencies within their customer base, and it falls to retailers and their employees to negotiate these different pressures when they order products, schedule events, and organize the physical premises of their shops.

We begin by briefly reviewing the history and political economy of comic book retailing in North America. The direct-market distribution system of specialty retail stores is virtually synonymous with "comic book culture," yet many have observed that some conventional retail practices tend to marginalize women and other participants who fall outside narrow stereotypes of the "comic book fan." Thus the LCS has rich possibilities as a strategic point of intervention. We close with a profile of the Valkyries, a network of women comic shop employees engaged in a project of "retail reform" that seeks to redefine comics culture as an open, inclusive community. Valkyries members, as women working in comic book stores, occupy a position between the competing interests of publishers, critics, and fan publics as they struggle to define what comics mean and who they are for.

Origins of Comic Book Stores

The contemporary comic book field is defined by a series of compromises between publishers' needs and the fan culture that comic shops both enable and emblematize. But this was not always the case; for much of the American comic book's history, comics were not for "fans," and there were no comic book stores. Rather, comic books were sold with magazines and other periodicals at newsstands, corner stores, and drug stores. This granted early comic book publishers tremendous reach; however, distributors—not publishers nor individual newsagents—determined which titles appeared for sale and in what quantity. There were no guarantees that the next issue would be available at the same location, nor were back issues available, since unsold comic books were supposed to be destroyed in exchange for a refund from the publisher. This mode of marketing comics—as an adjunct of the magazine industry via newsagents—assumed they were cheap ephemera for an undiscerning audience. Readers could only choose among whatever comic books happened to be available at a particular newsstand, and practices of collecting and connoisseurship that are now synonymous with comics fandom required a great deal of commitment.

As long as short, episodic stories dominated and publishers could assume that their youthful audiences would regularly be replaced by new cohorts of children, the newsstand model was largely satisfactory. But comic book sales began a long decline in the 1950s under competition from television and a series of price increases.[4] In order to survive, the comic book publishing industry needed better ways to reach the older, more "serious" readers who wanted longer stories and to follow the same characters from month to month, but since several major publishers were subsidiaries of magazine distributors, it was unlikely that they would develop an alternative.[5] Rather, it was the community of comics fans, nurtured within science-fiction fandom and emerging as a distinct group in the 1960s, that developed the new paradigm of comic book retail.

By the late 1960s, there were as many as two hundred specialty stores that sold comic books, but they were not comic shops as we know them today. Many were actually used book stores or purveyors of other print ephemera. Dan Gearino's interview with comic retail pioneer Dick Swan gives a flavor of this social world:

DS: We got the stock from the HoustonCon which ran from June 20–22 in 1969. We drove home, went out and rented a store the same week.

DG: I can see *Amazing Fantasy* #15, *Panic* #6, a Tarzan paperback, signs for *Zap* and *Red Eye*, and a Batman and Robin decal. Any specific memories about any of those items?

DS: Just trying to show a selection of what we had. *San Jose Red Eye* was a San Jose hippie newspaper. I know we paid a few bucks for an ad in their paper. The only other place we put an ad was in *Rocket's Blast/Comicollector* fanzine. The AF # 15 was probably about $10 at that time. We all loved ECs.[6] One interesting note is that there were three stores within two blocks of each other in San Jose (Frank Scadina's Marvel Galaxy which had been Seven Sons, and Bob Sidebottom's Comicollector Shop), and none of us carried NEW Comics, just old stuff. I remember Milligan, the distributor wouldn't sell to us because none of us were 18.[7]

Three points are worth noting. First, Swan and his contemporaries were engaged with existing, translocal networks of communication and exchange—conventions like HoustonCon and fanzines like *Rocket's Blast / Comicollector*. Second, the photograph that prompted his reminiscences shows several points of connection with the counterculture: Swan advertised the *San Jose Red Eye* and *Zap Comix*—examples of underground newspapers and underground comix, respectively. Hatfield notes that head shops, as the main outlet for underground comix, were integral to the early history of the comic shop, and Swan's storefront evidences this articulation.[8] Third, these comic book stores did not really compete with existing newsstands and corner stores. Most were oriented to the collector's market for "old stuff," not current comics.[9] Here, we see the origins of comic book stores as an alternative retail channel for comic books, one that is deeply imbricated in *fannish* rather than *industrial* forms of knowledge and already beginning the process of articulating otherwise distinct groups of consumers together through their own sense of what products "go together" in this emerging retail space. But most importantly, these early comic book shops demonstrated that there was an audience/market in search of a different way to buy their comics.

The key transformation in comics retailing came from high school teacher, comic book dealer, and convention organizer Phil Seuling, who used his industry connections to negotiate distribution deals with individual comic book publishers. Called the "direct market" because it initially involved printers shipping directly to stores, bypassing magazine distributors and the newsstand market, it in fact created a new middleman—Seuling and partner Jonni Levas's Sea Gate Distribution. Seuling's grand bargain rationalized comics marketing: publishers granted significant discounts when stores ordered and paid for comics in advance and on a nonreturnable basis and could, therefore, print to the orders, reducing waste; retailers could order specific quantities of specific titles, reflecting their best guesses at demand; and consumers had more reliable access to the comics they wanted in one place. Other, regionally based distributors soon followed, with ten major distributors active by the 1990s.[10] However, Marvel upset this ecosystem when, late in 1994, it attempted to purchase Heroes World and make them their exclusive agent in the direct market. The gambit led rival DC to sign an exclusivity agreement with Steve Geppi's Diamond Comics Distributors and set off a chain of consolidations. Marvel eventually closed down Heroes World and signed with Diamond, granting it a de facto monopoly on distribution that persists to this day.[11] As a result, Diamond has immense gatekeeping power, and its decisions and policies profoundly shape what comics are available in the market.

Direct distribution to comic book stores was initially a sideline for publishers, but it steadily grew in importance as the most effective way to reach their core audience. Today, with the exception of Archie's foothold in supermarket checkout aisles, periodical comic books have essentially retreated to direct-market comic book stores. M. J. Clarke proposes three major unintended consequences of the adoption of this retailing model. First, direct marketing required publishers to "solicit" their publications to store owners and managers months in advance, introducing a new temporality to comic book publishing. Second, because the direct market required lower print runs than newsstand distributors and the potential audience was more clearly delineated, it "opened up the industry to new entrants."[12] Independent publishers demonstrated that comic shop customers could support titles that would not survive in the broader periodical marketplace, and Marvel and DC experimented with specials and limited series featuring obscure or untested characters exclusively distributed to the direct market. Third, competition from new, direct market–oriented publishers improved the terms of creative labor. Because comic shops' fan clientele "more easily embraced formal experimentation, baroque story lines and explicit content," some creators were able to attain greater creative autonomy and introduce more diverse content to the field.[13] But this configuration privileged certain kinds of diversity—diversity of products *within* a set of aesthetic constraints—over others. The direct market both expressed and accelerated a demographic shift away from a broad, mass audience to a narrow one "steeped in devotion for the medium," which also tended to be disproportionately white, male, and middle class.[14] This subcultural audience made its home in local comic shops.

At the same time, comic shops became the industry's repository for risk. In exchange for lower costs, stores accept nonreturnable sales, so they must anticipate demand for individual issues, weighing considerations like character and creator popularity, advance reviews and promotion, tie-ins with larger-scale publisher "events," purchasing incentives, and so on—and they do it all months in advance. Underestimate demand and customers are unhappy; overestimate and the store is saddled with surplus copies that not only represent a financial loss but also take up limited inventory space until such time as they can be sold at a discount or given away.[15] Some commentators have suggested these dynamics account for retailers' perceived aesthetic conservatism. In 1998, Image Comics publisher Jim Valentino said, "The current market is not a comic-book market; it's a superhero market."[16] While this is changing, many an LCS remains principally, if not exclusively, oriented to so-called mainstream comics and are unable or unwilling to invest capital or devote scarce shelf space to untested properties and the audiences they might hypothetically attract.[17]

But the same dynamics also generate moral hazard. For economists, "moral hazard" describes when people undertake riskier behavior because they are insulated from the full costs of their actions' consequences.[18] When publishers experiment with new series or test the limits of how many variant covers the collectors' market will absorb, retailers bear the costs of their flops and missteps—at least in the short term. It is unsurprising, then, that Gearino's history of comic stores is a sequence of booms and busts. Today, there are approximately 3,200 comic book stores, compared with about 200 stores in 1977, 500 in 1987, 1,000 in 1990, and 10,000 in 1995.[19] Periodic contractions are often associated with publishers oversupplying the market: too many titles featuring a currently popular character (or copycats thereof), too many variant covers, too many crossovers and events, or too many copies in circulation, period.[20] Because the vast majority of comic shops are independent businesses that opened more out of fannish enthusiasm than market analysis, many owners lack sufficient capital to ride out market contractions.[21] Like all legacy media organizations, this retail model built for the needs of comic book collectors must now adapt to a transformed media landscape. In order to even out the variable demand for comic books, most LCSs have diversified product lines, selling not only comics and graphic novels but also games, toys, and other pop-culture merchandise and collectibles. As a result, "comic book" stores have become key points of articulation between multiple communities of practice making up the "geek culture" media subsystem. But this is not only a matter of making lateral moves into adjacent product categories; the social field of comic books is itself changing, having arguably split into two major subfields, neither of which necessarily needs comic book stores as they evolved since the 1970s.

First, some publishers have been drawn into closer alignment with the broader entertainment industries. While comic book publishing was once part of the magazine industry and then briefly stood more or less on its own, the two largest contemporary comic book publishers are now subunits of "entertainment" companies owned by large media conglomerates (DC Entertainment by Warner Bros. and Marvel Entertainment by Disney). Licensing deals with film, television, or video game producers are also important to many midrange publishers. For example, IDW was the fourth-largest publisher in the direct market in 2016 but, having also produced two television series, an award-winning graphic novel, and a line of board games, these sales only represented 15–20 percent of its revenue.[22] The "comic book industry" is arguably no longer a publishing industry at all but a character licensing industry that produces media brands.[23] When a best-selling comic book—say, an issue of *Batman*—sells approximately 130,000 copies in a given month, representing just shy of $400,000 in sales revenue at $2.99 a copy,[24] but a film like *Batman v Superman: Dawn of Justice* (2016) generates nearly $900 million in worldwide box-office returns and a Batman video game like *Arkham Knight* (2015) sells more than five million copies at about $100 each, it is difficult to maintain that DC is in the business of making comics. Comic books are one way to test out characters and story concepts before developing them into valuable franchises for larger, mainstream audiences, but it is unclear whether they and the apparatus that produces and sells them are essential to conglomerates' plans for the resulting properties. Indeed, the traditionally homosocial culture of the comic shop—and its extension into the production cultures of some creators and publishers or into online spaces—may represent a liability rather than an asset. On the one hand, subcultural audiences are not always reliable indicators of how other groups will respond. On the other, the risk of disgruntled fans behaving badly online, launching harassment campaigns or boycotts, may outweigh their value as consumers.[25]

Second, the rise of graphic novels and trade paperbacks (collections of material previously serialized in periodical "floppies") over the last two decades suggests a path for comic book publishing that ends in trade bookstores. Figure 11.1 compares sales revenue for the top-twenty publishers of comic books and graphic novels through the trade bookstore and direct-market channels, respectively. While the three largest publishers continue to derive the lion's share of their sales from the direct-market channel, fourteen of the top-twenty publishers receive more of their sales from bookstores than comic shops—none of which are traditional comic book publishers.[26] Looking exclusively at the bookstore channel, industry leader Marvel—notorious for its inconsistent line of trade paperbacks—is not only overtaken by long-time rival DC but drops all the way to fifth place. As noted previously, Marvel Comics' disproportionate reliance on direct-market comic shops may not reflect Marvel Entertainment and Disney's priorities, but the fact that many comic shops are disproportionately reliant on sales of Marvel comics is a point of vulnerability for the entire economy of comic book retailing whenever the publisher struggles.[27]

The LCS is no longer the only game in town. For many consumers, superhero characters are as much—if not more—creatures of film, television, and

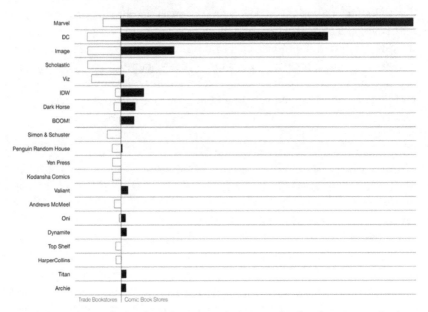

FIG. 11.1 Sales revenue breakdown for the top-twenty comic book and graphic novel publishers by distribution channel (2016). Bookstore sales from Brian Hibbs's analysis of Nielsen BookScan sales reports. Comic book store sales from John Jackson Miller's sales estimates based on Diamond monthly reports. Data are available for download: http://dx.doi.org/10.5683/SP/R5ISLU.

video games as of comic books. The regularization of the graphic novel format in the book industry enabled bookstores and libraries to carry comics. Meanwhile, after the trail was blazed by illicit comics scanners and independent webcomics creators, major publishers adopted digital distribution at scale, with Amazon's Comixology serving as the "digital Diamond." Nonetheless, direct-market distribution, specialty comic book stores, and the audiences they consolidated are responsible for much of the comics world we inhabit today. The community created by knowledgeable comic book shop owners and loyal customers not only helps mitigate some of the risks experienced by retailers but is also, for many, an end in itself. To the extent that there is a comic book culture—and not just an aggregate of individual readers—it can be found in comic shops that have served for decades as a social space and retreat for fans, most of whom have been boys and men.

Comic Shop Crisis

Ethnographic studies of comic book stores emphasize the central role they play, not merely as places to buy comic books but as culturally significant spaces. They are likened to "clubhouses" for fans, places of refuge from pre-sumed stigma against adults interested in comics.[28] Suzanne Scott has rightly called attention to the neglect of women's experiences in this tradition of comic shop ethnography, noting that negotiating one's "belonging" is much more fraught for those who fall outside the normative profile of a comic book fan.[29] While publicly available surveys (which are not above methodologi-cal critique) frequently confirm taken-for-granted assumptions about comic book readers, other evidence suggests a substantial audience of women fans. When Brett Schenker attempted to use data mined from social media to con-struct a picture of comic book fans, for instance, he found a gender split much closer to parity.[30] Problems of exclusion do not only affect women—many of the same critiques could be leveled on behalf of people of color and gender-nonconforming, queer, and trans individuals—but Schenker's findings raise an uncomfortable question: If Facebook "likes" show many more women fans than surveys conducted in comic shops, what keeps them away from their friendly neighborhood LCS?

Many critics focus on the content of mainstream comics themselves. The relative lack of titles foregrounding female characters presumably impacts the industry's ability to appeal to large numbers of women readers, but the nature of the content that *is* available for sale and is likely to be prominently displayed in the average comic shop is also worth interrogating. To many, female characters in comics seem designed for the sexualized gaze of male read-ers. One content analysis found that virtually every issue and one-quarter of all panels contained objectified representations of women.[31] These images appear on covers, on posters that are offered for sale and that decorate shops, and on licensed merchandise (in some cases, literally made plastic). Indeed, they are so normalized that they may not even register to longtime *habitués* of comic book culture. For example, retailer and industry commentator Brian Hibbs recently wrote about a wall of original art in the bathroom of his San Francisco store, which includes some sexually explicit and arguably violent images. In his col-umn, Hibbs attempts to think his way through the conflicts between his desire to create a welcoming environment in the store, free-speech principles, and the fannish desire to justify the artwork. But he acknowledges that he only belatedly realized they represented a source of discomfort for some of his female employees after a visiting cartoonist made a comment.[32] We do not want to deny that women readers can negotiate their own way through such texts or, indeed, find pleasure in them, but their overwhelming ubiquity in retail envi-ronments seems to signal who comic shops imagine themselves to be for.

Others might point to gatekeeping or outright hostility by staff and other customers as the major limitation on women's participation. In Gearino's book, veteran editor Diana Schutz recalls a customer bypassing her on her first day as a comic store clerk to ask the owners, "Who's the skirt?"[33] This seems a case of the "fake geek girl" avant la lettre. The trope first emerged as a way to suggest that women in geek culture spaces, including comic shops and conventions, were not real fans but only pretending to care about comic books, video games, and cult media. In the hands of women fans, this label was refashioned as a way of naming the exclusionary, boundary-policing practices that male fans used against them.[34] In many fields, "hardcore" fans construct themselves as superior to those they construct as "casuals" or "poseurs," but dominant discourses in comic book culture assumes all women are casuals a priori.[35] Many women fans have stories of being assumed to be shopping for a boyfriend or husband or of being peppered with knowledge-testing questions by staff and fellow customers to "prove" their credibility.

Other barriers and disincentives to women's participation in the field are less obvious—to men, at least. As Arielle Johnson, owner of Philadelphia's Amalgam Comics and Coffeehouse, put it in an interview with *Ebony*, "A lot of times, when you go into a comic book store, it feels like you're walking into someone's basement. As a woman, going into situations like that can be uncomfortable."[36] That is, gendered exclusions may be built into the shop itself. Many comic shops are physically small premises, and they are typically crammed with stock—betraying their origins in their owners' own collecting mania. It is almost de rigueur for them to cover their windows in posters of comic book characters, and comic books (especially the week's new issues) are frequently placed toward the rear of the store, while space at the front is devoted to toys, T-shirts, and collectibles.[37] To top it all off, some stores require patrons to leave their bags at the counter as a measure against shoplifting. Even if applied "equally," such policies disproportionately impact customers wearing women's clothing, which typically has fewer, smaller, and less functional pockets: "By taking a woman's bag, a comic book store is essentially taking away her freedom to escape from harassment. . . . How could she possibly feel completely comfortable browsing or engaging with the staff and other patrons?"[38] Taken together, this means that a new reader or customer has to enter the shop without being able to see what or who is inside and knowing they will themselves be hidden from view; surrender any bags they are carrying, which may contain their wallet, phone, and keys; and navigate their way to the back of the store through narrow aisles that restrict their free movement. Subjected to gender-based analysis, this way of organizing a comic shop appears not just uncomfortable but unsafe. The perception that comic book stores may not be welcoming environments for women and other customers who feel marginalized by the dominant fan culture—and the reality that some aren't—remains a significant obstacle to diversifying comic book culture.

But if comic shops are part of the problem, they can also be part of the solution. Cultural histories of the department store, supermarket, and shopping mall have pointed to the role these retail environments played in remaking gender relations, affording spaces for work and leisure that women could legitimately occupy.[39] Specialty media retailers like comic shops have (albeit on a smaller scale) arguably provided similar uses for men engaged in connoisseurist subcultures, and they could do so again for participants who have felt excluded from comic book culture in the past. It is perhaps not coincidental that one of the major voices for professionalizing comic stores was a woman. Marvel Comics direct-market sales director Carol Kalish, who died suddenly in 1991, was posthumously awarded the ComicsPRO Industry Appreciation Award and was inducted into the Eisner Awards Hall of Fame at the 2018 San Diego Comic-Con.[40] She is remembered for her discerning eye to the retail environment: under her leadership, Marvel subsidized the purchase of cash registers and advertising,[41] and Hibbs recalls her coming into a store to offer advice while on vacation.[42] Some of these initiatives dovetailed with her employer's interests, but they also aimed to remake the LCS into a clean, well-organized, and efficiently run retail environment—the kind of space, we are suggesting, where people excluded from the normative definition of comics fandom would feel safer and more comfortable.

As Pierre Bourdieu argues, the most important struggle in any social field is the "classification struggle" whereby participants seek to impose their definitions of the field and "correct" practice on others.[43] Every comic shop is a concrete manifestation of this field of forces. The products it carries as well as its design, layout, and policies all make an argument about what comics are and who they're for. Moreover, it carries the residue of past struggles—debates between and among publishers, creators, retailers and their employees, critics and journalists, and fan communities with different aesthetic and political sensibilities. In the next section, we examine one such "pressure group" as a case study, a network of women comic book retailers called the LCS Valkyries. Inspired by Scott's arguments about the gendered "politics of (in)visibility,"[44] we see the Valkyries as the most visible evidence that comic book stores are the Archimedean lever that can move the comics world.

Valhalla Is Calling

Instigated by the cartoonist Kate Leth, then a clerk at Halifax, Nova Scotia's Strange Adventures, the Valkyries were founded in 2013. Starting as a Facebook page and later growing to a private message board, the Valkyries enabled women working in comic book retail to discuss their experiences and share best practices. The Valkyries comprise more than six hundred members, multiple administrators, and a parallel network for former employees and women working in adjacent fields.[45] In addition to the forum, the Valkyries run panels and meet-ups at conventions and maintain a public-facing social media presence that enables them to engage with supporters. When we spoke with one of the group's administrators, the Houston, Texas–based retailer Annie Bulloch, she described the early buzz around the group: "'What is this secret cabal of women?' I wish I could say we were really in there doing something super subversive, but sometimes just getting women together at all [*laughs*] is kind of viewed as subversive by people." That is to say, the group's very "secrecy" rendered it highly visible in the context of the field.

The Valkyries' use of social media platforms amplified their influence beyond their own membership. A major feature of their social media work, especially on Twitter, where they are currently most active, is promoting dialog about upcoming releases. The Valkyries as a network does not endorse specific titles, but individual members and followers frequently share recommendations using the hashtag #ValkRecs. While comics by and about women are certainly common in these tweets, no single kind of comic dominates. In a retailing context where customers often need to request a comic months in advance, the Valkyries facilitate conversations that make specific comics visible to their colleagues (ideally convincing them that the comics are worth the risk to order) and to potential readers. In doing so, they also make women visible as a potential audience and as participants in the comics world. Here, they join a chorus of voices that have emerged from the implicitly masculine "geekosphere" to provide news and criticism oriented to women consumers. Given the lack of a substantial trade press for critical coverage of industry issues, news and review websites and individual critics' social media accounts are the forum for a "politics of visibility."[46] The discourse they generate around new releases constitutes a form of audiencing that *both* draws attention to titles outside the "mainstream" subfield—to a broader range of genres and formats, to independent and small-press publishers, to manga and other world comics, and to work by marginalized creators—*and* shows that people other than the normative straight, white, middle-aged cisgender male fan are buying and reading mainstream superhero comics.[47]

The online community created among the Valkyries has had real impacts in brick-and-mortar stores. As coadministrator Ivy Noelle Weir puts it, "The Valkyries shows that hey, if there's not a handbook for being a comic book retailer, we're a group of women who say at least there needs to be a standard for representation, for diversity, and for progressivism and inclusion."[48] They are actively reframing what it means to participate in comic book culture. However, this work has not gone uncontested. For example, the #ValkRecs hashtag was spammed by a parody account, @LCSValkyries_, associated with the so-called ComicsGate "movement." Inspired by GamerGate, a group of readers disgruntled with what they see as a political agenda of "forced diversity" in comics have taken to Twitter, YouTube, and other channels. Although the parody account had fewer followers than the real @LCSValkyries account by an order of magnitude and has since been deleted, its use of the #ValkRecs hashtag (along with #ncbd, or "new comic book day") in tweets containing transexclusive and white-nationalist content may have confused users who did not notice the subtle underscore and made the recommendations hashtag all but useless for those who hadn't blocked @LCSValkyries_.

That one or more ComicsGate supporters singled out the Valkyries as symbols of cultural change in the field signals that their project of retail reform has traction. However, Bulloch also highlighted constraints on members' abilities to effect change. Referring to the safety issues discussed prior, she observed that "not all shops are friendly, and that's one of the reasons why [the Valkyries] ended up existing." While the network enables members to share advice on how to "make your shop a good place to go to, a safe space or the next best thing to it," and those who are owners or managers can put these suggestions into practice, others "are just clerks who work in the shop." They may be one of several women employees or the only one; their employer may be supportive, indifferent, or actively hostile to the diversity agenda; and their clientele may be more or less receptive. Moreover, they operate in a complex, ever-changing field. For example, while Marvel was momentarily seen as supporting inclusion through changes in its lineup of books, to the point that it invited criticism from sectors of fandom and some retailers, as in the NYCC panel described earlier, it has also signaled that its support has limits, with comments that the diversity initiatives were responsible for declining sales and the cancellation of all their GLAAD award–nominated titles.[49]

The classification struggle over the meaning of subcultures and their practices usually takes place out of sight. When these debates and struggles do burst forth into the wider public realm, the loudest voices define mainstream perceptions. Recent controversies in other geek-culture fields are cases in point, with some fans' reactionary politics risking tarring all participants with the brush of misogyny, homophobia, transphobia, and racism. Headlines like "How the Alt-Right Invaded Geek Culture" or "Beta Testing Fascism: How Online Culture Wars Created the Alt-Right" give the impression that the identification of these fan cultures with toxic masculinity is a fait accompli,[50] but a social field is never just one thing, and it never stays still. In addition to concrete efforts to build community and share expertise among women working in comic retailing, to make women and other underserved audiences visible to publishers, and to reform the space of the local comic shop itself, the Valkyries demonstrate—to the outside world as much as to other participants—that the battle for comic book culture is still ongoing.

Conclusion

Aaron Kashtan has drawn attention to what he calls "direct-market centrism," a reactionary posture that accepts only comics sold within direct-market comic book stores and to their imagined audience of "true fans" as legitimate comics.[51] However, comics and graphic novels oriented toward broader, more diverse readerships have become increasingly important to the industry, creators who started out producing webcomics they distributed for free on Tumblr are signing major book deals, and the demographics of comics readers and of society in general are shifting. As a result, the middle-aged, straight, white man who loves superheroes will not be the average comic book fan—or retailer—for long, if indeed he still is.

The comic shops of tomorrow may not look like the crowded clubhouses of the past either. To name only a few examples: until its 2015 closure, Brooklyn's Bergen Street Comics provided the platonic ideal of an "elegant and family friendly" store;[52] Philadelphia's Amalgam and Toronto's Sidekick both combine comic shops with cafés—a case of both product diversification as well as signaling a different kind of retail culture—and both are owned by women;[53] and the Beguiling in Toronto has also been at the heart of several initiatives to broaden comics' appeal and reach, including sponsoring the Toronto Comic Arts Festival, developing a school and library sales program, and opening Page and Panel in the central branch of the Toronto Public Library as well as Little Island, a store focused on comics for young readers.[54] Additionally, more LCSs are incorporating periodic "Ladies Night" events, which give women and girls space and time in the shop as a safeguard against fears of gatekeeping or harassment from male customers. Such experiments show how different approaches to the idea of a comic shop can operate within the context of the direct-market distribution system.

Despite these hopeful signs, more can still be done to increase diversity in comic book retail and, through it, in comic book culture more generally. We say this not only as participants in the comics world who are committed to antioppression politics but also as industry observers. The value added by diversely skilled, knowledgeable retailers and the comfortable, welcoming environments they can create represents LCS's main competitive advantage against online shopping and digital distribution. We see a continued role for cultural intermediaries like these in negotiating the often-conflicting needs of producers and audiences, guiding new readers drawn in by comics' mainstream prominence, curating the best of publishers' back catalogs and increasingly diverse lines, and providing the material and organizational infrastructures necessary for fans to make inclusive communities around popular media.

Notes

1 Billy Henehan, "NYCC '17—Inside Marvel's Closed Door Retailer Presentation," *Beat*, 6 Oct. 2017, http://www.comicsbeat.com/nycc-17-inside-marvels-closed-door-retailer -presentation/; "Retailer Outrage at the Marvel Retailer Panel!," *Beat*, 6 Oct. 2017, http://www.comicsbeat.com/nycc-17-retailer-outrage-at-the-marvel-retailer-panel/.

2 Pierre Bourdieu, *Distinction: A Social Critique of the Judgement of Taste*, trans. Richard Nice (Abingdon, Va.: Routledge, 2010); Keith Negus, "The Work of Cultural Intermediaries and the Enduring Distance between Production and Consumption," *Cultural Studies* 16, no. 4 (2002): 501–515.

3 Benjamin Woo, *Getting a Life: The Social Worlds of Geek Culture* (Montreal: McGill-Queen's University Press, 2018), 141–144.

4 Jean-Paul Gabilliet, *Of Comics and Men: A Cultural History of American Comic Books* (Jackson: University Press of Mississippi, 2010), 30, 140–141.

5 Gabilliet, *Comics and Men*, 139.

6 EC Comics was the publisher of *Panic*.

7 "Comic World, 1969," *Dan Gearino: Writing and Reporting*, 5 Sept. 2017, https://dangearino.com/2017/09/05/comic-world-1969/.

8 Charles Hatfield, *Alternative Comics: An Emerging Literature* (Jackson: University Press of Mississippi, 2005), 21.

9 Some interviewed retailers recall when new comics were merely a way of generating regular traffic into the store rather than a real revenue stream in themselves. See Benjamin Woo, "The Android's Dungeon: Comic-Bookstores, Cultural Spaces, and the Social Practices of Audiences," *Journal of Graphic Novels and Comics* 2, no. 2 (2011): 125–136; Woo, *Getting a Life*.

10 Dan Gearino, *Comic Shop: The Retail Mavericks Who Gave Us a New Geek Culture* (Athens, Ga.: Swallow Press, 2017), 13–52.

11 Matthew P. McAllister, "Ownership Concentration in the US Comic Book Industry," in *Comics and Ideology*, eds. Matthew P. McAllister, Edward H. Sewell, and Ian Gordon (New York: Peter Lang, 2001), 24–25.

12 M. J. Clarke, "The Production of the *Marvel Graphic Novel* Series: The Business and Culture of the Early Direct Market," *Journal of Graphic Novels and Comics* 5, no. 2 (2014): 195.

13 Clarke, "Production," 195, 203.

14 Clarke, 196; "DC Comics—the New 52 Product Launch Research Results," *Newsarama*, 2011, http://www.newsarama.com/14637-the-full-nielsen-dc-s-complete-new-52-consumer-survey.html.

15 In recent years, some publishers have offered limited returnability on some titles as a way of reassuring retailers before a major departure in creative direction.

16 McAllister, "Ownership Concentration," 23.

17 Scott McCloud, *Reinventing Comics: How Imagination and Technology Are Revolutionizing an Art Form* (New York: HarperCollins, 2000), 115–116.

18 Tom Baker, "On the Genealogy of Moral Hazard," *Texas Law Review* 75 (1996): 237–292.

19 Gearino, *Comic Shop*, 85, 133. Gearino cautions that many of the ten thousand stores at the sector's peak were sports card and memorabilia shops that moved into comics when it was a "hot" collectibles market. In addition, these figures may count dealers who do not operate a storefront.

20 Bart Beaty, "Superhero Fan Service: Audience Strategies in the Contemporary Interlinked Hollywood Blockbuster," *Information Society* 32 (2016): 320–321; Gabilliet, *Comics and Men*, 87.

21 Gearino, *Comic Shop*.

22 Albert Ching, "INTERVIEW: IDW CEO on What Made 2016 the 'Best Year' in Company History," *CBR*, 4 Jan. 2017, https://www.cbr.com/interview-idw-ceo-ted-adams-on-the-best-year-in-company-history/.

23 Ian Gordon, *Superman: The Persistence of an American Icon* (New Brunswick, N.J.: Rutgers University Press, 2017); McAllister, "Ownership Concentration," 26–33; Mark C. Rogers, "Licensing Farming and the American Comic Book Industry," *International Journal of Comic Art* 1, no. 2 (1999): 132–142.

24 An average of estimated sales of *Batman* to comic book stores during 2016.

25 See Bethan Jones, "#AskELJames, *Ghostbusters*, and #Gamergate: Digital Dislike and Damage Control," in *A Companion to Media Fandom and Fan Studies*, ed. Paul Booth (Oxford: Wiley-Blackwell, 2018), 415–430; Katie Wilson, "Red Pillers, Sad Puppies, and Gamergates: The State of Male Privilege in Internet Fan Communities," in *A Companion to Media Fandom and Fan Studies*, ed. Paul Booth (Oxford: Wiley-Blackwell, 2018), 431–446.

26 These are a mix of trade publishers like Scholastic, Simon and Schuster, and Macmillan that have created lists or imprints devoted to graphic novels and companies translating Japanese manga for the Anglophone market like Viz Media, Yen Press, and Kodansha Comics.

27 Todd Allen, "If You Wondered Why Comic Stores Are in Trouble—DC vs. Marvel vs. Image Sales Distribution Charts for December 2017," *Beat*, 1 Feb. 2018, http://www.comicsbeat.com/if-you-wondered-why-comic-stores-are-in-trouble-dc-vs-marvel-vs-image-sales-distribution-charts-for-december-2017; Graeme McMillan, "2017: The Year Almost Everything Went Wrong for Marvel Comics," *Hollywood Reporter*, 29 Dec. 2017, https://www.hollywoodreporter.com/heat-vision/2017-year-almost-everything-went-wrong-marvel-comics-1070616.

28 Matthew Pustz, *Comic Book Culture: Fanboys and True Believers* (Jackson: University Press of Mississippi, 1999); Brian Swafford, "Critical Ethnography: The Comics Shop as Cultural Clubhouse," in *Critical Approaches to Comics: Theories and Methods*, eds. Matthew J. Smith and Randy Duncan (New York: Routledge, 2012), 291–302; Woo, "Android's Dungeon."

29 Suzanne Scott, "Fangirls in Refrigerators: The Politics of (In)Visibility in Comic Book Culture," *Transformative Works and Cultures* 13 (2013), DOI: 10.3983/twc.2013.0460.

30 Brett Schenker, "Demo-Graphics: Comic Fandom on Facebook—US Edition," *Graphic Policy*, 1 Nov. 2017, https://graphicpolicy.com/2017/11/01/demo-graphics-comic-fandom-facebook-us-edition-3/.

31 Carolyn Cocca, "The 'Broke Back Test': A Quantitative and Qualitative Analysis of Portrayals of Women in Mainstream Superhero Comics, 1993–2013," *Journal of Graphic Novels and Comics* 5, no. 4 (2014): 420.

32 Brian Hibbs, "Tilting at Windmills #265: #MeToo—When a Bathroom Makes Women Uncomfortable," *Beat*, 8 Nov. 2017, http://www.comicsbeat.com/tilting-at-windmills-265-metoo-when-a-bathroom-makes-women-uncomfortable/.

33 Gearino, *Comic Shop*, 74.

34 Alyssa Rosenberg, "Fake Geek Girls Are Not Coming to Destroy You," *Slate*, 15 Jan. 2013, http://www.slate.com/blogs/xx_factor/2013/01/15/fake_geek_girls_no_they_are_not_coming_to_destroy_you.html; Joseph Reagle, "Geek Policing: Fake Geek Girls and Contested Attention," *International Journal of Communication* 9 (2015): 2862–2880.

35 David Muggleton, *Inside Subculture: The Postmodern Meaning of Style, Dress, Body, Culture* (Oxford: Berg, 2000); Scott, "Fangirls in Refrigerators."

36 A. J. Springer, "Arielle Johnson Is Making Comic Book Stores More Inclusive," *Ebony*, 29 June 2016, http://www.ebony.com/career-finance/comic-books-arielle-johnson#axzz4yWBFTXAd.

37 Woo, "Android's Dungeon."

38 Kathryn Hemmann, "Attack of the Purse Snatchers: Gender and Bag Policies in U.S. Comic Book Stores," *Geek Feminism*, 3 July 2014, https://geekfeminism.org/2014/07/03/attack-of-the-purse-snatchers-gender-and-bag-policies-in-u-s-comic-book-stores/.

39 See William R. Leach, "Transformations in a Culture of Consumption: Women and Department Stores, 1890–1925," *Journal of American History* 71 (1984): 319–342; Erika Diane Rappaport, *Shopping for Pleasure: Women in the Making of London's West End* (Princeton, N.J.: Princeton University Press, 2000); Tracey Deutsch, *Building a Housewife's Paradise: Gender, Politics, and American Grocery Stores in the Twentieth Century* (Chapel Hill: University of North Carolina Press, 2010).

40 "The ComicsPRO Industry Appreciation Award," Comics Professional Retail Organization, 2017, http://www.comicspro.org/content.aspx?page_id=22&club_id=843470&module_id=88978; Heidi Macdonald, "Kalish and Ormes Inducted to Eisner Hall of Fame; Six More Women Nominated," *Beat*, 15 Jan. 2018, http://www.comicsbeat.com/kalish-and-ormes-inducted-to-eisner-hall-of-fame-six-more-women-nominated/.

41 Gearino, *Comic Shop*, 92–94.

42 Bryan Hibbs, "Tilting at Windmills," 31 Mar. 2010, *CBR*, https://www.cbr.com/245389-2/.

43 Bourdieu, *Distinction*, 481.

44 Scott, "Fangirls in Refrigerators."

45 Gearino, *Comic Shop*, 71–77; Lisa Granshaw, "Meet the Valkyries: A Community of Women Working in Comic Book Stores around the World," *Syfy*, 11 May 2016, http://www.syfy.com/syfywire/meet-valkyries-community-women-working-comic-book-stores-around-world; Victoria McNally, "Rise of the Valkyries! How This All-Female Group Is Changing Comics, One Shop at a Time," *Revelist*, 27 June 2016, http://www.revelist.com/pop-culture/valkyries-comics-group/3230; Kara Pauley, "Valhalla: A Safe Space for Women Librarians Who Love Comics," *American Libraries Magazine*, 25 June 2016, https://americanlibrariesmagazine.org/blogs/the-scoop/valhalla-safe-space-women-librarians-love-comics/.

46 Scott, "Fangirls in Refrigerators."

47 John Fiske, "Audiencing: A Cultural Studies Approach to Watching Television," *Poetics* 21 (1992): 345–359; Derek Johnson, "Participation Is Magic: Collaboration, Authorial Legitimacy, and the Audience Function," in *A Companion to Media Authorship*, eds. Jonathan Gray and Derek Johnson (Malden, Mass.: Wiley, 2013), 135–156.

48 McNally, "Rise of the Valkyries."

49 Jacob Bryant, "Marvel Exec Backpedals after Suggesting Diversity to Blame for Comic Book Sales Slump," *Variety*, 3 Apr. 2017, https://variety.com/2017/biz/news/marvel-exec-blames-diversity-women-comic-sales-slump-1202021440/; Rich Johnston, "All 3 Marvel Comics Nominated for GLAAD Awards Have Been Cancelled," *Bleeding Cool News and Rumors*, 1 Jan. 2018, https://www.bleedingcool.com/2018/01/19/marvel-glaad-award-noms-cancelled/.

50 Damien Walter, "How the Alt-Right Invaded Geek Culture," *Independent*, 29 Aug. 2016, https://www.independent.co.uk/voices/how-the-alt-right-invaded-geek-culture-a7214906.html; John Michael Colón, "Beta Testing Fascism: How Online Culture Wars Created the Alt-Right," *In These Times*, 27 June 2017, http://inthesetimes.com/article/20275/online-culture-wars-created-the-alt-right-nagle-kill-all-normies.

51 Aaron Kashtan, "'Those Aren't Really Comics': Raina Telgemaier and the Limitations of Direct-Market Centrism" (paper presented at the International Comic Arts Forum, Seattle, Washington, 3 Nov. 2017).

52 Heidi Macdonald, "Bergen Street Comics Is Closing," *Beat*, 26 Aug. 2015, http://www.comicsbeat.com/bergen-street-comics-is-closing/.

53 Springer, "Arielle Johnson"; Diane Peters, "Entrepreneur Fulfills Life's Ambition with The Sidekick," *Toronto Star*, 6 July 2015, https://www.thestar.com/business/2015/07/06/entrepreneur-fulfills-lifes-ambition-with-the-sidekick.html.

54 Gearino, *Comic Shop*, 221.

12

From Dealers' Room
to Exhibit Hall

• • • • • • • • • • • • • • • • • • • •

Comic Retailing and the
San Diego Comic-Con

ERIN HANNA

Early in Morgan Spurlock's 2011 documentary, *Comic-Con Episode IV: A Fan's Hope*, we meet longtime comic book dealer Chuck Rozanski. Though he owns one of the most successful comic shops in North America, Mile High Comics, Rozanski explains that he regularly struggles to break even at the San Diego Comic-Con (SDCC).[1] He attributes his underwhelming sales numbers to the steady disappearance of comics from the event: "Even though they have comic in the name of the event, very little of the convention anymore is actually comics." This oft-cited lament reflects SDCC's growth from a small fan convention to a key promotional site for the media industries that now attracts more than 130,000 attendees each year. But SDCC's fate has been intrinsically linked to the comic book industry since the event was founded by a group of San Diego fans, dealers, and aspiring professionals in 1970. So as comics entered into increasingly symbiotic relationships with media conglomerates in the twenty-first century, comic book retailers like Rozanski had the most to lose.

Nonetheless, as the film closes, even the downtrodden dealer can't help but proclaim that instead of heaven, "I wanna die and go to Comic-Con." Rozanski's ambivalence about SDCC raises questions about the historical connection between retail and comic fandom at the convention and gestures, however pessimistically, toward its future. In examining this relationship, I trace SDCC's retail space as it evolved from Dealers' Room to Exhibit Hall and connect this history to parallel developments in comic retailing—from the retail origins of the convention, to SDCC's response to changing retail models, to SDCC's contemporary economy of exclusive collectibles. This story is part of a much larger constellation of industry and fan interactions at SDCC, but the historical relationship between comic fandom and retailing represents a crucial entry point into the complex and contentious relationship between affect and economics that has come to define the convention. As this history demonstrates, SDCC, with its ties to the media industries and roots in comic culture, has long blurred the line between retail as an industrial practice and fandom as a consumer activity.

The "Capitalist Spirit" of Comics Fandom

In order to understand SDCC's relationship to retailing, it is necessary to consider the prehistory of the event and its roots in the "golden age of comic fandom" during the 1960s.[2] It was during this period that comic book readers began forming what Paul Lopes called "an organized social network."[3] Connecting through letter columns, fanzines, and conventions, many of these fans shared a central concern: collecting.[4] Of the more than six hundred fanzines published during the 1960s, *Rocket's Blast Comicollector*, an "adzine" where fans could buy, sell, and trade comics by mail, was by far the most popular.[5] And out of 169 people listed in 1964's *Who's Who in Comic-Fandom*, the "Official Directory of the Academy of Comic-Book Fans and Collectors," 153 identified themselves as "collectors" as opposed to "general fans."[6] Not only did these fans accumulate comic books; they also indexed, tracked, bought, sold, and traded them, cementing what historian Bill Schelly referred to as "the capitalist spirit" of comic fandom.[7]

This "capitalist spirit" was not an inherent attribute of comic book fans everywhere. Rather, collecting and its associated practices arose in response to the industry's mass-market distribution model. Like other periodicals at that time, comic books retailed primarily at newsstands, and because they were so inexpensive, they were often treated as interchangeable and disposable. Distributors would deliver "random assortments of titles," and retailers would return unsold comics for credit by tearing off the covers and presenting them as a "receipt."[8] And because publishers shouldered the cost of unsold comic books, neither retailers nor distributors had much incentive to keep track of their stock or sales.[9] As a result, readers struggled to follow their favorite new titles and back issues were difficult to locate.[10]

Under these conditions, collecting became something of a prerequisite for comic fandom. But it also became a potentially profitable endeavor. As scarcity drove up the value of old comics, the absence of reliable retailers left a gap that numerous enterprising fans filled by becoming dealers themselves.[11] In addition to the growing number of mail-order dealers who advertised in fanzines and comic books, a smattering of used bookstore owners began stockpiling old comics, usually because they were fans themselves.[12] This nascent collectors and dealers market, which functioned outside of the institutionalized structures of comic distribution and retail, was the context in which the earliest comic conventions, like the Detroit Triple Fan Fair and the New York Comic Con, emerged in the mid-1960s.[13] These conventions provided what collectors and dealers so desperately needed: a physical space where they could buy, sell, and trade their old comic books. It comes as little surprise, then, that comic collecting and comic dealers would prove instrumental to the founding of the San Diego Comic-Con in 1970.

SDCC's official history describes "an amazing confluence of fan groups" that emerged in San Diego during the late 1960s to found the convention, but what really brought these fans together was comic collecting and retail.[14] Shortly after SDCC's founder, Shel Dorf, relocated from Detroit to San Diego in 1969, he decided to sell some of his comics while he looked for work.[15] Back in Michigan, Dorf was part of a thriving fan community, but San Diego's comics scene was virtually nonexistent.[16] So Dorf turned to several area dealers and collectors, all of whom were just teenagers at the time. The most successful among them was Richard Alf, a seventeen-year-old entrepreneur who ran ads in the pages of Marvel Comics and stored his inventory of approximately twenty thousand books in his parents' garage.[17] Dorf had spent several years as a convention organizer in Detroit and was eager to continue that work in San Diego.[18] Intrigued by the prospect of a convention, Alf introduced Dorf to some of his friends.[19] Not only would a convention strengthen San Diego's fan community; it would also give local dealers, like Alf, a place to sell their wares.

Meanwhile, a group of science-fiction fans was holding regular gatherings in Ken Krueger's Ocean Beach bookshop, Alert Booksellers.[20] As a retailer and independent publisher, Krueger had a significant business background, but he also had a lifetime of experience in fandom, having attended the first World Science Fiction Convention in 1939.[21] When a chance encounter brought these two groups together, Krueger welcomed the opportunity to mentor a new generation of fans, and his bookstore became the base of operations for the first SDCC.[22]

Although Shel Dorf is widely recognized as SDCC's founder, his co-collaborators are quick to point out that it was the group's successful dealers, Richard Alf and Ken Krueger, who kept the event afloat in those early years. Alf's mail-order business enabled him to front crucial funds for the convention, and Krueger drew on his business experience to liaise with the hotel venue, handle contracts, and "keep things rolling along."[23] Given their importance to early comics fandom and the establishment of the San Diego Comic-Con, it comes as little surprise that a few years later, Shel Dorf would highlight retailers, alongside fans and comic artists, in the event's souvenir book: "The fan and the pro have a lot to offer each other. The sellers of rare material serve an even more important function—they help us fill the gaps in our collection and make available the stuff that has gone before. By studying the work of those who have laid the groundwork for the industry, we can learn to seek out new directions and help to build and diversify the field of comics."[24] Scholars have widely identified the importance of comic shops as "cultural spaces" of fandom.[25] But before the emergence of these specialty stores in the 1970s and 1980s, Ken Krueger provided a gathering space for San Diego's burgeoning fan community. Similarly, as a mail-order dealer, Richard Alf helped feed and sustain the collectors market outside the institutionalized newsstand model of distribution and retail.[26] But ultimately, it was SDCC—and other conventions like it—that brought these places, practices, and people together and, in doing so, imagined a new kind of retail space for comic books: the Dealers' Room.

"A Lot of Deals Were Made"

The earliest iteration of the San Diego Comic-Con, the March 21, 1970, "Minicon," was built on the template laid out by the first comic conventions in the mid-1960s and included "dealer's tables" that could be rented out for five dollars each and were open throughout the day.[27] The designation of special spaces for the sale of comics and memorabilia at SDCC continued that summer and, drawing on the nomenclature of an overlapping and more established fandom around science fiction, the program playfully referred to these spaces as the "Hucksters rooms."[28] An early flyer for the August event encouraged attendees to "come prepared for countless bargains you'll find at the dealers tables. . . . Comics of every description! Artwork! Sci-Fi magazines and pulps! Posters, fanzines, what the heck! . . . But—be sure to bring plenty of money, because at a convention, you'll want a lot of it."[29] This flyer is notable for two reasons. First, it highlights SDCC's eclectic retail environment, which, according to Richard Alf, was a deliberate strategy intended to boost attendance numbers.[30] Second, it foregrounds the importance of retail transactions at the event by encouraging attendees to seek out "bargains" and "bring plenty of money," ultimately connecting these practices to the ontology of the comic convention.

As it turned out, shopping in the Dealers' Room was such a popular feature during the first SDCC that it threatened to eclipse the rest of the convention. The *San Diego Union* reported that "the 'hustlers rooms' where the dealers tables were set up were so popular they had to be closed during the speeches and lectures,"[31] and Shel Dorf added, "We couldn't get the people out of there to listen . . . they just wanted to keep on dealing and buying."[32] The popularity of the Dealers' Room was, no doubt, a direct response to the scarcity of comic books—and back issues, in particular—in fans' everyday lives. If being a fan of the material necessitated meticulous collecting, it comes as no surprise that buying and selling would become a driving force at the convention. But as this episode illustrates, the preoccupation with buying and selling material often threatened to eclipse more intangible, affective practices associated with comics fandom.

By 1973, problems with overcrowding in the Dealers' Room would prompt organizers to once again reconfigure the event. In a rapid reversal of their 1970 strategy, organizers explicitly prioritized retail transactions over convention programming intended to educate and entertain attendees. The 1973 Wrap-up / 1974 Progress Report provides a detailed explanation of events:

> We're really grateful for the support our many fine dealers gave us this year. They had to put up with a lot, but we're sure they think it was worth it, considering the business they did! Our original set-up for the dealers' room was fine for Wednesday, but quickly proved infeasible on Thursday as more and more people arrived and crowded in; the fire marshal became very upset. We finally had to expand the dealers' room moving it into what was formerly the speakers-films room and reserving one corner of the former dealers' room for speakers and films! The expanded room was filled to capacity with both dealers and buyers throughout the convention, and, needless to say, a _lot_ of deals were made.[33]

From the very beginning, the Dealers' Room was a central part of the SDCC experience—so central that organizers were willing to make significant changes and reconfigure the space midway through the event. Their direct address to dealers in the report, along with their willingness to compromise other programming tracks in order to facilitate buying and selling, laid further groundwork for how the Dealers' Room (and subsequently, the Exhibit Hall) would function in the future—as a space that frequently prioritizes fandom as a business over the business of being a fan. That contradiction was far less pronounced in 1973, when the lines between fan, collector, and dealer were blurry, if not imperceptible. But that same year also marked a watershed moment in comics history—one that would ultimately make these lines much easier to trace at SDCC.

By the early 1970s, the problems with mass-market distribution and newsstand retailers had reached a critical mass. Fans were finding ways to work around these problems, but the comic book industry wasn't reaping the full benefits of the marketplace. To make matters worse for the industry, fan-dealers regularly exploited the mass market's honor system of returns by buying up popular titles from independent distributors and selling them by mail and at comic conventions for massively inflated prices. Distributors, in turn, would report these copies as unsold and seek refunds from comic book publishers.[34] These scams only exacerbated the comic book industry's problem with dwindling sales, and by the early 1970s, even Marvel, the industry leader, was only profiting on three to four out of every ten comics they printed.[35] It was fan, dealer, convention organizer, and high school teacher Phil Seuling who ultimately developed a solution. In 1973, Seuling approached comics publishers with a plan that would allow them to distribute comics directly to dealers like him. Seuling asked for the same discount offered to newsstand distributors, roughly 60 percent. In exchange, he would do away with the return system, and retailers would sell any leftover comics as back issues.[36] This direct-market distribution system meant shifting the risk from publishers to retailers, but it also meant that comic retailers and their customers would have a more reliable inventory of comics to buy and sell.[37] As Seuling's experience as a convention organizer suggests, the viability of this model had already been proven many times over in the flourishing marketplaces provided by Dealers' Rooms around the country.[38]

"Cash Register Receipts and Ledger Columns"

As fan-dealers like Phil Seuling began to work in distribution, a small number of stores specializing in comic books were opening across North America. By the mid-1970s, there were approximately thirty comic specialty shops in the United States and Canada. Ten years later, demonstrating the success of the direct-market model, the count skyrocketed to upwards of three thousand stores.[39] While there had been plenty of fan-dealers selling comics through mail order and conventions, opening brick-and-mortar stores required a much greater commitment of time and capital. Selling comics was no longer just a pastime; it was a profession.

The impact of these changes on SDCC was twofold. First, the opening of comics specialty shops around the country meant that the Dealers' Room was no longer the *only* place and time fans could rifle through old back issues and fill gaps in their collection. And second, SDCC became a place where publishers, distributors, and retailers could connect with not just fans but also each other. As the industry and fan culture surrounding comics changed, so too did the convention's retail space. While retail remained the central feature of the Dealers' Room, by the late 1970s, comic book publishers had also taken an interest in the promotional potentials of the convention. In 1979, Rick Marschall, the editor of Marvel's magazine division, convinced the company to set up a table in the Dealers' Room to promote their comic anthology magazine, *Epic Illustrated* (1980–1986), which, he claimed, may have "helped to start the ball rolling" and opened the door to an increasing number of publishers promoting their books at the event.[40] In 1983, SDCC's organizers, recognizing the professional scene that was developing, reached out to the industry and rented "hospitality suites" to "comics companies and other interested parties."[41] That year, thirteen comic companies were represented at SDCC, including Marvel, DC, and World Color Press, which printed almost all the comic books distributed in the United States.[42]

This promotional presence extended beyond fan outreach, however, and networking became equally important at SDCC. As writer Mark Evanier put it in 1983, "professionals are simply afraid to *not* show for a San Diego Convention because *this* is where it's happening."[43] In 1984, SDCC introduced the Comic Book Expo, a response to the increasing professionalization of fan-dealers as they moved from mail order to specialty shops. Differentiating itself from the fan convention, the Expo was held two days before SDCC and offered "a retailer-based schedule of programs including everything from company presentations about new products to detailed information on how to help run a small business, including personal time management, employee and tax advice, technology, marketing, and much more."[44] This trade-show arm of SDCC engaged more explicitly with the business side of comics culture, making a direct appeal to retailers by claiming to help "strengthen the direct sales marketplace where it counts, the cash register receipts and the ledger columns!"[45] SDCC even situated these goals within the parameters of its nonprofit mission, a justification that echoed Dorf's 1973 assertion about the importance of dealers to comic fandom: "Comic-Con and Comic-Book Expo are non-profit entities dedicated to furthering appreciation of popular culture in America. We recognize the specialty retailer as the means by which this exciting and important entertainment will reach a significant portion of the American public. We want to work with the comic book industry to provide an annual event that will strengthen and expand the marketplace, thus furthering our greater goals."[46]

This parallel trade show offered what John Caldwell calls "industrial geography lessons" by reproducing the institutional borders and boundaries that separate different segments of the industry while simultaneously mapping out ways for professionals to navigate and cross these thresholds.[47] Keeping the trade show "open to bonafide retailers and those affiliated with the industry" but "not the general public" created a spatial and temporal division that allowed SDCC and the Comic Book Expo to work symbiotically while maintaining an ideological gap between them.[48] Fans could mingle with representatives from the comic book industry during SDCC—dealers, artists, writers, and publishers, all of whom offered tables and booths in the Dealers' Room—but the Comic Book Expo was "<u>not</u> geared for the general fan" (original emphasis) and would therefore allow business to be conducted "without the interruptions of a large fan convention."[49] Where early comic fandom and the founding of SDCC relied on overlaps among dealers, collectors, and fans, the discourse surrounding the Comic Book Expo delineated the differences among these groups by privileging the economic interests of retailers, distributors, and publishers who profited upon the activities of fans. However, keeping this trade show separate from SDCC itself allowed this to happen in ways that would be nearly imperceptible during the main event. At the same time as fans were being explicitly excluded from this new industry trade show, the retail tables in SDCC's Dealers' Room were joined by a steady influx of industry booths, many of whom came for the expo and stayed for SDCC, where they could reach out to consumers too.[50]

This shift toward a greater industry presence manifested spatially in the convention's move from its longtime home at the El Cortez Hotel to the Convention and Performing Arts Center (CPAC) in the early 1980s.[51] The move to the CPAC meant that the event was now housed in a convention-center venue, geared toward meeting the needs of a more industry-oriented trade show. Not only were the facilities able to house SDCC's growing schedule of programs, but the CPAC also offered extensive exhibiting space, accommodating both the promotional and retail sectors of the comic book industry.[52] By the time SDCC moved to its current home, the San Diego Convention Center, in 1991, the Dealers' Room moniker had almost completely disappeared; it was replaced by the "Exhibit Hall," then a 92,000-square-foot space filled with a combination of "exhibitor's booths and dealers tables."[53]

This new title indicated an expanded space for consumption at SDCC in the form of not just retail sales but also promotion. It is not surprising, then, that ten years later, as the convention's attendance numbers and square footage continued to grow, SDCC stopped holding its annual comics trade show. Organizers said it had become somewhat redundant as "much of the business that had been taking place at the Expo began to shift to the larger event," which now offers a special "retailers only" space and programming track sponsored by the Comics Professional Retailer Organization.[54]

The end of the Comic Book Expo in 2001 came after a decade of setbacks for the comic book industry. Though the direct market helped shore up the industry in the 1980s and early 1990s, it also made comics more insular.[55] And with the books and their fans mostly relegated to specialty shops, story lines and continuity grew increasingly complex, convoluted, and inaccessible to outsiders.[56] At the same time, comic book publishers were eager to capitalize on another boom in the collectors market. As speculation drove comic sales, publishers fed this demand by spreading their most popular characters across multiple titles, orchestrating publicity stunts, and releasing variant covers and limited editions.[57] As comics alienated new readers and the speculation bubble burst, every sector of the industry found itself in dire straits by the mid-1990s.

Marvel filed for bankruptcy protection in 1996, and by 1998, countless small distributors had folded. So had more than half of the comic shops in North America.[58] SDCC, on the other hand, was more popular than ever.[59]

"Seismic Changes"

SDCC's elevated profile began with the comics boom but solidified with the significant recalibration of the comic book industry as it recovered from the bust of the 1990s.[60] As sales plummeted, the licensing and franchising of comic books as intellectual property became the industry's most reliable source of revenue.[61] So when the press began remarking upon SDCC's increased popularity, it was not because the event was the center of comics culture but because it was rapidly becoming "the center of the entertainment universe."[62] SDCC's retail environment in the twenty-first century reflects these changes in two significant ways: first, in the organization of the Exhibit Hall space, which highlights large, corporate exhibitors, and second, in the market for "Comic-Con Exclusives"—toys, comics, and other collectibles sold in limited quantities and only available at the convention—which allows such exhibitors and their customers to circumvent smaller dealers and retailers altogether.

There is, perhaps, no better illustration of the current status of comic books and retail sales at the convention than in the organization and mapping of SDCC's Exhibit Hall. At more than 460,000 square feet, the hall contains upwards of seven hundred exhibitors.[63] In this frenetic environment, small retailers must compete with film and television studios, comic book publishers, video game companies, and large toy and collectible manufacturers for attendees' dollars and attention. Tables and booths are arranged in aisles but are often clustered together based on the size and popularity of the display, the kinds of products being promoted or sold, and the companies (or individuals) doing the selling.[64] The result is a concentration of booths devoted to different—or in the case of media conglomerates, overlapping—sectors of the media industries. Such conglomerate displays are easily identifiable due to their size (most are several aisles wide or several stories high) and conspicuous corporate branding. The two-story Warner Brothers booth, for example, features the corporate logo surrounded by dozens of screens displaying promotional material and live footage of autograph sessions (figure 12.1). The promotional nature of these displays causes significant congestion in the hall, as they attract large crowds who linger for celebrity appearances and free giveaways. In contrast, the tables rented by smaller retailers and artists tend to blend in with one another in more-generic aisles. Because there is less crowding in these areas, it is easier to stop and browse without being pushed or pulled into the tide of thousands of constantly moving bodies (figure 12.2). But smaller crowds, of course, also mean fewer sales.

FIG. 12.1 Warner Brothers Booth, SDCC 2016 (photo by author)

FIG. 12.2 Gold and Silver Comics Pavilion, SDCC 2017 (photo by author)

The Exhibit Hall map reproduces this spatial hierarchy by prominently displaying brand logos belonging to larger companies. Smaller retail, dealer, and artist tables, on the other hand, are labeled with a three- to four-digit code that corresponds to the "Around the Booths" section of the events guide. So while booths belonging to media giants are rendered highly visible, navigating the smaller but more abundant retail tables requires significantly more effort on the part of attendees. Although these retailers—many of whom stock comics alongside toys and other collectibles—have had to contend with an influx of film and television promotion in the Exhibit Hall in the twenty-first century, comic book companies have long operated there in a promotional capacity. More disruptive, then, has been the increased presence of large toy and collectible manufacturers such as Hasbro, Mattel, and Funko, who have joined the comic book industry in promoting *and* selling their products at the event.

Three years after he appeared in *Comic-Con Episode IV*, dealer Chuck Rozanski was still struggling at SDCC. In 2014, he estimated a $10,000 loss at the convention and blamed the "seismic changes" brought about by the influx of Comic-Con exclusives offered by publishers and manufacturers in the Exhibit Hall.[65] Though some companies began offering exclusives in the 1990s, the practice took off when Rozanski helped institute Preview Night in 2001. When Rozanski first suggested the idea, he thought that allowing a limited number of dealers and artists to mingle on the show floor the night before the convention would bring "back a little of the old personal nature of the convention that made it so unique."[66] But coming as the Comic Book Expo ended, organizers seemed less interested in instituting another exclusive time and space for professional networking and more invested in cultivating exclusivity, in general. While the expo had separated retailers from "the general fan," Preview Night was open to professionals *and* attendees. In this new context, comics and toy companies, intertwined through licensing deals and media franchising, began to offer exclusive collectibles that attendees could only purchase from their booths.

Because dealers in the Exhibit Hall are forced to compete with other segments of the media industries—publishers, manufacturers, and studios—they find themselves in a challenging position when it comes to the buying and selling of collectible merchandise. As Rozanski put it, "The very organizations we most support are those who can cause us the most harm. . . . Not only do they divert revenues into their own pockets, but they also diminish our standing in the fan community by making us appear incomplete."[67] For some time, it was standard practice for dealers to use their Preview Night access to buy as many exclusives as they could and resell them at inflated prices. SDCC discourages these practices but has largely left it up to individual companies to regulate their sales, as Hasbro and Mattel did in 2013 when they began restricting exhibitor purchases.[68]

This all amounts to a significant shift in SDCC's retail environment in that it allows corporate producers to circumvent retailers and sell directly to consumers. By restricting access for independent dealers, companies like Mattel and Hasbro send the message that they are aligned with the interests of the consumer, while the exclusivity of the product guarantees increased demand.[69] Once these sales are made, the exclusives move to a secondary collectors' market, where their value is inflated, thus producing greater demand for subsequent exclusives. This same industrial strategy—the creation of false scarcity through the mass production of variants and limited releases—built upon the "capitalist spirit" of comics fandom in order to drive speculation and fuel the boom and bust in the comic book industry during the 1990s. But while this proved tenuous as a day-to-day business practice, it is right at home in the already exclusive context of the San Diego Comic-Con. In recent years, companies such as Mattel began offering preorders and selling select Comic-Con exclusives online. If anything, these practices demonstrate how rapidly this strategy of manufactured scarcity has been institutionalized and branded as part of the SDCC experience, even as it is deployed to drive sales beyond the convention floor.

In 2016, the *Verge* ran a story on the growing number of collectors who pay for their annual pilgrimage to the convention—and turn a profit—through "toy flipping."[70] But where collectors and speculators in comics fandom tended to treat their acquisitions as long-term investments, Comic-Con exclusives inflate in value almost immediately due to the excitement surrounding the event and the limited availability of the merchandise. These collectors pay for their habit by buying up Comic-Con exclusives and becoming dealers in their own right—through eBay, Craigslist, Facebook groups, and message boards.[71] This practice is roundly criticized by many, particularly those who wait for hours or days for a single item, only to see quantities dwindle as they're bought up by flippers. But in many ways, this trend brings the history of SDCC's retail space full circle, as it blurs the line between retail as an industrial practice and fandom as a consumer activity. When SDCC began, fans acted as dealers, driving the market for collectibles. Today, those same dealers are in jeopardy, as producers, distributors, and fans all occupy the role of retailer, capitalizing on the demand for exclusives during and after the convention.

Conclusion

In 2017, Rozanski made good on his threat to sever ties with SDCC. The decision was the result of a variety of factors—rising costs, increased competition, and poor management—but he ultimately concluded, "When you are in a relationship out of love and passion, but the other party could care less whether you live or die, you have to realize that it is time to move on."[72] It remains unclear if Rozanski's 2017 departure will be permanent or merely a temporary hiatus, but it is, nevertheless, significant. When SDCC arose from the golden age of comic fandom in the 1960s, collecting was a direct response to conditions of scarcity produced by the comic book industry's flawed distribution and retail model. Eager to capitalize on this secondary market, fans became retailers themselves, and dealers' rooms at conventions like SDCC were among the first physical spaces that allowed these practices to flourish. However, as the introduction of the direct market opened up new avenues for comic retailing, SDCC's space adapted to include an increased industry presence and support the professionalization of fan-dealers and specialty shop owners through the Comic Book Expo. Many of these developments were driven from the bottom up to the extent that fans *and* small retailers held a less privileged economic place in the hierarchy of the media industries, even as they affected the most change. But in recent years, these developments have given way to a top-down model, hinging on manufactured scarcity and driven by media conglomerates, franchises, and licensing deals. This historical relationship between comic retailing and SDCC helps explain the present state of the convention, but it also provides some clues about the future. SDCC's Dealers' Room once provided an environment that retailers and collectors could only find at a smattering of conventions and stores around the country. But the hundreds of local and regional conventions and comics specialty shops that arose alongside the San Diego Comic-Con now fill that same void. In 2011, Chuck Rozanski said that instead of heaven, he wanted to die and go to Comic-Con. But for many fans, collectors, and dealers, heaven might look less like SDCC's Exhibit Hall and more like Mile High Comics' 65,000-square-foot warehouse, filled to the brim with Rozanski's life's work: millions and millions of comic books.

Notes

1 Rozanski's massive inventory of comics supports an online store and three retail locations in Denver, Colorado. Randy Duncan, Matthew J. Smith, and Paul Levitz, *The Power of Comics: History, Form, and Culture* (New York: Bloomsbury, 2015), 289.

2 William Schelly, *The Golden Age of Comic Fandom* (Seattle, Wash.: Hamster Press, 1995).

3 Paul Douglas Lopes, *Demanding Respect: The Evolution of the American Comic Book* (Philadelphia, Pa.: Temple University Press, 2009), 93.

4 Lopes, *Demanding Respect*, 98.

5 Jean-Paul Gabilliet, *Of Comics and Men: A Cultural History of American Comic Books* (Jackson: University Press of Mississippi, 2005), 263; Schelly, *Golden Age*, 33, 61; Lopes, *Demanding Respect*, 98.

6 Larry Lattanzi, *Who's Who in Comic Fandom* (Warren, Mich.: Academy of Comic-Book Fans and Collectors, 1964).

7 Schelly, *Golden Age*, 87.

8 Some retailers took advantage of this system and resold coverless comics in sec-
ondhand markets. Michael Dean, "Fine Young Cannibals: How Phil Seuling and a
Generation of Teenage Entrepreneurs Created the Direct Market and Changed the
Face of Comics," *Comics Journal*, no. 277 (2006): 50.

9 Duncan, Smith, and Levitz, *Power of Comics*, 276.

10 Duncan, Smith, and Levitz, 61.

11 Lopes, *Demanding Respect*, 94–6; Matthew Pustz, *Comic Book Culture: Fanboys
and True Believers* (Jackson: University Press of Mississippi, 1999), 46–47.

12 Bill Schelly, *Founders of Comic Fandom: Profiles of 90 Publishers, Dealers, Collectors, Writers, Artists and Other Luminaries of the 1950s and 1960s* (Jefferson, N.C.:
McFarland, 2010), 40.

13 Schelly, *Golden Age*, 71, 77.

14 San Diego Comic Convention Inc., *Comic-Con: 40 Years of Artists, Writers, Fans
and Friends* (San Francisco: Chronicle, 2009), 22.

15 San Diego Comic Convention Inc., *Comic-Con*, 20–23; Peter Rowe, "From Little
Shows Big Cons Grow," *San Diego Union-Tribune*, 19 July 2009, http://www
.sandiegouniontribune.com/sdut-lz1a19comicco181351-little-shows-big-cons-grow
-2009jul19-htmlstory.html.

16 Angela Carone and Maureen Cavanaugh, "The First Comic-Con," *KPBS*, 22 July
2010, http://www.kpbs.org/news/2010/jul/22/first-comic-con/; Schelly, *Founders*,
102; Dean, "Fine Young Cannibals," 51.

17 Rowe, "From Little Shows."

18 Dorf spent several years organizing Detroit's Triple Fan Fair and used the convention as a model for SDCC. Schelly, *Golden Age*, 77.

19 Mike Towry, "Richard Alf," Comic-Con.org, 3 Dec. 2012, https://www.comic-con
.org/frontpage/richard-alf.

20 "San Diego's Golden State Comic-Con Program Book 1970," Series I: Programs and
Souvenir Books, folder 1, box 1, Shel Dorf Collection, San Diego History Center,
San Diego, California, Aug. 1970; San Diego Comic Convention Inc., *Comic-Con*;
Scott Shaw, "Cartoonist-at-Large #1: The 'Secret Origin' of San Diego Comic-Con
International," *Jim Hill Media*, 6 July 2005, http://jimhillmedia.com/blogs/scott
_shaw/archive/2005/07/07/1717.aspx.

21 Krueger also worked in comic distribution during the 1980s. "In Memoriam: Ken
Krueger 1926 2009," *Comic-Con Magazine*, Fall 2009, 6.

22 Greg Bear, "Biography," *Ken Krueger Tribute*, Nov. 2009, http://www
.kenkruegertribute.com/biography/.

23 Mike Towry, "Richard Alf"; "In Memoriam," 6.

24 Shel Dorf, "San Diego Comic-Con Program Book 1973," Series I: Programs and
Souvenir Books, folder 4, box 1, Shel Dorf Collection, San Diego History Center.

25 Pustz, *Comic Book Culture*; Benjamin Woo, "The Android's Dungeon: Comic-
Bookstores, Cultural Spaces, and the Social Practices of Audiences," *Journal of
Graphic Novels and Comics* 2, no. 2 (2011): 125–136.

26 Alf would go on to open one of San Diego's first comic shops in 1975 but later left
the profession and sold his mail-order business to Chuck Rozanski. Mike Towry,
"Richard Alf."

27 This one-day event functioned as a fundraiser for the first official SDCC that
summer. "San Diego's Golden State Comic-Minicon Flyer," Series IV: Comic-Con
Advertising, folder 1, box 3, Shel Dorf Collection, San Diego History Center;
Schelly, *Golden Age*, 65–74, 77.

28 "Comic-Minicon Flyer" (original emphasis); Donald Franson, "A Key to the Terminology of Science-Fiction Fandom," National Fantasy Fan Federation, 1962.
29 "Comic-Con Flyer, 1970," Series IV: Comic-Con Advertising, folder 1, box 3, Shel Dorf Collection, San Diego History Center.
30 Carone and Cavanaugh, "First Comic-Con."
31 "Hustlers room" is likely a mistaken reference to the aforementioned "Hucksters rooms." Andrew Makarushka, "Comics Connoisseurs Here for Golden State Convention," *San Diego Union*, 2 Aug. 1970.
32 Shel Dorf, quoted in Makarushka, "Comics Connoisseurs."
33 Chuck Graham and Barry Alfonso, "San Diego Comic-Con Progress Report No. 1 and 1973 Wrap-up Report," Series III: Progress Reports and Newsletters, folder 40, box 1, Shel Dorf Collection, San Diego History Center.
34 Lopes, *Demanding Respect*, 99.
35 Dean, "Fine Young Cannibals," 50.
36 Dean, 51.
37 Dean.
38 Seuling organized a number of comic conventions in New York beginning in the late 1960s. For more on his contributions to comic fandom, see Schelly, *Founders*, 106–108. For more on Seuling's role in creating the direct market, see Dean.
39 Dean, 51, 54.
40 Rick Marschall, "Rememberances of Cons Past," in *1984 San Diego Comic-Con*, ed. Jackie Estrada (San Diego, Calif.: San Diego Comic Convention, Inc., 1984).
41 Jackie Estrada, "1983 San Diego Comic-Con Progress Report No. 2.," San Diego Comic-Con, May 1983, Michigan State University Library Comic Art Collection.
42 "1984 San Diego Comic-Con Progress Report No. 1.," San Diego Comic-Con, Dec. 1983, Michigan State University Library Comic Art Collection (original emphasis).
43 Mark Evanier, "Comics: Ny2la," in *1982 San Diego Comic-Con Inc. Souvenir Book*, ed. Shel Dorf (San Diego, Calif.: San Diego Comic-Con Inc., 1982).
44 San Diego Comic Convention Inc., *Comic-Con.*
45 "Comic Book Expo Flyer, 1986," San Diego Comic-Con, 1986, Michigan State University Library Comic Art Collection.
46 "Expo Flyer, 1986."
47 John T. Caldwell, "Industrial Geography Lessons: Socio-professional Rituals and the Borderlands of Production Culture," in *Mediaspace: Place, Scale and Culture in a Media Age*, eds. Nick Couldry and Anna McCarthy (New York: Routledge, 2004), 163–190.
48 "Comic Book Expo Flyer, 1987," San Diego Comic-Con, Michigan State University Library Comic Art Collection.
49 Mike Pasqua, "Con-Tact #2," San Diego Comic-Con, 1984, Michigan State University Library Comic Art Collection; Fay Gates, "Comic Book Expo 84 Letter," San Diego Comic-Con, 21 Mar. 1984, Michigan State University Library Comic Art Collection.
50 San Diego Comic Convention Inc., *Comic-Con*, 60.
51 The convention was held at the CPAC in 1979 and 1980 and returned to the El Cortez for a final year in 1981. David Glanzer, Gary Sassaman, and Jackie Estrada, eds., *Comic-Con 40 Souvenir Book* (San Diego, Calif.: San Diego Comic-Con International, 2009), 72, 78–87, 94–95.
52 San Diego Comic Convention Inc., *Comic-Con*, 60.

53 Bill Stoddard and Janet Tait, eds., *1991 San Diego Comic-Con Convention Events Guide* (San Diego, Calif.: San Diego Comic Convention, Inc., 1991), 4.

54 San Diego Comic Convention Inc., *Comic-Con*, 87; "Retailer Programs," Comic -Con.org, 6 July 2017, https://www.comic-con.org/cci/retailer-programs.

55 Dean, 49.

56 Pustz, *Comic Book Culture*, 131.

57 Lopes, *Demanding Respect*, 115–116.

58 Lopes, 117; Matthew P. McAllister, "Ownership Concentration in the U.S. Comic Book Industry," in *Comics and Ideology*, eds. Matthew P. McAllister, Edward H. Sewell Jr., and Ian Gordon (New York: Peter Lang, 2001), 24.

59 Between 2000 and 2007, attendance grew from 48,500 to more than 125,000. San Diego Comic Convention Inc., *Comic-Con*, 154.

60 San Diego Comic Convention Inc., *Comic-Con*, 97–98.

61 McAllister, "Ownership," 29.

62 Karla Peterson and James Herbert, "Around Here, the Geeks Decide What's Cool," *San Diego Union-Tribune*, 19 July 2006.

63 Christie D'Zurilla, "By the Numbers: San Diego Comic-Con International 2016," *Los Angeles Times*, 21 July 2016, http://www.latimes.com/entertainment/la-et-hc -comic-con-updates-by-the-numbers-san-diego-comic-con-1469118665-htmlstory .html; and "Aisles of Smiles! Comic-Con's Massive Exhibit Hall Rocks!," in *Comic-Con International Update 3*, ed. Dan Vado (San Diego, Calif.: Comic-Con International, 2005).

64 Artists, small companies, and dealers typically use uniformly sized "tables," while "booths" denote larger and more costly blocks of space.

65 Chuck Rozanski, "San Diego Comic Con Report #2," *Mile High Comics*, 25 July 2014, http://www.milehighcomics.com/newsletter/072514email.html; Chuck Rozanski, "San Diego Comic Con Report #3," *Mile High Comics*, 26 July 2014, http://www.milehighcomics.com/newsletter/072614wemail.html.

66 Chuck Rozanski, "San Diego Update—Thursday, 18 July 2001—Mile High Comics," *Mile High Comics*, 18 July 2001, http://www.milehighcomics.com/sdcc071801 .html.

67 Rozanski, "Report #2."

68 Rich Johnston, "Hasbro and Mattel Stamp Down on Professional Scalpers at San Diego Comic Con," *Bleeding Cool*, 17 July 2013, http://www.bleedingcool.com/ 2013/07/17/hasbro-and-mattel-stamp-down-on-professional-scalpers-at-san-diego -comic-con.

69 Eileen Meehan, "Leisure or Labor? Fan Ethnography and Political Economy," in *Consuming Audiences? Production and Reception in Media Research*, eds. Ingunn Hagen and Janet Wasko (Cresskill, N.J.: Hampton Press, 2000), 83–84.

70 Jacob Kastrenakes, "Meet the Collectors Who Resell Toys to Pay Off Their Comic-Con Addiction," *Verge*, 25 July 2016, https://www.theverge.com/2016/7/25/ 12269660/comic-con-2016-resell-toy-flipping-collection.

71 Kastrenakes, "Meet the Collectors."

72 Chuck Rozanski, "Mile High Comics Withdraws from San Diego Comic-Con after 44 Years," *Mile High Comics*, 5 July 2017, http://www.milehighcomics.com/ newsletter/070517email.html.

13

The Changing Scales of Diasporic Media Retail

• • • • • • • • • • • • • • • • • • • •

EVAN ELKINS

Walk down a set of steps into a basement-level cluster of shops in Jackson Heights, Queens, and one is liable to encounter a particular kind of establishment. A sign over the door says, "Tip Top Professional Tailor: We make Salwar Kameez, Blouses, and do Alterations on Various Kinds of Dresses." Other signs promote CDs, DVDs, and Blu-ray discs. Inside the room, a woman sits in the corner sewing while a younger man stands behind a counter running the cash register and offering movie and music recommendations to customers. The walls are stocked with hundreds of Bollywood DVDs—many imported from India but a few clearly manufactured in-house, as evidenced by another woman sitting at a computer just outside the door, printing off DVD covers and sliding the covers into cases containing burned discs. Across the East River, stroll down a street in Spanish Harlem and you may encounter a street vendor hawking bootleg DVDs—many of mainstream Hollywood movies still in theaters but some of Spanish-language films and television programs from throughout Mexico and South and Central America. Further west, in Harlem's Le Petit Sénégal neighborhood, a media store owned by Senegalese Americans specializes in films from that country as well as from Nigeria and other sub-Saharan nations. Lest this seem like a coastal phenomenon, cities and towns throughout the country maintain similar establishments. An Indian grocer in Madison, Wisconsin, stocks a massive shelf of Indian DVDs next to imported food—and not just Bollywood movies but films from Hyderabad and West Bengal as well as other regional cinemas. These kinds of retailers exist in many places marked by a high concentration of migrant communities, and while there are significant differences among them, they all sell the same kind of wares: media products created by and for particular diasporas. Likewise, in spite of their many differences, the people who work in these stores tend to envision their customers embodying an intersection of two particular cultural-geographic vectors: denizens of the immediate local neighborhood and members of a transnational migrant community.

Prominent discussions in the United States about the state of the video store often underemphasize businesses like these. Rather, academic, industry, and popular discourse regarding the shift in U.S. video retail from brick-and-mortar establishments to online media delivery has tended to focus on two different genres of retailer: the first being major chains like Blockbuster Video or Family Video that offer(ed) home video rentals and sales of primarily Hollywood movies and the second representing independently owned stores specializing in cinephile fare such as indie and foreign art films.[1] A heavier focus on these kinds of retail locations rather than diasporic video stores can be explained by a number of possible factors: an American/European frame that remains dominant throughout media studies; the informality of many of these stores, which makes them more difficult to track and discuss; and the tendency of such establishments to use and sell media technology that to many might seem obsolete (and thus, given the cult of the new, unworthy of comment). In the age of digital delivery, DVDs are likewise considered by many to be old-fashioned, despite their still-common presence in everyday life.

In an attempt to shift this focus, this chapter investigates the impacts of video-on-demand (VOD) services on local diasporic video stores. It does so to complicate commonly held understandings of digital delivery's effect on media retail. Drawing on media-industry analyses of VOD services (both major global entities like Netflix and Hulu as well as diaspora-targeted niche platforms like DramaFever and iRokoTV) in addition to ethnographic interviews with owners and employees of U.S. video stores catering to various Global South diasporas, I show that contemporary diasporic video retail is marked by opportunities and anxieties regarding the geographic size and scale of the audience. Specifically, I argue that while both general and diaspora-targeted VOD platforms treat migrant communities as a primarily transnational audience, video stores serve a customer base envisioned as at once transnational *and* local. Anna Tsing emphasizes the importance of scale in the global economy when she discusses how states, corporations, and other institutions engage in "scale-making projects," or "projects that make us imagine globality . . . locality, or the space of regions or nations."[2] Traditionally, video stores have engaged in such projects to scale their operations not just transnationally, by tapping into formal and informal international video distribution networks and serving communities who identify with transnational diasporas, but also locally, by maintaining a customer base of people living in heavily diasporic neighborhoods. As an extension of their local dynamics, they also operate translocally, by functioning as nodes or, to use Michael Curtin's term, *switching points* in the flows of people and media commodities between and across various cities and immigrant neighborhoods within and beyond the United States.[3]

As VOD becomes increasingly viable as a mode of diasporic media distribution and retail, however, these scales are changing. There is a perception among those who work in video stores that streaming has led to a decrease in clientele interested in videos. Whether true or not (and it is a difficult thing to prove in a video retail economy marked by informal trade), it indicates a redefinition of the geographic scale of diasporic media markets. As the transnational paths of diasporic video distribution become formalized through video platforms funded by venture capitalists and entrepreneurs, they become at least partially disarticulated from the local. Instead, political-economic shifts result in the definition of diasporic viewerships as transnational entities and/or part of a mass global viewership.

In making this argument, this chapter takes diasporic media culture and retail as a loose cluster of media sale and consumption practices taking place among many immigrant communities. At the same time, it recognizes that not all diasporas are the same and thus cannot all be fully understood through one explanatory or analytical framework. I understand "diasporic" here as a useful category for both media studies and media industries that enables broad reflections about how human migration, media retail, and digital culture have all impacted each other. Instead of a sustained analysis of one particular ethnic or (trans)national culture or community, then, this chapter points toward broad, general trends in diasporic media retail centralized in the United States. Its larger goals are to ask what we can learn about the state of diasporic retail in an era of intensified global connection, assess how this might add to or revise commonly held axioms in diasporic media research, and carve out additional space for diasporic media alongside more commonly heard assessments of local media retail's viability.

Diasporic Media Retail

As a genre of retail establishment, the diasporic video store grew out of a combination of postcolonial human migration and the home video industry that emerged in the 1970s and came of age in the 1980s and 1990s.[4] As immigrants opened grocery stores, convenience stores, and other local retail establishments during this time, the nascent industry of home video distribution and emergent practice of videotape dubbing and copying made film and television available as objects to rent and sell in stores. Many of these stores emerged in cities and communities in North America with particularly high numbers of immigrants—cities like New York, Minneapolis, and Los Angeles—but also particular enclaves and neighborhoods within these cities that contained high concentrations of specific migrant populations. Thus the diasporic video store exemplifies what Timothy Shortell refers to as the "immigrant professional services" that are so prominent in diasporic neighborhoods. These services are generally run by and for members of immigrant communities defined by commonalities of language, ethnicity, nation, and/or region (e.g., the aforementioned DVD shop in Le Petit Sénégal offering videos from throughout the African continent but specializing in Senegalese cinema).[5] As opposed to, say, an independently owned video store offering independent films and art cinema from all over the world, the diasporic video store is usually narrower in its focus (though there is some overlap between the clienteles of these two kinds of establishments).

These establishments have served important roles in the circulation of shared diasporic culture. Numerous scholars have pointed to media's role as a *cultural resource* that diasporic people and communities use to negotiate identities, construct subjectivities, connect with local and dispersed communities, and as Glen Lewis and Chalinee Hirano put it, maintain "cultural continuity."[6] Indeed, the video store's role in ensuring that people have access to these resources points to media retail's significance in not just the business of diaspora but its cultural dynamics as well. At times, this can mean connecting the diasporic viewer back to a homeland—even an imagined one. As Youna Kim has shown in her study of Chinese, Japanese, and Korean women living in London, media can paradoxically encourage a sense of "diasporic nationalism" within people who lead transnational lives.[7] At the same time, the fact of diasporic media's encouragement of national belonging should not suggest that it *only* serves to connect people back to an imagined national identity. Rather, diasporic media culture is characterized by the cultural hybridity of transnational living.

As this suggests, diasporic video stores are as much transnational entities as they are local ones. They serve many migrant customers who often identify as hyphenates or part of a community that exceeds the scale of one nation. For example, a store might cater to a broader Latin American clientele rather than, say, a Mexican American or Dominican American one. They are also connected to formal and informal circuits of media distribution and trade that flow from country to country, as in the case of one Milwaukee-based Indian grocer who receives Bollywood DVDs from a wholesaler in Chicago that imports them from India. What distinguishes this from the international reach of an online streaming platform is how video stores' transnational dynamics connect to smaller-scale forms of local community. Stuart Cunningham characterizes diasporic media as a kind of "public sphericule" that can "provide a central site for public communication in globally dispersed communities."[8] We can think of this as media symbolically connecting people across space, but we can also think of the site of communication more literally: as a gathering space like a movie theater or video store. While the diasporic video store is a site in international media networks, it also sustains and is sustained by the more immediate local community in which it exists. This becomes particularly clear when we consider that many of these establishments exist in neighborhoods that figure as ethnic enclaves for people and families who live migrant lives. Many scholars of diasporic culture are as attuned to the local as they are the transnational, and canonical work by James Clifford emphasizes the importance of traveling cultures that live in and move between immigrant neighborhoods— neighborhoods that Arjun Appadurai calls part of "ethnic projects" that mediate transnational and local cultures.[9] The diasporic media store's relationship to its immediate neighborhood as well as the larger diasporic community residing within it enables us to understand how the "transnational" figures within particular local contexts in media culture.

Because diasporic video stores often serve as outposts of media culture in local enclaves of migrant communities, they are analogous to the small-town American video stores that Daniel Herbert has researched. As he says, these stores "interweave movie culture with a wide variety of local conditions and concerns."[10] Thus video stores are (or were) not simply the ends of the Hollywood product pipeline; they also reflect the tastes and values of their clientele. By primarily serving particular, localized, and usually ethnically specific groups, diasporic video stores operate much the same way. They are saturated with and help structure the tastes and cultures of the surrounding community. For instance, a video store in a primarily South Asian community will likely be stocked with a fair amount of Bollywood films as well as cinema from other regional Indian and South Asian cinemas. In some ways, this is a rather traditional practice of marketing media products that have some measure of proximity or similarity to the viewer's own cultural situation. This approach to media distribution and exhibition is similar to the definition of a diasporic market as a transnational mass community, but it is different in its dual address to diasporic customers who make their homes in the local neighborhood within which the video store is embedded.

As this suggests, it would be reductive to view these businesses' aims through the coldly rational lens of economic exigency. Like small-town video stores, local diasporic video stores serve particular *communities* defined through complex alignments among geography and other forms of cultural identity such as ethnicity. For instance, a Middle Eastern DVD store in Dearborn, Michigan, may see itself as serving an intersectional clientele comprising Lebanese Americans, residents of Dearborn, a transnational Pan-Arab American community, or some combination thereof. In serving such communities, these stores circulate products imbued with particularly rich cultural resonance. In some ways, this is similar to the Indian grocers in San Francisco that Purnima Mankekar calls "fecund sites for the proliferation and negotiation of affective regimes pertaining to India and Indianness" through the evocation of sense memories and other connections to transnational Indian culture.[11] Food, clothing, and other products redolent with strong "cultural odor" are emblematic of the diasporic experience more so than more culturally neutral products.[12] We might think about how film and media bring about similar affective relationships, albeit through different sensory registers. Even if a DVD box does not animate the same immediate olfactory response as, say, a rack of spices does, art and entertainment are significant sites of emotional and cultural resonance pertaining to diasporic positionality. Keeping in mind the role that diasporic grocers serve in migrant communities and particularly considering that many of these communities' video stores double as grocery stores, media retailers serve as spaces that animate any number of emotional responses to diasporic existence: nostalgia, pride, belonging, exile, and so forth.

In contrast, VOD's lack of connection to a local neighborhood points to a broader redefinition of the category of the "transnational" within diasporic media cultures. Whereas in the local retail markets, such a category speaks to the reverberations of transnational culture within local life, in VOD industries, the "transnational" implies more of a media-industrial construction of the audience as a particular market segment. Specifically, it is more akin to what Joseph Straubhaar refers to as the "transnational cultural-linguistic" markets that are "less than global but more than national."[13] As he points out, these markets often result from migration patterns—with the global Indian diaspora being one notable example. And while he focuses on cultural-linguistic markets in global television specifically, this extends to the video retail and online distribution sectors discussed here. The increasing centrality of VOD to diasporic media suggests an intensified focus on this large-scale cultural-linguistic market and the decreasing significance of more localized markets built around particular cities or even neighborhoods. Put another way, Hulu is understandably more interested in exhibiting telenovelas in order to reach a group defined broadly within a Latin American diaspora as a whole than it is in focusing specifically on, say, Mexican American viewers living in the West Side of Chicago. This different approach to the audience indicates how the ties between the transnational and the local are disappearing in the advent of digital video on demand. Within this environment, diasporic retail establishments retain that connection between transnational flows and local culture.

From Retail to VOD

The video store's centrality in diasporic viewing has shifted as the broad trend in media consumption has moved to online platforms. These shifts show not only how local media retail is increasingly supplanted by online retail and streaming; they also speak to the redefinition of the diasporic consumer as part of a more broadly defined transnational group. While at a larger level, the difference in services offered by video stores and VOD platforms may seem like one of degree rather than kind—after all, both offer viewers the opportunity to watch movies and television programs at home—they animate different understandings of the "diasporic" as a category. The video store by necessity must keep the concerns of its more immediately proximal community in mind as it chooses what to stock on its potentially limited shelf space, how much inventory to order/produce, and so forth. Because of a lack of scarcity of product (as opposed to a video store that may only have one or two copies of a movie) and potentially international reach, VOD services have no need to take such considerations into account.

Such changes have been spurred by major platforms getting into the diasporic media business. Starting in the mid- to late 2000s, services like Netflix, Hulu, and iTunes entered into high-profile distribution deals with non-U.S. or otherwise diaspora-oriented media companies. Netflix in particular has made a number of agreements to produce and distribute content aimed in part at non-U.S. and diasporic viewers. For instance, the company is readily building its library of South Asian cinema, and in late 2016, it signed a distribution deal with Bollywood star Shah Rukh Khan's company Red Chillies Entertainment to provide Bollywood films to viewers.[14] In the summer of 2017, Netflix also engaged in talks (along with Apple and Amazon) to stream Bollywood producer and distributor Eros International's film library.[15] Especially following the platform's highly publicized 2016 expansion into almost every country in the world, news, trade, and fan sources pointed to the availability of non-U.S. and diaspora-oriented content—telenovelas, Korean dramas, and Nollywood films—available on Netflix.[16] In addition, throughout the mid-2010s, Netflix incorporated diaspora-targeted content into its original programming. While in the United States, series like *House of Cards*, *Orange Is the New Black*, and *Stranger Things* have taken up the bulk of attention with regard to Netflix original programs, Spanish-language original productions like *Narcos* and *Club de Cuervos* are designed to appeal to viewers throughout Latin America as well as Spanish-speaking members of Latin American diasporas.[17] Netflix is far from the only major VOD service to increasingly cater to various diasporic clienteles, as many streaming and sell-through services have recently expanded global offerings. Hulu, the streaming platform owned and operated by three of the four conglomerates that own major U.S. television networks, maintains an extensive library of what it calls "international" film and television—Korean dramas, telenovelas, Chinese television programs, and more. Amazon Video's and iTunes' U.S. libraries carry many Bollywood films, with each potentially about to offer even more, per the aforementioned Eros talks as well as

Amazon's recently announced deal with Salman Khan Ventures.[18] Both services stock telenovelas and other Spanish-language content as well.

In addition to major services like Netflix and Amazon, niche-oriented platforms also serve diasporic audiences across various national and transnational cultures. Many of these have been developed by startup entrepreneurs connected in some way to the diaspora—a twenty-first-century analog to the diasporic video store business owner, perhaps—and/or are backed by venture capitalists and media corporations. Some, in fact, are designed to compete with the major VOD services described earlier. For instance, in 2017, Lionsgate and Hemisphere Media Group launched Spanish-language VOD platform Pantaya, directed toward U.S.-based Latina/o viewers.[19] The now-defunct DramaFever primarily offered Korean serial dramas but also contained Japanese programming and telenovelas. In 2016, Warner Bros. (WB) purchased DramaFever from Japan's Softbank Group, which had acquired the service two years earlier. In its announcement about the purchase, WB signaled that it planned to use DramaFever as part of a broader initiative to create new over-the-top (OTT) services offering content from outside the United States.[20] In part as a response, KPC Global, a U.S.-based joint venture of three major Korean broadcasters, launched streaming service Kocowa (which stands for "Korean content wave") to provide Korean television to American viewers.[21] In 2018, however, WB shuttered DramaFever, due in part to competitors like Netflix and Amazon driving up licensing costs for American distribution of Korean dramas—an indication of how major U.S.-based platforms are affecting transnational streaming.[22]

One particularly prominent diaspora-aimed streaming platform is iRokoTV, a VOD service that specializes in Nollywood videos. Given its founding in 2010 as a YouTube channel called NollywoodLove before it launched as its own platform the next year, the service's origins suggest a tension between ground-up entrepreneurialism and mainstream digital platforming.[23] iRokoTV's cofounder Jason Njoku in particular is a paradigm of a diasporic VOD entrepreneur, often placing himself front and center in public discourse about the platform. Balancing global ambitions with an acknowledgment of an African viewer base, Njoku frames his desired viewership in a mixture of regional, continental, and transnational terms, with a refrain often repeated in the trades that the site is—or aims to be—the "Netflix of Africa."[24] In doing so, he emphasizes the importance of a pan-African body of viewers. As he argues, "There's a billion people in sub-Saharan Africa. I think it's really important those people are served really well first, before we start looking for recognition from other places."[25] At the same time, Jade Miller has pointed out that as iRokoTV waits for Nigeria to adopt better internet infrastructures, the service has become popular with a broader diasporic viewership.[26] As a result, this major Nollywood VOD service imagines its audience in loosely regional terms while also envisioning it as a global entity.

The Changing Scales of Diasporic Media Retail

Consistent across all these examples is that "diaspora" as an audience category—whether envisioned as Desi, Pan-African, Latin American, or East Asian—is often considered in primarily transnational terms. Even when diaspora-oriented VOD platforms segment markets along ethnic or national lines, they open themselves up to considering an audience from beyond just one particular diasporic community. This suggests that the geographic scale of "diaspora" within media sales sectors has expanded. DramaFever is a notable example, as it regularly pointed out that its audience extended well beyond diasporic viewers and even touted the "universal" value of its programs' stories.[27] Such rhetoric indicates that contemporary diasporic video flows are increasingly scaled well beyond the local/transnational agglomeration of the neighborhood video store. VOD's geographic ties are more transnational and globalized in nature than those of the retail sectors that rent or sell physical products to people in a particular town or neighborhood. In other words, VOD's ties to place are shaped by a platform's availability within certain national or world-regional markets—a geographic dynamic shored up through technological phenomena such as geoblocking and high-speed internet availability. In contrast, the very nature of brick-and-mortar retail involves some connection to the local. Even outposts of a multinational corporation like Walmart are, on some level, local (here, many readers' minds will assuredly turn to "their" Walmart). Faceless and uniform as such locations may seem, they nonetheless become at least partially integrated into the local towns and neighborhoods in which they exist (notwithstanding their own suppression of a more organically local retail sector). The same is not as easily said for, say, an online retailer like Amazon or a streaming video platform. Thus a general shift from brick-and-mortar retail to online delivery has the effect of disarticulating consumer culture from one's local geographic environment.

These dimensions of scale both feed and reflect a particular industrial dynamic: VOD's *formalization* of diasporic video flows and its integration of diasporic media culture more thoroughly into mainstream media economies. This has occurred through the earlier-discussed emergence of major corporate money into diasporic video. In contrast, diasporic brick-and-mortar video stores maintain a more contingent relationship to formal industries, and they are not buoyed by the kind of capital that keeps a platform like iRokoTV running. Contrasting also with the digital metrics and data analytics typically associated with the formal VOD industry, it is difficult to get firm numbers on exactly how VOD sites have impacted the video stores' bottom lines. After all, as Ramon Lobato and Julian Thomas have argued, "Informality is essentially about the unmeasurable, the uncertain and the unsettled."[28]

At the same time, the hypothesis that streaming platforms have a negative impact on diasporic video stores was often repeated in my discussions with people who own and/or work at these stores. Furthermore, this refrain was largely consistent across stores serving different communities. That is, while there are specific dynamics of industry and culture that would suggest that we cannot identify "the diasporic video industry" as one singular entity, the broad perception that VOD is harmful to video stores is consistent. The manager of the aforementioned video store in Harlem says that DVDs just "don't move anymore," and the owner of a South Asian video store in Jackson Heights suggested that his sales have gone down 50 percent because of streaming services.[29] An employee of a Milwaukee-area Indian grocer told me that DVD sales "have gone down completely. [We] used to have lots of audio CDs and everything. Now it is just a side thing."[30] The idea that streaming was harming local retail became a kind of dogma repeated across my conversations, even if much of the evidence was more anecdotal than it was backed up by empirical data or firm numbers.

The decreasing significance of DVDs is occasionally evident in their location within stores that purvey more than just video, like grocery stores, for instance. At the aforementioned Milwaukee-based Indian grocer, the DVDs were nearly inaccessible behind a rack of kitchenware. The media become unnecessary clutter—a hassle—for some store owners. As another Indian DVD seller in Milwaukee noted, "Nobody buys CDs, DVDs anymore. We used to have a big DVD section, but now we're just trying to get rid of them."[31] For some, physical media has become a totem to erstwhile and increasingly obsolete forms of consumption—something akin to a clearance sale or inventory liquidation rack at a soon-to-close video store. Like the mostly empty shelves of physical media that Jeffrey Sconce details in his 2008 piece on a closing Circuit City location, the haphazardness of the DVD shelves compared to the cleaner and more precisely stocked shelves of spices and canned food in part indicates the decline of physical media as a saleable commodity.[32] But whereas Sconce presciently sees the death of Circuit City as symptomatic of the excesses of late capitalism and the collapse of retail markets, such reasoning can only partially explain what is happening in diasporic media retail. After all, the economic and cultural functions of a store like Circuit City are quite different from those of, say, a Jackson Heights South Asian grocer that also stocks a shelf of DVDs. The less-organized nature of DVD stock in some diasporic stores can also be explained by a relative lack of sales staff, an overabundance of stock relative to space, and/or the privileging of other sales items over media. Still, the fact remains that DVDs' increasingly neglected character in some stores speaks to the medium's decreased significance. If, as Herbert suggests, the layout of a video store reflects a particular "geography of taste" that "comingles with the tastes and values held by the larger community in which it exists," then the shrinking and increasingly messy state of the DVDs in some of these stores suggests viewing and taste cultures that increasingly forsake these nominally "physical" media for VOD services that are less immediately connected to local concerns.[33]

Time and time again, the store workers I interviewed suggested that streaming was the culprit of these depressed sales. Whether true or not, that store owners and employees perceive this to be the case speaks to the strength of the "decreased localization" narrative within a variety of diasporic media sectors. The same Indian DVD salesman who lamented decreasing DVD retail blamed it on a cluster of digitally networked technologies: "The computer has taken the place of everything. . . . With those smart TVs, you can just get on YouTube and Netflix on your TV. You don't even need a computer."[34] Indeed, the internet and convergence often took much of the blame for depressed sales, as in one Jackson Heights Indian DVD store where the manager told me that they "don't sell DVDs anymore because of the net."[35] An employee of a Spanish-language video store in East Harlem said the same thing almost verbatim: they "don't sell many DVDs anymore" because his customers are "watching over the Internet."[36] To quote an employee of one of the aforementioned Milwaukee-based Indian grocers: "Demand [for DVDs] has gone down, because now you can watch on Netflix and online; you can watch unlimited movies for fifteen bucks."[37]

Such statements articulate a broader anxiety about the death of the video store as symptomatic of a larger trend away from so-called physical media and also from a particular articulation between one's local community and love of film.[38] This follows the logics of market and culture in diasporic cultural industries explored throughout this chapter, wherein major media industries and diasporic media entrepreneurs are less invested in seeing diasporic viewers as communities that are simultaneously local and transnational, instead treating them as part of a broadly scaled transnational cultural-linguistic market. As a "scale-making project," or a cultural-economic project that conjures and articulates the scales of its operations, diasporic streaming as a media distribution enterprise conjures the scale of the diaspora differently than the more local reach of the video store. Broadly, this reflects a twenty-first-century shift that Aswin Punathambekar has pointed to, wherein television and digital media initiatives serving South Asian diasporas "sought to reimagine the diaspora as a commercially viable scale of media production and circulation."[39] The VOD platforms previously described function similarly, and they often do so in ways that scale the diasporic as a primarily and almost exclusively transnational market segment. As I have been arguing, one potential result of this is the minimized importance of the local nodes in the circulation of diasporic media culture.

Conclusion

On the one hand, imagining a population of viewers as broadly scaled niche market segments erases differences at local levels and ensures that media as a cultural resource loses some of its connections to local life within and across localities. On the other hand, it is perhaps too easy to romanticize video stores as localized outposts of informal economies, as these informal economies occur as a result of long histories of colonialism and the marginalization of particular groups of people—a phenomenon that Lobato and Brian Larkin have both pointed to.[40] Further, many of the video stores I've discussed exist in cosmopolitan centers and media capitals, and the circulation of diasporic media through transnational VOD platforms could open up access to these cultural resources for viewers living outside of these zones. So while the impacts of VOD for many U.S.-based diasporic media viewers and retailers alike suggest a potential crisis in the arena of diasporic brick-and-mortar media retail, the conclusions for now are more ambivalent. Whatever the impact, if we look at how various players within circuits of media retail conjure the scale of diaspora in particular ways, this enables us to avoid taking these cultural-geographical categories for granted. Rather, we can interrogate *how* they are mobilized, by whom, and to what ends.

Notes

1 See Joshua M. Greenberg, *From Betamax to Blockbuster: Video Stores and the Invention of Movies on Video* (Cambridge: MIT Press, 2008); Daniel Herbert, *Videoland: Movie Culture at the American Video Store* (Berkeley: University of California Press, 2014).

2 Anna Tsing, *Friction: An Ethnography of Global Connection* (Princeton, N.J.: Princeton University Press, 2004), 57.

3 Michael Curtin, "Media Capital: Towards the Study of Spatial Flows," *International Journal of Cultural Studies* 6 (2003): 204.

4 On the history of diasporic video establishments, see Bart Beaty and Rebecca Sullivan, *Canadian Television Today* (Calgary: University of Calgary Press, 2006), 123; Sangjoon Lee, "From Diaspora TV to Social Media: Korean TV Dramas in America," in *Hallyu 2.0: The Korean Wave in the Age of Social Media*, eds. Sangjoon Lee and Abé Markus Nornes (Ann Arbor: University of Michigan Press, 2015): 172–193; Glen Lewis and Chalinee Hirano, "Mi Arai Mai Mai Mai? Thai-Australian Video Ways," in *Floating Lives: The Media and Asian Diasporas*, eds. Stuart Cunningham and John Sinclair (Lanham, Md.: Rowman and Littlefield, 2001), 199–200; and Aswin Punathambekar, "Bollywood in the Indian-American Diaspora: Mediating a Transitive Logic of Cultural Citizenship," *International Journal of Cultural Studies* 8 (2005): 154–155.

5 Timothy Shortell, *Everyday Globalization: A Spatial Semiotics of Immigrant Neighborhoods in Brooklyn and Paris* (New York: Routledge, 2016), 138–140.

6 See, for instance, Stuart Cunningham, "Popular Media as Public 'Sphericules' for Diasporic Communities," *International Journal of Cultural Studies* 4 (2001): 131–147; Marie Gillespie, *Television, Ethnicity, and Cultural Change* (London: Routledge, 1995); Lucas Hilderbrand, *Inherent Vice: Bootleg Histories of Videotape and Copyright* (Durham, N.C.: Duke University Press, 2009), 73–76; Lewis and Hirano, "Mi Arai Mai?"; and Hamid Naficy, "Narrowcasting in Diaspora: Iranian

Television in Los Angeles," in *Planet TV: A Global Television Reader*, eds. Lisa Parks and Shanti Kumar (New York: New York University Press, 2003), 376–401.

7 Youna Kim, "Diasporic Nationalism and the Media: Asian Women on the Move," *International Journal of Cultural Studies* 14 (2011): 133–151.

8 Cunningham, "Popular Media," 133.

9 James Clifford, "Traveling Cultures," in *Cultural Studies*, eds. Lawrence Grossberg, Cary Nelson, and Paula Treichler (London: Routledge, 1991), 96–116; Arjun Appadurai, *Modernity at Large: Cultural Dimensions of Globalization* (Minneapolis: University of Minnesota Press, 1996), 183.

10 Herbert, *Videoland*, 123.

11 Purnima Mankekar, *Unsettling India: Affect, Temporality, Transnationality* (Durham, N.C.: Duke University Press, 2015), 71.

12 Koichi Iwabuchi, *Recentering Globalization: Popular Culture and Japanese Transnationalism* (Durham, N.C.: Duke University Press, 2002), 27.

13 Joseph Straubhaar, *World Television: From Global to Local* (Los Angeles: Sage, 2007), 7.

14 Nancy Tartaglione, "Netflix Teams with Shah Rukh Khan's Red Chillies to Stream Bollywood Icon's Pics," *Deadline Hollywood*, 15 Dec. 2016, http://deadline.com/2016/12/netflix-shah-rukh-khan-red-chillies-movie-streaming-deal-bollywood-1201871263.

15 Todd Spangler, "Bollywood Giant Eros in Talks with Apple, Netflix, Amazon to Sell Film Library (Report)," *Variety*, 7 Aug. 2017, http://variety.com/2017/digital/news/eros-apple-netflix-amazon-bollywood-film-library-1202517573.

16 Macy Daniela Martin, "29 Telenovelas to Add to Your Netflix Queue Right Now," *Popsugar*, 13 July 2017, https://www.popsugar.com/latina/Telenovelas-Netflix-40737923; Aramide Tinubu, "You Can Watch Nollywood's Highest Grossing Film Ever on Netflix Right Now!," *Jet*, 25 Apr. 2017, https://www.jetmag.com/entertainment/can-watch-nollywoods-highest-grossing-film-ever-netflix-right-now.

17 Anna Maria de la Fuente, "Netflix Steps Up Production on Spanish-Language Original Series," *Variety*, 3 Apr. 2015, http://variety.com/2015/digital/global/netflix-steps-up-production-on-spanish-language-original-series-to-lure-latin-american-subscribers-1201464816.

18 Nancy Tartaglione, "Salman Khan, Amazon in Global Streaming Deal for Bollywood Star's Movies," *Deadline Hollywood*, 31 July 2017, http://deadline.com/2017/07/salman-khan-amazon-streaming-deal-bollywood-movies-1202139089.

19 Etan Vlessing, "Lionsgate Launches Spanish-Language Subscription Streaming Service," *Hollywood Reporter*, 1 Aug. 2017, http://www.hollywoodreporter.com/news/lionsgate-launches-spanish-language-subscription-streaming-service-1025704.

20 Todd Spangler, "Warner Bros. Acquires DramaFever, Plans to Launch Other OTT Services," *Variety*, 23 Feb. 2016, http://variety.com/2016/digital/news/warner-bros-dramafever-1201713038.

21 Todd Spangler, "Korean Broadcasters Launch U.S. Streaming Service, Taking on Warner Bros.' DramaFever," *Variety*, 24 July 2017, http://variety.com/2017/digital/news/korean-streaming-service-kocowa-us-1202502916.

22 Todd Spangler, "Warner Bros.' DramaFever Korean-Drama Streaming Service Is Shutting Down," *Variety*, 16 Oct. 2018, https://variety.com/2018/digital/news/dramafever-k-drama-shutting-down-warner-bros-1202982001.

23 Jade Miller, *Nollywood Central* (London: BFI, 2016), 134.

24 Ahish Thakkar, "Meet iRokoTV, the Netflix of Africa," *Variety*, 26 Sept. 2015, http://variety.com/2015/digital/news/meet-irokotv-the-netflix-of-africa-guest-column-1201602051.

25 Conor Gaffey, "Nollywood's Biggest Streaming Service Isn't Afraid of Netflix," *Newsweek*, 27 Jan. 2016, http://www.newsweek.com/nollywood-biggest-streaming -service-afraid-netflix-iroko-420096.

26 Miller, *Nollywood Central*, 132.

27 Stephanie Bai, "'Universal Stories' Help Korean Dramas Find International Success," *NBC News*, 26 Jan. 2017, http://www.nbcnews.com/news/asian-america/ universal-stories-help-korean-dramas-find-international-success-n698511.

28 Ramon Lobato and Julian Thomas, *Informal Media Economy* (Cambridge, U.K.: Polity Press, 2015), 12.

29 Employee of Senegalese video store in Harlem, Manhattan, New York, interview by the author, 19 June 2014; Manager of Indian DVD store in Jackson Heights, Queens, New York, interview by the author, 16 June 2014.

30 Manager of Indian grocery store in Milwaukee, Wis., interview by the author, 22 July 2014.

31 Employee of Indian grocery store in Milwaukee, Wis., interview by the author, 22 July 2014.

32 Jeffrey Sconce, "Circuit City Unplugged," *World Picture Journal* 2 (2008), http:// www.worldpicturejournal.com/WP_2/Sconce.html.

33 Herbert, *Videoland*, 6.

34 Manager of Indian DVD store, interview by the author, 16 June 2014.

35 Manager of Indian DVD store, interview by the author, 16 June 2014.

36 Employee of Indian grocery store, interview by the author, 22 July 2014.

37 Employee of Spanish-language DVD store in East Harlem, Manhattan, New York, interview by the author, 19 June 2014.

38 For just a few examples, see Connor Simpson, "Blockbuster Is Dead. Long Live the Video Store," *Atlantic*, 6 Nov. 2013, https://www.theatlantic.com/entertainment/ archive/2013/11/long-live-video-store/354947; Andrew van Dam and Jeffrey Sparshott, "The Coming Extinction of the Video-Store Clerk," *Wall Street Journal*, 31 May 2016, https://blogs.wsj.com/economics/2016/03/31/the-coming-extinction -of-the-video-store-clerk; and Matt Singer, "Why We Still Need Video Stores," *Dissolve*, 6 Nov. 2013, http://thedissolve.com/news/853-op-ed-why-we-still-need-video -stores. See also Herbert, *Videoland*.

39 Aswin Punathambekar, *From Bombay to Bollywood: The Making of a Global Media Industry* (New York: New York University Press, 2013), 173.

40 Ramon Lobato, *Shadow Economies of Cinema: Mapping Informal Film Distribution* (London: Palgrave Macmillan, 2012); Brian Larkin, *Signal and Noise: Media, Infrastructure, and Urban Culture in Nigeria* (Durham, N.C.: Duke University Press, 2008).

14

Delivering Media

●●●●●●●●●●●●●●●●●●●●●

The Convenience Store
as Media Mix Hub

MARC STEINBERG

The convenience store is a ubiquitous part of the Japanese urban and rural landscape. In commuter towns proximate to urban agglomerations, convenience stores are clustered around train stations, where commuters drop in on their way to work to buy a coffee or energy drink, children and teenagers come to buy snacks and peruse magazine racks, and workers stop off en masse at the end of the night for prepared foods as they return home. In densely populated urban areas, they are spread throughout the landscape: in train stations, on street corners, and inside office towers. In rural areas, they equally form a central stopping point for those on bikes or cars. Wherever they are located, they have turned themselves into the hubs of daily life, through the freshly prepared foods they provide or through their stock of amenities for those who suddenly need a toothbrush during their business trip or some tape for their school project. They are places where one can pay one's electricity, gas, or telecom bills; deliver one's online purchases; or print a school assignment. As David Marutschke writes, the Japanese convenience store (CS) is "part of local community life, not only selling merchandise, but also providing bank, postal and delivery services, acting as ticket agents, accepting utility payments and even handling laundry, home cleaning services, printing services, garbage pick-up tickets and online shopping."[1] Representative of the new logistical regime of just-in-time delivery and service, the CS is also the symbol of the tough job market and the increasing reliance on casualized, low-paid labor that people must turn to in these more challenging economic times. It is also a site of massive waste production as it disposes of its fresh foods daily.[2]

The convenience store's place as part of everyday life has also percolated into media figurations as well. A series of Japanese films and novels has recently put the convenience store at the center of daily life. In July 2017, the anime series *Convenience Store Boyfriends* (*Konbini Kareshi*) aired on Tokyo Broadcasting Network (TBS). Debuting as a drama CD for girls (a voice-only drama, similar to radio serials) and cocreated by publisher Kadokawa's *B's Log Comic* girls' games magazine and the Lawson convenience store chain, *Convenience Store Boyfriends* is perhaps one of the first media franchise or "media mix" narratives anchored not around the school but rather around the convenience store as a site for amorous encounters between high schoolers.[3] It's there that the main characters have their first encounters while perusing magazines and reading girls' manga and continue meeting over the course of the series. The CS is similarly the nexus of Murata Sayaka's prestigious Akutagawa prize-winning novel, *Convenience Store Human* (*Konbini ningen* [2016]; English translation is *Convenience Store Woman*) that features a woman who has worked at a convenience store for eighteen years and thrives on its regimented, manual-driven order. Murata's novel highlights the mechanical quality of convenience-store life, the predictability of its rhythms, the regularity of its sounds, and the routine of incoming deliveries and peak times for customers.

Together *Convenience Store Boyfriends* and *Convenience Store Human* highlight the most important aspects of the convenience store for this article: the *logistical regime* of regular delivery in the latter and the convenience store's *media regime* in the former. By media regime I refer to the way that convenience stores function as hubs for media promotion, consumption, and diffusion. From the "standing and reading" (*tachiyomi*) of magazines and the latest manga weeklies, to newspapers and sports news, to a selection of novels and manga books, they offer an array of reading possibilities. A 2016 report notes that a full 30 percent of all book and magazine sales in Japan are through convenience stores, with convenience stores in rural areas in particular making up for the decline in small bookstores by providing a wider magazine and book selection.[4] In the candy section, one finds tie-ups with the latest children's anime programs. In the drink section, there is the inevitable Coca-Cola or Pocari Sweat tie-up campaign with the latest music or movie sensation. And often close to the candy section, one finds a selection of toys and collectible goods for the latest anime media mix, aimed at both children and older enthusiasts. Convenience stores function as hubs for the promotion of goods within the latest transmedia or media mix franchises.

Yet despite its prominence as a site of media retail and promotion, the CS's media regime remains something of a blind spot both in literature on the stores and in studies of the media mix. Studies of the CS tend to focus on its top sales items—namely, fresh foods and fast foods. Given that fresh foods account for both a large amount of sales (bento lunches, onigiri rice balls, and original fast-food items account for 28 percent of sales at 7-Eleven, for instance, and 57 percent of sales in the smaller-scale Family Mart stores located in train stations) and a large proportion of the product development strategies of the CS chains, the focus on this side of their business is understandable.[5] Indeed, convenience store chains see their biggest competitors to be supermarkets and fast-food chains.[6] Yet by focusing solely on food, we miss the crucial media-promotion function that convenience stores have.

Alternatively, work on convenience stores from business studies focuses on their logistical deftness, their manner of handling supply chains in a just-in-time (JIT) manner that makes them the next step in moving from JIT production to JIT delivery. This connection between JIT production (Toyotism) and JIT delivery (7-Elevenism, we might dub it, after the largest chain in Japan) is critical. Marutschke notes, "The Japanese CS industry effectively solved extraordinary problems of selling a large variety of fast changing products and services on very limited store size by creating a lean management system—similar to Toyota's production system—effectively linking store operation, product development, distribution and information system."[7] This raises the question as to the impacts of JIT circulation logics on media consumption and the manner in which the just-in-time circulation logic supports ad and merchandise campaigns that accompany the latest anime or television series.

Work on media such as anime and manga tend, in turn, to focus mostly on their consumption (i.e., on fan practices), their form, or their production. If retail is addressed, it is often only in relation to the meccas of fandom, the Tokyo districts of Akihabara (for male-oriented fandoms) and Ikebukuro (for female-oriented fandoms) where fans congregate, consume, and exchange goods.[8] Some theorizations of anime, manga, and televisual media touch on the role of candy crazes associated with particular media franchises. The chips and Kamen Rider episode of the 1970s or the Bikkuriman Chocolate craze of the 1980s are notable for being focal points for general hysteria about young consumers. Children famously buying Bikkuriman Chocolates simply for the sticker included therein and throwing the chocolates on the streets are focal points of early theories of media mix consumption, such as Ōtsuka Eiji's *Theory of Narrative Consumption*.[9] And yet the focus in Ōtsuka's work is on the consumption patterns rather than on the places they were being purchased—the corner store candy shop in the Kamen Rider case and the convenience store in the case of Bikkuriman. My own work on the media mix focuses on the media specificity of anime and its associated forms, as well as the industry organization around the media mix, but has not yet paid analytical attention to the implications of the spatial aspects of the media mix and media retail in particular.[10]

Missing from the earlier analyses is hence an assessment of the convenience store's critical role in promoting and supplying franchise or media mix goods. The aim of this chapter is, first, to put the convenience store on the radar for researchers of media, mapping a few of the many intersections of media and the convenience store. Second, I will argue that *the convenience store operates as a media mix hub*, suggesting its placement at the intersection of media flows, point-of-purchase encounters, and quotidian media consumption. A third aim of this chapter is to call attention to the formal intersection between logistics and the media mix. A fourth aim is to suggest the continuing importance of physical retail amid a shift toward e-commerce that, while significant, has perhaps unduly skewed research away from the crucial physical points of purchase. I will begin by suggesting some angles for exploration of the convenience store within current concerns around the environmentalization of media and the logistical trend of analysis within critical geography and media studies. I will subsequently offer three brief analyses of particular sites around which we find the intersection of media flows and the convenience store: character goods and candy toys, manga magazines and books, and the recent media mix *Snack World*, in which the convenience store itself features as a node within the narrative and game space.

Logistics of Circulation, Architectures of Promotion

The environmentalization of media is one of the principal effects of the media mix.[11] The Japanese media mix works through the ubiquity of advertisement and of brand extensions. This is one of the reasons that character-based images and objects are everywhere within Japan's visual landscape. The media mix is the art of making things circulate, organized around a given character, narrative, or franchise, and making people respond to and participate in this circulation. The convenience store is one enabler of this circulation. There is in turn nothing more ubiquitous and quotidian in the Japanese landscape than the convenience store. This convenience store's production of media life is in turn dependent on its logistical support.[12]

Logistics is the art and science of managing the movement of things and people. As Deborah Cowen notes in *The Deadly Life of Logistics*: "The revolution in logistics saw transportation conceptualized as a vital element of production systems rather than a separate domain or the residual act of distributing commodities after production; it thereby put the entire spatial organization of the firm, including the location of factories and warehouses, directly in question."[13] Logistical thinking enables just-in-time delivery systems to emerge, systems that support the development and functioning of the

Japanese convenience store. The "anytime, anywhere" availability of goods on which the CS depends is only made possible by the thorough integration of logistical thinking into every aspect of these stores' business planning. Cowen's observation likewise extends to the very distribution of stores within the city space, wherein proximity to the distribution center and to other stores (frequently plotted in a roughly triangular pattern for ease of reach during delivery) results in savings on delivery costs and times.

Logistics alters both city space and store space, drawing on a longer tradition of retail space management. Jesse LeCavalier has suggested the need to rethink the very spaces of retail inasmuch as they coincide with logistical logics. Walmart stores, in his account, are designed according to principles of continual circulation, and hence "Walmart designs stores to function more as valves regulating flow than as reservoirs capturing it; they are containers, but they are also conduits."[14] Walmart's physical spaces are constructed around the logic of flows of merchandise that pass through them. Convenience stores are similarly modeled as hubs for the circulation of people and things—valves or *mediums* of sorts for circulation and promotion.

In this regard, one of the more fascinating points Ōtsuka makes in his book noted in the previous section is that essentially, media companies use chocolates as a means of distribution of media properties. The chocolate was a mere vehicle, or *medium*, a supply-chain route by means of which to reach the store and, ultimately, the child consumer. Ōtsuka writes, "In the case of Bikkuriman Chocolates, the product took the form of 'chocolate' for the sole reason that its producer was a candy maker and of necessity sold the products by riding on the food distribution line. The main product of the commodity was the sticker; the chocolate was only there to play the role of a medium (i.e., a container for the sticker)."[15] This side note focuses our attention to the function of the convenience store itself as a medium for the circulation of character goods, and a hub for media mix promotion.

Indeed, the very phenomenon of the media mix requires us to expand the concept of "media" beyond the typical mass media of communication studies—newspapers, television, magazines, and so forth. Indeed, with the media mix we find a *mediatization* of objects and commodities, from the lowly sticker that becomes a promotional object drawing consumers to and keeping them in a given franchise to the toy whose materiality syncs up with the media rhythms of the characters onscreen. Similarly, the convenience store itself functions as a medium for the circulation of media and people, playing down its built materiality as much as possible, presenting itself as a vessel for circulation. The convenience store supply chain itself is mobilized for its speed and visibility, used as a promotional medium for the media mix commodity.

The conception of the convenience store as a promotional medium is common among marketers and media rights holders in Japan.[16] Ōta Kensuke, the rights promotion team manager for the animation production company Sunrise, calls the convenience store itself a "medium" and a "user touch point" in the context of promotions around its properties and the *Tiger & Bunny* series in particular.[17] Square Enix executive producer Saitō Yōsuke in turn describes the convenience stores as being "second to none" as an advertising medium and "equivalent to the power of the television commercial in terms of the 'diffusion of information,'" in the context of promotions around its *Dragon Quest* game series.[18] For those who want their media franchises to gain traction, having them featured in a nationwide convenience store franchise campaign is the way to go. In its promotional function as well as its distributive or logistical function, the convenience store has the potential to sync the nation's media time. Extending everywhere throughout Japan's territory and keeping each store in sync with media time, the convenience store is the transmedia equivalent to national television—a national, terrestrial, and in this case, physical broadcaster of media extensions, a point through which goods and people meet on a quotidian basis. While differences in stock patterns mean that the degree to which a given item is promoted may vary from store to store, the deployment of some CS chain head-office-mandated goods means that the convenience store functions as a node for syncing national media times.

Following from this, the convenience store itself should be understood as a medium or an *architecture of promotion*.[19] The CS involves a meticulous organization of space; a carefully curated array of chocolate, toy, comics, and other components of the media mix; and a judicious placement of physical point-of-purchase displays and placards throughout the store. Its logistically supported JIT delivery systems ensure that these media goods arrive in time for the larger promotion campaign that occurs outside the store walls. When these elements are taken together, the convenience store promotes a given media franchise. With its tie-ins with drink companies to the newest magazines, manga volumes, Blu-rays, and spin-off toys, the convenience store becomes a veritable point of purchase (POP) display at the heart of Japan's media mix. The convenience store is hence a vessel for everyday promotion, a place of constant availability, and a just-in-time logistically supported, ready-to-hand apparatus of sale and display.

Ubiquity by Number

The impact of the convenience store is in large part due to their environmental ubiquity. Japan has more than fifty thousand convenience stores operating nationwide, which translates into approximately one store for every 2,540 people.[20] Around eleven new stores open every day in Japan, and there are an estimated 16.7 billion visits to a convenience store per year, meaning the average person visits once every three days.[21] Convenience stores mostly operate on a franchising model. The franchisee either owns the property or pays a large royalty in cases where the store chain owns the property. The store chain is responsible for provisioning, for developing new products, for providing the elaborate point of sales (POS), and for ordering software systems that allow the store owner or manager to make the best decisions in how to restock their store. The implications of this are a degree of autonomy in the selection of goods from one store to the next. This also has an impact on how much a particular store carries media goods, given that an owner or manager of a given CS franchise would have to be keyed into popular media franchises to know whether or not to order their related products for their store.[22]

There is, moreover, an incredible turnover of merchandise from one year to the next; more than 70 percent of merchandise in the store changes from one year to the next, meaning that sales depend in large part on either a smaller number of long-selling items or a large number of novelty items that must be regularly refreshed.[23] This means that product development is overseen by the store chain head office, and in many cases, the store chain cooperates to develop merchandise with goods producers. Representative of this is 7-Eleven in particular. As Hendrik Meyer-Ohle notes, "Seven-Eleven works closely together with a whole range of brand manufacturers in efforts that are called team merchandising."[24] Increasingly, merchandise development is at the core of the CS franchise headquarters' activities.[25] Makers collaborate with the convenience store chains in the development of goods—often so-called private brands, which are goods that are branded with the names of CS chains, such as 7-Eleven or Lawson. There is a fierce battle to have one's product included in the convenience store's private brand lineup, which could mean massive orders as goods are adopted nationwide.

Character Goods in the Store

Character-goods makers also vie to be selected to take part in this team merchandising, either to make private brand goods or exclusive products for a given CS chain campaign. This occurs in the context of a chain planning a campaign around a particular media franchise. For instance, 7-Eleven will run a monthlong campaign of *Detective Conan* goods, wherein many goods will be exclusively available in its stores. Such a campaign would be negotiated on one level between the rights holders for the *Detective Conan* property and the CS chain. On another level, the negotiation will be between goods makers and the CS chain. Fans of *Conan* will have to go to these stores to access these limited-time-offer goods. This is an example of the *Conan* goods working to attract customers to 7-Eleven stores, but it may also have the effect of introducing uninitiated or younger consumers to the *Conan* franchise.

For instance, the toy company Chara-Ani (known for its quality renditions of popular anime characters and for its licensing and production of anime goods for special promotions, whether for anime-specific retailers like Animate or general retailers like convenience stores) produced small, packaged file folders that each come with a candy inside. While billed as "Conan Fruits Candy," the six small candies inside were incidental; the lure of the product was the collection of all eight special-edition postcard-sized plastic file folders with the images of *Conan* characters. Similarly, Chara-Ani produced limited-time "Osomatsu Terucot" figurines related to the popular *Osomatsu-san* franchise, joining hands with 7-Eleven to put exclusive *Osomatsu-san* items in the stores. (*Osomatsu-san*, or *Mr. Osomatsu*, is a cheeky exploration of what happened to the six male sextuplets from the 1960s manga *Osomatsu-kun—Little Osomatsu*—as they grew into adulthood.) Like the *Conan* goods, these *Osomatsu* figurines were collectibles; unlike the *Conan* goods, these were higher quality and higher priced, made for mostly teen or adult collectors, most of whom bought entire boxes of six for approximately thirty-five U.S. dollars, rather than buying the figures one by one. For Chara-Ani this was a chance to make a product that would be guaranteed distribution throughout the country; for 7-Eleven it was an opportunity to attract customers to their stores, particularly older ones who wanted to buy entire six-pack boxes to complete their sextuplets collection.[26] And these in turn formed part of the general media mix around the *Osomatsu-san* property.

One of the most visible character-related goods in convenience stores is without a doubt the *shokugan* (literally, "eating toy"), a combination of a collectible toy or card or figurine with a candy snack. The "Conan Fruits Candy" is a great example of this. The degree of importance of the snack portion differs depending on the product in question; sometimes the candy itself could be important, but more often than not, the toy aspect of the shokugan is the motivation for its purchase. The candy is merely a means of packaging the toy into a sellable commodity and for assuring it a place in the candy section.

A second kind of character toy found in convenience stores as of the early 2000s is what is called the *hobī toi* (hobby toy), which is much more clearly oriented toward an older market segment, willing to pay higher sums of money for the selected character goods (see figure 14.1).[27] These goods are at the upper end of what is considered the average price for convenience store goods—namely, five hundred to six hundred yen ($4.50–5.50 USD); CharaAni's Osomatsu Terucot is an example of this latter category. They are often collectible goods, and collectors are known to buy entire boxes and sometimes multiple boxes of a given good to complete their collection. According to one account, these goods were first introduced into convenience stores by 7-Eleven in April 2002, with the Gatchabox series, after which there was a peak of popularity for these stand-alone, collectible toys.[28] By 2017, the market for these toys seemed to be

FIG. 14.1 7-Eleven magazine rack mixing hobby goods and shokugan in Enoshima, Kanagawa prefecture, on August 8, 2017 (photo by author)

on the decline, and one is less likely to come across collectible character toys in convenience stores, where space has been ceded to food products and everyday goods. Indeed, both the general manager of the sales division of character-goods maker Chara-Ani, Kokubo Hiroshi, and Tamura Akifumi, the CEO of Chara-Ani, note the downturn in sales of character goods in contemporary convenience stores. Kokubo estimates that whereas during the 2000s, some 60 percent of convenience stores carried some kind of hobby toy, by 2017, only about 10 percent of convenience stores did, marking a sharp decrease in the permeation of hobby goods (even if not of shokugan).[29] What this means for the future of the convenience store as media mix hub remains unclear, since this may be a temporary slump or indicative that other retailers—such as the anime-goods specialty chain Animate—have begun to replace the CS as sites for acquiring character goods.

Still, while recent years have seen the decline in the total number of goods within stores on the one hand, on the other hand, the chance to capitalize on hit anime shows has also seen the convenience chain Lawson invest in anime productions as part of a "production committee system," in which a number of companies (from publishers, to television stations, to ad agencies and DVD makers) collectively invest in the production costs for a series. Their aim is to have part of the rights over any income that comes out of it and, most importantly, priority access to use the characters as part of their own merchandising efforts or ad campaigns.[30] Indeed, Lawson has for some time been involved in a keen use of characters for its own sales. Renowned manga author Koike Kazuo has penned a book-length analysis of Lawson's effective use of both its own characters and other characters as promotional tools. To Koike, the convenience store is the best place to understand "the current state of characters."[31] "Convenience stores are overflowing with recent characters and hit characters," he writes, noting that he visits the stores daily—and Lawson in particular—to find out what is happening in the world of characters.

Magazines of Convenience

Customers reading magazines in the convenience store is one of the most common sights of in-store media consumption. That stores allow this "standing and reading" (*tachiyomi*) practice is a sign of the importance of the magazines as a tool for attracting customers to the store. Even during what appears in 2018 to be a relative lull of other media goods in the convenience stores as compared with the early to mid-2000s, magazines still occupy the same location they always have: the position by the window, generally to one's right as one enters the store. They are part of the "golden triangle" of the stores: magazines, bento boxes, and drinks. Even the smallest convenience stores— often kiosks within a train station—stock the latest editions of newspapers, weekly news and commentary magazines, and manga magazines.

Magazines are also unique in that they are one of the product categories whose stock is mostly out of the hands of the store owner. Japan's uniquely powerful book and printed materials distributors (called *toritsugi*) use a given store's point-of-sales data to calculate which magazines (or manga books) to distribute to the store. More than 80 percent of the magazines in a store are placed there by the distributors, to some extent in consultation with a given chain's magazine division, leaving about 20 percent of stock up to the individual choice of the store owner.[32] Each *toritsugi* distributor has a convenience store division responsible for delivering magazines to the stores and for negotiating with the chains. One of the trade-offs of the distributors' power is that unsold books and magazines are returned to the distributors at no cost to the store. Finally, amid the downturn in book and magazine sales, convenience stores have increasingly taken to stocking books as well as magazines, as I will describe later. According to a 2006 report, 7-Eleven alone accounted for

9.5 percent of all magazine sales that year and 20 percent of all manga magazine sales. Hence even as convenience stores depend on magazines for sales and attracting customers, publishers and distributors depend on the convenience store networks for their magazine sales.[33] This close relationship between CS chains and print distribution explains why Tosho Printing, a subsidiary of the *toritsugi* giant Tohan, appears as a member of the *Convenience Store Boyfriends* anime production committee, wherein characters regularly read manga at the convenience store.

There are also manga magazines and manga books that are exclusively sold in convenience stores and which deserve brief consideration (see figure 14.2). A fascinating example of the magazines exclusive to the CS is the *Hero's Monthly* (*Gekkan Hīrōzu*) magazine, a six-hundred-page magazine published monthly, sold exclusively at 7-Eleven stores for the low price of two hundred yen ($1.75 USD).[34] Published in collaboration with the established publishing house Shogakkan, the project is led and financed by the entertainment company Fields Corporation, which is best known for its pachinko parlors, which are variants on the slot machine that have their own franchise-centric media ecology. Fields Corporation's second-most significant business appears to be buying the rights for older characters and selling the rights to pachinko machine makers. Given that pachinko machines often incorporate characters into their design as a means of attracting users, this character intellectual property (IP) purchasing makes some sense. It also appears that the next step in mobilizing its IP was to create and launch *Hero's Monthly*, the first installment of which appeared in November 2011. Its two-hundred-yen price tag and ubiquity within 7-Eleven stores both lend the magazine value while at the same time promoting its IP and forthcoming media mixes. This magazine was the source of the 2017 reboot of what was arguably the first anime to fully deploy the character-merchandising strategy that is now a staple of the industry, *Tetsuwan Atomu* (*Astro Boy*). *Atomu: Za Biginingu* (*Atom: The Beginning*) was written and illustrated by Kasahara Tetsuro and was serialized as of January 2015 in *Hero's Monthly*. The anime version was originally broadcast on NHK, then subsequently streamed on Amazon Prime in Japan, pointing to the role of the CS-distributed media as a starting point for media mix productions.

A second kind of printed manga is what are known as "convenience store version bargain manga," "conbini comics," or "bargain version comics." Manga critic Ōnishi Shōhei notes that there has been a "rise of a 'readership that only buys manga from convenience stores.'"[35] While these started off as reprints of long-running classics, they have since become a subgenre of original manga written specifically for the convenience store. The latter, a "second generation of convenience store manga," has seen the rise of exclusive manga written for the format.[36] Some of these are manga versions of V-cinema, a direct-to-video genre of lower-budget films that often afforded directors greater creative

FIG. 14.2   7-Eleven magazine rack, with *Hero's* POP display at the top left, as seen in Enoshima, Kanagawa prefecture, on August 8, 2017 (photo by author)

control; others are stand-alone works or series.[37] While these convenience store manga are not necessarily part of the promotional apparatus of the media mix, they do point to the distinct media distribution circuit of the CS, as well as the need for more research into CS-specific media production.

Convenience Stores and *Snack World*

No media mix better highlights the critical role of the convenience store in the circulation of children's media than *Snack World*, a franchise that debuted in 2017 and comes from the producers and the playbook of *Pokémon* and *Yo-kai Watch*.[38] *Snack World* is notable for its goods being prominently displayed in convenience stores during the summer of 2017, as well as for having a convenience store as one of the main elements of its franchise narrative—the generically titled Hero Mart, which one can enter in the "town" sections of the Japanese role-playing video game (JRPG) and that features in the opening credits to the television series. *Snack World* is a game incarnation of the shoku-gan concept, mixing snacks and play into its own world, a world that combines the quotidian (smartphones and convenience stores) and the fantastical (dragons, quests, and princesses) in equal measure. As the English-language opening lyrics of the anime go, "Snack World, the hallowed ground of dreams and adventure. A world full of dragons, smartphones, and convenience stores. It's a pretty cool place." The characters' names derive from food groups; the monsters or allies that one meets and collects during one's quests are called "Snacks" (analogous to the collectible creatures called "Pokémon" or "Yokai" in previous JRPG games).[39] Convenience stores populate the game's town and the anime landscapes as hubs for nourishment and revival.

Given the series' built-in reference to the convenience store system and the deliberate blurring of the boundaries between characters and food items ("Snacks"), it isn't surprising that the game has given rise to shokugan toy-snacks. The *Snack World* game allows and indeed encourages users to buy and input NFC-enabled (near-field communication) "trejares" (weapons) or "light snacks" (NFC game tokens) into their Nintendo 3DS *Snack World* game to advance in the game world. These are similar to the "toys-to-life" feature used in some games but with the difference being that these are simple NFC chip–enabled, keychain-sized, three-dimensional plastic swords and tokens. Just as one finds treasure boxes during gameplay that contain new weapons or items, the contents of these real-life treasure boxes can be inputted into the game, unlocking weapons and friends that would be otherwise inaccessible (or alternatively accessible only with a great deal of luck). These NFC-enabled trejares and light snacks are, unsurprisingly, sold as shokugan in convenience stores in blind boxes. The NFC tokens essential to game play in *Snack World* hence mobilize the food delivery system, even as the single chicklet-sized piece of gum that comes in the package belies their real function as NFC token sales rather than food sales.

Like the convenience store itself, *Snack World* brings together three things Japanese children are socialized to adore: eating, play, and characters (figure 14.3). Unlike other media mixes, however, *Snack World* calls attention to the hublike function of the convenience store within the contemporary media milieu. Just as the *Snack World* characters can go to Hero Mart to be restored or to buy treasure boxes, the convenience store in real life is a site where media mixes can go to be promoted and gain critical health points through circulation. While *Snack World* is no doubt an exceptional example, it points to the critical function that the convenience store plays in the everyday circulation of media mix goods and child consumers.

FIG. 14.3 Convenience store from opening sequence of *Snack World* anime, episode 1. The text reads, "There are dragons, and also smartphones and convenience stores" (screen capture).

Delivering Media

This chapter has examined the convenience store's place as a hub within the media mix. The convenience store delivers and promotes shokugan and hobby character goods, magazines, and books, some of which use the convenience store (or even a single CS chain) as their sole supply line. *Snack World* sums up this function of the convenience store *as* media hub within its game world and animation, bringing together shokugan, character toys, and promotion. Other media objects could also be the subject of further consideration. CDs started to be distributed in 7-Eleven stores in 1992 and video games since 1996.[40] As of the year 2000, multimedia terminals were introduced in multiple chains, with Lawson's "Loppi" machines leading the way.[41] These terminals were to be the physical distribution centers for digital contents of all kinds, from video games to music and e-books, and were seen as a key element of a distinctly Japanese e-commerce strategy in which convenience stores were to be the physical hubs.[42] Rather than being opposed to e-commerce, then, convenience stores were from an early moment positioned as an essential part of the wider informatization of retail. Recent visions of the convenience store have seen Japan's largest social media platform, LINE, pair up with Family Mart to announce the future opening of a LINE-mediated convenience store experience, wherein all payment and purchases would be made through the LINE app. Much like the Amazon Go–model convenience store, this vision places digital platforms at the center of the CS imaginary.[43]

While these deserve further attention, this chapter has focused on the types of goods that are both most common to the daily consumer experience in the convenience store and most closely tied into media mix franchise strategies, mobilizing the CS and its distribution supply chains as a medium for promotional strategies. As such, this chapter highlighted the ways the logistical regimes of the CS intersect with Japan's media regimes. As Marutschke puts it, "No retailer has featured a faster changing product line-up, more frequent delivery times and a more sophisticated information system."[44] This in turn recalls LeCavalier's description of Walmart stores in the United States as "valves" and "conduits" regulating flow.[45] The CS occupies a parallel position to Walmart within the Japanese landscape, one even more deeply woven in the patterns and habits of everyday life. The CS functions as a crucial node within the physical space of the media mix, a site to daily encounter the latest developments in media franchising, and the space through which flows information and promotions around given media mixes. With a daily delivery of snacks foods and the delivery of magazines six days a week, the convenience store is a logistical hub for media delivery and distribution.

No surprise, then, that the convenience store is also centrally figured within media mixes like *Snack World*, which calls attention to the centrality and everydayness of the convenience stores, which is as ready-to-hand as the smartphone the series also features. If this book rightly emphasizes the central (and despite the rise of e-commerce, persisting) role of the store in media engagement and consumption, then this chapter has hopefully contributed to this expansion of our understanding of media retail by suggesting the critical place of the convenience store as a physical media hub and as the purveyor of its own, often unique forms of character merchandise and media. As companies like Lawson actively enter production committees and put funds toward animation production, we must also ask how much agency these chains have in the very creation—and not merely circulation—of media. As the delivery vehicle, conduit for, and indeed producer of media flows, the convenience store demands attention as a crucial site for the study of media retail and a veritable hub of the media mix.

Notes

1 David Marutschke, *Continuous Improvement Strategies: Japanese Convenience Store System* (Basingstoke, U.K.: Palgrave, 2012), 5. For a study of the convenience store from the angle of its younger users, see David Marshall, "Convenience Stores and Well-Being of Young Japanese Consumers," *International Journal of Retail & Distribution Management* (2018), https://doi.org/10.1108/IJRDM-08-2017-0182.

2 Gavin Hamilton Whitelaw, "Shelf Lives and the Labors of Loss: Food, Livelihoods, and Japan's Convenience Store," in *Capturing Contemporary Japan*, eds. Satsuki Kawano, Glenda Long, and Susan Orpett (Honolulu: University of Hawai'i Press, 2014), 135–159.

3 The *media mix* is the Japanese industrial and popular term for what in North America goes by the term *transmedia storytelling* or *media convergence*.

4 "Konbini wo kagaku suru," *Daimond*, 29 Oct. 2016, 33; Nejō Tai and Hiraki Kyōichi, *Konbini gyōkai no dōkō to karakuri ga yoku wakaru hon* (Tokyo: Shuwa System, 2015), 64.

5 Nejō and Hiraki, *Konbini gyōkai*, 21, 108.

6 See, for instance, the article "Sebun Erebun ga sūpā ni kawaru hi" ("The Day When 7-Eleven Will Replace Supermarkets"), *Konbini*, July 2013, 10–13.

7 Marutschke, *Continuous Improvement Strategies*, 23.

8 P. W. Galbraith, "Maid Cafés: The Affect of Fictional Characters in Akihabara, Japan," *Asian Anthropology* 12, no. 2 (2013): 104–125; Marc Steinberg and Edmond Ernest Dit Alban, "Otaku Pedestrians," in *Wiley Companion to Media Fandom and Fan Studies*, ed. Paul Booth (Oxford: Wiley-Blackwell, 2018).

9 Ōtsuka Eiji, "World and Variation: The Reproduction and Consumption of Narrative," trans. Marc Steinberg, *Mechademia* 5 (2010): 99–116.

10 See my *Anime's Media Mix: Franchising Toys and Characters in Japan* (Minneapolis: University of Minnesota Press, 2012); Thomas Lamarre, *The Anime Machine: A Media Theory of Animation* (Minneapolis: University of Minnesota Press, 2009); and Lamarre's *The Anime Ecology: A Genealogy of Television, Animation, and Game Media* (Minneapolis: University of Minnesota Press, 2018).

11 In *Anime's Media Mix*, I suggest that the environmentalization and proliferation of the character image are two key functions of character merchandising and, ultimately, the media mix.

12 I take inspiration from the work of Anna Tsing, "Supply Chains and the Human Condition," in *Rethinking Marxism* 21, no. 2 (Apr. 2009): 148–176; Deborah Cowan, *The Deadly Life of Logistics* (Minneapolis: University of Minnesota Press, 2014); and Jesse LeCavalier, *The Rule of Logistics: Walmart and the Architecture of Fulfillment* (Minneapolis: University of Minnesota Press, 2016).

13 Cowan, *Deadly Life*, 40.

14 LeCavalier, *Rule of Logistics*, 13.

15 Ōtsuka, "World and Variation," 105.

16 Stores are also, Anna McCarthy points out, conceived as promotional tools by North American retail industry writers, one of whom suggests that "stores are not simply places to buy anymore, but the last medium that can persuade people to buy." *Ambient Television* (Durham, N.C.: Duke University Press, 2001), 164.

17 Koike Kazuo, *Lawson no sosharu kyarakuta senryaku* (*Lawson's Social Character Strategy*) (Tokyo: Koike Shobo, 2013), 191.

18 Koike, *Lawson*, 198.

19 This formulation borrows from Jesse LeCavalier's description of Walmart as an "architecture of fulfillment" in *The Rule of Logistics*.

20 "Konbini wo kagaku suru," 28.

21 "Konbini wo kagaku suru," 32.

22 Kokubo Hiroshi, Chara-Ani general manager of the sales division, interview with the author, 4 Aug. 2017. Chara-Ani is a maker of figures that has had regular collaborations with convenience stores in the creation of special goods for convenience-store character tie-ins and promotional events—for instance, *Conan* and *Osamatsu-san* events at 7-Eleven.

23 Kazuhiko Fukunaga, "Konbini," *Look Japan*, July 1999, 4.

24 Hendrik Meyer-Ohle, "Collaborating for Change in Japanese Consumer Goods Distribution," in *Japanese Distribution Strategy*, eds. Michael Czinkota and Masaaki Kotabe (London: Thomson Learning, 2000), 128.

25 Katō Naomi, "Kaihatsu iyoku takamaru 'originaru shōhin' kyōsō jidai," in *Gekkan Konbini* (*Convenience Store Monthly*), Apr. 2002, 50.

26 Kokubo Hiroshi interview; Tamura Akifumi, Chara-Ani CEO, interview with the author, 4 Aug. 2017.

27 Kokubo Hiroshi interview.

28 Takasawa Kunihito, "Baiyazu ai: 7-Eleven Japan gangu," *Gekiryū* 29, no. 1 (Feb. 2004): 108–109.

29 Kokubo Hiroshi interview.

30 Sugimoto Riuko, "Nekkyō! Anime keizaiken" ("Going Nuts! The Anime Economic Zone"), *Shūkan Tōyō Keizai* (*Orient Economics Weekly*), 1 Apr. 2017, 38. Also mentioned here is JR East Railways' involvement as a member of the production committee.

31 Koike, *Lawson*, 28.

32 "Minaosō! 'konbini no zasshi, shoseki, komikku,'" *Gekkan Konbini*, Nov. 2006, 37, 45.

33 "Minaosō!," 44.

34 I thank Ōtsuka Eiji for the suggestion to look into *Hero's* and for background information about its merchandising strategies, which forms the substance of the following paragraph.

35 Ōnishi Shōhei, "Konbini muke kakioroshi renka manga no genzai" ("On the Current State of Cheap Comics Written for the Convenience Store"), *Kino*, July 2008, 70.

36 Ōnishi, "Konbini muke kakioroshi," 71.

37 For an account of V-cinema, see Alexander Zahlten, *The End of Japanese Cinema* (Durham, N.C.: Duke University Press, 2017).

38 For an analysis of *Yo-kai Watch*, see Marc Steinberg, "Media Mix Mobilization: Social Mobilization and Yo-Kai Watch," *Animation* 12, no. 3 (2017): 244–258. On *Pokémon*, see Anne Allison, *Millennial Monsters: Japanese Toys and the Global Imagination* (Berkeley: University of California Press, 2006).

39 Mia Consalvo analyzes the game production company Level 5, responsible for *Yo-kai Watch* and *Snack World*, in *Atari to Zelda: Japan's Videogames in Global Contexts* (Cambridge: MIT Press, 2016).

40 "Konbini 25nen" ("25 Years of the Convenience Store"), *Konbini*, Oct. 1999, 34.

41 "'Tomerarenai basu': ATM, netto bijinesu no yukue" ("An Unstoppable Bus: On the Direction of ATM and Net Business"), *Konbini*, Feb. 2000, 110.

42 "E-bijinesu kyōsōkyoku" ("E-business rhapsody"), *Konbini*, Apr. 2000, 15–16.

43 "Famima to LINE ga jisedai tempo de teikai, Nihon-ban no 'Amazon Go' ga tanjō ka" ("Family Mart and LINE Teaming Up to Create the Next Generation Store: A Japanese Version of Amazon Go?"), *Mynavi News*, 16 June 2017, https://news .mynavi.jp/article/20170616-famima/.

44 Marutschke, *Continuous Improvement Strategies*, 18–19.

45 LeCavalier, *Rule of Logistics*, 13.

15

Retail Wizardry

●●●●●●●●●●●●●●●●●●●●●●●

Constructing Media Fantasies
from the Point of Sale

DEREK JOHNSON

Since the publication of the *Harry Potter* book series and the multibillion-dollar media franchise it spawned, countless children (and many adults) have fantasized about receiving letters of admission to the Hogwarts School of Witchcraft and Wizardry. The letter that protagonist Harry Potter receives via owl post in chapter four of *The Sorcerer's Stone* promises passage from the dreary existence of nonmagical "muggles" into a new and fantastic world. The fan who receives a similar letter (perhaps as an invitation to a Potter-themed birthday party) can similarly anticipate crossing over from the mundane to something magical (where the party truly becomes a special occasion). Yet in the *Harry Potter* narrative, it is not the letter of academic admission so much as the accompanying shopping list that actually *orients* the protagonist and reader to this fantasy. With an inventory of necessary school supplies in hand, Harry enters into the Wizarding World in chapter five as a first-time consumer of magical retail merchandise. With his guide, Hagrid, Harry explores the shopping district of Diagon Alley in search of robes, course books, wands, cauldrons, animal familiars, and other wizarding paraphernalia all Hogwarts students need. The fantasy of entering the Wizarding World, in this first instance, operates through retail practices, experiences, and environments.

The tourist experience of visiting the Wizarding World of Harry Potter similarly depends on retail as a point of entry and means of support for immersive media fantasy. At the Universal Studios theme park in Orlando, Florida, visitors follow in Harry's footsteps, exploring the shops of Diagon Alley both as described in J. K. Rowling's original novels and as visualized in cinematic production design. Selecting wizards' robes at Madam Malkin's Robes for All Occasions, buying magic wands at Ollivander's, and browsing enchanted pranks at Weasley's Wizard Wheezes, visitors to the Wizarding World can engage in the same transactions they have seen Harry and his friends conduct in Diagon Alley. With separate admission to the adjacent Islands of Adventure park, tourists can visit the shops of Hogsmeade village too. Fans can wait in line to tour the nearby Hogwarts school as part of the "Forbidden Journey" ride, but they will likely spend far more time (and money) exploring the surrounding shops of Hogsmeade, including Honeydukes candy shop and wizard gear supplier Dervish and Banges—all recognizable locales from the story in which the consumer can spend their own money. In both Diagon Alley and Hogsmeade, retail offers the primary point of entry to tourist participation in the franchise.

To the extent that Warner Bros. as the media rights holder and Universal as its theme-park partner have capitalized on the potential for merchandising built into *Harry Potter*, these experiences are fairly typical of "media franchising" strategies.[1] However, to the degree that author J. K. Rowling created a fictional world that could be so directly translated into a tourist fantasy of narrativized shopping, the franchise offers an extreme case of entrepreneurial brand management that foregrounds retail as a means of engaged participation in popular media. In this entrepreneurial extremism, the Wizarding World centers retail and shopping experiences within the consumer fantasies of media fandom. The Wizarding World taps into the pleasures and identifications of media consumers as *buyers of things* within capitalist economies, where some of our most fundamental relationships with media come at the transactional level of retail. Retail shopping is at once an everyday experience and a gateway for meaningful, symbolic relations between consumers and industry. Retail is a transformative phenomenon through which consumers can most basically participate—or enjoy a fantasy of participating—in commercial media cultures. At the point of sale, shoppers purchase not just access to media product but also a transactional participation that embeds them within an economy of media relations in which agency and autonomy extend from the capacity to spend money within a meaningful cultural field. The immersive tourist fantasies offered by media franchises like *Harry Potter* thus deploy the transactional dynamics of retail to support the interactional feelings of immersion and participation.

Emphasizing the often-unexplored power of retail in media culture and consumers' participatory engagement with it, this chapter examines how entertainment franchises—including but not limited to *Harry Potter*—position retail as a transactional point of entry into and participation in fantasy worlds. Reflecting on world building as a creative and industrial practice, the chapter first considers how narrative media texts like *Potter* foreground retail spaces and institutions as points of pleasure, identification, and participation. Second, I trace the corporate strategies and partnerships that envision retail as the industrial linkage between franchise texts and theme park spaces. Finally, drawing upon January 2017 fieldwork at the Wizarding World of Harry Potter at Universal Orlando—as well as comparisons to experiences at Walt Disney World—I explore how consumers can encounter and experience imagined retail environments as part of material spaces and economies. More than arguing that the point of the theme park is to position consumers for retail purchases in the gift shop, this participation in retail economies provides direct and meaningful forms of access to a fantasy world, where the act of buying and selling in a retail space affirms consumer agency within that mediated imaginary. Beyond a theme park "ride," shopping itself becomes the participatory media fantasy in spaces like Diagon Alley and Hogsmeade. In total, this chapter argues that the mundane consumer experiences of shopping can powerfully underwrite participation in media fantasy; retail is not just the end point in a chain of media circulation but also a meaningful and transformative space of narrative and meaning. Our participation in the magical worlds of media through retail reveals the embeddedness of the point of sale within commodity culture and the need to pay greater attention to the design and experience of shopping across media production and consumption.

Building Retail Fantasies

A significant body of scholarly research has investigated the construction of fantasy worlds—particularly as contemporary media convergences capitalize on the compatibility of world building with industry imperatives and fan cultures alike. Henry Jenkins defines world building as a project wherein "artists create compelling environments that cannot be fully explored or exhausted within a single work or even a single medium. The world is bigger than the film, bigger even than the franchise—since fan speculations and elaborations also expand the world in a variety of directions."[2] In this way, media worlds support the needs of converging media industries that leverage brands repeatedly across the many different film, television, and digital holdings of entertainment conglomerates while at the same time appealing to consumers through detailed, familiar, and participatory environments for investing their desires. The potential for participation possessed by media worlds thus operates across production and consumption alike. Adopting a "systemic perspective" to emphasize spatial dimensions of world building, Marti Boni argues that "the sum of different uses and interpretations creates a result that exceeds the original work—in size, in shape, and in its intentions and directions—thereby creating a complex world."[3] Given this potential for investment and collaboration from a wide variety of creators, Mark J. P. Wolf has similarly described as "sub-creation" the capacity of worlds to support successive and subsequent revisitation by numerous contributors.[4]

This emphasis on creative practice often considers how designers build worlds to sustain collaborative participation over time. This world building depends on "contextualizing devices"[5] and distinctly identifiable "objects, artifacts, technologies, customs, institutions, ideas, and so forth"[6] that establish specific cultural spheres for participation in narrative space. The most iconic media worlds therefore turn significantly on specific institutions that shape and govern participation in that environment: in *Star Trek*, the institutions of the United Federation of Planets and Starfleet provide a set of utopian principles and quasi-military structures under which characters act and fans too can aspire; not to be outdone, *Star Wars* offers the Rebel Alliance and the Galactic Empire. The Marvel Cinematic Universe has S.H.I.E.L.D., *The Hunger Games* elaborates a complex backstory for its districts, and the Wizarding World of Harry Potter, of course, includes the bureaucracies of the Ministry of Magic.

Yet while contextualizing institutions can operate at this governance level, the economic organizations of retail consumer culture can also support media worlds. For example, the world of Springfield as experienced by viewers of *The Simpsons* is significantly defined by its retail context. Stores like the Kwik-E-Mart and The Android's Dungeon and Baseball Card Shop function as settings for exploring the core characters of Homer, Marge, Lisa, and Bart while elaborating the world through the various supporting characters who run these businesses (like Apu and Comic Book Guy, respectively). As the *Simpsons* brand is managed across media platforms, moreover, these stores become key loci of consumer participation: licensed video games like *The Simpsons Game*, *The Simpsons: Hit and Run*, and *The Simpsons: Tapped Out* invariably present these shops as spaces for play and exploration, while consumer-products licensee LEGO marketed a Kwik-E-Mart construction kit. Figured so heavily in the media texts and paratexts of *The Simpsons*, the retail store is more than just one of the many institutions critiqued by the series—including school, capitalism, and family—but also part of what Jonathan Gray identifies as the series' parodic critique of media culture.[7] As the site where characters buy and sell magazines, comics, and more, the retail store supports critical commentary on and engagement with that media. Indeed, the LEGO Kwik-E-Mart comes complete with printed bricks representing media products. Other television series have elaborated their worlds through the construction of retail institutions too. *Chuck* figured its eponymous protagonist as an employee of big-box electronics store Buy More, a retail front for secret espionage operations.

Other stores in this retail community—like the frozen yogurt shop Orange Orange—reveal additional spycraft façades, while efforts at online promotion embraced retail's potential as a participatory environment. On a Buy More website, viewers could apply to become store employees, joining a community of fan productivity identified with mundane retail tasks.

Among these other examples of retail-based world building, the Wizarding World is not unique in its construction of distinct shopping environments within branded narrative experiences. However, *Potter* books and films do accord retail a certain centrality. Because Harry has a consumer imperative to acquire his school supplies, his initial shopping trip introduces key elements of the Wizarding World. His first stop at Madam Malkin's Robes for All Occasions, for example, immediately leads to an encounter with one of his primary antagonists, Draco Malfoy. In Rowling's prose, Draco's demeanor as part of a privileged (and sinister) wizarding elite is immediately communicated through his family's shopping plans: his mother is "up the street" looking at wands, while Draco himself plans to "bully" his father into buying him a Quidditch broom in violation of school rules.[8] This representation of retail—experienced differently based on class hierarchies—establishes the ongoing narrative conflict between Harry and Draco. Through the remainder of this shopping excursion, moreover, Harry first learns about the wizard sport of Quidditch, encounters spells and curses in his stop by Flourish and Blott's bookstore, and gleans a hint of his destiny to do "great things" when Ollivander sells him a wand linked to the evil Voldemort.[9] With every shop visited, the reader learns a little more about the core series mythology.

Moreover, the book series continually reexamines the retail landscape to reorient the reader and evince institutional changes within the narrative world over time. The second installment, *Harry Potter and the Chamber of Secrets*, revisits Diagon Alley as the characters prepare to return to Hogwarts. A planned trip to Flourish and Blott's to buy new textbooks goes awry, however, when a teleportation accident lands Harry instead in Knockturn Alley, a seedier shopping district frequented by practitioners of the dark arts. Expanding retail space beyond Diagon Alley, the series widens the scope of villainy with which Harry will have to contend, establishing that dark wizards have their own shopping spaces and practices. Amid the sinister wares of the Borgin and Burkes shop, Harry encounters another Malfoy—Draco's father, Lucius, whose interactions with the shopkeeper link the retail transactions of dark wizardry to ideologies of racial supremacism. For a second time, shopping reveals, by inversion, the social morality of the Wizarding World, where ideologies of race and class align with specific retail spaces, choices, and clienteles. Although an emphasis on the consumer pleasures of shopping in Diagon Alley continues—Harry particularly covets a new Nimbus 2000 broom in the third book—it gives way in later books to a decline in the wizarding retail economy reflective of social change and political struggle as the story unfolds. With the focus of consumer fantasy for Hogwarts students having shifted in the fourth and fifth books to locales like Honeydukes candy shop in the Hogsmeade village adjacent to the Hogwarts campus, Diagon Alley returns in *Harry Potter and the Half-Blood Prince* as an indicator of public unrest amid Voldemort's return to power. Once-idyllic and spectacular shops like Florean Fortuscue's Ice Cream Parlor are now boarded up, replaced by "shabby-looking stalls."[10] Ollivander's too has been closed, with the shopkeeper kidnapped by Voldemort. The rise of the dark wizard, therefore, is reflected by the decline of wizarding retail institutions (a literal "retail apocalypse," perhaps). Meanwhile, the establishment of the Weasley's Wizard Wheezes joke shop by former Hogwarts students stands in defiant contrast to this deterioration, representing a new generation of heroic retail entrepreneurs who will stand up to evil.

The significance of retail institutions to the design of the Harry Potter world also unfolds in its adaptation across film and other visual media. Although retail locales like Florean Fortescue's are not introduced until much later in the book series, the first film adaptation seeds these future locations of import into the production design of Diagon Alley. In the ninety-second sequence that introduces Daniel Radcliffe's Harry to the shopping district in the first film, the camera shows his point of view as he marvels at each shop window, taking in all that this retail district has to offer. He sees sweets, owls, and racing brooms—including the new Nimbus 2000 that the literary Harry does not become aware of until the third book (published two years prior to the first film). With prior knowledge of the retail environments and objects significant to future book installments, the filmmakers construct long-term consumer fantasies that will pay off later. Moreover, as in the case of *The Simpsons*, retail locations play vital roles in the production of licensed products that allow media consumers to engage with, explore, and participate in the *Potter* universe. LEGO released two different playsets based on Diagon Alley between 2001 and 2011, as well as sets dedicated to Quality Quidditch Supplies and Knockturn Alley. For users of these products, retail is presented as an environment in which to construct and engage in the character role-play of shopping. The *LEGO Harry Potter: Years 1–4* video game, meanwhile, made Diagon Alley a gameplay "hub" from which players could freely explore, manage their characters and inventories, as well as make choices about what objectives to pursue. In these spaces, players also used the points they collected to buy special unlockable features in the game, making retail transactions into a play mechanic.

Retail is not, of course, the only form of contextualizing institution that can support the fantasy of fictional worlds produced across media. Yet when transposed into the environment of a theme park—and its orientation toward consumer fantasies—these retail institutions become a platform for consumers' meaningful and transactional participation in the world. Just as shopping structures the diegetic world, the merchandising of *Harry Potter* supports both the lucrative industry practice and the means by which consumer "muggles" might participate in that fantasy narrative.

Harry Potter and the Order of the Franchise

Universal launched its first Wizarding World of Harry Potter theme park attractions in 2010 with the opening of the Hogsmeade area at Islands of Adventure in Orlando. Diagon Alley followed at the Universal Studios park in 2014, linked to the first attraction by a Hogwarts Express ride shuttling visitors between them by train. That same year, Universal brought a Hogsmeade attraction to its park in Osaka, Japan, before doing the same at Universal Studios Hollywood in 2016. The *Potter* franchise has been an undeniable boon for Universal. Over the first seven years of operation, the attractions helped increase attendance at the Islands of Adventure theme park in Orlando by 80 percent, with some 47.4 million total visitors having passed through the turnstiles in that time.[11] With the price of admission to a single park in excess of $100 per adult or child, the Wizarding World has already supported park revenues in the billions of dollars even before considering the scope of merchandising operations within these parks. Within its first year, the Orlando Wizarding World attraction was estimated to have made $364 million in revenue for Universal.[12] While retail sales at theme parks represented only a piece of the $7 billion in merchandising revenues generated by the *Potter* franchise across many different markets, companies, and product categories, they nonetheless offered significant additional income potential for Universal. *Los Angeles Times* estimates suggest that theme parks can typically expect 30 percent of their revenue from food, beverages, and merchandise.[13] Moreover, industry analysts credited the *Potter* attraction with a 104 percent increase in food and beverage sales and 156 percent spike in merchandise sales at Universal's Orlando parks in the first year.[14]

Of course, these revenues are not pure profit for Universal. This themed Wizarding World experience extends from a web of licensing agreements that transfer creative and economic rights between corporate entities. Warner Bros. holds the media exploitation rights to the franchise following its agreement with author J. K. Rowling, but lacking significant theme park holdings of its own, the studio sublicensed themed attraction rights to fellow media conglomerate NBC-Universal. Industry analysts estimated that the license to build its *Potter* attractions cost NBC-Universal an upfront fee of $265 million.[15] While unclear exactly how much Warner Bros. takes from park revenues as an ongoing royalty on ticket, souvenir, and food/beverage sales, the conglomerate stands to profit even more from merchandising. Because Warner

Bros. Worldwide Consumer Products holds "all worldwide licensing and mer-chandising rights" as part of its "overall deal" with Rowling, it decides what manufacturers of toys, clothing, and other consumer goods can work under the *Potter* license.[16] Beyond extracting license fees and royalties from Universal at a retail level, then, Warner Bros. also takes in fees and royalties from manufacturing companies that supply Universal with retail products. These licensing fees are significant enough that theme park royalties funneled back to Rowling alone through Warner Bros. reach the "low double-digit millions" and represented the second-largest source of income for the author in 2016.[17] Beyond license payments to Warner Bros., Universal also faces construction and maintenance costs. Whereas single ride experiences can cost between $100 and $200 million to design and construct, entire themed areas like the Wizarding World require investments on the scale of $500 million.[18] Due to a long-standing pact with Steven Spielberg, Universal also parts with 2 percent of all park admissions and concessions in exchange for his historical services as a design consultant.[19]

Despite this collision of economic interests, the design of the Wizarding World attractions trades in appeals to creative unity. Warner Bros. serves not only as the central manager of the license but also as the aesthetic baseline against which immersion is created and authenticity measured. Promotional discourses consistently emphasize the continuity of labor across the adaptation of Rowling's books into the film series and subsequently the translation of that production design into interactive theme park environments. Trade reports and popular entertainment journalism suggest that the parks benefit from the creative participation of the entire art department behind the Warner Bros. film, involving input from production designer Stuart Craig as well as the craftspeople who collaborated with him—including Miraphoa Mina and Eduardo Lima, credited for the look of the *Daily Prophet* newspaper as well as many other props and signage in the films.[20] Such stories emphasize the authenticity of the environment by asserting that various props throughout the parks actually appeared on-screen in the films; meanwhile, those objects "that weren't in the movies come from the same designers."[21] Even *Architectural Digest* promises that the parks are the vision of the "same team" that produced the films.[22] The Wizarding World theme park business thus depends on recreating the space of the cinematic production—and as we will see, it is the fantasy of retail experience in that space that becomes paramount to consumer participation in it.

The Retailing World of Harry Potter

That sense of cinematic authenticity was palpable upon my visit to the Orlando park in 2017. Although the tourist must walk around a brick privacy wall to enter Diagon Alley—somewhat less fantastically than the way Hagrid parts the wall magically for Harry in *The Sorcerer's Stone*—the effect of stepping through the threshold and having one's vision filled with the busy shopping street nevertheless echoes the on-screen reveal. In one moment, the wall blocks the tourist's view, and in the next, the gaze down a long and busy shop-filled street reveals Diagon Alley in depth (figure 15.1). As the flow of the crowd compels the visitor to move down the street, each storefront catches the eye; looking from side to side at the sights, the visitor's orientation to the space evokes the sequence of shots during Harry's first trip to Diagon Alley in the film (which moves from a long shot of the whole street to point-of-view glances at each shop window). In this way, the Wizarding World attractions provide a sense of not just the films' production design but also its cinematography as a way of moving through that space.

Crucially, this movement through space is directed toward and around retail. Stepping into Diagon Alley, Universal visitors see signs for The Leaky Cauldron, Slug and Jiggers Apothecary, and Magical Cures and Preventions on the left, with Scribbulous and Wiseacres Wizarding Equipment on the right. As described in the *Los Angeles Times*, the layout of Wizarding World attractions "is designed to promote retail sales by funneling visitors past the shops and eatery before they can get to the two featured rides. Guests also exit

FIG. 15.1 Stepping into Diagon Alley (photo by author)

the rides into stores."[23] At one level, this quote reflects a banal truism of theme park design, where the rides exist to move consumers into gift shops at the end of the themed experience. Yet this consideration of retail as an experience that *precedes* the ride also reveals a potential inversion of that logic: retail is not a bait-and-switch exit from themed fantasy back into the everyday world of capitalist consumption but instead a primary means of entry for consumer fantasies of immersive authenticity. Retail becomes the medium for navigating the Wizarding World.

While recognizing the potential pleasures of this experience, previous critical analyses of the Wizarding World attraction juxtapose its retail commercialism to fan participation in theme park space. Carissa Baker interrogates Universal's promises of immersion and authenticity, zeroing in on how rides like "Escape from Gringotts" contribute to those pleasures while acknowledging too the retail pleasures of buying Hermione's wand at Ollivander's wand shop.[24] Her engagement with retail consumption, however, contrasts these industrially produced experiences to the practices of fandom. "Despite the underlying profit motive, which most corporate Potter expressions possess," Baker writes, "WWoHP has gone outside this to become a site of fan activity."[25] Baker is thus less interested in industrialized retail transactions than how theme park environments can support bottom-up fan practices of cosplay, role-playing, and what Nick Couldry, Will Brooker, and Matt Hills call media pilgrimage.[26] In her own examination of immersion in the Wizarding World, Rachel Gilbert engages more directly with the consumerism of the park but similarly holds it in tension with a competing sense of authenticity produced by fans themselves. Likening the objects in the theme park environments to the "portkeys" that characters in the *Potter* universe use to travel between different locations, she cleverly considers how theme park objects transport consumers into a fantasy world.[27] While Gilbert focuses on what one sees while standing in line for a ride (such as Dumbledore's Pensieve along the way to the "Forbidden Journey"), she also explains how wand selection at Ollivander's serves as a "rite of passage" that consumers engage in to take up a position within the magical world.[28] Yet it is on the re-creation of the ritual from the book rather than the buying of the wand that her focus trains. Gilbert thus casts the retail aspects of the experience as counterproductive to ritual immersion: "The magical atmosphere evaporates when the fan realizes that the main purpose of the ritual is to sell the manufactured wands; conveniently, the visitors must exit Ollivander's through the gift shop."[29] While Gilbert engages more deeply than Baker with the scope of retail operations on-site, both contrast its focus on licensed merchandise with the greater productivity and participation of fans as industrious cosplayers, artists, and textile manufacturers in their own right. Retail is, in this view, an obstacle to the freedom of fan participation, only serving those who can pay.

These questions of access, consumerism, and the comparative productive potential of fans are important ones. However, in casting the participatory authenticity of fandom in opposition to that packaged and sold by Universal, we may miss how consumer fantasies of immersion operate through transactional participation, where retail relations enable fantasy rather than leading back to the mundane world of consumer capitalism. In that light, the retail experience of Ollivander's is *both* the egregious commodification of mass-produced magic wands and a transactional gateway into retail fantasy. Ollivander's is a scripted experience; after waiting in line to watch a brief show in which a resident wand-maker chooses a participant from the crowd to fit for a wand, visitors are funneled into the main showroom where they see boxes and boxes of wands to purchase. This is no mere exit into the gift shop but a continuity of experience in this scripted space. Furthermore, the signature objects on sale here are fifty-dollar "interactive" wands—available in a variety of styles—that promise consumers greater power over the environment of the park. Included with these wands are maps of the park denoting special points of interest at which the owner can use the wand—with the right amount of practice—to cast their own magic spells. On the one hand, this devious marketing scheme ensures that even after paying for admission, one must conduct another retail transaction to access the full park experience. On the other hand, this transaction is a crucial entry point to position-taking in and navigation of this retail-oriented fantasy world. First, the process of selecting a wand means browsing through walls of different boxes and deciding whether one wants a "replica" of a wand used by a "famous" wizard with whom one identifies or deciding what wand composition best suits the individual wizard shopper. Hazel? Willow? Oak? The choice is (only) meaningful to a shopper who considers their transaction as part of taking on a role within the fantasy world, where wand attributes communicate something about the wizard consumer.

Once the shopper acquires a wand, moreover, their orientation to retail space in the park significantly changes. While wand owners, like all park visitors, move from shop to shop, the transaction of buying the wand opens the door to "magical" participation within that retail space (see figures 15.2 and 15.3). Shoppers visit the Honeydukes shop in Hogsmeade to buy licensed *Harry Potter* candy, for example, but with wands in hand, they become magically empowered to enchant retail wares and displays, casting spells to make a chocolate frog pop out of a candy box in the shop window. Most points of interest on the interactive wand map lead to similar shop windows or store signage where shoppers can wave their wands to trigger practical magical effects over retail displays. Make no mistake—this participation in wizarding retail serves the strategic goal of funneling visitors from storefront to storefront (with each move activating the possibility of subsequent transactions in the spellcasting location). In this way, the wand is a high-tech evolution of Duffy the Disney Bear, the "passport" that

FIGS. 15.2 AND 15.3. Casting spells over retail merchandise (photos by author)

kids take to be stamped at various locations within Epcot Center, a journey that winds through numerous gift shops. Yet the transaction of buying the wand refigures navigation of the Wizarding World, where the visitor no longer consumes licensed souvenirs in the mundane consumer-products market of muggles but instead participates and exerts agency in the environment of a magical retail economy. Whether that is worth fifty dollars remains debatable.

Notably, many retail storefronts in the Wizarding World are merely façades, not functional gift shops (figure 15.4). Despite the oversaturation of gift shops within these parks, the presence of retail façades in themed lands suggests that park designers perceive points of diminishing returns. Elsewhere at Universal, a themed Kwik-E-Mart store in the *Simpsons* realm offers visitors the chance to engage in their participatory transactions, engaging in the same convenient, on-the-go purchases of branded products enjoyed by the series' characters—most significantly, Duff Beer. A block away, The Android's Dungeon comic book store holds similar potential to be a themed repository of Simpsons collectibles, yet it is only a façade marked by the ever-present "Sorry We're Closed For Bi-Mon-Sci-Fi-Con" sign in the window. The Kwik-E-Mart must therefore pull double duty as in-world convenience store and out-world branded *Simpsons* collectible emporium. Similar façades pepper Diagon Alley and Hogsmeade. The shop window of Tomes and Scrolls in Hogsmeade might be a particular point of interest for fans given its display of the many printed works

FIG. 15.4 The "closed" media retailer in the media theme park (photo by author)

of Defense Against the Dark Arts instructor Gilderoy Lockhart. Yet the door to the space is barred by a perpetual "closed" sign; the texts are not for sale, and there is no opportunity for real economic transactions. While dozens of such façades fail to offer transactional participation, the shopper can engage with many of them nonetheless through the prior transaction of buying the wand. In these moments, retail is a space for participation (admittedly, a limited one preprogrammed by park designers) even when not a fully functional site of economic activity.

The door to the Flourish and Blotts bookstore also could not be opened, ironically suggesting that bookselling was beyond the limits of retail in a theme park experience owing to a book series. Attention to what is—and isn't— sold in these retail spaces thus provides a sense of the boundaries of retail as a meaningful fantasy experience. Particular forms of *Potter* media—namely, the books and movies inspiring the spectacle of the park experience—were extremely difficult to locate and purchase during my visit to Universal Orlando in 2017. This sat in contrast to other media franchises promoted elsewhere at Universal and competing parks. At the Tatooine Traders gift shop in the *Star Wars* area of Disney's Hollywood Studios in 2017, for example, shoppers could buy DVDs, soundtrack albums, novelizations, children's board books, and comic books. At Universal, the E.T.'s Toy Closet gift shop offered DVDs to visitors disembarking from the "E.T. Adventure" ride. By contrast, I could find *Potter* books or DVDs in only two locations throughout the Universal Orlando parks. First, hidden behind the counter in the Wiseacres Wizarding

Equipment gift shop were three lone copies of the recently released *Harry Potter and the Cursed Child* stage play script. Notably, this store also seemed to trade in more out-world merchandise than its fellow gift shops, carrying items like phone cases and earbuds. The second location was fully outside the Wizarding World in the Islands of Adventure Trading Company at the central hub of the eponymous park. Set alongside displays for *Minions*, Marvel, and the many media brands retailed at Universal, books and DVDs were more overtly positioned as consumable goods and key commodities in the *Potter* franchise. Outside the immediate boundaries of its themed fantasy environment, *Potter* could be more easily positioned as a media object rather than an embodied, mediated retail fantasy of buying things.

Indeed, the retail objects alternatively on offer in the Wizarding World privileged a fantasy of buying retail products from a position of narrative participation within the fantasy world rather than fan allegiance to a media franchise from a consumer position on the outside. Although park-branded "Wizarding World of Harry Potter" T-shirts and other gear acknowledging the status of *Potter* as a media commodity could be found, such merchandise was overshadowed in number and prominence of retail placement by goods bearing logos and iconography from in-world products, practices, locales, and institutions—from butterbeer to Grimmauld Place to the Death Eaters tattoo. Instead of the souvenir pens readily available at Disney World (for securing autographs from costumed characters), Diagon Alley and Hogsmeade sold a wide variety of quills and parchment paper enabling the buyer to imagine themselves writing as the characters do. Beyond the souvenir T-shirt, visitors were encouraged to engage in cosplay by purchasing robes and donning clothes adorned with the logos of rival Hogwarts houses Gryffindor, Slytherin, Ravenclaw, and Hufflepuff.

The individual offerings and identities of different shops also constructed boundaries and imposed in-world logics on consumer transactions. For example, although we denied my daughter's requests for a phoenix plush during our initial visit to the Magical Menagerie in Diagon Alley, we eventually relented, promising to find one during our visit to Hogsmeade the next day. After checking several Hogsmeade shops, however, we learned the item was only available in the Menagerie. It seemed it should not be so hard to spend money. However, the potential for elusive, exclusive retail objects could motivate the purchase of multiple park passes to access the varied shopping experiences offered by Diagon Alley and Hogsmeade. This sense of specialization also helps funnel the fan consumer through every shop, rather than just one, to see all the merchandise on offer. For example, the Borgin and Burkes shop in Knockturn Alley (just off the main Diagon Alley thoroughfare) uniquely offers high-end Death Eater masks and collectibles, serving as a special point of interest for fans identified with the franchise's evil dark wizards.

The Wizarding World is not unique in nesting the retail experience within the established retail trappings of an on-screen world. The *Frozen* ride at Epcot in Disney World, for example, abuts a Wandering Reindeer gift store that enables visitors to imagine themselves shopping in the same locale where Anna buys hiking gear and meets Kristoff in the film. However, the shop's wares focus on Anna and Elsa dolls and plastic toys. The mountain gear one would narratively expect to find in such a store adorns the walls but only as decoration, not for sale. By contrast, Universal's Wizarding World structures the retail experience by creating boundaries between the commodities of the media world that can be consumed as part of a shopping fantasy and the media commodities that can be purchased as part of the everyday media economy. This also distinguishes the Wizarding World from retail outlets like the Disney Store and Warner Bros. Studio Store that in the 1990s foregrounded corporate brands and studio logos as objects of consumer desire.[30] Here, retail is driven by institutions of fantasy and the promise of transactional participation in their narrative space. Disney's more recent theme park expansions, however, suggest that the principles of bounded retail fantasy undergirding the Wizarding World have become even more widely embraced as industry strategy. For the *Star Wars*: Galaxy's Edge attraction launched at Disney parks in 2019, the company promised a tourist experience in which real-world brands would be filtered out in favor of a purely in-world retail experience. Visitors in need of refreshment would find Coca-Cola products repackaged and rebranded in bottles designed to look like something that might be found in the *Star Wars* universe, while shops would sell the kinds of goods that an inhabitant of that world might purchase (from droids to lightsabers) rather than branded products featuring the *Star Wars* logo that resist transactional immersion.[31]

Perhaps most clearly evincing the potential meaningfulness surrounding such retail transactions in the Wizarding World is the Money Exchange in the Carkitt Market area just off of Diagon Alley. Visitors interacting with the animatronic goblins working here trade their U.S. dollars for the in-world currency of Gringotts Bank Notes equally accepted by restaurants and shops throughout the Wizarding World. Economically, this exchange served no purpose: the bank notes offered no greater buying power, and at the end of vacation, the visitor could even be stuck with whatever change remained from their initial ten- or twenty-dollar-denomination exchange. Yet the value proposition, such as it was, rested in the potential to further situate one's retail transactions within the economy of the fantasy world rather than mundane consumer existence. For many consumers, this exchange—like the interactive wand—might not be a good bargain, and the concerns that Baker and Gilbert express about unequal access to retail fantasy based on the consumer's ability to pay still resonate as crucial issues. Yet the retail transactions toward which Universal funnels its visitors do not impede fantasy; instead, they are privileged forms of participation in which structured practices of buying and selling support meaningful and interactive engagement with environments of consumption.

Conclusion

The Wizarding World of Harry Potter foregrounds retail as part of its fantasy world and has seized on that potential to generate a profitable theme park experience. However, underlying this story about the magical shopping experiences of muggle consumers role-playing as wizards is perhaps a more fundamental finding about the significance of retail to media culture and our study of it. Our retail transactions by all means reflect our participation in a consumer economy where media objects are commodities bought and sold in the manufacture and exploitation of fantasy by capital. At the same time, our retail transactions also provide crucial sites of investment where meanings, identities, and fantasies can all be negotiated. Under capitalism, retail becomes a mundane practice in media culture but also a site of extraordinary power at which we imagine ourselves and participate in practices that promise consumer transformation. Through the retail transaction, we exchange our economic capital while gaining entry into the realms of culture and power in which media operates—whether that is the narrative fantasy of *Harry Potter* or the ideology of consumerism more broadly. Indeed, the exorbitant expense of participating in the Wizarding World through theme park retail reveals the consumerist structures of the retail economy that in this and every other case shape access to media fantasy. Rather than consider retail as an obstacle or distraction from more authentic forms of fan participation, we might productively reflect upon its transactional nature as a powerful (and thus privileged) gateway to fantasy, meaning, and cultural participation.

As a means of understanding the economics and politics of world building, this emphasis on the institutions of retail in media franchising might also benefit from a closer dialogue with digital game studies that foreground the role of virtual economy in supporting and sustaining participation with virtual worlds. Examining massively multiplayer games, Edward Castronova identifies the presence of market institutions and a transactional economy between players as a crucial ingredient for players' identification, investment, and participation in synthetic game worlds.[32] In other words, it is in part the ability to engage in economic activity that makes the fantasy of these game worlds meaningful. For theme park tourists—and many other potential types of media consumers—the ability to nest shopping experiences within the fantasy world of branded franchises can have similarly significant implications for how, why, and under what constraints and privileges they participate in media culture. We must take care not to confuse consumption within the industrially structured capitalist economies of retail with fan cultures that could push against them; instead, in taking retail seriously, we might increasingly look to consumption not in opposition to participation but as a crucial, uneven, and transactional form of interaction in media's cultural economies.

Notes

1 Derek Johnson, *Media Franchising: Creative License and Collaboration in the Culture Industries* (New York: New York University Press, 2013).
2 Henry Jenkins, *Convergence Culture: Where Old and New Media Collide* (New York: New York University Press, 2006), 114.
3 Marta Boni, "Introduction: Worlds Today," in *World Building: Transmedia, Fans, Industries*, ed. Marta Boni (Amsterdam: Amsterdam University Press), 9–27.
4 Mark J. P. Wolf, *Building Imaginary Worlds: The Theory and History of Subcreation* (New York: Routledge, 2012).
5 Jenkins, *Convergence Culture*, 116.
6 Wolf, *Building Imaginary Worlds*, 35.
7 Jonathan Gray, *Watching with the Simpsons: Television, Parody, and Intertextuality* (New York: Routledge, 2006), 5.
8 J. K. Rowling, *Harry Potter and the Sorcerer's Stone* (New York: Scholastic, 1999), 77.
9 Rowling, *Sorcerer's Stone*, 85.
10 J. K. Rowling, *Harry Potter and the Half-Blood Prince* (New York: Scholastic, 2005), 110.
11 Hayley Cuccinello, "How JK Rowling Earned $95 Million in a Year," *Forbes*, 19 June 2017, https://www.forbes.com/sites/hayleycuccinello/2017/06/19/how-j-k-rowling-earned-95-million-in-a-year/#6c3b0c4d4291.
12 Madeleine Kruhly, "Harry Potter, Inc.: How the Boy Wizard Created a $21 Billion Business," *Atlantic*, 15 July 2011, https://www.theatlantic.com/business/archive/2011/07/harry-potter-inc-how-the-boy-wizard-created-a-21-billion-business/241948/#slide1.
13 Hugo Martin, "With Harry Potter Land, Universal Banks on Merchandising Magic," *Los Angeles Times*, 1 Mar. 2016, http://www.latimes.com/business/la-fi-harry-potter-merchandise-20160302-story.html.
14 Jason Garcia, "Universal Attendance Soars Even Higher," *Orlando Sentinel*, 13 May 2011, http://articles.orlandosentinel.com/2011-05-13/business/os-universal-orlando-earnings-20110513_1_universal-orlando-wizarding-world-guest-spending.
15 Brooks Barnes, "Universal Lifts the Veil on a Harry Potter Park," *New York Times*, 15 Sept. 2009, https://www.nytimes.com/2009/09/16/business/media/16harry.html.
16 "Warner Bros. Worldwide Consumer Products Awards Harry Potter Worldwide Master Toy License to Mattel," *TimeWarner*, 10 Feb. 2000, http://www.timewarner.com/newsroom/press-releases/2000/02/10/warner-bros-worldwide-consumer-products-awards-harry-potter.
17 Cuccinello, "JK Rowling."
18 Marc Graser, "From *Harry Potter* to *Hunger Games*, How Theme Parks Have Caught Franchise Fever," *Variety*, 5 June 2014, http://variety.com/2014/film/news/from-harry-potter-to-hunger-games-how-theme-parks-have-caught-franchise-fever-1201210671/; Martin, "Harry Potter Land."

19 Martin, "Harry Potter Land."

20 Carey Dunne, "Re-creating the Magic of Harry Potter in the Real World," *Co-Design*, 23 July 2014, https://www.fastcodesign.com/3033356/recreating-the-magic-of-harry-potter-in-the-real-world.

21 Seth Porges, "How 'The Wizarding World of Harry Potter' Uses Easter Eggs to Reward Its Biggest Fans," *Forbes*, 12 July 2016, https://www.forbes.com/sites/sethporges/2016/07/12/how-the-wizarding-world-of-harry-potter-uses-easter-eggs-to-reward-its-biggest-fans/#172639186cb6.

22 Elizabeth Stamp, "Behind the Scenes at the Wizarding World of Harry Potter," *Architectural Digest*, 4 Apr. 2016, https://www.architecturaldigest.com/story/wizarding-world-of-harry-potter-design.

23 Martin, "Harry Potter Land."

24 Carissa Ann Baker, "Universal's Wizard World of Harry Potter: A Primer in Contemporary Media Concepts," in *Harry Potter and Convergence Culture: Essays on Fandom and the Expanding Potterverse*, eds. Amanda Firestone and Leisa A. Clark (Jefferson, N.C.: McFarland, 2018), 55–66.

25 Baker, "Universal's Wizard World," 62.

26 Will Brooker, "Everywhere and Nowhere: Vancouver, Fan Pilgrimage, and the Urban Imaginary," *International Journal of Cultural Studies* 10, no. 4 (2007): 432–444; Nick Couldry, *The Place of Media Power: Pilgrims and Witnesses in the Media Age* (London: Routledge, 2000); Matt Hills, *Fan Cultures* (London: Routledge, 2002).

27 Rachel Gilbert, "A Potterhead's Progress: A Quest for Authenticity at the Wizarding World of Harry Potter," in *Playing Harry Potter: Essays and Interviews on Fandom and Performance*, ed. Lisa Brenner (Jefferson, N.C.: McFarland, 2015), 24–37.

28 Gilbert, "Potterhead's Progress," 28.

29 Gilbert, 32.

30 Paul Grainge, *Brand Hollywood: Selling Entertainment in a Global Media Age* (London: Routledge, 2007).

31 Ed Mazza, "Disneyland Unveils Its Massive Star Wars: Galaxy's Edge Expansion," *HuffPost*, 30 May 2019, https://www.huffpost.com/entry/disneyland-star-wars-opens_l_5cef9490e4b00cfa19663cef; Scott Trowbridge, "Specially Designed Coca-Cola Products Coming Exclusively to Star Wars: Galaxy's Edge," *Disney Parks Blog*, 13 Apr. 2019, https://disneyparks.disney.go.com/blog/2019/04/specially-designed-coca-cola-products-coming-exclusively-to-star-wars-galaxys-edge/.

32 Edward Castronova, *Synthetic Worlds: The Business and Culture of Online Games* (Chicago: University of Chicago Press, 2005).

Index

Notes on Contributors

Elizabeth Affuso is the academic director of intercollegiate media studies at the Claremont Colleges, where she also teaches media studies at Pitzer College. She received a PhD from the School of Cinematic Arts at the University of Southern California. Her work has been presented at conferences such as Society for Cinema and Media Studies (SCMS) and Console-ing Passions and been published in *Jump Cut*, *Discourse*, and *The Routledge Companion to Media Fandom*.

Tim J. Anderson is an associate professor of communication and theatre arts at Old Dominion University. Among his publications are two monographs: *Making Easy Listening: Material Culture and Postwar American Recording* and *Popular Music in a Digital Music Economy: Problems and Practices for an Emerging Service Industry*. His latest research project focuses on recordings, musicians, listeners, and the public sphere.

Meredith A. Bak is an assistant professor in the department of childhood studies at Rutgers University-Camden. She writes on both historical and contemporary children's media, visual, and material culture. Her work has appeared in publications including *Early Popular Visual Culture* and *Film History* and is forthcoming in *The Velvet Light Trap* and *The Moving Image*, as well as several collections. Her book *Playful Visions: Optical Toys and the Emergence of Children's Media Culture* is under contract with the MIT Press. A second project in development considers the history and theory of animated toys, from talking dolls to augmented reality apps.

Courtney Brannon Donoghue is an assistant professor in the department of media arts at the University of North Texas. Her research areas include conglomerate Hollywood and international operations, local-language productions, Brazilian media, management and distribution cultures, feminist media industry studies, and blockbuster franchising. Brannon Donoghue is currently working on a book about gender inequity and female-driven films in Hollywood and the global film industry. Her first book, *Localising Hollywood* (BFI Press, 2017), explores the localization of Hollywood operations across Europe and Latin America since the 1990s based on industry interviews and international fieldwork in eight countries. Brannon Donoghue's publications have also appeared in *Cinema Journal, Media, Culture & Society*, and various edited collections.

Lynn Comella is an associate professor of gender and sexuality studies at the University of Nevada, Las Vegas. She is the author of *Vibrator Nation: How Feminist Sex-Toy Stores Changed the Business of Pleasure* and coeditor of *New Views on Pornography: Sexuality, Politics, and the Law*. She's written extensively about gender, sexuality, and marketplace culture for academic outlets that include *Porn Studies, International Journal of Communication, The Feminist Porn Book, Commodity Activism, Sex for Sale*, and *New Sociologies of Sex Work*. Her research has been featured in the *New York Times, Washington Post, Rolling Stone, The Atlantic, Jezebel, BUST*, and more. She is the recipient of the 2015 Nevada Regents' Rising Researcher Award in recognition of early career accomplishments and is a frequent media commentator.

Evan Elkins is an assistant professor of media studies at Colorado State University who specializes in digital media industries and technologies, globalization, access, and cultural difference. He is the author of *Locked Out: Regional Restrictions in Digital Entertainment Culture* (NYU Press, 2019), and he also occasionally writes about transgressive humor, aesthetics, and media authorship. Current and future research projects examine and critique Silicon Valley's practices and politics of global development and modernization. His work has appeared in the *International Journal of Cultural Studies, Television and New Media*, the *Fibreculture Journal*, the *Historical Journal of Film, Radio, and Television, Critical Studies in Media Communication*, and several edited collections.

Erin Hanna is an assistant professor of cinema studies at the University of Oregon. She is the author of *Only at Comic-Con: Hollywood, Fans, and the Limits of Exclusivity*, and her work also appears in *CineAction, Television and New Media*, and the *Journal of Fandom Studies*.

Daniel Herbert is an associate professor in the department of film, television, and media at the University of Michigan. He is the author of *Film Remakes and Franchises* and *Videoland: Movie Culture at the American Video Store*. His essays appear in the *Canadian Journal of Film Studies*, the *Creative Industries Journal, Film Quarterly*, the *Journal of Film and Video*, the *Millennium Film Journal*, and the *Quarterly Review of Film and Video*, as well as in several edited collections.

Derek Johnson is a professor of media and cultural studies in the department of communication arts at the University of Wisconsin–Madison. His most recent book is *Transgenerational Media Industries: Adults, Children, and the Reproduction of Culture*. He is also the author of *Media Franchising: Creative License and Collaboration in the Culture Industries*, the editor of *From Networks to Netflix: A Guide to Changing Channels*, and the coeditor of *A Companion to Media Authorship* as well as *Making Media Work: Cultures of Management in the Entertainment Industry*.

Nasreen Rajani is a PhD candidate in communications and media studies at Carleton University with an MA in women's and gender studies. Her research area broadly centers around online feminist activism.

Avi Santo is the director of the Institute for the Humanities at Old Dominion University. He is the author of *Selling the Silver Bullet: The Lone Ranger and Transmedia Brand Licensing* and coeditor with Derek Johnson and Derek Kompare of *Making Media Work: Cultures of Management in the Entertainment Industries*. His research focuses on retail as a contested storytelling medium for entertainment brands.

Olli Sotamaa is an associate professor of game culture studies at Tampere University's Game Research Lab. Sotamaa has a PhD in media culture from the University of Tampere, and he is a docent of digital culture methodologies at the University of Turku. His more than seventy academic publications cover user-generated content, player cultures, player-centered research methods, and cultural and historical analysis of the game industry. Sotamaa has published in and edited special issues for several scholarly journals including *Convergence, Fibreculture, First Monday, Games and Culture, Game Studies*, the *International Journal of Arts and Technology*, and *Simulation and Gaming*. His current research interests include coproduction, creative labor, and regional gaming scenes.

Marc Steinberg is an associate professor of film studies at Concordia University, Montreal. He is the author of *Anime's Media Mix: Franchising Toys and Characters in Japan* (University of Minnesota Press, 2012), its Japanese expanded version *Naze Nihon wa "media mikkusu suru kuni" nano ka* (*Why Is Japan a "Media Mixing Nation"?*) (Tokyo: Kadokawa, 2015), and *The Platform Economy: How Japan Transformed the Commercial Internet* (University of Minnesota Press, 2019). He is the coeditor of *Media Theory in Japan* (Duke University Press, 2017).

Gregory Steirer is an assistant professor of English and film and media studies at Dickinson College. He is currently completing a monograph, funded in part by the National Endowment for the Humanities, on U.S. intellectual property law and the origins of the narrative-based franchise. His book on the American comic book industry and Hollywood, coauthored with Alisa Perren, will be published by BFI/Bloomsbury in 2020.

Ethan Tussey (PhD, University of California–Santa Barbara, 2012) is an assistant professor of communication at Georgia State University. His book *The Procrastination Economy* examines mobile-device use in the context of the workplace, the commute, the waiting room, and the living room. His work explores the relationship between the entertainment industry and the digitally empowered public. He has contributed book chapters on creative labor, online sports viewing, connected viewing, and crowdfunding to the anthologies *Saturday Night Live and American TV*, *Digital Media Sport: Technology and Power in the Network Society*, *Connected Viewing: Selling, Sharing, and Streaming Media in a Digital Era*, and *Crowdfunding the Future: Media Industries, Ethics, and Digital Society*. He is also the coordinating editor of *In Media Res* and the cofounder of the Atlanta Media Project. He teaches classes on television analysis, cultural studies, and digital media. He has presented his research at multiple conferences including SCMS, Consoling Passions, and Flow.

Heikki Tyni is a PhD candidate at Tampere University and has been working at UTA Game Research Lab since 2010. With a focus on cultural studies, Tyni's work has centered on various game industry mechanisms and their consequences on game culture, including downloadable-content strategies, the free-to-play model, and hybrid games and toys. His ongoing PhD work studies games crowdfunding as an alternative publishing model and a cocreative channel for gamers.

Emily West is an associate professor of communication at the University of Massachusetts Amherst. Her areas of research are promotion, technology, and culture; media audiences and users; and critical approaches to health communication. She is the coeditor of *The Routledge Companion to Advertising and Promotional Culture* and author of articles and book chapters on greeting cards, affective advertising, mediated nationalisms, and discourses of health in media. Her forthcoming book with the MIT Press is titled *Branding Ubiquity: Amazon, Digital Distribution, and Platform Capitalism* (2021).

Benjamin Woo is an associate professor in the school of journalism and communication at Carleton University (Ottawa, Canada). His research examines the production, circulation, and reception of comic books, graphic novels, and related media. He is the author of *Getting a Life: The Social Worlds of Geek Culture*, coauthor (with Bart Beaty) of *The Greatest Comic Book of All Time: Symbolic Capital and the Field of American Comic Books*, and coeditor (with Stuart R. Poyntz and Jamie Rennie) of *Scene Thinking: Cultural Studies from the Scenes Perspective*.